JAMES   GOULD   COZZENS

ALSO BY MATTHEW J. BRUCCOLI

The Composition of *Tender Is the Night*
As Ever, Scott Fitz—(*editor, with Jennifer Atkinson*)
F. Scott Fitzgerald in His Own Time (*editor, with Jackson Bryer*)
F. Scott Fitzgerald: A Descriptive Bibliography
Supplement to F. Scott Fitzgerald: A Descriptive Bibliography
F. Scott Fitzgerald's Ledger (*editor*)
The Great Gatsby: A Facsimile of the Manuscript (*editor*)
Apparatus for a Definitive Edition of *The Great Gatsby*
Bits of Paradise: 21 Uncollected Stories by F. Scott and Zelda Fitzgerald
(*editor, with Scottie Fitzgerald Smith*)
The Romantic Egoists (*editor, with
Scottie Fitzgerald Smith and Joan P. Kerr*)
"The Last of the Novelists": F. Scott Fitzgerald and *The Last Tycoon*
The Notebooks of F. Scott Fitzgerald (*editor*)
The Price Was High: The Last Uncollected Stories of
F. Scott Fitzgerald (*editor*)
Correspondence of F. Scott Fitzgerald (*editor, with Margaret Duggan*)
F. Scott Fitzgerald: Poems 1911–1940 (*editor*)
Some Sort of Epic Grandeur: The Life of F. Scott Fitzgerald
Scott and Ernest: The Authority of Failure and the Authority of Success
Ernest Hemingway, Cub Reporter (*editor*)
Ernest Hemingway's Apprenticeship (*editor*)
Hemingway at Auction (*editor, with C. E. Frazer Clark, Jr.*)
Kenneth Millar/Ross Macdonald: Descriptive Bibliography
Raymond Chandler: A Descriptive Bibliography
Chandler Before Marlowe (*editor*)
Ring Lardner: A Descriptive Bibliography (*with Richard Layman*)
Some Champions: Sketches & Fiction by Ring Lardner
(*editor, with Richard Layman*)
The O'Hara Concern: A Biography of John O'Hara
"An Artist Is His Own Fault": John O'Hara on Writers and Writing (*editor*)
John O'Hara: A Descriptive Bibliography
Selected Letters of John O'Hara (*editor*)
Just Representations: A James Gould Cozzens Reader (*editor*)
James Gould Cozzens: New Acquist of True Experience (*editor*)
James Gould Cozzens: A Descriptive Bibliography

TO ME, LIFE IS WHAT
LIFE IS.

JAMES GOULD COZZENS

A LIFE APART

MATTHEW J. BRUCCOLI

A HARVEST/HBJ BOOK

HARCOURT BRACE JOVANOVICH
PUBLISHERS
San Diego · New York · London

HBJ

Requests for permission to make copies of any
part of the work should be mailed to: Permissions,
Harcourt Brace Jovanovich, Publishers,
Orlando, FL 32887

Excerpts from the writings of James Gould Cozzens are reprinted
by permission of Harcourt Brace Jovanovich, Inc., copyright 1940,
1942, 1952, 1957, 1964, 1968, 1970 by James Gould Cozzens; copyright 1924
by B. J. Brimmer Company.

Library of Congress Cataloging in Publication Data
Bruccoli, Matthew Joseph, 1931—
James Gould Cozzens: an interior life.
"The publications of James Gould Cozzens": p.
Bibliography: p.
Includes index.
1. Cozzens, James Gould, 1903– —Biography.
2. Novelists, American——20th century—Biography.
I. Title.
PS3505.099Z59 1983   813'.52   82-23312
ISBN 0-15-146048-5
ISBN 0-15-645952-3 (pbk.)

Designed by Margaret M. Wagner

Printed in the United States of America

First Harvest/HBJ edition 1984

A B C D E F G H I J

CONTENTS

ILLUSTRATIONS

*For Fannie Collins
and for Julian Muller*

INTRODUCTION

I WOULD like to be able to boast that this biography is a labor of friendship. But James Gould Cozzens claimed he had no friends. I honored him, and he endured me. Although we regularly communicated by mail and phone during the last three years of his life, I never met Jim. If not a labor of friendship, then it is a work of homage and restitution. This effort was not undertaken for his sake: Cozzens insisted that he cared nothing for mortal fame or posthumous reputation. His masterpieces are to be cherished for their own sake; yet readers are being deprived of his work because they have never heard of it. In the long run justice will be done to Cozzens, with or without this book. My intention is to accelerate the process.

This volume assesses Cozzens's career through the events of his life. The organization and emphases are provided by his work. As Dr. Johnson decreed, "The gradations of a hero's life are from battle to battle, and of an author's from book to book."[1]

I have written a biography of a man who discouraged biographers. Moreover, it is a biography of a reclusive writer whose life was his work. Cozzens was a pure novelist, a writer only. He didn't associate with other writers. He didn't grant interviews. He signed no manifestoes, attended no cocktail parties, made no speeches, joined no faculties, supported no causes, divorced no wives, courted no columnists, punched no reviewers, advised no Presidents. He stayed home and wrote. Cozzens was withdrawn in private life and as a literary figure (he didn't want to be one). Privacy and indifference to fame started as a defensive strategy; but the role became increasingly comfortable, and the act may well have taken over the actor.

Commentators refer to "the enigma of James Gould Cozzens," meaning his secession from the outside world proceeding from his conviction that he was different—and better. It was a tranquil misanthropy, devoid of Swiftian excoriation. He believed in the aristocracy of literature and in the aristocracy of intelligence, and he found that he could best serve them in seclusion. There is nothing in his background to endorse this sense of aristocracy; neither is there any way to explain how the son of a stablekeeper knew that "a thing of beauty is a joy forever." It is instructive to learn how a talent was nurtured, but genius is single and singular.

Cozzens's seclusion proves to be one of the best-documented authorial lives, through his diaries, notebooks, and letters. I began this biography worrying how I would fill the gaping holes in the public record; but I discovered more material than I could use—most of it from Cozzens. He not only prepared the documents: he preserved them at the Princeton University Library. Perhaps he found that having written his diaries and notebooks he could not bring himself to destroy them in his later years. I don't think so. Given the evidence that these records really were written for the record, with persistent care for truth, I am convinced that—whatever use he intended to make of them in his fiction—Cozzens preserved them for posterity. He had a clear sense of John Milton's "self-esteem founded on just and right"—a phrase he relished. What might be a disproportionate use of documentary excerpts in the biography of a more public figure is justified in the case of Cozzens because he lived an interior life on paper. His thoughts resist paraphrase. The force of his mind is conveyed by the force of his expression.

Cozzens's novels fit no convenient category in American fiction. He has been classed with John P. Marquand, Louis Auchincloss, and even William Dean Howells as a social (not sociological) novelist; yet he differs from them more than they differ from each other. He is closer to John O'Hara in subject though not in tone or technique—without O'Hara's emotion but lacking O'Hara's dialogue skills. If it is obligatory to place Cozzens in a literary tradition, he probably belongs with the English novelists of manners from Jane Austen to W. Somerset Maugham—two writers he admired. Yet his fiction was solidly American. Literary taxonomy can be a useful endeavor, but great writers form their own categories.

The paradox that the antisocial man was one of our best social novelists does not require development beyond noting that his isolation accords with the impersonality of his fiction. Readers found him cold or clinical, and no doubt the more sensitive were wounded by his contempt for their emotions. Cozzens recognized that his work seemed to be "a kind of writing that must have some emotion-arousing quality that makes those who like it unable to see its faults; and those who don't like it, unable to see its merits. The result is no critical middle ground. The likers, in effect, love it and give it the highest praise; the dislikers are not just bored or indifferent. In effect, they hate it; actively and loudly they assert it's as bad as possible."[2] Despite five Book-of-the-Month Club selections—one of which, *By Love Possessed,* was a prodigious best seller—his books failed to please enough of the right people.

Literary reputations are not made by book clubs or sales figures; they are promulgated and enforced by the professorial-critical axis operating in collaboration with spokespersons for what is regarded as the intellectual establishment. Pedagogues exert great influence simply by exposing unread students to certain books. Cozzens's novels are hard to teach because they require so little explication—leaving the teacher with the problem of filling up class time. One reason why William Faulkner is a classroom staple is that his novels provide the teacher with so much to explain or clarify. Nonetheless, F. Scott Fitzgerald and Ernest Hemingway, whose work is notably clear, have kept teachers gainfully occupied.

It is too simple, then, to claim that Cozzens's novels do not recommend themselves to academia only because they provide little for teaching and criticism to do. A better explanation is that his material is inimical to the academic temperament as well as inaccessible to the immature. Cozzens's principal theme was expressed by Fulke Greville: "passion and reason self-division cause." His subjects are deontology (the ethics of duty) and the limitations of will. He recognized an elite of the intelligent and fortunate, insisting on the obligations of the privileged. Cozzens's protagonists are educated, successful, upper-middle-class men who accept responsibility within the limits of choice. This role model is not fashionable on campus.

While honoring intelligence, Cozzens regarded most intellectuals with suspicion; and he was scornful of liberalism. The result of this position has been to alienate or infuriate the most vocal portion of the intellectual hegemony. Cozzens has been classified as a conservative or a reactionary; but his work has no political message. His conservatism—toryism is a better term—was social, for he recognized hierarchies and respected traditions. The compulsion to concentrate on Cozzens's apolitical conservatism impedes the proper assessment of his high achievements as a writer.

Cozzens did not accept the duty of a writer to elevate the race or ameliorate the ills of civilization. The only thesis he admitted to was that "people got a very raw deal from life. To me, life is what life is."[3] When he discussed his aims he sometimes cited Johnson and Milton, stating that he wrote as accurately as he could to achieve "just representations of general nature"[4] and thereby provide "a new acquist of true experience."[5]

The University of South Carolina
19 March 1982

ACKNOWLEDGMENTS

M Y greatest single debt is to Fannie Baumgarten Collins, who trusted me and shared her memories and material with me. This biography really could not have been written without the generous aid of the staff of the Princeton University Library Manuscripts Department: Professor Richard Ludwig, Jean Preston, Mardel Pacheco, Charles Greene, Ann Van Arsdale, Barbara Taylor. These people at Harcourt Brace Jovanovich provided crucial assistance: William Jovanovich, Julian Muller (my editor), Joan Judge, Carol Meyer, Rita Vaughan, Dan Wickenden, Karin Crine. Meredith Walker and Catherine Coleman not only typed and retyped, but also asked many irritating questions. My research assistants, Heather Barker, Michael Mullen, and John Clewis, were indispensable. The able Interlibrary Loan staff at the Thomas Cooper Library, University of South Carolina, found almost everything I needed: Harriet Oglesbee, Lori Finger, Susan Bradley, and Beth Woodard. The help of Samuel W. John, Kent School Librarian, was crucial. Edward Newhouse was patiently helpful in many ways. Arlyn Bruccoli vetted the typescript and corrected the dangling modifiers—urging me to seek another line of endeavor.

The following Kent School old boys responded to my inquiries: Walter V. Aldridge, William F. R. Ballard, Jacob D. Beam, Henry W. Bragdon, Koert D. Burnham, Thompson B. Crane, John P. Cuyler, I. Davis Hall, James P. Humphreys, W. Draper Lewis, Edward M. Littell, Prescott Mabon, Lewis Nichols, William L.

Pryor, Jr., Lawrence Rose, Alexander T. Taft, C. Henry Weymer, Frederick P. Weymer, Parker Wilson, William Worthington, and, especially, Robert W. Richardson.

These people provided assistance: Dr. John A. Abbott, Dr. William Abey, W. R. Anderson, Carlos Baker, Walter Jackson Bate, Millicent Bell, Edward G. Biester, Jr., Stephen Birmingham, Frederick Bracher, William S. Braithwaite, Jr., Carol Brandt, Zelma Brandt, Ward W. Briggs, Jr., Robert F. Brugger, Joseph Bryan III, William F. Buckley, Jr., Kenneth Bull, Hortense Calisher, Colin Cass, John Chamberlain, Jo H. Chamberlin, Mary Chamberlin, C. E. Frazer Clark, Charles Clegg, Cary C. Conn, Joan Crane, Thayer Cumings, William H. Cunliffe, Rodney G. Dennis, Captain Rick P. DuCharm, James Dunkly, Ellen Dunlap, Joyce L. Eakin, James N. Eastman, William Emerson, Philip Eppard, Philip Faherty, Jr., Philip A. Farris, George Feather, Paul W. Ferris, Cornelia Fitts, Russell Fraser, Edmund Fuller, Mary Rose Gagné, Brendan Gill, Robert Giroux, Suzanne Gleaves, Dr. Donald W. Goodwin, Shirley Ann Grau, Ralph Graves, Maj. James A. Grimshaw, Jr., Marilla B. Guptil, Gordon Haight, R. Cargill Hall, Muriel Hamilton, Charles L. Harding, Jr., A. L. Hart, Avis E. Harvey, G. E. Hasselwander, Lillian B. Hettling, Serrell Hillman, Mrs. Stanley H. Hillyer, John Iggulden, Rhoda Jackson, Judith Johnson, Nancy Johnson, T. E. Kalem, Virginia T. Kearns, Col. Frederick T. Kiley, Donald Klopfer, Dr. George Lacovara, Kay Lally, Margaret E. Law, Nellie M. Law, Kathleen Lazare, Michael Lazare, Roberta Leighton, Denver Lindley, Frances Lindley, Lt. Col. Henry F. Lippincott, Jr., Robert A. Lovett, Townsend Ludington, Dwight Macdonald, Mary McCarthy, Ken McCormick, Allan McDowell, Margaret Johnson McNamee, Peter Matthiessen, Amy Eggleston Mayfield, James A. Michener, Margaret M. Mills, Kathleen Morehouse, Anton C. Masin, James Meriwether, Jack H. Mooney, Frank Morley, Dr. David J. Myerson, Lt. Col. John H. Napier III, Roger O'Connor, Dr. William Ober, Theodore Oxholm, Edward C. Parish, Jr., James A. Parrish, Jr., Stewart Perowne, Jean Peters, Charles W. Phillips, Luise Porter, Dr. Anthony Privatera, Joseph Rees, Anne Reubold, Dorothy Reynolds, Mary Robert, Natalie Rogers, Philip Rollinson, Mary Shaffer, Malcolm B. Sheldrick, Charles Schlessiger, David Schoem, David E. Schoonover, Budd Schulberg, Donna J. Shelleberger, Al Silverman, Joan Southworth, Dr. Michael Sribnick, Ray Stark, Willard Stark, Vernon Sternberg, Roger Stoddard, Robert Thomsen, Senator Strom

Thurmond, C. Norris Tilton, Sidney N. Towle, Lester Trauch, Maj. John Vermillion, Susan Walker, John William Ward, Virginia Reiland Watson, Henry Wenning, William W. Whalen, Christopher Whelen, Alden Whitman, R. A. Whitaker, Cara White, Patricia Stemler Whiley, Rev. Carl E. Wilke, Robert Woolf, Ella Worthington.

The following institutions made material available: Albert F. Simpson Historical Research Center, Maxwell Air Force Base; Alderman Library, University of Virginia; All Saints Episcopal Church; American Academy and Institute of Arts and Letters; Beinecke Library, Yale University; Houghton Library, Harvard University; Humanities Research Center, University of Texas; Newport Historical Society; New York Athletic Club; Office of Air Force History; Oral History Collection, Columbia University; and St. Thomas Episcopal Church, New York City.

I am indebted to my colleagues and masters at the University of South Carolina, who have allowed me to do my work. Professor George Geckle, Chairman of the English Department, provided all the help I dared ask for.

CHRONOLOGY

19 August 1903	Birth of James Gould Cozzens to Henry William and Bertha Wood Cozzens, Chicago, Illinois.
Fall 1910	Enters Staten Island Academy, New York City.
September 1916	Enters Kent School, Kent, Connecticut.
March 1920	"A Democratic School" appears in the *Atlantic Monthly*.
September 1922	Enters Harvard University.
April 1924	Publication of *Confusion*.
Spring 1924	Leave of absence from Harvard; does not return.
Summer–December 1924	Nova Scotia. Writes "Ignorant Armies" (unpublished) and *Michael Scarlett*; edits "The Criticisms of John Keats on English Poetry" (unpublished).
September 1925–Spring 1926	Teacher at Tuinucú, Cuba.
November 1925	Publication of *Michael Scarlett*.
August 1926	Goes to France with mother.
Late 1926–Spring 1927	Tutor in Europe. Writes "The Minor Catholicon" and begins "The Careless Livery" (both unpublished).
Spring 1927	Returns to America; St. Thomas Chapel vicarage in Manhattan. Completes "The Careless Livery."
Fall 1927	Librarian at the New York Athletic Club.
31 December 1927	Marriage of Sylvia Bernice Baumgarten and James Gould Cozzens in New York City.
1928	Apartment at 48 Charles Street, New York City.

September 1928	Publication of *Cock Pit*.
March 1928	Employed by M. P. Gould & Co., New York City.
August 1929	Publication of *The Son of Perdition*.
Fall 1929	Apartment at 325 East 79th Street, New York City.
August 1930	Publication of "S.S. 'San Pedro': A Tale of the Sea" in *Scribner's Magazine*.
August 1931	Publication of *S.S. San Pedro*.
January 1933	Publication of *The Last Adam*.
Spring 1933	Purchases Carrs Farm, Lambertville, New Jersey.
1934	Works on Civil War novel (unpublished).
September 1934	Publication of *Castaway* in London; American publication in November.
January 1936	Publication of *Men and Brethren*.
January – October 1938	On *Fortune* staff in New York City.
June 1940	Publication of *Ask Me Tomorrow*.
May 1942	Enlists in the Air Force; Officers' Training School at Miami, Florida, August – September.
July 1942	Publication of *The Just and the Unjust*.
September 1942	Assigned to the Training Aids Directorate (TAD), Gravelly Point, Washington, D.C.
November 1942	TAD moved to Orlando, Florida.
May 1943	TAD moved to 1 Park Avenue, New York City.
October 1943	Transferred to Office of Technical Information, Air Forces headquarters, Arlington, Virginia
October 1945	Discharged from the Air Force with the rank of major.
September 1948	Publication of *Guard of Honor*.
1948	Plans "Fast Falls the Eventide" (unpublished).
May 1949	Awarded Pulitzer Prize for *Guard of Honor*.
June 1952	Awarded honorary doctor of letters degree by Harvard.
August 1957	Publication of *By Love Possessed*
September 1957	*Time* cover story.
January 1958	Rents "Windingdale," near Belle Haven, Virginia.
1958	Plans "A Skyborn Music" (unpublished).
Fall 1958	Purchases "Shadowbrook," Williamstown, Massachusetts.
July 1964	Publication of *Children and Others*.
August 1968	Publication of *Morning Noon and Night*.
1969	Plans "A Thing of the Past" / "The Wind and the Rain" (unpublished).
May 1971	In car wreck in Williamstown.
Fall 1971	Moves to Stuart, Florida.

1973 Buys condominium at Beacon 21, Rio, Florida.

30 January 1978 Death of Sylvia Bernice Cozzens in Rio, Florida.

9 August 1978 Death of James Gould Cozzens in Stuart, Florida.

JAMES   GOULD   COZZENS

1957

T H E R E used to be "the *Time* jinx" when an athlete appeared on that magazine's cover. The portrait of James Gould Cozzens appeared on the 2 September 1957 issue of *Time* when *By Love Possessed* was published. The cover story was a hoodoo. Headed "The Hermit of Lambertville," it noted that at fifty-four and after eleven novels he was "the least known and least discussed of major American novelists." Quoting Cozzens's decree that sentimentality is "the underlying principle that has ruined American fiction," it portrayed him as a misanthropist—describing him or his work as *classical, dry, cerebral, pessimistic,* and *temperamentally aristocratic.* Cozzens, the unsigned article indicated, was emotionally deficient and kept both himself and his readers at a distance from life.

Although the article helped to make *By Love Possessed* a bestseller, the *Time* characterization of James Gould Cozzens outraged many readers—and was probably intended to do so. Cozzens was at least partly to blame. Ignorant of the ways of interviewers, he violated the rule of experienced public figures: never employ irony when talking for publication. Above all, never try to kid the reporter. Thus, *Time* printed his comment that "I still feel I'm better than other people." ("That's a joke, Son," Cozzens noted on his copy of the article.) On the subject of his thirty-year marriage to literary agent Bernice Baumgarten, Cozzens was reported to have observed: "I suppose sex entered into it. After all, what's a woman for? . . . Mother almost died when I married a Jew, but later when she saw I was being decently cared for, she realized that it was the best thing that could have happened to me." Acknowledging that his wife had brought in most of their income, he said, "It could have been a humiliating situation, but I guess I had a certain native conceit and felt that her time was well spent." Speaking of the Kent School and its headmaster, Cozzens stated: "But Kent marked me for life. If there's hard work to be done and I get out of it, I feel extremely guilty. That's the attitude Father Sill inculcated in us."

The *Time* writer buttressed his portrait of James Gould Cozzens as a cranky reactionary snob by warning that *By Love Possessed* would be "controversial" because of its patronizing treatment of Catholics, Jews, and Negroes. Liberal critics responded by denouncing Cozzens as the voice of middlebrow culture and the spokesman for the complacency of the Eisenhower years—as well as a pretentious writer who falsified human nature. The name of the writer who for three decades had avoided publicity and eschewed all causes—except the cause of writing truthfully—became a shibboleth. Cozzens observed in 1960: "To fill emotional partisans . . . with fury there's nothing like a careful exercise of detachment, or an attempt to write nothing but the truth." [1]

The *Time* article remained the only biographical sketch of Cozzens and influenced the assessments of him for the next twenty-five years. Inevitably, the writer's personality and the value of his work were conflated. Critics who were upset by the impression of Cozzens as an anachronistic bigot found ample cause to reject his work; critics who disliked his work reinforced their dismissals by appeal to the received facts about the writer. That some of these critics otherwise regarded Henry Luce and his magazines as pernicious did not seem to matter.

James Gould Cozzens withdrew into his privacy, publishing two more books. At his death in 1978 he was the least read and the least regarded major American novelist.

MORNING

ONE

Boyhood and Kent

T H E only child of Henry William and Bertha Wood Cozzens was born in Chicago at 8:15 P.M. on 19 August 1903 and was named for his great-uncle. Although James Gould Cozzens insisted that the place of his birth was a matter "pure peradventure,"[1] his father was employed there by the Campbell Press Company. "Whoever was born in Chicago? It used to embarrass me like hell at school."[2]

Both parents were of New England stock. The English Cozzenses (Curzon, Cozzen, Cussin, Cousins, Cosen, Cousens)* claimed descent from Geraldine de Curson or Curzen, a Breton follower of William the Conqueror; but James Gould Cozzens remarked that he was descended from a distinguished line of indentured servants. The Cozzens family was established in Newport, Rhode Island, by Leonard Cozzens of Wiltshire (the infant's great-great-great-grandfather), who was admitted to Rhode Island as a freeman in 1711. He may have been a religious refugee from the Bay Colony but was more likely a runaway servant. William Cole Cozzens, a dry-goods merchant, became mayor of Newport and for three months in 1863 was governor of the state. His son—the grandfather of James Gould Cozzens—lost the family money. The Cozzens family made no contribution to American arts and letters except for Frederick S. Cozzens (1818–1869), author of the once-popular *Sparrowgrass Papers*.

* The verb *cozen* means to cheat.

Bertha Wood
(*Princeton University
Library*)

Henry William Cozzens
(*Princeton University
Library*)

Bertha Wood was born in Conning, Nova Scotia, in 1875. Her ancestors had been Connecticut Tories who migrated to Canada at the time of the Revolution. It was a matter of family pride that they had remained loyal to the king. Bertha detested "cheap people." She was educated at a seminary in Wolfville, Nova Scotia, and, although her family was Episcopalian, probably attended a convent school in Montreal. When her father became captain of the Vanderbilt yacht *Conqueror* he moved his family to Newport, where she met Henry Cozzens, who was ten years her senior. Henry had left Brown University after one year for financial reasons and worked for the sales departments of printing-equipment manufacturers. He was thirty-eight when their son was born. James Gould Cozzens would attribute his stolid qualities to his father's family; the Woods were high-strung.

James Gould Cozzens at three months,
19 November 1903

The infant's first word, reported by his grandmother, was "Hark!" at the age of one year.[3] By 1906 the family was at St. Austin's Place, West New Brighton, Staten Island, which was then in the countryside. There were six houses (designed by Stanford White for rising executives) on the street when the Cozzenses settled there. Henry Cozzens commuted to the Intertype Corporation, 50 Court Street, Brooklyn. He became general sales manager of the firm but was "no more than modestly well-to-do."[4]

ABOVE. *With father*   BELOW. *With mother*

Henry and Bertha Cozzens were firm Episcopalians, and he was a member of the St. Mary's vestry. Her deepest interest, which her husband did not share, was rose gardening, and their son would become a serious gardener. In his foreword to *Roses of Yesterday* (1967) Cozzens recalled his mother's rose garden.

Long shafts of declining warm sun, the stir of shady air under the little pergola and trellises, the enclosing thickets of well-grown roses in bloom (those like Mrs. John Laing, American Beauty and Paul Neyron were as tall as I then was), the gleam of silver tea things and the rose patterned (of course) Spode cups and muffin plates, the two or three women in their light dresses chatting and resting in ease of friendly familiarity (yet in those days sure to be sitting quite straight) make the picture in my mind. I think then I may very well have imagined that everything was going to be like that all the time always. . . .

My one retained picture of my father among the roses shows him on a Sunday morning when he was to usher at church (members of the vestry in pairs took turns). For the purpose he puts on a morning coat and striped trousers. He places on his head a shiny top hat taken from a leather box lined with red silk. Ready to go over to church, he walks down to the end of the garden. . . . He was of old Rhode Island extraction and I have cause to know this can make for austerities of practice, especially in small matters. Using a gold-cased penknife attached to his watchchain, he cuts himself a gravely selected Frau Karl Druschki bud. As we all know, this rose, opening to the most splendid white there is, has, alas, no fragrance. Austerity gets its sop.[5]

From childhood Jim manifested an emerging solipsism, which he later attributed to his early realization that there was "no plan in

this world." In 1952 he explained to his mother: "—I think it came to me on the occasion when you informed me that everyone was going to die. I don't know how old I was but such a notion had never crossed my mind before, and the impact was enough to fix the instant—my own disconcerted alarm, your own efforts (to my child's eye pretty feeble) to make light of the matter. I suppose I realized quite soon, or perhaps instantaneously, that so it was, it was true; and if it was true, it must follow that all ideas of certainty and security were illusions; and I think that within at most a day or two after that I abandoned all thoughts of either."[6]

He entered the Staten Island Academy in 1910. "I was ruined for life in one sense, in that you didn't have to do anything you didn't want to do. When I write in my books about doing your job and sticking things out, I'm the one who knows best because I failed myself."[7] He later noted: "The parable I always liked best, possibly because it is so short, is the one in St. Matthew: A certain man had two sons: and he came to the first and said; Son, go work today in my vineyard. He answered and said I will not: But afterward he repented and went. And he came to the second and said likewise. And he answered and said, I go, sir: and went not."[8]

Writing came easily to him. This childhood composition arguably presages Cozzens's interest in factual material:

RUSSIA

Russia is cold Country. The capital is St. Petersburg. The streets are good and wide. The city is made of brick or stone. And it is very enteresting. At each coner of an important Ave. there is a small house. This

Age four, 1907
(*Princeton University Library*)

is a policeman's house. About the next to largest city is Moscow. Their buildings are not stately and the people are shy for when Napoleon marched to capture the city they were burning the city, but this was bad luck for Napoleon, for he had to march all the back. And nearly half the number died of want of food. Warsaw is another city too but that is a good deal like the others.[9]

At about eleven he was an expert on the Napoleonic Wars and was considered a show-off by his playmates. When he and neighbor Bob Richardson were taken on a tour of an ocean liner, Jim "paraded" his knowledge of ships. He also experimented with shoplifting and took change from his father's pockets—but was never caught.

Indifferent to sports, Jim had to be persuaded to join baseball or soccer games when he was needed to make up a team, and then would annoy the other boys by refusing to take the game seriously. He knew that he was a disappointment to his father, a proficient tennis player and strong swimmer. An assessment of their relationship appears in "Child's Play," a 1937 story in which a disgusted father tries to teach his timid son to swim: "I felt, if not exactly the shame I ought to have felt, something no pleasanter— a familiar distracted hopelessness—for while I could see how easy it was to win favor and admiration, I knew that I would never be able to do it. Because of my considerable conceit, this was a distressing notion."[10] At the time of *By Love Possessed* the fifty-four-year-old novelist admitted: "All creative arts are compensatory in that everyone who practices them is trying to prove something to someone, and usually it's his father. . . . He was a practical man and he didn't like me at all, if the truth were told. He was bitterly disappointed in me and would be today. . . . He didn't think writing was a man's work. I still think he was right, if the truth were told."[11] Nonetheless, Henry Cozzens wrote humorous verses for his nieces and nephews.

Bertha Cozzens was regarded as outspoken and was admired in the St. Austin's Place enclave for her sharp wit as well as for her cultural interests. She pumped away on the classics at her player piano, but her son couldn't carry a tune. Jim's intelligence delighted his mother, who encouraged him to write accounts of his outings. Well read and a good judge of writing, she may have been compensating for her own thwarted literary ambitions. If that was the case, it was not necessary for Bertha to force her son into the mold she had prepared for him. By the time he was ten Jim Cozzens knew that he was going to be a writer.

Like most writers, he became a steady reader at an early age. In 1924 he told an interviewer: "The first thing I ever remember reading was *Pinocchio* and *The Faerie Queene*. I must have read all of *The Faerie Queene* through before I found it bored me. It was three or four years before I became entranced with it. About the same time I read *Don Quixote*." [12] Since he was playing the brilliant undergraduate novelist at this time, these claims may well have been exaggerations. When he was fifty-nine Cozzens responded to the question "What books did most to shape your vocational attitude and your philosophy of life?" by listing the Oz books, the Motor Boys series, the Henty books, Kipling's *Jungle Books, The Swiss Family Robinson,* and Macaulay's *Lays of Ancient Rome* [13]—a more convincing mix.

Jim's first appearance in print was with "The Andes," published by the Staten Island Academy *Quill* in 1915, when he was eleven.

> The morning dawns, the light supreme,
> The condor lifts its waking scream,
> The shadows flee before the dawn
> Of golden beam, for night has gone.
>
> James Cozzens,
> Grade 6. [14]

A year and a half later his twelve-line tribute to Lord Kitchener appeared in the *Digby* (Nova Scotia) *Weekly Courier*.

> Ho! ye swarthy Arabs
>   On Sudan's burning plain!
> The hero of grim Khartum there
>   Ye ne'er shall see again. [15]

In the summer of 1913 Henry Cozzens went to Britain and Germany on business, accompanied by his wife and ten-year-old son. Other summer vacations were spent at Alden's Farms and Camps, near Watertown, Maine, and in Nova Scotia. Jim went to Camp Wake-Robin in the Catskills in 1916. His father visited him there and recited "Casey at the Bat," which embarrassed Jim but made a hit with the other boys. He also sent an illustrated poem to his son at camp.

> Look here son!
> If I had a gun
> I might point it straight at you.
> And I guess you'd skip
> At a lively clip
> To write your Dad a few
> Selected lines
> 'Bout birds and vines
> And those things you're going to do.
>
> . . . .
>
> So write me a few
> Choice words oh, do!
> Of you work and your hikes and your play.
> Use a pencil stub
> And spell like a dub
> You're sure to grow up someday.[16]

During the summer of 1916 it was decided to send thirteen-year-old Jim to boarding school, because, he suspected, his mother had found mash notes written to him by girls at the Staten Island Academy. (His final marks for the seventh grade at the Academy were: reading, A; composition, 75; grammar, 82; writing, B; spelling, 94; arithmetic, 75; geography, 90; history, 95; French, 75; drawing, B; manual training, C; deportment, fair.)

The Kent School in Connecticut recommended itself because it was High Church and because the fees were lower than for the better-known and older New England prep schools. Kent was filled, but room was made for Jim upon his mother's plea. After her son was admitted, Bertha wrote to the headmaster explaining her persistence: "In fact, to tell the whole entertaining truth, I believed it would be a mutual loss if he never reached Kent. It was nice of you not to explain. I've got it now without help. *He is just an ordinary little kid*."[17] The ironic tone of Cozzens's prose can be detected in these sentences, including his custom of following a formal statement with a colloquial conclusion.

Kent had been founded in 1906 by Frederick Herbert Sill. Born in 1874, he joined the Anglican Order of the Holy Cross, a celibate missionary order, in 1900. One of that legendary breed of New England headmasters whose schools were extensions of their characters, Father Sill established Kent "to provide at a minimum cost for boys of ability and character, who presumably upon gradua-

Father Sill's study

tion must be self-supporting, a combined academic and scientific course. Simplicity of life, self-reliance, and directness of purpose are to be especially encouraged." Located on the Housatonic River at the town of Kent, the school had some 160 students—or "fellows," as they referred to themselves.

Kent was regarded as a "new school" because the fellows did the chores and discipline was theoretically maintained by student prefects. The school was particularly proud of its unsupervised study halls. In addition to waiting table, the fellows maintained the grounds, hauled coal, and harvested crops on the school farm. This work reduced the recommended fee to $700 per year in 1916; but parents paid what they could afford. Henry Cozzens was able to pay $400.

Kent boasted of its self-government system; but Father Sill supervised every aspect of school life, and the enrollment was small enough for him to know every fellow. The familiar cry at Kent was "the old man's on a rampage!" At these times Pater—as he was known to students and faculty—would explode into anger and go through the buildings seeking malefactors. Despite his sometimes arbitrary or outrageous behavior, Father Sill had an intuitive genius for knowing what was right for Kent. "He felt the feelings of a boy. He could accept as real the values of a boy. A boy's wants were obvious to him; a boy's intentions were readily foreseeable." [18] Cozzens later described him very carefully in the character of Dr. Holt in a series of short stories about the Durham School, which was Kent.

Doctor Holt had a magnificent, solid, convex profile. The type is often small-boned, intellectual, but Doctor Holt's face was like something outstanding and lordly cut from a cliff. His blue eyes, keen, haughty and wise, waited, ready to leap. His tangled blond eyebrows—these were a sandy, strong blond, and similar hairs grew out of his massive nostrils—resembled somehow the illustrations in the fourth-form Caesar, showing a cross section of the Gallic defenses—ditch, glacis and a hedge of uprooted trees. Rather round-shouldered, he was not tall enough to have a hollow appearance. He was intensely solid; a considered, terrible energy. Also, he was slightly deaf. This seemed sometimes a stratagem, for whatever it was disastrous or expedient for him to hear, he heard. Involved explanations, trembling evasions and artless falsehoods he could not hear. He roared for their repetition—a task beyond many a guilty conscience. [19]

This was the man who dominated Jim Cozzens's days for six years at Kent.

Primarily concerned with building character, Father Sill did not develop an innovative academic program or particularly encourage individual talent. Adolescent introspection disturbed him. The curriculum was meant to prepare the fellows for college entrance exams. Latin, English, math, and history were required in every year. The only electives came in the fourth, fifth, and sixth forms (sophomore, junior, and senior years of high school), when the fellows were allowed to choose Greek, modern languages, or sciences in preparation for college.

Father Sill endeavored to keep the fellows too busy to get into trouble and was determined to channel their emerging sexual drives into healthy activities. The Kent day began with the 6:15 rising bell. The first class was at 8:00, and classes ended for the day at 12:45, after six periods. Dinner was at 1:00 P.M., after which the fellows engaged in sports or other outdoor activities until the 4:45–5:45 study hall. (Jim preferred to spend his afternoons walking in the countryside with a book, often Swinburne's verse. In the spring he brought back blossoms for his room.) Chapel was at 6:20, followed by 6:30 supper. Evening study hall began at 7:30 and ended with lights-out at 9:00. (Jim habitually read after lights.) The school chores occupied half an hour, twice a day.

Each fellow was limited to an allowance of twenty-five cents a week. There was no social life off the school grounds, and permission was needed to cross the bridge into town. The religious atmosphere was strong but not overpowering. Attendance at chapel and Sunday services was mandatory, and Father Sill heard voluntary confession. There was a stream of visiting missionaries, bishops, and monks. Pater, who wore the white robe of his order, taught required classes in sacred studies. A favorite theme of his discourse was "Can Cosmos have Chaos for its Crown?"

Jim loved Kent in his own way; but he was not the familiar case of the old boy who loves his school for the rest of his life because he was happy and admired there. An indifferent scholar (his name appeared on the honor role only once, when he achieved an 85% average in December 1920), he violated the rules and rejected the life of muscular Christianity—not because he was a natural rebel, but because his own values were the only ones that mattered to him. All the fellows were required to participate in sports, and the football, baseball, and hockey captains were the school gods. Jim played intramural football and was a member of the 1917 championship junior team; but he was not big enough or tough enough

Kent School, 1922

Kent School Championship Junior Team, Fall 1917:
Cozzens, top row, second from right

to win a letter. His later insistence that writing was a compensation for his athletic deficiencies was an expression of the habit of ridiculing the pretensions of literary life. He was a born writer, and his aspirations were formed before he ever saw Kent.

In "Some Day You'll Be Sorry," one of his Durham stories, he wrote about a boy very much like himself at Kent.

The raw material for that disturbing and so unpleasant quality called genius may have been distinct in Benson Smith, but, as sometimes it does, it happened to look very much like laziness, bad temper and deliberate, insolent contrariness. . . .

. . . Although his health was actually excellent, he looked somewhat sickly—a combination which Durham could only excuse on the basis of outstanding scholarship. He had nothing approaching this, but to make Durham's trial more grievous, he was inescapably clever in a moody, reticent, rather insolent way. Most of all he was agonizingly vain.[20]

The prefects were authorized to administer corporal punishment in cases of incorrigible recalcitrance. Jim was paddled for reading indoors during a flu epidemic when Father Sill had ordered the fellows to stay out in the fresh air.

Jim's first major crisis with Father Sill came when he was sixteen, after a summer 1919 canoe trip on Lake George during which he read Thomas Paine's *The Age of Reason*. He returned to start his fourth-form year at Kent in the fall and informed Pater that he could no longer attend chapel because he did not believe in God. When Jim declined to discuss his loss of faith, Father Sill roared: "Get out of this room! I'm sick of the sight of you! Report yourself on detention for a month. If you're absent from chapel, the prefects will take care of it. Get out of my sight!"*

On 21 October 1919 Father Sill informed Henry Cozzens of his problems with Jim.

I feel I ought to write and tell you that Jim's attitude is distressing me very much. I started out when he came back with a most friendly attitude, telling him that I appreciated the intellectual difficulties he was facing and telling him that I did not want to force him to adopt any of my opinions. I went so far as to buy the book by Paine which he said had been his chief reason for his losing his Faith. When the book came I read it over carefully and asked him to come up and see me in order that I might show him how impossible some of Paine's arguments were, in view of the truths substantiated by modern scholarship through what is called the critical study of the text of the scriptures. He then said that Paine's book had not affected him very much after all and evaded an interview. Meanwhile he adopted in Sacred Studies class such an antagonistic and supercilious attitude that I was obliged to tell him that if he could not act as a gentleman he better not come to the study for those classes. He has also resented every word spoken to him in the way of correction and, as two or three men on the faculty have mentioned him as being most obnoxious and fresh in the class room, I felt it necessary to speak to him in a kindly way in regard to this. He is what the boys call a "crabber" that is he is continually criticizing the School and everybody who in any way disagrees with him. I am determined to eliminate this element from the School. James is practically the only representative of the crabbing set at present but this like a disease is apt to spread. Any body who is corrected for a fault gravitates toward the champion "crabber". We had a bunch of them last year and as a result I dropped five boys at the end of the School year on the ground that they were not worth carrying on. Now unless there is a distinct change in Jim's attitude

---

*Quoted from "Some Day You'll Be Sorry." The *Time* account of this episode was provided by Cozzens's roommate Charles Gleaves. Cozzens wrote on the copy of *Time* he annotated for Princeton: "Not F.H.S speaking nor even actual words, I can feel sure, of the reported relator who naturally knew FHS as well as I did. How FHS did speak and behave are set down with every care for accuracy in several C&O [*Children and Others*] short stories picturing 'Dr. Holt.' "

the same result will be inevitable in his case. He is in no sense being made a martyr as he says. I have told him that it is immaterial to me whether he comes to Chapel or not, that feeling as he does I do not want to impose a burden on what I call conscience but which he says does not exist. I just write you this in order that you may know that it is necessary for Jim to change his attitude very soon if he is to return to us after Christmas. This is in no way due to any views the boy may have on religious matters, along that line he must work out his own salvation, but his attitude toward the School and toward authority is such that his presence at the present time is a blemish on the good tone of the place. No doubt he will write you that he is misunderstood, that I have been picking on him, etc. but I am backed up in this opinion by some of my fellow workers. The boy strikes me as being more or less spoiled, he has an exalted opinion of himself and thinks he is superior to all those around him. This is a most unfortunate attitude for an unsophisticated youth to maintain. I hope you will write him a very strong letter on the subject. I regret the necessity of writing as I do.[21]

Henry Cozzens's reply was conciliatory, reporting that his wife was coming to spend a week in Kent. Bertha wrote Father Sill: "I sent him to you three years ago as thorough a little Churchman as any mother ever turned out. I call it up to you—"[22] After her visit, Father Sill informed Henry that he felt encouraged about Jim.

Jim did not return to the fold, although he conformed to Kent religious practice. His sense of decorum, or perhaps it was his indifference to what others thought, quelled the impulse to pros-elytize. In time he would conclude that religious belief was a matter of temperament and that he simply lacked the spiritual temperament. Nonetheless, religion became a permanent interest in its Anglican and Roman disciplines.

He was not bullied or ostracized. His school days were not miserable, although he engaged in a six-year running battle with Father Sill. He read books that the other fellows had never heard of* and held ideas that they never thought of; but his sturdy con-

---

*During his fourth and fifth forms in 1920 Cozzens read Hugo, Ibsen, Miracle Plays, Swinburne, Dumas, Maupassant, Butler, Austen, Balzac, Nietzsche, France, Gogol, Tolstoy, Masefield, Villon, Andreyev, Voss, *Piers Plowman,* Meredith, Cervantes, Lindsay, Bjornson, Hardy, Voltaire, Swinnerton, Francis Thompson, Macaulay, Amy Lowell, Borrow, Chesterton, Thackeray, Dickens, Browning, Ibáñez, Marlowe, Bacheller, Wells, May Sinclair, Hubbard, Rolland, Van Dyke, Shakespeare, Tennyson, Kipling, Aristophanes, Hugh Walpole, Jonson, Moore, Santayana, Dunsany, Turgenev, Dowson, Strachey, Stevenson, Verga. His favorites were *The Way of All Flesh, Jean-Christophe,* Jane Austen, H. G. Wells, and George Meredith.

ceit relieved him of the necessity to prove anything to them. He was not unpopular, and in time won grudging respect for his confidence and displays of brilliance. Of the thirty-three fellows in his graduating class, only Charles Gleaves, a reserved Virginian, became a lifelong friend. Gleaves, his sixth-form roommate, nicknamed him "Gouldy Gouldy Coz Woz."

There were thirteen masters, most of whom shared Father Sill's dedication to the aims of the school. Jim was influenced by three of his masters—Landon Robinson, George Bartlett, and Cuthbert Wright—who lent him books and encouraged him to write. Wright, who impressed Jim as the most interesting figure he had met, left Kent in 1919 to become a writer; but his career was spoiled by alcoholism and personality problems. Robinson resigned in 1920, and Bartlett died that year.

When Jim was interested in a book, he read it in class. Math he regarded as a waste of time, and his Latin was shaky. He managed to stay in Kent by virtue of his ability to concentrate on a subject when forced to and usually cram enough to get through an exam. But when he learned something that interested him, he really learned it. All of his life he would be able to assimilate information and retain it.

Some of Jim's gestures became school legends that classmates could recall fifty years later. For an algebra exam he wrote an essay on the folly of studying algebra. He withheld his topic for one of the required Saturday-evening speech sessions, flipping a coin to decide while walking to the platform, and spoke brilliantly. The topic of another Cozzens speech, "The Degradation of the Democratic Dogma"—from Henry Adams—became a school catchphrase. It was rumored that he had been seen riding in the Stutz Bearcat of a young divorcee who lived in the Kent area. His style set him off from the other fellows; he impressed them by appearing at Grand Central Station to take the "Queen of the Valley" train back to school smoking a Melachrino and followed by a porter carrying his bags.[23]

In January 1920 the *Atlantic Monthly* published E. W. Parmelee's article "A Boarding School Inquiry," which charged prep schools with commercialism, with arbitrary discipline, and with failure to develop serious attitudes about college. Father Sill and sixteen-year-old Jim both wrote replies. The *Atlantic* published Jim's "A Democratic School" in March. He refuted each of Parmelee's points with examples from Kent and concluded with a tribute to Pater.

May I suggest as our crying need, rather than Mr. Parmelee's "American Cecil Rhodes," more men of the type of the head-master of this school, who conceived the educational system. He has endowed American boyhood with a great gift—a gift not yet fully understood by present-day educators, but one which we who have benefited by it must believe to be the coming school, the true, democratic American school.[24]

This article was subsequently distributed as a pamphlet by the Kent Building Fund Campaign Committee. The March *Atlantic* also published a letter from Jim, in which he added a defense of Kent against philistinism. ". . . I have never known anyone to be seriously ridiculed because he enjoyed nature, good pictures, or good music. The boy who really cares for these things is not worried by disparaging remarks from those who don't understand."[25] He had not intended his article as a ploy; nonetheless its publication made it difficult for Father Sill to dismiss him. There were frequent confrontations, with threats on both sides, but Jim remained at Kent.

Jim's consciousness of his literary destiny may have prompted him to begin keeping diaries in 1920. Most gifted youths are aware of their uniqueness and stimulated by the drama of their emerging genius. Despite his resistance to discipline, Jim maintained detailed diaries through 1923, making full entries in ink and never skipping days. He often appears to be writing for the record—that is, for posterity—and he was clearly stockpiling material.*

The Kent diary entries begin with a note on the weather; he always responded to the sky and to the change of seasons. The diaries combine an account of his school activities (particularly his encounters with Pater) with broodings on his ambitions and his sense of urgency in fulfilling his promise. "I have the same fear of inability as I used to have of death" (27 July 1920).†

During his fourth-form year Jim became eligible to "heel" the two school publications—the weekly *Kent School News* and the *Kent Quarterly*, the literary magazine (which banned fiction). There were no *News* by-lines; but twenty-nine of his unsigned contributions have been identified from his diaries.‡ His usual *News* assignment was to report on the Saturday-night speeches, and he regularly supplied editorials. Since the contents of each issue were approved

---

* Cozzens kept diaries in the thirties, but these were mostly weather logs and gardening notes. He again compiled full diaries in the Air Force and during the last years of his life.
† Parenthetical dates in the text refer to Cozzens's diaries, Princeton University Library.
‡ See Bruccoli, *James Gould Cozzens: A Descriptive Bibliography*.

by Father Sill, there were occasions when Jim's articles were killed over his protestations: "But, sir, this is unfair. . . ." One of his *News* editorials was regarded as so extraordinary that some of his classmates remembered it half a century later.

There is a great god called coal. He slumbers under whole states in many ridges and broad fat veins. By grey day and flare-lit night; to the thunder of the breakers and the crunch of shattered rock, to the hoarse roar of long chutes, to the click, click of the wheels in dark tunnels, to the snarl of electric drills and rasp of shovels; year after year men labor in the entrails of the giant.

Twenty million hungry fires absorb the black mounds spewed forth; white crested streamers with faint smoke in their funnels, crack eighteen hour trains roaring Chicago-ward, lofty stacks of fenced-in factories, innumerable dusty cellars whose brick chimneys protrude on shingled roofs; all these, ever greedy, crying for more coal, and more.

It won't be long before that cry cannot be answered. There are plenty of people who are being uneasy about that fact already. They point out with indignation just how rough a deal the public gets when a strike happens. Their concern is not for the workers in the dingy towns where a black dust smothers the flowers and where all sorts of nasty living on insufficient wages goes on. Nor for the men sitting far into the night over papers and columns of figures behind the frosted windows marked private. The men lying behind car wheels in West Virginia, firing and firing until from behind a fence a man raises his rifle and there is presently one less, an unlucky chap with a bullet in his head, detectives who drive armored cars, and ragged men who dynamite the mine entrances— "What is that to us?" says the public, "let them see to that."

Coal, give us coal!

Our ships are idle in port, train after train is laid off, the factories shut down, We must have coal. There is no coal.

That great god coal must stir with laughter under his hills seeing the confusion he has wrought. Men cry for him, suffer for him, they slave in his bowels, fight for him, their lives are built around the fury of his flames. And yet ever and again all we who live by coal cannot get coal. Then the keepers of the fires remember those who work in the earth.

Perhaps some day men will think it worth while to introduce forethought into their affairs. Until then the joke is on them, and a wretched joke it is.[26]

Jim's first *Quarterly* appearance was the republication of his *Atlantic* article in March 1920. It was followed in May by "The Trail of the Lakes," an account of his summer canoe trip—which omitted his discovery of Paine. His other signed *Quarterly* contributions were an essay on Emerson, a criticism of Sinclair Lewis's *Main Street* (which he had not bothered to read), "Religion for Beginners: A Nova Scotian Sketch" (a story disguised as an essay), and his 1922 prize essay, "A Study in the Art of the Novel." He also provided unsigned editorials. While at Kent, Jim submitted stories to magazines, but none was accepted. His most ambitious literary project, begun in the spring of 1920, before his seventeenth birthday, was a long story or the start of a novel set in North Africa. This work developed into his first novel, *Confusion* (1924).

Henry Cozzens died at fifty-four of mastoiditis on 24 January 1920. His sixteen-year-old son was not deeply moved, noting in his diary that day: "Really for the best as he would have at the least been totally deaf."* His father's death freed Jim of a burden of disapproval, for Bertha encouraged the interests that disappointed her husband. In his fifties Cozzens admitted, "I often feel I ought to be in an honest profession. I can hear my father say: 'Jim, you've tried writing for years and you're not a success. Why not give it up?' "[27] Except for the figure of the austere man of reason, the presence of Henry Cozzens can scarcely be detected in his son's novels. Yet, when James Gould Cozzens matured, he moved steadily closer to his father's standards. The romantic boy became a man of reason.

His father's disapproval, compounded with that of Father Sill, inculcated a sense of duty and guilt in Jim. In *Morning Noon and Night,* his last novel, Cozzens analyzed the operation of the Puritan conscience:

Persuasions of his upbringing and environment won't all be eradicable, even when contradicted (and quite a few are likely to seem confirmed) by later experience. An implanted deontology, they put him to a ceaseless passing of moral judgments. Sometimes he may come to manage not to pass judgment on others; he will never manage not to pass judgment on himself.[28]

---

*On 26 January 1921 he wrote in his diary: "It was a year ago today, I think, father died. I was just beginning to know him. It is strange I should not understand him better. Beyond his voice & face I have little recollection, he was never very real, somehow. However he believed in God. How ends the wise man?"

This process found its expression in Cozzens's private term of self-contempt: "You son-of-a-bitch!"

Henry Cozzens left an estate of perhaps $50,000, which was sufficient to provide a comfortable, if economical, life for his widow. There was enough to continue Jim's education without luxuries; but Jim resented being what he regarded as a poor boy. He upset his mother by insisting that money was the most important thing in life and later claimed that nothing so clearly influenced character as the deprivation of money in youth. After her husband's death Bertha received Jim's promise that he would write to her regularly. For the rest of her life he sent long letters on a strict schedule—twice a week until he joined the Air Force in 1942 and every week thereafter.

By the time of his father's death Jim had come under the influence of the Reverend Richard M. Doubs, curate of St. Mark's-in-the-Bouwerie Episcopal Church in Manhattan. Some fourteen years older than Jim, Dickey Doubs was a bachelor with wide artistic interests. He encouraged Jim's literary ambitions, developed his taste in music, and introduced him to the milder forms of Greenwich Village bohemian life during school vacations. Jim was too independent to become his protégé, but the schoolboy was impressed by Doubs's friends and flattered by his attention. Jim eagerly awaited Doubs's letters at Kent. In one Doubs wrote:

It is always a longer or a shorter road to that poise which real people gain after a time. The length of shortness of the road depends on the

The Reverend Richard M. Doubs (Courtesy of All Saints Episcopal Church)

incline. But the height is always the same. It's cold up there. Brand to his ice-palace—Zarathustra to his mountains—each of us to his Pisgah and his Mount of Vision. But long or short, there is no royal road (to be trite). The Royalty is what is on the road. I shall never try to ease your mind or your soul of its burdens. The hopeful part is that you have a mind and a soul meant for burdens. That discovered, the problem becomes: WHAT BURDENS. Re-read the last chapters of "Marius" and the conclusion to "The Renaissance", if you can get an edition in which the Conclusion intact is published. That says it for us all. Appropriate it to your peculiar person and needs.[29]

Doubs was homosexual, which Jim did not realize until much later. Though he was scarcely aware of it, homosexuals were attracted to the handsome, gifted youth. Jim's own appetites were staunchly heterosexual.

Bertha Cozzens moved to the town of Kent in the spring of 1920. Jim managed to see her almost every day, usually going for tea. He was not ridiculed by his schoolmates for his close relationship with his mother; no one seems to have regarded it as unusual. She was admired by his friends, who often came to tea with him. In any case, he was not a mama's boy. He respected her intelligence, trusted her literary judgment, and valued her devotion to him. "When she was allowed to grow up with her power to write neglected a real crime was unwittingly committed. She has a great heart" (6 February 1921). Jim was not dominated by his mother or anyone else. Their closeness was based on mutual interests and a shared belief in his genius.

Although he abandoned the enthusiasm after college, during his student years Jim enjoyed music, attending concerts and subscribing to the *Symphony Society Bulletin* and the *Opera Weekly*. He later said that he really did not understand music, claiming that his interest in it had been prompted by a desire to seem cultured. At Kent he also subscribed to the *New Republic* and was briefly a self-described "boy radical," producing solemn speeches and editorials on world problems.

In the summer of 1920 Jim was a counselor at Camp Wake-Robin, where he had previously been a camper. There he worked on his North African story and wooed "the adorable Helen." Strongly attracted to girls because they gratified his vanity, he was successful with them partly because he was an accomplished dancer. Jim enjoyed kisses and sought them, but his sexual drive was hindered by fastidiousness. He avoided promiscuous girls, whom he regarded as common, and did not try to go beyond kissing the young ladies he wooed. His diaries carefully record his teen-age broodings over the problems of sexual appetite and his desire for idealized intercourse.

He went out for football when he returned to Kent in the fall of 1920 to begin his fifth-form year, but he was dropped from the squad and played on an intramural team. A new series of crises erupted with Father Sill, inspiring emotional diary entries. "I distrust him, his petty tyranny disgusts me, his hypocricy is damnable. And yet this school means so much to me I *will* stay. The pater will never come to reckoning, but the things I know & have seen will someday come to light. He is a paradox, insidious & incredible; great & mean, kind & cruel, sincere (possibly) but lying at every word. I await his award" (26 October 1920). And, "trouble with Sill reaches a new level. It's no use, he simply hates the sight of me, & try as I may I hate the sight of him. Told me I must drop Eng. Hist unless I can pass algebra. I'm am not a deist, but if there is a God I hope some day reckoning will come. Mother is perfectly miserable, he thwarts every effort I make, I'm under his thumb & he knows it. Mother is here & I must think of her first. It would break her heart for me to be fired, I can do nothing except curse Sill. He is monsterous. Short talk with him & tried to come to an understanding but he turns on me in a way that makes me boil. I wish I could tell him what I thought of him. My helplessness drives me to dispair. The future threatens to be impossible" (6 November 1920). On Father Sill's side of the case there were the circumstances that Jim's grades were poor, that he cut classes, and that he broke the study rules for his own reading and writing. Sill could not prove, but rightly suspected, that Jim spent class and study time sneaking smokes. That fall Jim worked hard at organizing and cataloguing the library, expecting to be put in charge of it; but Father Sill gave the job to another fellow, causing a lingering resentment.

Jim's confrontations with Father Sill continued in 1921. In February the headmaster informed him that he had arranged for Jim to transfer to Exeter. The explanation was that his geometry grades were poor; but Jim suspected that the real reason was Father Sill's annoyance because he had spoken out against unsupervised study halls. Jim did not believe that the danger of dismissal was great.

*The Reverend Frederick Herbert Sill, Litt.D., S.T.D., O.H.C.;
portrait by John C. Johansen (Courtesy of Kent School)*

"Of course it is Kent or nothing for me" (23 February 1921). He informed his mother that everything depended on his getting the editorship of the *News*. If Father Sill gypped him out of that, he would leave.

Like many boys who hear the drums of destiny, Jim worried about his lack of achievement. "I must do something soon or I shall lose faith in myself, I wish I knew whether my faith is futile and a waste of time. If I cannot write I shall have lived my life worth nothing, leaving the world no better no wiser for me. I must go on and I hope with my whole soul that Dickey is right when he says I have something. The horror of failure has been present for a long time in the back ground of my life, it is not strong nor troublesome, but it is present. I hope it is empty and harmless" (6 March 1921). His career anxieties were often combined with his sexual ponderings as he recognized the conflict between his rational nature and his desire for ideal love. "I wish I could get more organised, the fear of futility is ever present. I wish I could do something that was worth while, something that would be of some use to the world. The value of life is of course only a relatively important matter, but I can see that there is a great deal to do to make it more pleasant for those who have to go thru with it and I feel that perhaps I can do something. It is so hard to tell. I seem to deliberately thwart my purpose from time to time, to act like such an ass, to be absolutely self-centered. My sex inclinations would be of a dreadfully selfish nature, I can almost say, God pity the girl who gets in my power, at times. And then again there develops a species of real spiritual exaultation, of a fine wonder and yearning, a sense of the divinity of it all. And all thru a sort of horror of degraded sentiment and such, I hardly know what. There are things that it seems to me other people muddle and profane, things that I cannot bear to be touched. It is the same with anything that seems to me really beautiful. It is intolerable to hear anyone comment on it. What a damn ass I am" (26 March 1921).

"My idea is that there is in sexual intercourse a certain priceless mental and spiritual experience and fine sensibility that vanishes after youth (18–24), at least I judge it must from what I have seen & heard. The line between a mere screen (or vehicle, as F.H.S. would say) for lust is hard to draw and harder for some to believe even after it is drawn. The theory would only do for a few people who really have a soul and some inherent delicacy. The idea of a 'sacrament' is abominably trite, but it is hard to find a better word" (28 March 1921). "I lay here almost two hours in the twilight watching the wind and rain in some pale green maple leaves and tried to get over the idea of inherent futility (I am adicted to that word, it is the only one that carries my meaning) Vanity suggests a worthlessness in regard to gain, personal gain, that's what the Preacher was thinking about without a shadow of doubt. Futility is worthlessness in regard to any enduring service to the world. The 'He also serves—' doctrine would be intolerable to me. There is the element of personal ambition, and I don't know how commendable it is. I am not content merely to serve, I want to serve in a pleasant way, I want to see myself doing something, to hear other people—that damned public opinion element—say I'm doing something. Fortunately it's clear that only way I can do much good is by writing, which would be pleasant, at least, and might do all that personal ambition could dictate" (23 April 1921).

Jim continued work on his North African novel in 1921, writing 30,000 words, which he burned in May. He began again in October. His heroine was named Cerise, and the title *Confusion* came when he found a "dandy bit" in the *Meditations* of Marcus Aurelius:

Wipe off all idle fancies and say unto thyself incessantly; Now if I will it is all in my power to keep out of this my soul all wickedness, all lust, and concupiscences, all trouble and confusion. But on the contrary to behold and consider all things according to their true nature and to carry myself towards everything according to its true worth. Remember then this thy powers which nature hath given thee.

He expected to be named editor of the *News* for his sixth-form year because he was the best writer at Kent and had worked hard on the paper. The appointment was made by Father Sill in consultation with the editorial board, and on 1 May 1921 Jim learned that he had lost the editorship to Senior Prefect Frederick Weymer. Instead, Jim was given the *Quarterly*—"a job for which I have no use." His initial reaction was bitter disappointment. "At breakfast it seemed to me that everything was broken and shattered, the light and worth gone out of my school career. Now I think perhaps it has not. There is still a great deal to be done, an infinite amount and in one or two lines I am seeming to win out. I tear up all my carefully composed plans for setting the news on its feet and try to get organised. The Quarterly has, of course, no interest at all. A Prep school paper is such a damn waste of time. It is too bad everyone can not be put to doing the right thing. I believe Shaw says "Get what you like, or you'll begin to like what you get" well—(the quotation is thru Barbellion, by the way, I am enjoying the 'Disappointed Man a great deal.)"*

Jim's 1921 College Board results distressed his mother: English history, 90; American history, 74; Latin, 75; French, 61 and 57; English 55. "I think thats awfully amusing, that 55 in English The damn fools—I suppose it was because I made a few profane comments on some of the subjects we were to write on" (12 July 1921). Bertha was not a nagger, but there were infrequent quarrels when she reminded him of his failure to distinguish himself at Kent. He recognized that he had been a disappointment, particularly in view of the devotion she had invested in him, but he knew that he would continue to be directed by his sense of destiny. "I tried to explain what I have to fight against in an overwhelming force which seems to run me for its own ends. I hesitate to write that as I am mortally afraid it will be misunderstood.† It is not a question of not being able to keep from picking up my reading in a study period as an unreasonable rage at the idea of not doing what I want. To study appears in that light as as senseless as the wanton self-mutilation of some Hindu fanatic. The overwhelming force is myself. If I want to read Plato, I want to do it, & if I read it, it is because I have decided that Plato is more worthwhile than my present lesson. I am not absolutely sure here myself but I seem to be unable to explain it better" (29 June 1921).

Bertha and Jim spent the summer of 1921 at Digby, Nova Scotia, visiting her sister, who was married to Dr. Willard Reade. There Jim conceived a literary hoax, planning to write an imitation of a miracle play which he would claim had been brought to Nova Scotia by English soldiers. His idea was to publish it in the *Kent Quarterly* as a transcription from a manuscript he discovered in the possession of an old sailor. When he lost interest in the scheme he wrote Father Sill that the sailor had died and the manuscript was no longer available.

During the Nova Scotia visit his mother and others warned Jim about his coldness or selfishness, which he acknowledged. "Of course with the exception of Dicky I haven't a real friend in the world. Why? Well because partly at least, I have never found anyone who I could care to have as a real friend, no one who under-

---

*W. N. P. Barbellion, *The Journal of a Disappointed Man* (1919).
†Cozzens's awareness that his diaries might someday be consulted by researchers is obvious here.

stands, who has the sympathy that my mistakes demand. Now as I write about it it doesn't seem so serious and important, yet I know it is. That is Eugene O'Neil's fault, that lack of 'love and kindness,' the thing that stands between him and real genius. I fear it may be mine, and a very hard one to fight as the indifferent feeling is almost impossible to attack" (21 August 1921). His emotional insufficiency concerned him only as an impediment to the fulfillment of his literary ambitions.

At eighteen Jim was prepared to forgo friendship, but not the pleasure of female beauty. His principal interests that summer were dancing and Aileen Elliot, a summer visitor who moved him to transports of romantic effusion. "I really never knew what it was to kiss a girl who wanted you to before and now that I do I have nothing to say that is in any way adequate that will not sound like rot. The sensation of her warm lithe body in your arms and her cool lips on yours, and am perfectly and completely certain there is nothing better in life—there could not be. She clasped my hand in hers and whispered Jimmy softly. I should think my kisses would have burned her, they seemed shot thru with flame and for the moment I felt a sort of unearthly extasy and sheer overwhelming joy that she was at least then wholly and completely mine. . . . She turned her face softly up to me, her throat white in the darkness and took my kiss full upon the mouth while her grip tightened on my hand—God—no one can tell me that it is not better than life, that it is priceless and incredibly splendid. . . . It is enough to make you believe in God for the sole purpose of having someone to thank" (25 August 1921). Jim did not see Aileen after that summer; during the fall and winter he spent hours brooding on her beauty and her kisses.

In the fall of 1921 Jim—at five feet eleven and 127 pounds—again went out for football and was again dropped from the squad. His final year at Kent began with an armed truce with Pater. Jim worked to improve the *Quarterly* and secured contributions by Cuthbert Wright and Robert Hillyer, '13. Contrary to the custom of prep-school editors, he did not make the magazine an organ for his own work. Only two pieces appeared under his by-line during the year—"Religion for Beginners" and his 1922 prize essay—but he provided most of the unsigned editorials.

At the end of 1921 Jim conceived an ambitious plan to write a long poem entitled "An Autumn Symphony, being a Prelude to an Accomplishment." It was "intended to be a summary of my present and recent past attitude of mind, attitudes of mind is more accurate, and general mental reaction of youth to the world in general. It keeps me very busy with the first movement which is to be the sombre one and I did a good part of it, some not bad. The second will be the more usual vein the lighthearted, careless attitude, the third an attempt at a calm summary, the attitude of hope, faith and the presentiments of accomplishment" (2 December 1921). His work ended after 146 lines, which open with a Swinburnesque overture.

> With sweetness of memory and slow sadness of love
> Stumbling word and disobedient phrase
> Untoutered thought, unmellowed recollection
> In sorrow now goes youth down autumn ways
>
> Back from a land of summer vistas and dear dreams
> The world turns winterward, and laughter seems
> To die away down the warm arches of the wood.
> Old gardens faded.
> The keen sorrow,
> Of things bravely begun, and dying not completed.
>
> Either to think
> Or, more blessedly,
> Not to think, not to remember, not to care
> Take which you will. See it awhile
> And feel the everlasting sadness there.
> When the sunlit thickets play at summer
> In autumn's noon
> A moments warmth and light
> For one short hour bright
> Does that atone for the ungracious night?
> What can October know of June? [30]

Bertha Cozzens left Kent in the fall of 1921 to take a job at Greenwich House, a Manhattan settlement house. Jim spent his Christmas vacation there and managed to kiss Betty Sanderson and Dot Kibbe during a dance at the Gotham Hotel. On New Year's Eve he was drunk for the first time.

After Christmas Jim decided to write a new version of his novel, setting it in Perpignan, France. On 13 January he noted that "the start I made on my novel, to be called tentatively 'Confusion' was not all together satisfactory. I am not able to explain why, but I know that the work was not distinguished and I must insist on its being just that, I must deliberately set out for that goal." He was planning to complete it in 50,000 words; and *Madame Bovary* provided the standard for his work: "It is of course the most exquisitely written thing I have ever read, the beautiful construction stands thru the translation, the clarity of thought and sincerity of feeling, all with the incomparable style, you sense it at once as an aristocrat of books, very close to *the* aristocrat. I know I shall be able to write better for knowing Madame Bovary, I could hardly help thinking better" (15 January 1922). At this time he was studying Jules Payot's *The Education of the Will* (1909) in the hope of reconciling his romantic and rational instincts. "There is nothing I am at present sure of. . . . Yet I feel confidantly that the time is not far off when it shall be plain, when a standard of value unbiased by novelty, untroubled by the spirit without discipline, and undarkened by words without understanding will come to me. I believe it so much that I started Confusion to be a novel to picture this mental state roughly for future use, to do it while, as friend Raliegh said, I can 'look into mine own heart and write' " (21 January 1922).

If Jim anticipated that Payot would provide the mental discipline for organizing his time into productive work, he was disappointed. His schedule of a representative day at Kent, made the next day, shows that classes interfered with his real concerns. Indeed, Payot provided distraction.

Sunday, January 22
From six oclock in the morning till eleven at night gives just seventeen hours which I manage to put in each day somehow and yet get remarkably little for them. Ordinarilly I start with a shower get dressed slowly and can sometimes glance over some papers before the morning assembly. ¾ of an hour. The assembly, breakfast, and the pleasant sixth form habit of lingering over the coffee afterwards. ¾ of an hour more. Fifteen minutes to make desperate efforts to get Chemistry done. 15 minutes of assembly. 15 more minutes when we drift to our rooms, turn on the Vic and bask in the sunlight with a Chemistry book more or less open. Classes for one hour and a half except Thursdays when French omits and Saturdays when Chemistry sometimes does. ¾ of an hour when I feel the necessity of doing Math. I look at the clock. 9.45. Then I decided whether or not I feel like Math. If I do I do it, if not I drag down what ever I am reading—Payot lately—or go the rounds to remind the Quarterly

contributers that I am on the map. It is a nice period, very warm and sunny. I could get a lot of writing work done if that was only my job. Math for two solid periods, 1½ hours, in the rather gloomy schoolroom B. That is the low point of the day and brings me up to 12.15. Lunch and things like that to one. At one I come over to the room, consider my prospects. If it is clear I cut whatever work demands attention and walk or skate or ski and I need the exercise so I never protest. 3.00 P.M. now. 3.45 assembly. That space has been taken in changing my clothes and doing the room. 4.00 to 4.30 or perhaps later, the study tea. 1½ hrs to chapel which are really the only profitable part of the day and they not always. Supper to 7.15, or a few minutes earlier. Loaf from then to 7.30. Dining Room from 7.30 to .40 work more or less steady from then to 10.30 or more usually eleven. And somehow there's awfully little to show. Another day gone, gone just as I write, the successive stages pass in review and presently it is always evening, while I reflect and try to choose between Payot and Chemistry.

Jim had staged Lord Dunsany's *The Lost Silk Hat* at Kent in 1921, and in January 1922 he tried to organize a drama club. Father Sill at first opposed a permanent organization, but then reversed himself. In March Jim produced and directed—but did not act in— Lady Gregory's *Spreading the News,* which most of the fellows did not understand. He tried to follow it with *Everyman,* but there was insufficient interest. Father Sill refused permission for a production of *Macbeth*.

When Jim sent his mother an article he was planning to publish in the *Quarterly,* she advised him:

Such clever writing, darling, but it's no go—I hate telling you, but to make it usable anywhere and especially in the Quarterly you'd have to cut out all intensity—Love, for those young things must be kept like your breeze "—impalpable, like the memory of a breeze."—so adolescent love must be only a vision thru moving mists—a lovely trembling dream of love. You were not doing a tea dance affair. Stick to the fireflies, shadowy wood, wavering like atmosphere—cut out, with intensity, all, or almost all the literary weight, and all dramatic action Blur the whole thing with a beautiful touching uncertainty and helplessness of youth. You don't like the beautiful—cut that out too, then—do not make it so real and crude—show them . . . you must not write *of love at present. Your imagination is too much inflamed"* [10 February 1922].

He admitted that she was always right about his writing and scrapped the piece.

Program for Spreading the News

His responses to nature intensified as he developed the ability to record them, as shown in a diary entry when he went out to sneak a smoke before chapel. ". . . I saw along the delicate mass of birch branches the most exquisite grey blue in the sky I have yet met. So I stood dumbly in the snow and stared. The branches like sparse tangled silky hairs above the almost black masses of green hemlock, clouds darkened, puffy grey and the sky. I brushed off a boulder and sat down, watching the drift of them, thin ragged clouds and the slowly changing shade of blue, marvelous half tones and colors. Presently white stars, appearing over the piles of cloud, like the lights of traveling ships. I sat and let the cigarette burn my fingers, being in a religious mood from Taylors exquisite paragraphs [*Holy Living*] thanked any god who might be responsible for allowing such things to be. Incidentally I missed chapel. I wanted very much to save it, to store it up, to leave some record here to perpetually remember it by. It seemed the rarest and most beautiful thing I had ever seen" (13 February).

The 1922 diary entries make it clear that he was using it to polish his skills; it was meant to serve as an exercise book, as well as a journal. "There is a weakness in this diary system—I think that I retain remarkably little interest here by an account of the innumerable petty affairs that fill the well ordered days. . . . I haven't yet learned to give myself a more subjective attitude and can still continue to fill pages with tommyrot of no earthly future interest, I can't remember that one isolated incident well described, one clear reflection, one concise statement of puerile opinion is worth weeks of the minute description of the weather. The damn diary is being kept because nominally at least I believe and hope it will one day be useful. Instead of writing it with that it mind I use it to exploit my sturdy egoism, I never have the sensation of catching scenes and putting them away it these pages. Instead I continually say I did so and so, I thought so and so, which might indirectly explain matters to a discerning reader but which waste a great deal of time. It is next to inconceivable that my daily abstractions should be important while it is relatively sure that what other people do and how they look doing it may be both useful and interesting" (16 March 1922).

During his last months at Kent in the spring of 1922 Jim was corresponding with both Betty and Dot while still brooding about Aileen. Betty was the most passionate girl he had known, and his thoughts about her excited sexual fantasies: ". . . the thought of returning to her at night to drown away the day, to find her soft and white stretched upon the cool sheets waiting for me, naked and unashamed, eager for my embrace, touching me with hot eager hands" (4 June 1922). At the same time he continued work on *Confusion,* which seemed to be writing itself.

In June Jim won the speech prize with "an idealistic one about Russia as an idea, an adventure" and the essay prize for "A Study in the Art of the Novel"—the first time that both prizes went to the same fellow. Father Sill did not remark on this accomplishment at commencement. "Instead I retain a harsh memory of his expressionless stare at the table and utter absence of applause with which he greeted all the other awards, just a sullen silence which breathed hate, the only word for it" (10 June 1922). Bertha, who had moved back to Kent, was delighted that her gifted son had finally distinguished himself at school.

Jim's prize essay rejected the padding of the Victorian novel and praised the economy and vitality of Galsworthy, Wells, Walpole's *Prelude to Adventure,* and Swinnerton's *Nocturne:* "I doubt if books more dear to me than Pendennis and David Copperfield; Richard Feveral and the Mill on the Floss; Pride and Prejudice and Kennilworth will ever be written, but I believe most firmly that the things we have done and are doing today in the novels of this generation will make clear the way and magnificent the progress of those great ones still to come."[31] He also wrote "The Class History" for the 1922 Kent *Year Book,* ending with an obligatory tribute to Pater, "who made the school, who is the school."[32]

The sixth formers remained at Kent after commencement to cram for college entrance exams, and on 20 June Father Sill denounced them as "an aggregation of Judases." When Jim asked if the reference was to him, Sill said that it was. Jim thereupon left the school and tried to return his diploma—with his mother's approval. Father Sill refused to accept it, and the quarrel was patched up.

Jim wrote a farewell to Kent in his diary on 25 June.

Kent School Year Book, 1922

It is irrevocably all over now and the thought gives me an intangible feeling curious and not to be defined with synonyms I couldn't say even were it glad or sad, it had no relation to anything, just a sensation of things over, things done and finished and the book already closed and set away in some forgotten shelf. I sat on the bed in an attempt to analyse the feeling and look back over the six years spent here without success. "So" I thought "it will feel when life is almost done, you sit wondering as you do now." I took it quite seriously and stared at the far wall in the darkness. "See to it" I said aloud "that the years to come teach as much and accomplish more than these now passed" I realised then that I was talking to hear myself with a preverted instinct for the dramatic and was properly chagrined, but the thought decently hidden, remains and I shall not forget, I trust. I can remember at the time that it seemed someone was saying it to me and I did not recognise my own voice for a moment. Really a curious and slightly silly incident.

Harvard was the only college Jim considered. He had hoped for financial assistance from the Price Greenleaf Aid Fund, but neglected to apply in time. Father Sill told him that he had sent Harvard a favorable report.* But Charles Gleaves saw Henry Pennypacker's letter to Sill in which the chairman of the Harvard Committee on Admissions wrote: "I have written to Mr. Cozzens that we desire a personal interview with him at his reasonable convenience. It looks to me from all the evidence that I have at hand as if we probably ought not to accept him into this Fellowship, but we shall reach such a decision only with great reluctance and after much questioning."[34] Jim went to Cambridge and talked his way into Harvard with a display of earnestness; but his admission to the class of 1926 was conditional upon his college entrance exam grades, which were inadequate: geometry, 60; algebra, 30; French, 61; chemistry, 81; Latin, 75; English, 94 (the hundredth percentile); American history, 74; English history, 90. He was three points shy of the required fifteen entrance points. He had hoped to spend the summer working on a ship. Instead, he remained in Kent and

*In "Ignorant Armies," an unpublished novel written in 1924, Cozzens provided the text of a letter to Harvard written by Dr. Holt of the Durham School about Stanley Meredith, which provides Cozens's view of Father Sill's assessment of him: "Dear Sir; in response to your communication I must reply with regret that Meredith will go up to the university without my recommendation. He is a boy of some cleverness, but he does not, and despite every effort, will not, apply himself. I have had trouble with him since his entrance at Durham. . . . Merdith's general attitude, founded on a contempt for rules, indifference to scholastic standing, and influence on boys of a similar type renders him unlikely to preserve the school's good name at the university."[33]

studied algebra and modern European history for make-up exams. His C in algebra and B in history cleared his conditions.

In addition to studying every day during August, Jim planned to finish *Confusion;* but the novel was interrupted for a story called "Tide." He pronounced another summer work, "The Conquest of the Corn," as "more splendid and beautiful than I thought possible for me to do. It goes off to the Dial tomorrow and acceptance or not it is a wonderful thing, a thing fraught with an unfamiliar genius which I hardly dare call my own" (27 August 1922). It was rejected by the *Dial* and was not preserved.*

Dot was at Camp Po-ne-Mah at South Kent, five miles from Kent, but Jim managed to see her only a few times. He was deflected by his interest in Consuelo Ford, a young married writer living in Kent. Jim did not become romantically involved with Mrs. Ford, but his attentions to her upset his mother. As always, he was preoccupied with his ambitions and introspections—playing the young genius while trying to form principles for his career. One evening in New York he saw tramps sleeping in the park and "concluded it couldn't be helped and the only thing to do was ignore it—not very satisfactory, but absolutely the best I could do after very long and careful thought. . . . God knows I'm ready to be radical, but I don't see any damn use in it. I class it with religion in a bracket labeled nice but silly" (19 July 1922). Beauty and the satisfaction of writing well were what he required. "Those who feel the urge to solve life's meaning gain their satisfaction in the stress of the hunt. I take mine from the blue evening hills, the moon the flowered fields, music at night and colored lights, the ensnared thought in a verse of of a half dozen lines, the satisfaction of the endless striving for personal accomplishment and perfection, candle light and blue cigarette smoke, the glow of wine glasses, a girl's lips and her laughing eyes, all the things which are spread out before in a tapestry of experience and memory and expectation" (6 August 1922).

*The *Dial* paid him for a book review, which was not published.

NOON

TWO

Fair Harvard

C o z z e n s ' s 1922 diary breaks off in September, before he entered Harvard. Because he was admitted late, dormitory space was not available. He took a room at 30 Mt. Auburn Street, where Kent alumnus Robert Hillyer, an instructor in the English Department, had an apartment.

Tuition was $250 per year, but Harvard was expensive for a young man who liked to eat well and enjoy himself. He found it impossible to manage on fifteen dollars a week. There were many agreeable ways to spend money in Cambridge and Boston, and Cozzens resented the necessity to economize—not that he really tried. For someone who demonstrated his indifference to other people's views, he was sensitive about seeming poor. There was a clear system of social stratification at Harvard, symbolized by the circumstance that Cozzens lived in a rooming house insultingly near the expensive "Gold Coast" dormitories. At the top of the heap were the exclusive final clubs—of which Porcellian represented the peak of Harvard success. Cozzens would come to feel that if he could not go through Harvard in style, then it was not worth going at all.

In 1922 Harvard could boast the most distinguished faculty in the United States, under President A. Lawrence Lowell. The stars of the division of humanities included Irving Babbitt, Charles Townsend Copeland, John Livingston Lowes, George Lyman Kittredge, Bliss Perry, and Alfred North Whitehead. As a freshman

Cozzens took five courses: English A (Rhetoric and English Composition), German A (Elementary), French 6 (General View of French Literature), History I (European History from the Fall of the Roman Empire), and Philosophy A (History of Philosophy). Cozzens entered Harvard with high resolves, expecting at least four A's. He would be able to concentrate on courses that interested him and was free from math requirements. However, his confidence was shaken by the realization that for the first time in his life he was competing with first-rate minds. At Kent he had convinced himself that he could excel in his studies if he took the trouble; but at Harvard he made the humiliating discovery that there were young men with superior resources of intelligence.

The freshman class impressed him as "the dirtiest, greasiest, most completely unattractive bunch I have ever seen assembled."[1] He was surprised by the heavy and consistent consumption of synthetic gin, but told his mother that she had no cause to worry about his drinking. Undergraduates cultivated what was known as "the Harvard manner." One did not make oneself conspicuous; the big man on campus was a figure of ridicule. One practiced understatement ("rather amusing" meant "very interesting"). One did not know many people. One did not know Jews, although 20% of the undergraduates were Jewish. Only Jews asked questions in class. (One of the Jews in the class of '26 was Robert Oppenheimer.) Cozzens's conditioned anti-Semitism developed beyond the fashionable snobbery of the time.

In October he sent his mother an account of his college days:

Monday Wednesday and Saturday I have that horror known as a nine oclock class and it necessitates my getting up at eight forty and hastening over to the new lecture hall. There is a little dump named Bond's on the littel street that I go up and they always have a hot chocolate malted milk ready in two seconds notice at a temperature that enables you to get to class in six minutes from the house. That's about nine (Tues., Thurs; Sat, about ten) and brings me thru to lunch at twelve in much better mental condition than when I have a formal breakfast. I don't get sleepy in the mornings any more and the doing without utterly unnecessary bulk in food does it, or at least so my friend Edwin A Locke in his boresome and undoubtedly correct volume on food values asserts. At any rate it works to perfection.

Then you dash down to the Georgian a spacious and rather interesting cafateria where every one has lunch. Then three afternoons a week you go and exercise. The other three I head over for the Historical Department library in the basement of the rather gigantic library building and take notes on my proscribed (excuse me, pre)) reading for two hours. That brings me to about three. Then I walk down to the house and Mr. Hillyer always drops into my room when he hears me come up then and suggests a walk which lasts until five or so. Then you have tea with his an amicable talk until half past six before his fire. Then you go out to supper, at the Cock Horse or the Pickwick Arms with him on leisurely evenings and at the Georgian on the others, which means usually. Almost always I meet Pres or Tommy then and have supper with them. I declare a holiday until eight oclock and run up to their rooms to talk to Pres and watch the amusing efforts of the rest to get an edge on before going out for the evening. That's one of the rules of the game. You get un-steady before you start and then carry a flask so you can get good and soused on an instant's notice. At quarter of eight I come down to my place and settle down religiously till eleven thirty or so when Hillyer generally gets in from some poetical adventure and asks me to come in and have a biscuit and a glass of his carefully collected wine, a sort of Chianti which he gets by the dozen from some secret source. Then you sit before the fire and talk about books and things and the art of the occult which has rather taken me by storm, and get to bed about twelve thirty.[2]

Cozzens's friends during freshman year were sophomores Tom Howard, John Abbott, and Press Mabon (Kent '21); he attended concerts and dined with history instructor Paul Schaeffer. He prided himself on knowing few of the men in the class of '26. His closest friend during 1922–23 was Hillyer, who, "civilized me as much as I could be civilized."[3] Nine years older than Cozzens, Hillyer had published four volumes and was regarded as one of the more promising American poets. Cozzens admired his fluent command of verse and was gratified by Hillyer's encouragement when they read each other's work-in-progress. An Armenian lodger at 30 Mt. Auburn supplied them with arrack, which they drank during their late-night sessions.

Cozzens was not a joiner. His only formal extracurricular activities were the Poetry Society and the History Club, which was supervised by Schaeffer and had only five members. He contributed to the *Harvard Advocate,* the literary magazine, but did not seek a position on the editorial board. His first appearance in print at Harvard was a sonnet in the November 1922 *Advocate.*

THE TRUST IN PRINCES

Lo, my Lord Summer is come stricken down,
His smouldering liveries strew the autumn street,
To lift and fall about my casual feet.
His garden palaces of late renown,
Are wasted wholly. His tall forest crown
Is stained and sere; he is long dead, men say.
From his rich trappings heaped in dank decay,
Rises blue smoke, the hills' funereal gown.

Mourn! Mourn! How shall I, who am dumb with pain?
Prey of spoiled hopes, of the cold wind despair,
Which browns the secret groves of my own brain.
I trusted him when he stood radiant there;
Prevail he must! I cried in my delight,
But now they burn his banners in the night.[4]

He appeared in the *Advocate* eleven times during his freshman year—seven poems, three book reviews (Joseph Hergesheimer's *The Bright Shawl*, Lord Dunsany's *Don Rodriguez,* and Jane Austen's *Love and Freindship*), and one story. The poem that attracted the most campus attention was "The Virginia Rose: A Ballad for Eunice," an eighty-line work in the May 1923 issue. (Eunice Johnson was a Boston girl with whom he was friendly, but not in love.) Reminiscent of Alfred Noyes's "The Highwayman," Cozzens's ballad narrates how a highwayman kisses Lady Anne Shelton,* known as the Virginia Rose. The final stanza reads:

> They tell of the six league running fight
> That Jerry fought one dark June night.
> A sliding board and a knot loose tied
> Was the end of Jerry's desperate ride.
> Men prayed he'd swing choking into hell
> But perhaps 'twas their way of wishing him well,
> Since paradise might seem pale to those
> Who had once kissed the Virginia Rose.[5]

The only work of fiction by Cozzens in the *Advocate* was "Remember the Rose" (June 1923), in which roses symbolize mutability. A young man and an elderly woman share a passion for roses, but he is deflected by a beautiful girl. He is too young to

---

* Cozzens also gave this name to the heroine in *Michael Scarlett* (1925).

believe the inscription on the garden sundial: "Remember the Rose how it doth fall."

Despite his resolution to study at Harvard, Cozzens continued his custom of neglecting assignments for writing and the reading that interested him. He attended concerts and the opera, dined in Boston, went to dances and parties, took long country walks, and boxed for exercise. His enthusiasm for music was largely feigned; and he later wrote of the autobiographical protagonist in *Ask Me Tomorrow:* "Music was not one of Francis's natural interests or pleasures, for he was practically tone-deaf; but the love of it is a mark of superior culture, and so he had heard a great deal of music while he was at college and supported with disciplined patience many concerts and evenings of opera rather than have his friends suppose he was in any respect their aesthetic inferior" (p. 24). As at Kent, he wrote a good deal of verse. Though not a conspicuous campus drunk, he regularly consumed prohibition booze and carried a gin flask to dances.

There were Boston girls who interested him during his freshman year, and he became romantically attached to one of them while maintaining his correspondence with Betty Sanderson and Dot Kibbe. When Cozzens reviewed his Harvard diary in 1977, he compiled a list of the girls mentioned and observed: "One sees with pain that I was really a little bastard, loving attention" (7 July 1977). Sex was still a steady concern, but he did not want to sleep with any of the girls he knew. Although he was normally randy, he required more from a woman than an orgasm. One of his Harvard friends performed fellatio on him, which Cozzens submitted to in the spirit of urbane curiosity. This experiment confirmed his preference for women—even though he had not yet had one.

The spring semester of his freshman year and the fall semester of his sophomore year are documented by diaries. In February 1923 Cozzens resumed work on the draft of *Confusion* that he had failed to complete during the summer before he entered college. The novel had been planned as a justification of the passage from Marcus Aurelius that supplied the title and theme: confusion of the spirit could be conquered. As he wrote Cozzens found that his conviction of "pleasant futility" was taking over. "I just feel that most of the main springs of human action are rot—that I don't know whether I can prove it without betraying the fact I don't believe what I say" (16 February 1923). While writing the novel he continued to think of himself as a poet: "I still know that my job

is to somehow interpret the essence of the age in verse and then, if ever, it will be clear sailing enough. I shall hit it sooner or later as the matter is constantly in mind" (20 February 1923). To help himself master the sonnet form, he memorized Shakespeare's sonnets, as well as many of Hillyer's poems. What he memorized he retained, and he would automatically drop phrases from Shakespeare into his speech and writing for the rest of his life.

On 24 February Cozzens finished the first draft of *Confusion,* which did not end as planned: "it seemed to take its-self out of my hands and after futile objecting and side stepping on my part made Cerise die, throwing my last years moral to the winds and giving an odd ironic flavor to the quotation from Marcus Aurelius." He had written his first novel at the age of nineteen years, six months. When Hillyer advised him to stop writing for a while Cozzens observed that it would be easier to stop eating. "There is just one thing I want in this world and that is to write well, to write as well as the thoughts form in my head. If I could ever catch the picture perfectly there would be nothing to it. . . . I don't know that I can ever write verse which will accomplish any— but I know the day will come when English prose is my devoted slave and I shall astound one or two people" (25 March 1923).

After seeing Dot in New York during the 1923 spring vacation Cozzens experienced spells of dejection which he treated with alcohol. "I know I love Dot, but I don't know what it will or could come to, I don't want to marry her, sex doesn't interest me in the least—I don't know what I want of her, or what I would do next having gained it" (23 May). He agonized when she did not answer his letters promptly. One May evening, having dosed himself with gin fizzes, he lay on Hillyer's floor and wept.

Although he was placed on probation for exceeding the cut limit in the spring of 1923, Cozzens finished his first year at Harvard in tolerable academic standing. He failed German; but earned B's in English, French, and philosophy, and an A in history. His summer schedule was to live at Kent with his mother and rewrite *Confusion*. Hillyer had found him a job revising a travel book, *Lanterns Junks and Jade* (published in 1926), by Samuel Morrill, for $150. Cozzens worked steadily on both projects—with time out for bridge. One of the influences on the new draft of *Confusion* was Compton Mackenzie's *Sinister Street* (1913–14), a quest novel that had inspired F. Scott Fitzgerald's *This Side of Paradise*. Cozzens sometimes worked on his novel ten hours a day, writing directly on the typewriter. (He was a fast two-finger typist.) His mother read and criticized his work. Father Sill was cordial. They had long conversations, and Cozzens suspected that the change in their relationship indicated the headmaster's concern to maintain the loyalty of an alumnus who showed symptoms of fame.

Dot was again at Camp Po-ne-Mah, but Cozzens managed to see her only a few times because she was carefully supervised. Bertha was hurt when her son decided to dedicate his novel to Dot; he had unfeelingly assumed that his mother did not expect to be the dedicatee. As he worked on *Confusion* during the summer of his twentieth year his confidence grew, and he understood that writing would be more important to him than love. "It's a damn cinch I never ought to marry because I foresee an existence wherein I shall want to do nothing but write, when no one, nothing will matter except that. . . . It doesn't seem to matter in the least whether this stuff ever gets published or not, I've been gravely asking myself how I shall feel if things go wrong and the prospect does not bother me in the least. I feel an absurd confidence in my own ultimate success, in my own future ability to write junk which will be good beyond question, which I will find satisfying. But Dot. As soon as I finish the work I somehow feel Dot will become again extremely important" (23 August 1923). And the next day: "I'd rather like to marry her and put her away somewhere I might be able to have her around when I got time." At the end of the summer he asked Dot to elope with him—perhaps in emulation of his novel. She declined, rather to his relief.

Before returning to Harvard for his sophomore year he visited Tom Howard at Ogdensburg, New York, where his family had a house on Po-ne-Mah Island in the St. Lawrence River.* There Cozzens met Wellesley student Wilifred White, the daughter of an Episcopal minister. It appeared that she and Tom had what was then referred to as "an understanding"; but Cozzens was strongly attracted by her "crinkly blond hair, the faintly husky tone of her voice, the tone of her skin, dusty, faintly freckled, about the same gold tone as her hair."[6]

Cozzens returned to Cambridge with an estimated twenty pages of *Confusion* left to write. His first priority was to finish the novel for submission to B. J. Brimmer Co., a small Boston firm that published Hillyer. He roomed with John Abbott off campus at 22 Plympton Street, next to the *Harvard Crimson* building. At the beginning of this year Cozzens was required to declare his field of concentration; he chose history and literature with the Renaissance as his special area. His courses during the year were History 5^1 (History of the Church to the Reformation), Philosophy $6a^1$ (Philosophy of Religion), Philosophy 15^2 (Kant), Philosophy $20a^2$ (Seminar in Metaphysics), French 10^2 (The Social Background in French Literature), Latin 8^2 (Cicero and Lucretius), and a repeat of German A. He registered for History 11 (History of England during the Tudor and Stuart Periods), which he was allowed to drop, and attended some of George Lyman Kittredge's lectures on Shakespeare. Kirsopp Lake's classes on church history and architecture in History 5^1 impressed him; but he neglected his courses for writing, carousing, and Willie White. After determining that she was not informally engaged to Tom Howard, Cozzens saw her frequently at Wellesley and in Boston. During the course of one alcohol-fueled spree he smashed the lights in Apley and Dana and put a road-closed sign in a friend's window. Father Sill saw him drunk at the Yale game and refused to speak to him. Cozzens's friends that year included S. Foster Damon, '14, and Dudley Fitts, '25, who became respected scholars.†

* Ponemah was the land of the hereafter in "Hiawatha." Cozzens later used the name in *By Love Possessed*.

† Fitts designed a bookplate for Cozzens showing a tortoise with a lily and a motto from Catullus, "Nescio sed Fieri Sentio et Excrucior." Cozzens later explicated the symbolism: "—the tortise is classically Time bearing away slow but sure the Lily (Beauty); so, yes; *I don't know why it's that way but I feel bad.*"[7]

Ex Libris
James Gould Cozzens

Harvard bookplate designed by
Dudley Fitts

Wilifred White at Wellesley

The revision of *Confusion* was finished on 10 October 1923, and Cozzens delivered it to the Brimmer offices at 343 Boylston Street. The president and editor of the firm was William Stanley Braithwaite, the Negro poet and anthologist. Two days later Cozzens was with Willie at Wellesley's Pomeroy House when he received a phone call from Braithwaite. Brimmer would publish *Confusion*. The contract, dated 18 October 1923, gave the publisher all rights to the novel and a nine-year option on the author's work. (Cozzens mistakenly assumed that the option clause meant that Brimmer would have to publish anything he submitted.) There was no advance. In any case, the contract was not legally binding because the author was too young to sign it. This triumph was capped by his first kiss from Willie on 30 October. "I was feeling wretched beyond words quite suddenly; chiefly that I did after all want to kiss Willie more than anything else on earth, and I knew I never could, first because Willie forbade me and second because I knew why she forbade me. I did feel rotten but I was taken wholly by surprise to find my eyes perilously and inexplicably full of tears— everything seemed wrong and too wretched. As we passed under one of the occasional lights Willie saw before I could brush them away. 'Oh, what is it?' she whispered, and it seemed to hurt her at least as much as it hurt me. 'Nothing' I said. She stopped short and stood looking at me in the dark. I wasn't going to kiss, I knew I couldn't and mustn't. Willie caught my scarf and drew my face down to hers, and so I shut my eyes and let her, until her trembling half parted lips were on mine. Of course that finished, she cried a little and kissed me and clung to me and God knows it was a blessed thing to hold her in my arms."

Two days after Braithwaite accepted *Confusion*, Cozzens began plotting a new novel, "The Cloudy Trophy" or "Cloudy Trophies."* intended to provide " a complete exposition of what I think about women" (7 November 1923) as well as an accurate assessment of Harvard—rereading *This Side of Paradise* "to learn how not to do it" (18 November 1923). But he soon abandoned it to start on "Ignorant Armies,"† a novel about prep school, Harvard, youth, love, and futility. On the eleventh of December Cozzens was sent to the Harvard infirmary with jaundice. There he worked on "Ignorant Armies" and planned a "scheme of books whereof both this and Confusion have a part. The others will be The Cloudy Trophy, and Avalon and I plan privately to cover in the four the whole case of youth as it appears to me. If all goes well I can certainly get the Ignorant Armies done this summer and once in mind the others should follow rapidly" (15 December 1923).[8] His Harvard diaries end with 1923.

Cozzens met Lucius Beebe early in 1924, probably in connection with the forthcoming publication of *Confusion*. The son of a Massachusetts banker and industrialist, Beebe was well launched on his career as an eccentric, dandy, and *bon vivant*. Having been dropped from the Yale class of 1926, he was spending 1923–24 as a reporter for the *Boston Telegram* before resuming his education, at Harvard. At six-foot-four Beebe was an imposingly well-clad figure whose vocabulary was larded with archaisms and esoteric learning. Cozzens did not realize that Beebe was homosexual (or perhaps bisexual at this time). Beebe's custom of being "majestically drunk" at 9:00 A.M. impressed him; Cozzens drank with him and imitated Beebe's aristocratic arrogance—a Harvard version of the damn-your-eyes, milord manner combined with Restoration wit and debauchery. Cozzens took to carrying a walking stick and sported a

---

* From Keats's "Ode on Melancholy": "His soul shall taste the sadness of her might, / And be among her cloudy trophies hung."
† From Arnold's "Dover Beach": "And we are here as on a darkling plain / Swept with confused alarms of struggle and flight, / Where ignorant armies clash by night."

raccoon coat that he bought (but did not pay for) from Beebe. He ran up bills with tailors and florists (he sent Willie flowers every day), expecting to finance the splurge with his anticipated royalties from *Confusion*. He hated "the small wounds to pride, the private chagrins, the anxieties of living, because you felt that you had to, willfully beyond your means."[9] Braithwaite probably encouraged Cozzens's high hopes, for he thought *Confusion* was brilliantly written and expected to make it another *This Side of Paradise*. (*Confusion* was a novel of youth, but it was not a novel of flaming youth; one of the best sellers of 1924 was Percy Marks's *The Plastic Age,* about collegiate drinking and wenching.) Within the limited resources of his firm Braithwaite publicized the novel and its author. Press releases about the twenty-year-old Harvard author resulted in newspaper coverage, especially in Boston, and Cozzens rather enjoyed playing the role of brilliant boy novelist.[10]

Published on 11 April 1924,* *Confusion* chronicles the education of Cerise D'Atrée, daughter of a French aristocrat and an English mother. Her father dies before she is born, and she is elaborately educated in Europe according to a plan supervised by her mother and the Russian Leon Tischoifsky, Prince Serganoff:

---

*Publication had been scheduled for February. Although he had stopped wooing Dot, he kept his promise and dedicated the novel "To Dorothea."

The author of Confusion

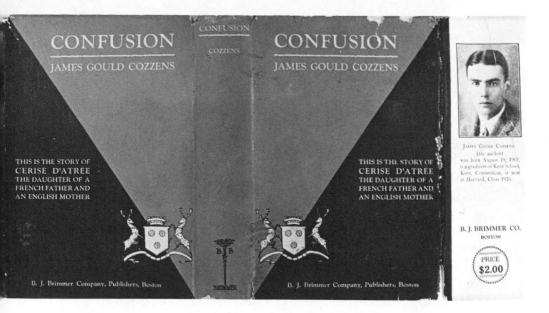

CONFUSION

JAMES GOULD COZZENS

THIS IS THE STORY OF
CERISE D'ATREE
THE DAUGHTER OF A
FRENCH FATHER AND
AN ENGLISH MOTHER

B. J. Brimmer Company, Publishers, Boston

CONFUSION

JAMES GOULD COZZENS

THIS IS THE STORY OF
CERISE D'ATREE
THE DAUGHTER OF A
FRENCH FATHER AND
AN ENGLISH MOTHER

B. J. Brimmer Company, Publishers, Boston

JAMES GOULD COZZENS
(the author)
was born August 19, 1903,
is a graduate of Kent School,
Kent, Connecticut, is now
at Harvard, Class 1926.

B. J. BRIMMER CO.
BOSTON

PRICE
$2.00

Jacket for first printing of Confusion

. . . at twelve she promised well for their plans. True, she was listless at such studies as Latin and Mathematics, but she spoke three languages fluently, and much more Spanish than people not Spaniards usually speak. Her reading had been fairly wide; she knew quite a surprising amount of history. Though she rebelled against practising on the piano, exhibiting no aptitude, even protesting with a fervency it seemed foolish to over-ride, she had a musical taste in the forming, and could talk pictures with wide knowledge. Yet even Tischoifsky must confess that with the exception of her talent for languages and admiration for history she did not offer more than average promise academically. But there were things she did very well indeed. She could do anything with a horse, she was a tireless swimmer, and all Tischoifsky's uncanny skill with rifle and foils had been exercised at her demand to make her shooting a local sensation, to provide her with a wrist of steel and no little dexterity in fencing. That much was definitely his work, his training and it was by his encouragement that Cerise followed what were apparently her own instincts. In all one could be more than a little proud of the accomplishments of the very lovely and very boyish Cerise [pp. 54–55].

Sent to America during the Great War, Cerise attends boarding school and a New England women's college. But she has been over-educated or overtrained: there is nothing to challenge her in America. Overwhelmed by futility, she elopes with an undergraduate. He is killed when a train hits their car, and Cerise dies of terminal confusion. When Bertha received her copy she wrote her son: "Its fault—if it be a fault—is that, like Cerise, it is over-educated— Your very unusual mental equipment is obvious—" Feeling that her devotion was finally yielding dividends, she declared, "I'm the proudest mother alive today." [11]

In Cozzens's apprentice novels Cerise is the first of the line of superior youths who are unable to find duties or causes commensurate with their abilities. She is not a rebel against convention, not the familiar twenties figure of youth in revolt. Rather, she is so superior to her environment that she has nothing to rebel against. Even though *Confusion* can be traced to the quest novels of Mackenzie and Wells, Cerise's quest is largely passive. She feels no call to a unique destiny, no controlling aspiration.

Confusion is loosely structured in scenes and episodes that do not link up closely. The style is lushly romantic by any standard—embarrassingly so by the gauge of Cozzens's mature prose.

"Cerise," said Blair lifting his head, "Marry me."

"Oh, please," cried Cerise, touching the hand which crushed hers. More than moonlight, more than that far music, and the heaviness of the primroses, the flash of reiterated pain in her fingers seemed to take her heart trembling and close over it so her breath faltered and her head reeled. It was as if she had been snatched up to the dim stars in the keen sweet pain of space, pain that seared the heart while the heart shuddered and laughed.

. . . .

Cerise slipped a finger under Blair's chin and held it a moment so she could see his eyes. "I love him," she thought, her heart in a shuddering ecstasy. She wondered if she were going to faint. It was like being on a mountain top, a mountain of all the splendor and spoil of ages heaped in gem and gilded mail, up into the vivid night, and Blair lay at her feet and the jeweled stars swung low to crown her lifted head.

"Marry me," whispered Blair.

"My dearest," said Cerise, laughing low and clear. She arose softly and turned yearning to the silver light. "Now," she thought, "let me die." Blair started to his feet and she was in his arms, she felt his lips, and clinging to him, closed her eyes against the madness of the moon [pp. 351–52].

The dialogue is self-conscious and unconvincing; the characters are given to pontification and often seem to be reciting set speeches in a play. *Confusion* allowed the sophomore novelist to display his remarkable store of erudition. What he did not know, he researched. He would always be able to assimilate information for

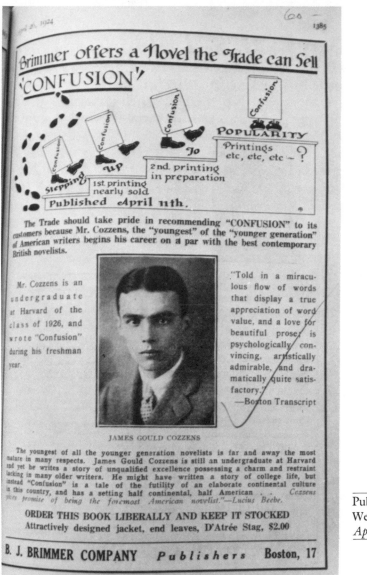

Publishers
Weekly, *26
April 1924*

the needs of his fiction, but he still had to learn how to use his research naturally.

In publishing his first novel Cozzens had produced a false start. *Confusion* is pretentious and overwritten; the characters are unbelievable; the whole thing has the secondhand quality of a novel written from books, not from experience or observation. (When Professor Copeland saw the novel he "virtually ordered" Cozzens to take his writing course in junior year.) Cozzens came to recognize that *Confusion* was a bad novel and that the good luck of its publication had been unfortunate. He had written it before he learned how to write and had therefore been confirmed in bad habits that took years to break. The only way in which *Confusion* can be said to foreshadow Cozzens's mature novels is that it deals with a search for values—here frustrated.

Confusion attracted review space in the Northeast, with most of the critics commenting on the novelist's youth. The *Boston Transcript, New Republic, Bookman, Time,* and *Harvard Advocate* were friendly. William Lyon Phelps declared in *Scribner's:* "It is an excellent story, and perhaps its chief triumph consists in this: the heroine is an absolute paragon, physically and intellectually, and yet is real." [12] But Joseph T. Shipley was condescending in the *Nation* ("That it should all be taken seriously is a tribute to Mr. Cozzens's skill at cozenage"), [13] and the *New York Times* was scathing:

. . . Mr. Cozzens is not yet a novelist. He has not learned from the Pater he mentions so glibly, or even Gustave Kahn, that the artist selects—even in all this confusion. Every artist of any significance has started out knowing that there is confusion—some indicating phases of it, some forgetting it, some laughing at it—but Mr. Cozzens just takes a hard grasp on Roget's "Thesaurus" and his pen writes quite truthfully on every one of his 404 pages "confusion." [14]

Cozzens was hurt by this review and never forgot Beebe's obvious enjoyment of it. Nonetheless, Beebe worked on his behalf, serving as a press agent and reviewing *Confusion* in the *Boston Telegram.* Comparing Cozzens with Fitzgerald, Percy Marks, and Cyril Hume, he declared:

Cozzens has plumbed the depths of human weakness with a facile agility which leaves his readers feeling in themselves the flat, stale, and unprofitable qualities bound up in the uses of this world. There is in his work the calculating introspectiveness, a little youthfully morbid, of a Conrad without his ponderous stylism.

Not only does Cozzens give promise of becoming the foremost American novelist. In many ways he has started already to justify that reputation. Far more of an artist than any of the other three novelists we have considered, he is the accomplished master of style and language as well as a scholarly and erudite writer. [15]

The size of the first printing is unknown, but it was probably 2,000 copies. A full-page ad in *Publishers' Weekly* on 26 April 1924 bravely announced that the first printing was "nearly sold" and that a second printing was "in preparation." There was no second printing, and some 500 copies of the first printing were remaindered. The royalty on 1,500 copies of a two-dollar book would have been $300—not enough to maintain Cozzens in the style to which he aspired, or even to settle his bills.

While Cozzens was enjoying his celebrity and carousing with Beebe his studies were neglected even more than before. Harvard placed him on scholastic probation during the spring of 1924, and at the end of the term he received grades in only two courses (C in history and B in philosophy of religion). Drinking and lack of sleep damaged his health; on 27 May he was allowed to withdraw from Harvard "in view of his physical condition." At the time of his departure he owed the college $262.39 and had debts to local tradesmen, including a sizable bill at August Brothers, tailors. Although he was eligible to return to Harvard, Cozzens probably knew that his college days were over. A feeler from Porcellian, which he could not afford to join, contributed to his decision to leave Harvard (7 January 1977). "I did not want to return to Cambridge unable to support myself financially on the scale I felt my 'fame' as a published writer required. . . . On the other hand, I saw how I could avoid all that and perhaps even improve what seems to be called today my 'image' by withdrawing myself to a place remote and improbable, dedicating a year's leave-of-absence to my 'art.' "[16] Willie White also figured in his decision to drop out of Harvard, for he was aware that another year of close proximity would probably bring about their marriage; and he was not ready to marry.[17]

In June Cozzens rusticated himself to Woodman's Point, Westfield Center, New Brunswick, Canada, where he lived with his uncle Milner Wood while he recovered his health and completed "Ignorant Armies." Impractical as the scheme seemed, Cozzens really did accomplish a great deal during his self-exile. He worked too fast, but he wrote. B. J. Brimmer had virtually turned into a press for Cozzens and his friends; and Dudley Fitts had become a sort of editorial adviser to the firm. The August 1924 Brimmer catalogue in *Publishers' Trade List Annual* announced *Ignorant Armies* (for February 1925), *Corydon and Other Poems* by Beebe, *The Historia De Petro Cvnicvlo of St. Florentivs Vinosvs* by Fitts, and two volumes in The Imperishable Series to be edited by Cozzens: *The Criticisms of John Keats on English Poetry Selected from his Letters* and *The Sonnets of Michael Drayton*. Only *Corydon*—dedicated to Cozzens—was published.*

The *Petro Cvnicvlo* volume was planned as a Latin translation of Peter Rabbit with a bawdy and blasphemous mock-scholarly apparatus by Cozzens; but the project collapsed when someone realized that Peter Rabbit was protected by copyright.† Cozzens's redaction. of Keats's critical views reached the dummy stage before it was abandoned.‡ The Preface explains:

> It is not the purpose of the present writer to devise new ones [theories] or reassert old ones, for in this small volume are set forth what he believes to be the theories and opinions which matter most, and they are those of John Keats himself, than whom few writers have possessed more capacity for self-perception and self-criticism. In their vigour of expression and colourful exactness of phrase the reader will find the surest guide to an understanding of all the significances and beauties of the man's work[18]

During the summer and fall of 1924 Beebe—whom Bertha regarded as a corrupting influence on her son —undertook to pacify Cozzens's creditors and manage his literary affairs. He arranged for Braithwaite to provide an allowance of eighteen dollars a week (Cozzens had asked for $150 a month) and sent frequent letters of advice as well as whatever money he could spare—which was not much, since he was on a tight allowance.

Dear Jimmy,
I received the enclosed notice in the mornings mail. Under all ordinary conditions this outlaws all outstanding cheques and the bank refused to do anything about. I, however, got together with Durant and his lawyer and managed to get them to withdraw the attachment. They promised they would do this and so I hope it has not interfered with the cheques drafted in Canada.

---

*Jacobo G. Cozzens/MAXIMA CUM ADMIRATIONE/NEC NON ET/AMICITIA PERENNE/HAECCE CARMINA/DEDICAT/AUCTHOR. [The author dedicates these poems to James G. Cozzens with the greatest admiration and indeed with everlasting friendship.]
†The working drafts of *Petro Cvnicvlo* are with the Fitts papers at Yale. The 24 May 1924 contract with Fitts and Cozzens for this volume was signed by Fitts only.
‡The unique copy is at the University of Notre Dame Library.

Durant was extremely decent about it and did not wish to inconvenience you at all. He proved it by promptly withdrawing his lein. What he was sore about is that he has sent you a registered letter asking at least for a reply even if you couldn't pay him. You didn't do this and so he tried to draw to your attention to the fact that you had neglected to do it.

I hope you will write him at once and explain all this, as I did some very hot talking for you and practically went as far as to guarantee your account personally.

By devious routes it has been reported to me that Billings and Stover (happy source of infinite supplies of bubble water) contemplate a similar action. I therefore pray that your cheques come through before I have another harrowing scene such as has just taken place with that attorneys of Durant.

Neither of those two matters are in themselves of serious account. What is serious is the cause of them. The word has somehow leaked out from Harvard headquarters, I believe through one of the under-secretaries, that you are in hot water with the university and probably won't return in the fall.

Rumors are borne to my unwilling ears of fifty seven varieties of hell that is going to break loose almost at once. There have been a good many veiled inquiries at Brimmer about you and one or two people are about to attempt to get your money there. I feel that as soon as the good old fashion panic starts there will be a very devil of a riot of abuse and yelling and dancing up and down and shouting of "You're no gentleman", mostly as a result of the story that has percolated from the bursar's office.

I'm getting to where the thing is out of my hands, and I can't personally go around making promises when I have no reason to believe they will be justified, at least not to all and sundry.

Now my advice is this. Note carefully as I may never again be sober enough to remember it.

Stay right where you are in Canada and don't for the life of you consider coming to this state before the game week-ends unless things clear up.

Go to your mother and let her pay what bills she can, and don't be lilly-fingered about it. The university will make an actual claim against her on your bond pretty soon and then she will have to do it.

Write to those tradesmen you can't possibly pay off with her help and tell them they'll have to wait a while.

Make your plans for the winter doubly secure by not cashing any cheques in Canada and not running into any debt.

If you want your stuff sent up from your rooms I'll have that done at once. I don't think the landlord will try to hold it since it is hardly worth his while.

Above all don't hesitate to let your mother help you out by whatever means she may see fit. Some of these bills like your college and rent will be brought against her legally where-ever she is anyway.

My usefulness is about at an end with the tradesmen here because they're on to even my lying and yessing, and I expect them to begin with direct measures without much delay now. Only August has your address and so they can't really pester you personally for a time, but they will get judgements and liens out against you no end, so that it seems time you took the bull by the horns and saw what can be done with the creature.

Perhaps my perfect bluntness of suggestion is a reflection of the spartan simplicity with which various tradesmen have spoken with me in the matter. I do not mean to suggest that you rely on your family if it can't actually be done. But her peace of mind will be vitally affected later by it and so she might as well do what is possible now.

You will, I'm sure, Jimmy, understand I should never mention such low matters to you but that they are now a crying need and I don't want your name to stink in Cambridge here over that sort of thing. I am nothing but a recording instrument passing on to you the dope that I pick up through a score of sources and it is quite impersonal.

Therefore, old toss-pot, think of me not as a ticker in a broker's office so much as

> your friend,
> Lucius [19]

Cozzens came to Boston for a meeting with Brimmer during the summer, and Beebe visited him in Canada.

Fitts reprimanded Cozzens in Latin and English epistles, excoriating him for his arrogance and warning him against betraying his genius.

What I am very much afraid of [is] that your carefully nourished attitude of studied indifference and contempt for the world as a whole will harm your work. You must not get the idea that you are divinely afflated, or whatever the term is, and somehow or other raised above all human obligations. . . . Why in hell should you, with no assets but your own genius (tremendous, I admit, but not infallible) tear about the peacefull streets of Cambridge, running up huge bills that you know you can never pay? And that someone else will have to pay? Why in Hell should you treat perfectly nice boys with such studied insolence as to make your name an anathema hic et ubique, and to jeapordize the reputation of those few friends of yours who do so love you and who would do any goddam thing in the world for you? What if Simeon Gook cannot scintillate conversationaly? So that he be a gentleman with the instincts of a good fellow, why in hell should you snot him in viis publicis and hail him as woolly? James, you are one of the princes of the Earth. You are the pride of my susceptible heart, and the joy of Lucius' life. But the fact remains that you are also one of the most monumental and epoch-making asses that ever brayed through a winged collar. (The rev Beebe says that the real source of the trouble lies not in the fact that you wear a winged collar, but that you wear a fourinhand tie, instead of a bow, in it. . . .) For Christ's sake, stop making easy blurbs, such as 'If I can't live like a gentleman, The game isn't worth it.' God! Does that mean any damned thing at all? Must you swindle merchants (and God knows I shed no tears over them) and ruin your mother's peace of mind, shout 'woolly' at nice-looking boys in Jimmies, urinate in Grotties' cars, and antagonize your University, to say nothing of getting dishonourably expelled from it—to live like a gentleman?[20]

Cozzens dispatched "Ignorant Armies" (which he considered retitling "Hebron House") to Beebe in installments during the summer. As the title indicates, "Ignorant Armies"—like *Confusion*—examines youth's search for values and goals.* It is inferior to *Confusion*—loosely structured, overpopulated with unconvincing characters, and freighted with soliloquies and disquisitions.

The central figure is Stanley Meredith—a minor character in *Confusion*—and the novel records his career through the Durham School and Harvard. A child of wealth and a gifted musician, Meredith is plagued by the same strain of futility that afflicted Cerise D'Atrée. During his sixth-form year at Durham he writes a novel expressing the message of "Ignorant Armies": ". . . youth isn't prepared for life from any view point. Humanity's debt to youth, or rather obligation toward youth, is being disregarded."†

One of the characters, clubman David Locke, the best-dressed man on two continents, appoints Meredith his literary executor. He spends a summer editing Locke's allegorical fantasy "Lazarus" (included in "Ignorant Armies"), which exacerbates his sense of futility. At Harvard he becomes sexually involved with Leda Holmes (another character from *Confusion*), who has been dismissed from Wellesley for smoking. When their relationship is discovered, Meredith decides to go to Africa as a soldier of fortune; but the conclusion is left open-ended, and he may be remaining

---

*Each of the chapter titles is taken from Arnold's "Dover Beach": I. Let Us Be True; II. The Land of Dreams; III. So Various; IV. The Darkling Plain; V. Night.

†The typescript of "Ignorant Armies" is with the Cozzens Papers at Princeton University.

with Leda. "Ignorant Armies" is the work of a brilliant young man who had not learned how to plan a novel or develop characters.

After dispatching his second novel, Cozzens reported on his situation to Braithwaite from Digby, Nova Scotia, where he was visiting his uncle Dr. Reade.

I've been waiting in some anxiety to get your opinion on Armies whose last parts Lucius has doubtless turned over to you by now. The possibilities of its being serialised are rather low, I fancy, for which I'm sorry as por Dios we do need cash. And shall need it more desperately at the end of this month. Any small sum over the eighteen dollars a week which you can squeeze out will go far toward saving my life as I sit here alone and destitute speculating on the possibilities of getting to Fredericton. Thirty dollars would get me there and even pay a few express charges and such like rot, likewise buy me five or six cigarettes and clear me for a brief week at least. I'm frankly up against it and must count definitely on your promise for a couple of months. By which time I really hope to get Avalon into your hands—I go up to the Acadia College Library at Wolfville at the beginning of next week where I can get a ripping collection of historical data on the period—I'll only be there a couple of days, so pray you write here. J. Keats is getting finished rapidly—I think you'll be impressed by its interest and value, it ought to sell quite powerfully if it can be got out fast, but if there is pressure in print shops, as I imagine, I think it rather more important to get the Drayton out first as there there is real danger of a forestalling. I shall have the Keats manuscript in the mails by a week from now if all goes well—I'm quite sure you'll like it. I neglected in the press of concluding Armies to thank Miss Jackson for the kind note on my brithday, I do it now and thank you for all your kindness to me. I await your comment on Armies with bated breath[21]

Braithwaite's reaction to "Ignorant Armies" is not known, but the novel was never published—partly because the firm was in financial trouble.

The allowance from Braithwaite—which terminated before Brimmer went bankrupt in June 1925—was inadequate to maintain Cozzens and allow him to pay installments on his Harvard debts. Beebe and Braithwaite advised him to write short stories for ready money, and Braithwaite recommended him to a New York literary agency, Brandt & Brandt. Cozzens did not succeed in selling a story until 1926, but the agency represented his novels after the collapse of Brimmer. One of the employees at Brandt & Brandt was Sylvia Bernice Baumgarten, a twenty-two-year-old secretary who was working her way up in the book department.

In the fall of 1924 Cozzens moved to a rooming house on University Avenue in Fredericton, New Brunswick. When he lent Aldous Huxley's *Antic Hay* to the daughters of Bishop Richardson, it was returned with a note from the Bishop saying that the book was not suitable for young ladies. During September he researched and abandoned a historical novel on Fort Louisbourg at the library of Acadia University in Wolfville. (Fort Louisbourg, Nova Scotia, was the site of two sieges during the war between France and England, in 1745 and 1758). He dropped his trilogy plan after "Ignorant Armies" and began *Michael Scarlett,* a novel set in Elizabethan England. Cozzens returned to Kent for Christmas 1924 and lived with his mother while he revised *Michael Scarlett.* In January he was trying to serialize "Ignorant Armies" in *College Humor* while Braithwaite was shopping the novel around to other publishers.

On 12 June 1925—nearly five months before his novel was published—Cozzens wrote an article for the *Daily Princetonian* headlined "Harvard Author Reviews New Work 'The History of Michael Scarlett,' " in which he stated that the dominant characteristic of Elizabethans was "the inability to see two sides, theoretically possessed by every problem"; he had tried to remove the whitewash from the age and show in Nashe, Marlowe, Jonson, and Donne "the untrammeled wholehearted blindness of those yet uninfected by the major disease of civilization, our much vaunted tolerance."[22] *Michael Scarlett* is an improvement over both *Confusion* and "Ignorant Armies." More tightly plotted, it eschews the digressions that marred his previous novels. Moreover, the sixteenth-century setting permitted Cozzens to display his erudition without ostentation, and the Elizabethan speech concealed his stylistic indulgences.

Like Cerise D'Atrée and Stanley Meredith, Michael Scarlett, the future Earl of Dunbury, is an elaborately educated youth. At Cambridge he forms close friendships with Thomas Nashe and Christopher Marlowe, who respect his literary gifts and need the protection of his name and wealth. After a bloody town-and-gown riot with the puritans, Michael and his friends move to London and take over the Golden Asse inn, where their familiars include John Donne, Robert Greene, and Ben Jonson. William Shakespeare figures as an opportunist who is not well regarded by the

university wits. Denied responsibilities at court because of his youth, although Queen Elizabeth favors him, Michael becomes the leader of the London anti-Puritan faction. He dies helping Nashe escape from being arrested for murder. The Latin epigraph for *Michael Scarlett,* from Lucretius's *De Rerum Natura,* applies more clearly to Cozzens's circumstances than to those of his hero: "Indeed, being shamefully disposed and suffering bitter poverty are manifestly far removed from the pleasant, steady life and, as it were, linger right at the gates of death. . . ."

Michael Scarlett is a convincingly brilliant performance for a twenty-one-year-old Harvard dropout. Cozzens shared the Elizabethan love of rich language and responded to the adventurous spirit of the age. Unlike many historical novels, in *Michael Scarlett* the attempt to reproduce the speech of the period does not seem quaint or silly. Cozzens obviously relished the opportunity to write dialogue for the masters of English verse, as in Marlowe's blasphemous peroration:

"Hell, hell, hell—why these words?" Marlowe slipped out his dirk, laid the keen point on the skin of his throat behind his windpipe. "One twist and push," he said, "an eye's wink, a mere twist of muscle—'Hic jacet this much useless tripe." Marlowe turned the point slowly till the skin broke and blood ran. Michael stared at him in the shadows. "Dost think, why saith he so much and doeth so little? God knows! Here's blood. A paper and a splinter." He reached out, the great shadows wavering, and took them from the table where Michael's Aristotle lay open by his writing materials. "Didst read my pretty lay how Jack à Wertenburg bonded his everlasting soul? God's Teeth, I'll shame the devil!" His great black shadow aping him on the wall, he bent forward, dipped the splinter in the blood on his neck. "No congealing there; it dost consent to my damnation. Marlowe gives to thee his soul. Excellent well writ." He stared at the tiny red marks on the paper. Suddenly he roared aloud, "Oh, peerless jest! I am consigned to hell! Mark you, Michael, how I frustrate Belzebub. Right here is hell, nor am I out of it. I've plumbed hell, I've toiled in hell! New hells for old! Veni, veni, Mestophile—he won't come. Why should he? He doth find his own hell hot enough without approaching mine! Dost fear fire Michael? Warm, comforting fire?" [pp. 101–102].

Miss Baumgarten got Cozzens out of his Brimmer option contract and placed *Michael Scarlett* with the new house of Albert &

OPPOSITE.
At the time of Michael Scarlett

Charles Boni, which published the two-dollar novel on 2 November 1925.*[23] The novel was elaborately dedicated to Willie.

MICHAEL SCARLETT
His History
BOTH WITH HOMAGE, AND WITH ADMIRATION AND
ESTEEM
TO
MISS WILIFRED WHITE

Madam:

   I call on you thus long after his inception to read and I hope countenance Michael Scarlett. Did I not think him close to your wit, that was his true begetter, I had taught him a less ambition than wear your name. Now he approacheth your censure, tricked with that care and skill I had, content shall any worth commend him, you will count it yours and cast the bye away

yours also,
J. G. C.

Michael Scarlett was not widely reviewed and sold only 707 copies. As unsigned favorable review in the *New York Times Book Review* annoyed Cozzens by pointing out chronological "blunders" he had intentionally committed to condense the time frame[24]; but he was gratified by a complimentary note from Professor Roger Merriman ("the grand old man of the Elizabethan Age"), whose English Renaissance history course he had dropped at Harvard. A revised edition of *Michael Scarlett,* published in London by Holden in 1927, sold 269 copies. (Thirty years later Cozzens recalled "one change I made in a hurry. It was pointed out to me that . . . Shakespeare was caused to praise highly some verses of which I was the actual author. Pretty thick, I had to admit.")[25] The *Times Literary Supplement* ridiculed the swashbuckling plot: "it evidently could not have gone on much longer with such a death rate."[26]

---

*Other 1925 novels were Fitzgerald's *The Great Gatsby,* Willa Cather's *The Professor's House,* John Dos Passos's *Manhattan Transfer,* Theodore Dreiser's *An American Tragedy,* and Sinclair Lewis's *Arrowsmith.*

THREE

Foreign Strands

I N September 1925 Cozzens was in Tuinucú, Cuba, near Sancti-Spíritus in Santa Clara Province (now Las Villas), 200 miles southeast of Havana, teaching the children of American employees at the Czarnikow-Rionda Central Tuinucú sugar mill. He had eight pupils under the age of fourteen, whom he divided into four classes, meeting from 8:00 A.M. to 3:00 P.M. He got along well with his charges, who were being prepared for further schooling in America, and was sufficiently proud of their progress to send his mother reports when they did well on tests. The children, whose educations had been neglected, responded enthusiastically to Cozzens's curriculum, which was strong on literature and history. On 17 December 1925 he gave this four-hour exam covering two weeks of classes to Mary Brooks Kirby-Smith and Earl Hine:

I

1. Sketch fully the events between 500–479 B.C. which brought about the ascendency of Athens in Greece.
2. Give an account of the men and methods concerned in the formation of the Delian Confederacy; its purpose, original organisation and evolution.
3. Notes on 18 of the following;

The Ionian Revolt	Aeschylus	Athenian Constitu-
Mardonius	Piraeus	tion under Pericles
Themistocles	Euripides	Phidias
Battle of Himera	Pausanias	Herodotus

Pylos   Cyrus   Brasidas
Alcibiades   Sophists   The Sicilian Expedition
404 B.C.   Pindar   The Athenian Theater
Sophocles   Nicias   as a means to culture

4. On the Map, locate: Athens, Syracuse, Sparta, Thermopylae, Sardis, the Hellespont
   show the route of either the Sicilian Expedition or Xerxes' Invasion.

II

1. Sketch briefly the life of Victor Hugo.
2. Write in detail on the character of Javert, selecting at least two incidents from Les Miserables to illustrate your point.
3. Outline the story from the arrival of the ship-of-the-line Orion at Toulon to the departure of Fauchelevent and Jean Valjean from the Vaugirard cemetery.
4. Deriving your material from the first book of Les Miserables, comment on the effect of the severe French criminal code of a hundred and twenty years ago on the criminals it was designed to correct.

III

1. Brief note on Sir Thomas Malory.
2. "And anon he led him to the Siege Perilous where beside sat Sir Launcelot, and found there the letters that said thus; 'this is the siege of . . . . . .'"
   (a) Of Whom?
   (b) Describe briefly his adventures from that point until the end of his quest.
3. "And when the knight felt him stung, he looked down and saw the adder, and then drew his sword to slay the adder, and thought of none other harm."   Describe the circumstances under which this took place and what followed to where the arm rises from the lake and catches Excalibur.
4. Identify 5 of the following Merlin, Beaumains, Knight of the Red Launds Sangreal, Sir Kay, Sir Mordred, Melias, the lady Lionesse, the Maid of Astolat, Guenever.[1]

He was pleased when Mary Brooks scored 90 and Earl 80. His favorite was Katherine Kirby-Smith, and he remarked that he would not mind having a daughter like her.

Life was agreeable for Americans in semicolonial Cuba. Cozzens lived at the American Club, which was amply staffed with servants, and had his pick of horses from the company stables. He rode

most afternoons, often with the children. The American men cus-
tomarily went into the countryside armed against bandits, and
Cozzens sometimes carried an unloaded revolver in his holster.
There was considerable socializing among the half-dozen American families; the handsome, well-spoken tutor was welcome at their
parties. He was popular with the wives and accepted by the men—
Eph Kirby-Smith, the Administrator; Joseph Eggleston, the Chief
Field Engineer; Hine, the Chief Mill Engineer; and R. O. Binet,
Manager of the Royal Bank of Canada in Sancti-Spíritus. Cozzens
admired the manliness of Eggleston and Kirby-Smith as compared
to literary types. He was impressed by the competence of Eggleston, who rode the crop and maintained company property. In his
early thirties, Eg was a hardheaded boss who could get anything
done. The men were drinkers and invited Cozzens to join their
sprees. He developed a fondness for Tropical beer and Royal Alex-
anders (Bacardi, goat's milk, honey, egg white, and absinthe).
Cozzens enjoyed himself in Cuba. He acquired a stable of fighting

*Cozzens at
Tuinucú,
Cuba:
Joseph
Eggleston on
his right*

cocks and made trips to Havana, after which he worried about venereal disease. He vomited after his first visit to a brothel.

Still paying off his Cambridge debts, he tried to supplement his salary by writing short stories for Brandt & Brandt to offer. "Letter to a Friend" was sold to the *Pictorial Review* for $250 and appeared in May 1926. Cozzens's first story sale was an obvious sop to the magazine market. A young man writing home boasting of his success in New York is chased from a hotel writing room for loitering. Cozzens's unpublished 1924–26 stories are known only by their titles: "The Miracle of St. Proteus," "The Gray Men Take a Purse," "The Disastrous Conflagration of the Steamboat Isis," "Earthworms," "The Song of India," "The End in View," "Fire and Candlelight," "The Good Fight," "The Leather Love of Henceforth Strephon," "June Night," "Five from Dos Fuegos," "La Gloria," "The River of Thieves." *

He corresponded with Willie from Cuba, and in November wrote to his mother:

I'll always regret from time to time that I didn't marry her, but such regret is really beneficient I expect. Which recalls unexpectedly one of the few good sonnets I ever wrote—sent up to her about a month ago

> Cherish, Belovéd, that so facile prize,
> Your Golden Now: whose slight, gay, colours go
> Like dust upon the moth-wing, sun-reached snow;
> Duller growing and grayer to weary eyes.
> Tighten your fingers on that precious flow
> Of aureate sand, too careless held, that buys,
> For all its sifting, spilling, melting so,
> The few immortal moments of the wise.
>
> Now when the sand is thinning more and more,
> And Time is freighting low the nether scale,
> While youth takes wing, and presently hopes pale,
> I will be blind and mute. Ah, spend youth's store,
> Dance out the music ere the late lights fail,
> And I, I will be waiting as before.[2]

Despite his seven-hour teaching schedule and the strenuous social life, Cozzens worked on novels, about which he corresponded

---

* Four unfinished Cuban stories—"Chinaman's Chance," "The Snake," "Old Order," "He Who Would Valiant Be"—are preserved in Cozzens's papers at Princeton; but it is impossible to date them.

with Bernice Baumgarten at the Brandt & Brandt agency. His principal project was "The Minor Catholicon," a novel "showing all about how life is empty and future ferocious a.d. 600 at Anitoch."[3] (A catholicon is a panacea, or a comprehensive treatise, or a lesson from the Catholic epistles.) On 1 November 1925 he sent his mother a nine-chapter plan "with the elegant subtitles done into English":

I. The Counsel of Esculentus.
   Thou, who from so great darkness wert first able to lift so shining a light, illuminating the blessings of life, thee, o glory of the Greek race, do I follow. (Lucretius, in De Rerum Natura)

II. The Behaviour of Acersecomes.
   When asked how he accounted for these man-loving fellows the sage explained: "That Prometheus, who made our race, came home one night very drunk and through the confusion of his heart and the error of drunkeness attached generi masculo to some girls." Phaedrus Fables of Aesop.

III. The Good Intention of Horans.
   What does it profit a man if he gain the whole world and destroy his own soul? And what shall a man give in exchange for his soul? (Roman Vulgate for Matthew 16, 26)

IV. The Appetite of Matella.
   Therefor is it fitting that a woman cover her head, because of the angels (Corinthians I, 11, 10 — also R.V.) (I can thank Willie for that)

V. The Response of Vacculus.
   Therefore young lady, when you get the man crazy about you by these means, you might acknowledge that Ovid was your teacher (Ars Amatoria)

VI. The Loyalty of Semprus.
   here are the tears of things. . . .

V. The Observation of Mentule.
   and mortal sorrows touch the soul. (Vergil in the Aeneid)

VI. The Faith of Philelephantus.
   Jesus saith unto him (her), I am the resurrection and the life whoso believeth in me, if he were dead, yet should he live (John 11, 25 also R.V.)

VII. The Conduct of the Praetorians.
   Therefor is death nothing and pertains to us not one jot, since the nature of the mind is mortal (Lucretius in De Rerum Natura)[4]

Much of Cozzens's effort went into refining or remaking his style. After translating André Gide's *L'Immoraliste* to keep up his French, he explained to his mother on 29 November: "Just what I want is harder to say, but a less ornate style for one thing. I have never, as I noted long ago, seen it in English, but it's Andre Gide's better stuff in French — perfectly stark, smooth and lucid, a result not so much of simplicity as of an agonisingly careful choice of words. I gave way inevitably to the temptation to write richly of a highly colourful and ornate setting, and while I think I've done the job well enough through three or four of the nine or ten chapters, I see now that it is not at all the book I had in mind, and still have in mind." Cozzens later insisted that a writer could only write the way he wrote; but there is ample evidence that he painstakingly reformed his early style away from the ornate. "The Minor Catholicon" was completed in 1927 and destroyed. While working on it in December 1925 Cozzens planned a short novel about Alcibiades, the Athenian politician and general (c. 450 –404 B.C.), to be called "Gifts." This work probably never progressed beyond the planning stage. He also replotted "Ignorant Armies," intending to salvage the material and characters for a new novel to be written in Germany during the summer of 1926.

In the spring of 1926 Cozzens felt bored with the pleasant but artificial life in Cuba and was concerned that his career was losing momentum because he was finding it hard to save time for writing. When he learned that Mrs. Doty—the niece of sugar tycoon Don Manuel Rionda and the queen of Tuinucú—was considering a pair of married teachers as possible replacements for him, he offered his resignation with a sense of relief. The separation was amicable, and Mrs. Doty promised to find a job for him in Peru. Cozzens left Cuba broke, and he still hadn't discharged his Harvard debts. Just before his departure he wrote his mother, on 15 May 1926, about his conviction of developing literary powers:

. . . I know without any need for comment or argument with myself or any one else that I have the power of writing as well as anyone at present on earth can, it's developing steadily and when it hits on all eight all the people who would wisely or cautiously doubt and deprecate such an insufferable statement from the Hero as Conceited Young Man will simply get knocked between the eyes—if it were a matter of any personal worth or worthiness I'd be more tolerably sceptical about it myself—this hasn't got anything to do with me as a person—my various virtues will not forward it (supposing any one has ever detected any) and my lamentable darwbacks (I wouldn't dignify them as vices) won't hinder it—it's simply in me and is on the way out—the most I can do is what I have done, write and write and write so that the mechanical side of it will not keep the other waiting. I'm practically ready now, but it won't be this year, I think and what successes I can manage will be aside from the actual point really, the product of accidental smooth functioning of the undirected but oiled up machine. Something is going to start it all of a sudden and I have no way of telling what it will be—as I've said before, I'll simply wake up one morning and discover it has begun—I'll knock everyone with sense for a row of empty bacardi bottles beginning with that moment.

Cozzens returned to America with the vague plan of going to Mexico after visiting his mother. They decided, instead, to spend a year in Europe, partly to take advantage of the favorable rate of exchange. (Bertha's income was $2,933.50 in 1928.) They sailed for France on the *Carmania* in August. A fellow passenger was the Reverend Killian Stimpson, chaplain to the U.S. Students & Artists Club in Paris, with whom Cozzens formed a friendship and later made an auto tour of Brittany and the château country. Canon Stimpson had a wealthy wife, a château at Versailles, and did himself extremely well—which prompted Cozzens to contemplate the advantages of marrying money. (Willie White was in France that summer, but his passion for her had cooled.) Since Dickey Doubs had served at the American Pro-Cathedral of the Holy Trinity in Paris, Cozzens had introductions there. He avoided the expatriate literary life and made none of the almost obligatory Left Bank contacts: he never met Gertrude Stein or Hemingway or Fitzgerald. Though well schooled in the art and history of Europe, his reactions to the populace were xenophobic.

Canon George Gibbs of the American Cathedral introduced him to Virginia Reiland, a 1925 Vassar graduate and the daughter of the Reverend Karl Reiland, rector of St. George's Episcopal Church in Manhattan. Virginia, Cozzens, Gibbs, and another girl made day excursions to the cathedrals around Paris. Cozzens fell in love with her "infinitely appealing hollow-cheeked face and wide but beautiful mouth";[5] but his courtship was hampered by his limited finances. He hated being poor and hated even more having to acknowledge his poverty.

An unpublished 1931 story, "An Introduction to Mammon," anatomizes Cozzens's sense of deprivation at the time he was in love

Virginia Reiland in 1925

Cozzens with Edward C. Parish, Jr.

with Virginia Reiland. Francis Ellery, the young author of two books, is in Paris feeling very superior to American materialism. He has about $500 left from a small inheritance, which is all he requires for his quiet life. He meets Lorna, an American girl just out of Vassar, and discovers that the inexpensive pleasures he shares with her cost money. He cannot afford to join her on a trip to Italy. Francis then resolves to make his future in business. "It might take time, it must take work, and perhaps good fortune, like Uncle George's help; but I would be back in Paris someday, able to go to Italy, to go anywhere my unremarkable desires pointed. After all, they were not, I saw, humble but happy in having learned it, desires of a sort to point to any high place where an abundance of this world's goods could not bring me."[6] "Introduction to Mammon" was the seed for the 1940 novel *Ask Me Tomorrow*—which retains the characters' names from the story—and provides a clue to the process that Cozzens underwent during his year in Europe, not a conversion to materialistic ambition, but the clear recognition that genteel poverty and Grub Street were intolerable. Wanting above all else to write, he nonetheless wanted to be comfortable and enjoy what seemed reasonable pleasures. Just as he had left Harvard rather than cut his garments to fit his pocketbook, so he was too proud—or too conceited—to compete in the humiliating struggle for literary fame.

Bertha was operated on for cancer at the American Hospital of Paris in September 1926. Cozzens remained at Neuilly during her recuperation, starting the "third or fourth version" of "Ignorant Armies."

In October he was showing Meudon Forest to an American girl and got into a dispute with a taxi driver, who grabbed his wallet and tried to drive away. Cozzens jumped on the running board and recovered his wallet; the driver tried to run down Cozzens and bumped the girl with his cab. Thereupon Cozzens pulled him out and punched him. They all ended up at the local *gendarmerie,* where depositions were taken. The *Paris Tribune* reported that "an American, said to be Jack Gould Coznes" had been charged with severely beating a taxi driver with a cane.[7] The case seems to have been dropped.

Bertha's illness cut into their funds, and in November Cozzens took a job as a traveling tutor while his mother remained in Florence. Mrs. Edward C. Parish, a well-off American, was touring Europe with her son and a maid while her daughter was attending a French finishing school. Edward C. Parish, Jr. was fourteen; he wore leg braces as the result of polio and suffered from asthma attacks. Cozzens prepared him for the St. Paul's School entrance exams and was required to serve as the boy's companion until dinner, after which he worked on "The Minor Catholicon." Although Cozzens found Edward "a nice kid" and performed his work well enough that his pupil was admitted to St. Paul's, Mrs. Parish felt that he was not sufficiently interested in her son. Cozzens resented his position as a servant and the limitations placed on his liberty. *Ask Me Tomorrow,* the novel based on Cozzens's months with the Parishes, shows that the author-tutor was sensitive about his ambiguous position, which pricked his twenty-three-year-old's pride. Mrs. Parish informed Bertha that she would not look with favor upon his romantic interest in her daughter—which was nonexistent. From the perspective of 1940 he regarded his attempts to cut a figure in Europe (he wore a cape and carried a cane) as painfully absurd.

After joining the Parishes in Montreux and accompanying them to Grindelwald, he persuaded Mrs. Parish to spend January 1927 at Cap d'Ail near Monte Carlo, where Virginia Reiland was visiting the birth-control crusader Margaret Sanger, a close family friend. Another guest at Sanger's Villa Bachlyk was English author Hugh de Selincourt, who exasperated Cozzens with his flow of verbiage.* The reunion with Virginia was disappointing, for his job interfered with his freedom to spend time with her. When he could not be with Virginia, he sent her sonnets.

> Your face is music in the listening night,
> Sharper and stronger than the ceaseless drums,
> Smoother and sweeter, softer than the slight
> Frail magic that the far violin becomes.
> Those things have carried me to vanished places,
> Stirred the rich dust of latent treasured things,
> Sliding a light across forgotten faces
> Clipping the feathers from Time's spread-out wings.
> Yet all they brought to mind is lost and dead,
> Shadow of shadows, roses under snow,
> Remembered sun with skies gray over-head;
> In pain, a pleasure faded long ago.
> Surer than song, your face, nor fine stone stronger,
> Clearer than night-bound music, lasting longer—
>
> J.G.C.
> Cap d'ail[8]
> Jan. 1927

Virginia recalls that Cozzens repeatedly asked her to marry him. She considered him brilliant and believed in his future; but she did not find him romantically attractive.

After the Riviera, the Parishes toured the Rhine Valley and then spent a month in Chamonix, where Cozzens finished "The Minor Catholicon" and was a terrified member of a bobsled team that competed for the Coupe de Président de France. In March they went to Berlin, where Cozzens revised *Michael Scarlett* for the English edition. It thenceforth became his custom to use the oppor-

---

* De Selincourt provided the model for McKellar in *Ask Me Tomorrow:* "Spoken by Mr. McKellar, the English language died in extremity, was solemnly buried, and rose again having put on incorruption. It became more English, not in the imitative sense of resembling an Englishman's speech—until Mr. McKellar took up his residence there such an accent could hardly ever have been heard in England—but absolutely, in the sense of resembling a Platonic ideal, with 'a's so nobly broad and feats of synaeresis so extraordinary that the most supercilious don would have to go down, and Mr. McKellar bore the palm alone" (p. 198).

tunity provided by English publication to correct errors and make spot improvements in the texts of his novels.

Bertha joined Cozzens a few times while he was traveling and was included in a papal audience arranged by Mrs. Parish. Edward Parish remembers Bertha as delicate and quietly ladylike, but he did not detect much mutual warmth in her relationship with her son. There seemed to be uneasiness on both sides. Her forbearance irritated Cozzens, who wrote in *Ask Me Tomorrow:* "he detested her patience as a humiliation in itself, a wound to pride reaching through her to him."[9]

In the spring Cozzens accompanied the Parishes to Italy and Sicily. At the Villa Igiea in Palermo he worked on "The Careless Livery," the new version of "Ignorant Armies" that he had planned in Cuba. He sailed to America with the Parishes at the end of April 1927.

FOUR

Sylvia

Cozzens had been planning to take another tutoring job in Mexico, which fell through. In New York he moved into the vicarage of St. Thomas Chapel on East 60th Street as the guest of Dickey Doubs.* That June Cozzens had a brief, exhausting affair with a married woman. He spent July with Doubs at East Marion, Long Island, where he completed "The Careless Livery." The subject of this novel was once again the defeat of a gifted youth.† The principal figure is Stanley Meredith of "Ignorant Armies," but Cozzens discarded Meredith's childhood and prep-school history to begin with his Harvard career. After Leda Holmes is dismissed from Wellesley, she becomes a successful novelist. Meredith leaves college and lives with her in Europe, where he stops composing and drifts. Leda dies in Spain, and it is evident that Meredith is ruined and will not fulfill his gifts.

"The Careless Livery" has a secondary plot, dealing with the marriage of Meredith's sister, bulking almost as large as the main plot—as well as subplots for Florian Walker and Charles Pelton, who are carried over from "Ignorant Armies." The replanned version of the novel covers a shorter time span and has fewer sideshows; but it

---

*The chapel and its settlement house were funded by the affluent St. Thomas Church on Fifth Avenue.

†The title was taken from the King's speech to Laertes in *Hamlet:* ". . . youth no less becomes / The light and careless livery that it wears / Than settled age his sables and his weeds."

is still a loosely structured work with a good deal of moving back and forth between groups of characters in different locations. Also retained from "Ignorant Armies" are the set-piece descriptions of music which attempt to evoke the effects of sound on the other senses, as when Meredith plays Wagner:

The remaining dusky glow through a stained parchment shade gave it all a legendary colour—some sublime Abensonnenshein on the battlements of Valhalla. Into it the prelude launched like a ship, a galley with froth and flash of music about the steady sweep of oars. There was the forest too, and the dark forge. A rich and magical forest, more like the stone forests of Chartres and Bourges and Milan, with distant coloured lights, with the peril of heights and the glory of depths and breadths. In the heart of it the gnome wielded the hammer on the sword.

Leda lay back in the chair, quiet, except for a small quiver which began in her instep and traveled to her shoulders at the sudden notes of the silver horn, remaining through the music of the sword and the gnome's persistent minor. She remembered a phrase of Browning's ". . . *a long cramped scroll, freshening*. . . ." You could feel it, as if a hand passed smooth and cool across your face, pressing away a thousand trivialities in a melting union of sense and sound, so powerful and entrancing that you could see the tight silk on your crossed ankles and wonder to whom they belonged.[1]

During the summer of 1927 Cozzens considered writing a biography of Queen Elizabeth or another Elizabethan romance, to be titled "The Voyage of Mathew April" about a minor figure from *Michael Scarlett*. He wrote an essay for a contest sponsored by the Woodrow Wilson Foundation.* "The Minor Catholicon" and "The Careless Livery" were turned over to Bernice Baumgarten (she had dropped "Sylvia" from business use), who tried to dissuade him from publishing them; but she offered "The Careless Livery" to Viking Press after getting him out of his Boni contract.

Bernice was seven months older than her twenty-four-year-old client. She was small, efficient, intelligent, determined, and an excellent judge of writing. Born in Washington, D.C., where her father manufactured rubber stamps (he died when she was seven), she had been a steady reader as a girl but expressed no literary ambitions. She graduated from Hunter High School in New York

---

*The assigned topic was a 2,500-word essay on "What Woodrow Wilson Means to Me." The two first prizes, of $25,000 each, and the two second prizes, of $1,000, were not awarded.

Sylvia
Bernice
Baumgarten
before her
marriage

City. At that time there was a type of goal-oriented young woman known as a "Hunter girl." Since family finances were inadequate to send her to college, she went to the Teresa Aub Secretarial School and briefly worked as a secretary in a law office before answering a want ad for a job at the Brandt & Brandt literary agency. She began as a secretary for Carl Brandt's wife, Zelma, in the book department; by the time Cozzens met her, probably in 1925, she was handling authors on her own.* Bernice had expected to marry a department-store executive in 1927, but the engagement was broken.

Cozzens took Bernice dancing, and once had to borrow the price of their dinner from her. He also saw her at the office "children's hour" on Saturdays, when Brandt provided bootleg gin for writ-

* Bernice's sister, Fannie Collins, recalls that Bertha Cozzens made the initial contact with Brandt & Brandt. The first mention of Bernice Baumgarten in Cozzens's letters to his mother was from Cuba on 28 October 1925; since he refers to her as "Bernice," it would appear he had already met her.

*Fannie and
Bernice
Baumgarten*

ers. Cozzens was often sitting on the stairs when Bernice left her apartment in the morning. That Bernice was a Jew seemed to make any commitment by Cozzens impossible. Apart from his streak of anti-Semitism, it was a time when "mixed marriages" were still regarded as remarkable—especially on the level of Episcopalian society that had shaped him. Yet they were soon in love, as documented by letters when one or the other was out of town. Bernice wrote Cozzens: "It's ghastly without you" and "I adore you."[2] He declared: "I love you very damn much and am not getting any better" and dispatched the sestet of a sonnet:

> So I come back bow blindly to your knee,
> Yet not quite fool enough to think that there
> The lowered face would only lean to me.
> The arms that clasp and close compassionately,
> The fingers kind and quiet in my hair,
> I need not take as showing that you care.[3]

Doubs found Cozzens a job in September 1927 as librarian for the New York Athletic Club at 58 West 59th Street. The position paid $150 a month and meals; but it was really a sinecure because the library was rarely used except by the occasional member who came in to read volumes of mild erotica such as *Casanova's Memoirs*. The librarian had ample time to read and write while watching the books. Cozzens recatalogued the 14,000 volumes by the Dewey decimal system and wrote bookish articles for the club magazine, *The Winged Foot*. In the first of these, a biographical note on the "young and able new librarian" announced that "The Careless Livery" was to be published in the fall and that he was currently working on a history of the Anjous in Naples and translating Andres Revesz's Spanish writings on Mussolini and De Rivera; none of them appeared.[4] His articles instructed the membership about the Dewey classification, the Hakluyt Society volumes, and the Loeb Classical Library; and he discussed current fiction, recommending Joseph Hergesheimer, Thornton Wilder's *The Bridge of San Luis Rey,* and Lion Feuchtwanger's *Power*. At this time Cozzens was working on another historical novel, "Joanna," in which Saint Catherine of Sienna figured, and he expected to translate Gide's *L'Immoraliste* for Knopf.

Seventeen-year-old Henry Wenning was trying to educate himself by reading in the N.Y.A.C. library. He was impressed by the librarian's stature as the author of two published novels, and Cozzens was pleased to have someone to lecture at. He was hard on Dreiser (no style) and the Russians and Germans Wenning admired (all German novels are 100 pages too long). Instead, he recommended Jane Austen. Wenning's admiration turned into something like awe when he saw Cozzens leave the club and enter a large foreign touring car driven by "one of the damndest best looking woman the eyes of youth could imagine."[5] The beauty may have been Virginia Reiland, who was in New York during the fall of 1927. When she sailed for France at Thanksgiving, Cozzens saw her off on the *Berengaria* but resisted making the marriage proposal that seemed to be expected. That evening he explained to his mother: "I suppose if I got right down to it, what's wrong with me is a total emotional sell-out to Bernice so I'd have great difficulty in seriously giving a damn about any other woman—despite my hectic career, I'm in a way deplorably faithful—or perhaps faithful as long as my imagination is completely captured. . . ."[6]

That fall Cozzens was reading French and Spanish books for

Brandt, earning four dollars each for his reports. Bernice tried to find free-lance editorial jobs for him. Funk & Wagnalls was prepared to pay him $10,000 to edit a series of "100 Great Love Stories"; he submitted a plan but withdrew when the publisher wanted the work done too rapidly. He had started a novel set in Cuba, and Bernice advised him to stick with it.

Bernice's powers of mind and character became steadily more impressive. He reported to his mother in December: "I had a moment to brood over Bellini's familiar portrait of the sultan Mohammed II, and a faint similarity of feature and expression explained to me why Bernice disapproved of marriage—she is really purely Levantine, and not Jewish, and must have had a very interesting descent, probably connected with the sixteenth century Turkish inroads about Vienna—it accounts at once for her perfect poise and easily aroused contempt."[7] The idea of her son's marrying a Jew was utterly unthinkable for Bertha. Bernice's family did not object to her marrying a gentile, but they felt that an unsuccessful writer was a poor prospect and suspected that she would have to support him. In view of Cozzens's later insistence that "virtually all marriages are arranged by the woman,"[8] it would appear that Bernice was not entirely reluctant. Neither was he, for he recognized that she was what he needed. In addition to having charms of mind and body, Bernice would take good care of him and his career. Moreover, marriage to Bernice would get his mother "off my neck."

Sylvia Bernice Baumgarten* and James Gould Cozzens were married on her twenty-fifth birthday, 31 December 1927, at City Hall after Doubs refused to perform the ceremony. Bertha was in Florida at the time of her son's marriage. There is a report that when Mr. and Mrs. Cozzens arrived at the hotel in the Poconos where they planned to honeymoon, they were turned away because she looked too Jewish. The newlyweds took an apartment—with separate bedrooms—at 48 Charles Street in Greenwich Village. There was no question of Bernice's giving up her career, for Cozzens planned to keep his library job only until he finished his next novel in February. She continued to be known as Miss Baumgarten or

---

*Cozzens called her "Sylvia" or "Bernice" interchangeably, but referred to her as "S" in his diaries.

B. B. in her work. They did not want children. Neither one was philoprogenitive, and Cozzens later remarked that he didn't want a son of his kept out of Porcellian because he was half Jewish. Bernice had an abortion when she became pregnant.

Bernice was determined to make a success of her marriage—and she was a very determined young woman. She understood Bertha's distress and avoided a cliché mother-in-law drama. Three days after the marriage she wrote to her husband's mother:

Dear Mrs. Cozzens—
Your note has added a great deal to my happiness! I have tried over and over again, in the last few weeks, to write to you, but whatever I attempted to say seemed miserably inadequate. I know your distress and I wanted desperately to have you understand something of my feeling for Jim.
I shall do all I can to make Jim happy and if I succeed, you may forgive me for a little of the pain I must have caused you.
We're absurdly pleased with our queer, small house, and although I'm much afraid that I shall be an erratic housekeeper, I'm enjoying it hugely.
I'm hopelessly inept at letters,—but I *am* so eager to know you—

> Gratefully
> Bernice[9]

The Cozzenses enjoyed playing house; and her salary, supplemented by his sporadic earnings, allowed them to have a good time in Jazz Age Manhattan. Bernice was an excellent cook and a dedicated decorator. Their prize possession was the Townsend-Goddard mahogany Chippendale secretary (c. 1750–1770) made for Matthew Cozzens of Newport, which had been in the family for five generations. They entertained and went to the theater and movies. (He enjoyed Harpo Marx.) One of their guests was Bernice's client Ford Madox Ford, whom Cozzens found "vastly amusing." Ford talked to him about Joseph Conrad and John Galsworthy; one evening Ford proposed a revolting-dish contest—which he won with "chocolate-covered oysters." Cozzens enjoyed the company of English novelist Alec Waugh; and he was impressed by William Bolitho, a South African journalist he described as the "Man from Mars" because "he sees everything with a sort of acute, appreciative wonder."[10] The Cozzenses attended the publicity parties for Brandt & Brandt authors, and he became familiar with the operations of literary ballyhoo. When Trader Horn, the writer of an enormously popular spurious book of African adventure, came to promote his book in America, Cozzens met him several times. Cozzens was proud of Bernice; there was no nonsense about concealing his Jewish wife from his WASP friends. Dickey Doubs came to dinner and announced that he was going to say what he thought about their marriage; "Bernice, of course handled it to perfection. . . ."[11]

Cozzens maintained his custom of writing to his mother every third day and tried to see her once a month in Kent, but she rarely visited him. His post-nupital letters expressed his continuing sense of discovery that he had married an extraordinary woman. Bernice had clear plans for his career and was determined to help him become a major writer. She believed that he was the most talented writer among her clients, but that his novels had been false starts — overwritten and unplanned. On 2 February 1928 he sent his mother the carbon copy of "The Crop" (published as *Cock Pit*), a novel set in Cuba:

I think Bernice is pleased with it, pleased to see me grasping so much more securely my means of expression, but I know that thinking on a large scale, she regards it as so much ground-clearing or healthy exercise in preparation for the books with which I am to knock them dead, and she will begin, as soon as I get my breath, trying to evoke a fuller sense of the distinction between incidents and events, prodding me critically and aesthetically into getting at what she wouldn't call,—but would probably think of as—the stuff of life. She sees such things with astounding clarity of mind and despite claims to the contrary, with a gift for accurate expression—one of those rare people who can look straight at a thing and say what it is instead of what they think about it, or how it reacts on them, or what it might be if it weren't something else. It's a type of mind that fascinates me, because it has trained itself in method instead of material—the results are amazing, not in what it knows, but in what it knows how to do—the speed with which it can grasp and understand anything at all without preparation or premeditation—to a degree that makes almost every other mind I ever saw seem inert, or merely cluttered to the bursting point with desperately clung-to facts of no real importance whatsoever—I suppose, fundamentally, it's the distinction between the ability—presented with a given object—to supply a quantity of previously learned facts *about* it and the ability, presented with the same object, to supply a quantity of facts or ideas *from* it. . . . She could not to save her neck give you the date of the battle of Marathon, but given the battle of Marathon, she could unassisted deduce the previous policies of the Persians and foretell the age of Pericles—just as she can light a cigarette, prop her feet on a waste-paper basket, and summoning a secretary, dictate under the pop-eyes of the elderly expert the method for an outline of his science, with which she will make him wealthy, or the principles for his biographical study with which she will make him notorious—indeed the number of learned gents who have drawn back hurt and affronted to find her early in her twenties and rather personable, remaining to stagger out with most of their work done for them before the cigarette is ended, grows daily more impressive. Not least impressed is, you may judge, your correspondent.

Bernice was not satisfied with *Cock Pit,* but she thought that it had served its purpose in achieving a more direct presentation and was good enough to publish. She said that he had failed to make his principal figure, Ruth Micks, a complete character; compared to her father she wasn't real. But Bernice did not want him to rewrite the novel; it would be better for him to go on to another work because he had learned most of what was to be learned from *Cock Pit.*

On 15 February Cozzens reported to his mother: "I think Bernice is really keener to keep my nose to short stories simply to discipline me to the degree of being able to keep a definite conception, once taken in hand to treat, running deep in a single and defined channel instead of leaking in facile writing all over the lot. Being the sworn enemy of what she calls the "What-of-it?" school, she can level at The Crop the devastating formula—simply saying, well, what of it? and maintaining stoutly that the writer has got to answer that adequately; first arouse the reader to a point where he cares, and then satisfy him, before the book can really be said to matter. After that it is time enough to take up the question as to whether what aroused and answered the interest is incidental or fundamental. . . ." He concluded: "I'm perfectly sure that if I have the stuff, or ever develop it, she'll get it out of me—she'll get it out of me with no friction and next to no fuss, and that will be that."

Cock Pit is set at a Cuban sugar mill operated by Americans. Most of the characters are recognizably drawn from the families Cozzens knew at Tuinucú, and the dedication page reads:

To Mr. and Mrs. Joseph Eggleston in
the happy memory of Tuinucú

Ruth Micks is invented. The final appearance of the gifted but frustrated youth figure in Cozzens's novels, Ruth is superior to the men who love her. Unlike Cerise d'Atrée, Michael Scarlett, or Stanley Meredith, she has a streak of cold determination. Ruth is the twenty-one-year-old daughter of Lancy Micks, the Chief Field Engineer. Based on Eggleston, Micks is highly competent, completely honest, and fearless. When Don Miguel, the Machiavellian sugar baron, arranges to have Micks murdered for refusing to make a false report, Ruth defeats the plot—which her father never suspects—by torturing the hired killer. Don Miguel graciously acknowledges defeat and admits Ruth into the fellowship of the world's realists. Yet she is not de-sexed. As Don Miguel observes, "You know, Miss Micks, even in your most magnificent moments, you manage, as you say, to show you're glad you're not a boy" (p. 298). Cozzens explained to his mother: ". . . psychologically—indeed every way—the man she could be entirely in love with is her father, of course. That, in a sense, is what the book is about. All her hardness and ruthlessness is rooted in this fundemental and hopeless frustration and the interaction of the other characters should be and was intended to be mere relief or emphasis, undertoning or under lining a situation emotionally awful and insoluable."[12] Bertha protested, "Well, who could think of such a thing unless the evidence was unmistakable?" Cozzens replied that it wasn't really necessary for the reader to detect the element of suppressed incest. ". . . I was explaining what I believed about her, to help you see what it looked like through my eyes . . . my whole desire was to leave it for the reader to interpret as he chose—presumably a good many nerves would jangle if I forced everyone to believe that she wanted him—I don't know that I believe it myself—I believe that it's of minor importance. In saying it was what the book was about I gave it too much emphasis because apparently it hadn't come to your attention.—The action of the book isn't affected by the subtle (and to me) unimportant distinction of whether she wanted him or merely could want no one else. The simple fact is that she is faced with a plain frustration by the part her father plays in her life, and I can't see that I need to inquire very deeply into the actual nature of that part."[13]

Ruth is a bit too much of a superwoman to be entirely convincing; but Cozzens tried to support his characterization by according her the approval of Britton (based on R. O. Binet), the antiromantic bank manager:

You missed Ruth altogether if you could see only that clean cutting power. That was superficial, a clear head working easily muddled ones. His own clear head could recognize that with admiration, but there was something deeper, he knew, for he felt, totally unsentimental, an attachment for Ruth, a sense of understanding her, of seeing what none of these people saw, not even her father. His mind with a clearing flash, like the dropping pieces of a kaleidoscope into perfect pattern, held it there.

By God! he thought, not surprised, for he had known it all along, he supposed; what a rotten shame! *Not even her father. . . .*

An unutterable and very simple sadness came over him. It turned from Ruth, for that was the end he saw, not temporary, but a final frustration [p. 169].

This passage provides the clearest clue in the novel to Ruth's feelings for Lancy.

Cozzens's third novel marked a fresh start, under the guidance of his agent. The style is cleaner and the plotting tighter than in his previous work, and it is the first novel that displays his ability to present an organization or occupation with apparent total familiarity. More significant, *Cock Pit* announces Cozzens's emerging commitment to the imperatives of reason against the mess of sentimentality—though qualified by Ruth's romantic impact on the reader, despite her unsentimental intelligence.

Cock Pit was published on 20 September 1928 at $2.50 by the recently formed house of William Morrow & Co.* Cozzens was on friendly terms with his editor, Thayer Hobson, but he was married to the only editor he trusted. The dust jacket carried endorsements by Grant Overton ("Real plot, real people, real action, real excitement, and the pure romantic feeling") and Ford Madox Ford (". . . if you are introduced by a book to a new world, your thinking about it does not stop with the covers of the work supposing what has been done has been done well and truly. Mr. Cozzens has done that"). The novel was not widely reviewed; but the notices were favorable, though most of them categorized it as a tropical adventure tale. Isa Glenn, of the *New York Evening Post,* had no trouble getting the point about "the frustration of a forbidden love" and declared that Cozzens "is on his way to becoming a great novelist."[14] The first printing, probably 2,000 copies, sold out promptly, and a second printing was required in Septem-

---

* Another novel published in 1928 was Aldous Huxley's *Point Counter Point,* which Cozzens greatly admired.

ber. *Cock Pit* went into a Grosset & Dunlap seventy-five-cent reprint in 1933.* It was Cozzens's most successful novel to date, but the royalty on 3,000 copies would have been $750. There was no English edition. A windfall came when Fox Studios paid $4,000 for the movie rights, which they were planning to make as "The Girl from Habana."†

Bernice urged Cozzens to write short stories for discipline. He studied the work of successful magazine writers (particularly Fitzgerald and John P. Marquand) and tried to produce commercial fiction; but his stories weren't what the slicks wanted. Only one was published before November 1929. "Foreign Strand," which appeared in the September 1928 issue of the *Paris Comet,*‡ is a slight story. An American millionaire is visiting Havana with his expensively educated daughter, who regards him as uncouth. Intimidated by her disapproval, he declines the opportunity to sleep with a night-club dancer. Cozzens explained that his stories weren't right for the commercial market because he didn't know how they would end when he started them.

Carl Brandt was planning to send the Cozzenses to London in the fall of 1928 to open an office for Brandt & Brandt—but the idea was dropped. Feeling that he needed business experience, Cozzens went to work in March 1928 for M. P. Gould (no family connection), an advertising agency at 45 Fourth Avenue, and was assigned to the United States Bond & Mortgage account. He enjoyed the challenge of learning about investments in a short time; at the end of his first week he was given a raise and an office. Bernice had urged him to try a real job, "claiming that I knew too many books already and hadn't any great need to encounter more writers and arty boys, but a few hard contacts with the people who made up the world, about whom I apparently knew nothing—would do me no end of good. . . . She wants me to stick it for six months and then, I gather, plans to jerk me out and put

---

*There were no American "mass-market" paperbacks before 1939. The Grosset & Dunlap reprints of *Cock Pit* and *Son of Perdition* in 1933 probably resulted from the success of *The Last Adam.*

†A movie called "The Girl from Habana" was produced by Fox in 1929, but it had no connection with *Cock Pit.*

‡*The Paris Comet* was published in New York and Paris. No copy of this issue has been located; the story survives in a clipping Cozzens preserved. Two unpublished 1928 stories are known only by their titles: "On the Way Down" and "Rien ne va Plus." The typescripts of three unpublished stories at Princeton may date from this period: "Purchase," "Heart's Desire," and "Year After Year."

me in somewhere else that will do me good—'of course,' she said, 'you won't exactly get ahead that way, but I don't believe you want to, and you're not going to turn into any damn advertiser under my eyes. You've simply got to get a little different angle on this world before you do any more writing—you've got the greatest talent for writing Brandt & Brandt handles and not one plausible or really real thing to write about—you haven't made contact. No one wants you to write about offices, but you've got to write about people and offices is where most people are.' "[15]

The advertising job upset Bertha, who wrote to Bernice that she would "simply die" if Jim gave up writing. Cozzens explained that his wife felt the same way. "It does puzzle me why you've never realised that I could no more giving up writing than change the colour of my eyes or tack on a cubit by taking thought."[16] He expected to move on to an editorial job with Macaulay, a publishing company, after getting what he needed from Gould. Bernice opposed the Macaulay plan because she wanted him to devote all his time to writing. He soon grew bored with advertising and quit in April to write another Cuban novel. Cozzens continued to undertake occasional short jobs. In 1928 he was hired by Judge William Cohen* to investigate the political activities of Judge Peter Schmuck. In 1929 he revised *Zoom!* (New York & London: Longmans, Green, 1931), an aviation handbook by George R. White.

Cozzens received a $250 advance from Morrow for his fourth novel, and he had a complete draft ready in October 1928. It had the working title "Five From Dosfuegos," which became "Dark Dominion," "Foreign Strand," and finally *The Son of Perdition* in February 1929. The source of the title is provided in the epigraph, from John 17:12: "those that thou gavest me I have kept, and none of them is lost, but the son of perdition." The reference is to Judas Iscariot. Cozzens had trouble with titles for his novels and let Bernice choose from the possibilities.

The typescript was sent to Bertha, and on 14 November Cozzens explained that the subject of the novel was the effect of machines on man. "What I mean by 'foreign strand' is naturally not Cuba. . . . The foreign strand is the new civilisation of order and

---

*"Judge Cohen is a venerable and white-headed old millionaire who seems seriously concerned over the corruption of the judicial system."[17]

machines. How foreign it is, and always must be to human beings, is what I am setting forth. Just as, literally, they are all gathered on a sand bar in the Caribbean; symbolically they are on an island in the new civilisation, in an environment foreign to the whole history of the race." Cozzens was not making the familiar point that machines eliminate or diminish man; instead, he contended that "they make his principles, his conduct, his thinking and manner of life infinitely more important." The system of technology is dependent on men for its operation. "Every human gesture the man makes endangers the machines. . . . Transferred from the purely material—steel, mechanism, and material forces of electricity and steam this theory will operate in what ever ways are inevitable to it in the world of morals, or more accurately, man's tastes and discriminations and volitions." The morality of the machine age requires responsibility. Since Oliver Findley, the son of perdition, recognizes no duties, he is "the principle of evil incarnate." Joel Stellow, the Administrator General of the sugar company, "is the principle of good in the machine age—symbolically, God." Having purged himself of his attraction toward romantic fiction, Cozzens had become involved in a rebound affair with the symbolic or allegorical.

Cozzens reported to his mother on 26 November that Bernice had reservations about Stellow, and admitted that he didn't understand Stellow as well as the other characters in *The Son of Perdition*. Bernice said that although Cozzens wrote "like no one else in America when I wrote about what I knew and understood," his treatment of Stellow demonstrated that he was not ready to handle such a character. "Briefly, if I'd keep my shirt on, she'd say that as far as she could see I had spent at least twenty-four of my twenty-five years in such a preoccupation with books and writing that I hadn't matured at all beyond a superficial coating got mainly from books. . . . I needn't expect to learn all there was to know about life and people in a year and a half." The twenty-six-year-old agent was making her husband a fully equipped novelist. Such was his trust in her judgment that the process was accomplished without wounding the ego of a young author. It would be bootless to speculate on what James Gould Cozzens might have become without Bernice Baumgarten; what he became during eighteen months of her tutelage is manifest.

The Son of Perdition considers the effects of American drifter Oliver Findley on Dosfuegos, the sea terminal of the United Sugar

Company. Findley is the embodiment of disorder; wherever he goes he is attended by death and destruction. His antagonist, Joel Stellow, personifies responsibility and is entirely motivated by "the morality of ruthless good sense" (p. 227). Dr. Palacio, a cynical intellectual, accuses Stellow of having become dehumanized—a company instead of a person. Stellow's only personal relationship is with Vidal Monaga, a proud fisherman. Monaga discovers—as the result of Findley's involvement with his daughter—that his son is guilty of incest and executes him: " 'Other people may do things which are not my business, but with which I will not have myself, my house, my name, when it is borne by a man dirtied. When I saw that he did not understand this, I thought to myself; my son is of age now, he is a man, grown up. Yet he does not know what it is to be a Monaga. . . . Being sure of this, I saw that he would be better dead' " (p. 248). Stellow arranges to drop the charges against Monaga, but the old man refuses: " 'It is not much to be a Monaga to any one but me, señor. But I will be turned over to the authorities, please' " (p. 303). Overhearing them, Findley sees the confrontation between Stellow and Monaga as exposing "the great joke of the machine's inhuman beauty, the reason and might of the machine confounded so inevitably by the rooted folly, the poor stubborn pride of man" (p. 304). The great joke is that while Stellow has tried to maintain the "necessary illusion" of the dignity of man in the machine age, Monaga's simple dignity belittles the Administrator's efforts and affirms the freedom of man. *The Son of Perdition* ends with Findley boarding the ship that is to take him away from Cuba. " 'There is a place prepared for you,' " he is told. This echo of Christ's comforting words to his disciples ("I go to prepare a place for you," John 14:2) is heavily ironic. There is no place in "my Father's house" for the son of perdition.* Comparison of the published novel with Cozzens's comments on the first draft indicates that he revised it to de-emphasize the message about the machine. Stellow became less of an allegorical figure; the point is made, but almost casually, when Findley asks, " 'Or do you just get sick of being God, Mr. Stellow?' " (p. 295)

The Son of Perdition was published by Morrow on 22 August 1929 at $2.50.† (The dust jacket was prepared from a sketch by

* Other possible Biblical sources for the phrase are Exodus 23:20, Matthew 25:41, and Revelation 12:6.
† Hemingway's *A Farewell to Arms* and Faulkner's *The Sound and the Fury* were also published in 1929.

Bernice's sister, Fannie.) It was dedicated *For Sylvia* with two lines from *Troilus and Cressida:* "Outliving her beauty's outward, with a mind / That doth renew swifter than blood decays."* The novel was widely noticed as a colorful tale of tropic adventure, but the critics missed the machine message while praising the characterizations. The strongest reviews were by William McFee, in the *New York Herald Tribune Book Section,* and Charles Poore, in the *New York Times Book Review.* Poore observed: "Like Webster, he is 'much concerned with death' and 'sees the skull beneath the skin.'"[18] William Bolitho wrote in the *New York World:* "This is an exciting book, a sincere book, and even an out-of-the-way good book, in that it manages remarkably the technical perfection of the novel (as apart from a romance), which is the creation of living characters in a convincingly real world." But he observed that the novel is not moving because the people are repugnant and because Cozzens's Cuba is "irascible rather than tragic, or truly passionate."[19] The publisher's ads asking "Who *is* the Son of Perdition? No three readers will agree" did not help the book. Morrow sold 1,979 copies in America and printed 1,000 copies for Longmans, Green to publish in London, of which 222 were sold. Milton Waldman, who took the novel for Longmans, had read it in typescript and made structural suggestions that Cozzens found helpful. Longmans reissued the novel in 1931, selling another 692 copies. There was a seventy-five-cent Grosset & Dunlap reprint in 1933; and World reprinted it in 1942 (10,000 copies) and 1943 (4,710) at forty-nine cents.

At the end of his twenty-sixth year—his fifth year as a published novelist—Cozzens had written seven novels and published four. He was getting known, but that was about all he could claim. Writers want to be read, and they want to make money. He had a well-developed taste for good food, good clothes, and pleasant surroundings; but he felt no financial pressure, because Bernice was doing well. In 1929 she placed 180 manuscripts and was becoming known as the best agent in New York.

Their marriage was comfortable. Though not a demonstrative man, he signified his affection for Bernice by patting her head or tugging her hair as he went past. Both regarded quarrels as undignified, and Fannie never heard them raise their voices. One topic

---

*Cozzens emended Shakespeare to insert *her*.

of quiet disagreement was money, for Bernice did not share her husband's view that "what I spent I had; what I saved I lost."

The Cozzenses went to Europe in the spring of 1929 on the proceeds from the movie sale of *Cock Pit*. They spent April and May in Naples, Florence, Rome, Venice, Vienna, Strasbourg, Paris, and London. That fall they moved uptown to an apartment at 325 East 79th Street.

On 10 November 1928 the *Vestris* left Hoboken, New Jersey, bound for South America. Captain W. J. Carey, sixty, commodore of the Lamport & Holt Line of Liverpool, was on the bridge. The first night out the vessel hit rough weather that turned into a gale. The *Vestris* began to ship water and list, but the captain delayed sending distress signals until 10:29 A.M. on the twelfth. The ship was abandoned at 1:25 P.M. and sank off the Virginia Capes, with a loss of 112 lives, including every child on board. Captain Carey went down with his ship, and his reasons for delaying the SOS eleven hours were never determined. An investigation by the British Board of Trade's Court of Inquiry found that the *Vestris* had probably shipped water through a coal port and that she had left Hoboken deliberately overloaded. The sinking of the *Vestris* was not one of the worst sea disasters, but it attracted considerable press interest because of what was regarded as a failure of command. Captain Carey seemed more concerned about salvage fees than about the safety of his passengers.

Cozzens began assembling notes on the *Vestris* while he was revising *The Son of Perdition*. On 10 December 1928 he wrote his mother that he was planning a novel to be called "Eternal Father" and listed the main ideas he expected to treat:

—Natural simplicity of the sea against the tremendous complexity of the ship's engines.
—Captain Clendening a sick man on a sick ship. This common affliction must be emphasised. The Captain much more seriously ill than he knows, just as the state of the ship to the hour of its foundering was far more serious than the Captain realised. I have been thinking here about the psychology of it—the Captain's refusal to admit his own breakdown connected obscurely with his refusal to admit the ship's danger. He has lived a tremendously hard and vital life—just as the ship has seen years of service.

OPPOSITE.
Paris, spring
1929

—Water in the machinery like literal destiny flooding the complicated lives of the passangers and crew. All this marvelous intricacy of no avail once the sea has poured in. Some many lives and careers about to founder, like the ship.[20]

At this time he planned a three-part division—part one dealing with the captain and crew, part two with passengers, and part three with the sinking. The novel was to include a close analysis of the officers, including the homosexual second officer.

Cozzens visited the *Vestris*'s sister ship, the *Vauban,* and discussed the sinking with his uncle, Captain Joseph Wood (who would go down with the *Mohawk* in 1935). He used Felix Riesenberg's *Men on Deck* for details about shipboard practice and studied the 2,000-page transcript of the New York District Attorney's investigation. By June 1929 he had decided that the novel would concentrate on the investigation after the sinking and that the central character would be the first officer, who "gets the whole thing resolved, realising that the world is going on, that people are not so bad, and neither is fate and neither is life—he has made his complete adjustment, there is nothing left now which can upset his poise or undermine his resignation."[21]

In August 1929, while Cozzens was still writing the sea novel—now titled "Mighty Ocean"—he began planning a companion novel about the recent riot at Auburn prison in upstate New York, which interested him as an opportunity to examine the problem of man's freedom from another angle. "Mighty Ocean is settled on the assumption that man is free except for the limitations his nature puts on him, and the mechanical limitations the structure of the universe imposes—if he once gets adjusted to those, all's serene. In the case of man in jail, however, it's instantly obvious in the most literal way that he isn't free even up to those rather large limitations. Further, and perhaps more important, he is put in a position where certain abstract or moral limitations are removed—there's no decency and no justice and no honor. If the implication of Mighty Ocean is that the world gets along surprisingly well without too much of any of them, I will now gracefully demonstrate that the human being can't get along at all without them, at least not so long as he's human—he has to be able to count on them to protect his inevitable weaknesses and inadequacies."[22] The prison novel was abandoned.

He had almost completed the first part of "Mighty Ocean" by

the twelfth and was ready to write the second part, in which he planned to develop the idea that although the sinking of the *San Pedro* was a devastating event for First Officer Anthony Bradell, it was just a business matter for the company. (After studying Erich Zimmerman's *Foreign Trade and Shipping,* Cozzens remarked that he knew enough to form his own company, "since I see so easily what's wrong with them all.")[23] Bradell's "progress is a long fight against what he considers wrong—he defends the company, conceals and distorts the evidence, considering his personal loyalty to the deceased captain and people employing him of prime importance, until he realises inescapably that businesses are out to make money, that he's being used, that everything his sense of decency or loyalty has made him say or do simply helps to strengthen the company's position for making money, which is their only concern at bottom. . . ." Offered command of the *San Pablo,* Bradell intends to resign; but his conception of his importance is deflated when he visits the *San Pablo.* "He recognises his capacities and limitations, sees in front of him the ship which will be his and knows his simple obligation and job will be to run it to the best of his ability. So seeing, he grasps definitely the truth that to understand all is, if not to forgive all, to recognise the million factors of man's behavior, understand their urges and necessities, and bear steadily in mind the knowledge that what matters is not what other people do but what he does himself."[24] The working drafts were not preserved.

By December 1929 Cozzens had completed another opening section, limited to the three days of the sailing and sinking of the *San Pedro*. He had been working on the novel for almost a year and a half. Carl Brandt decided to enter the first 23,000 words in the *Scribner's Magazine* short-novel contest. "S. S. 'San Pedro': A Tale of the Sea" was the first work published in the competition, in the August 1930 issue. *Scribner's* paid $1,000 for it; but the $5,000 prize was awarded by judges Gilbert Seldes, Malcolm Cowley, and John Hall Wheelock to John Peale Bishop's "Many Thousands Gone," which Cozzens thought had little merit. Cozzens decided to break off the sea novel after the first section appeared in *Scribner's*. At this time Bernice moved him from Morrow to Harcourt, Brace and Company because William Morrow wanted him to write in a more popular vein. *S.S. San Pedro* was published on 27 August 1931 at $1.50. The dedication page read: "For my Mother in Memory of Nova Scotia sea captains." The 133-page novelette was the Sep-

tember selection of the Book-of-the-Month Club, along with Sheila Kaye-Smith's *Susan Spray*. BOMC paid a $2,000 advance and claimed to have distributed 50,000 copies.*

S.S. *San Pedro* opens on Friday, 7 June, as the ship is preparing to leave Hoboken. Anthony Bradell, the senior second officer, is surprised when Captain Clendening tells him to show the ship to Dr. Percival, who is in the captain's cabin—a violation of presailing routine. Dr. Percival, a grotesque figure, warns Bradell that Clendening is worn out. Before going ashore the doctor observes that the ship has a list. The first night out a flirtatious flapper tells Bradell that she was spooked by seeing Dr. Percival and thinks he is still aboard. That night the ship hits rough weather, and Bradell meditates: "Only, the *San Pedro* was built for stress; the great turbines turning could never grow tired; the renewed watch above was always sleepless. Men, it seemed to Anthony, were not so well made for living. Energy, power, the vital confidence, grew low as the void grew larger, the ocean mightier and more immense. Eyes wore out with watching; they neither saw nor cared finally—" (p. 55). As the storm heightens, the ship's list increases; but the officers cannot discover the cause or correct it. By Saturday night

---

* Bibliographers have identified one Harcourt, Brace printing. According to the publisher's records, 10,500 copies were printed, of which 5,373 were sold to BOMC and 1,550 were destroyed.

the *San Pedro* is in trouble. Captain Clendening is unable to function properly but refuses to send a distress signal. None of the officers is able to act for the captain, who still maintains his authority. The first SOS is not sent until the morning of Sunday, the ninth, when preparations are made to abandon ship. Bradell is knocked unconscious trying to jettison deck cargo; he later watches the sinking of the *San Pedro* from a lifeboat.

Although *Cock Pit* and *The Son of Perdition* anticipate the voice of his later work in sections where Cozzens describes the operation of the sugar mills, *S.S. San Pedro* is the first novel in which he consistently maintained the objective tone and detached point of view that define his major fiction. The process of rewriting the novel through successive versions had brought control over his material and style. Having published four self-indulgent novels, he moved at twenty-eight into his unembellished middle style. Heretofore Cozzens had been a rapid writer who enjoyed the sense of discovery afforded by the act of composition. After 1931 he would be a methodical writer, increasingly concerned with the structure of his work. Cozzens was satisfied with *S.S. San Pedro,* which he regarded as his first mature work; and it became the first book that he claimed in the by-the-same-author lists of his subsequent books. Nonetheless, *S.S. San Pedro* is marred by the blatantly symbolic use of Dr. Percival to foreshadow death and disaster—a carryover from *The Son of Perdition.* After one more experiment with allegory in *Castaway,* Cozzens permanently forsook it.

S.S. San Pedro was well received despite its uncommercial length. Reviewers compared Cozzens to Joseph Conrad and Stephen Crane. (He had not read Crane at this time.) William McFee announced in the *Saturday Review of Literature* that "this is probably as near genius as a writer in our time can attain."[25] (In 1944 McFee included the novelette in his anthology *World's Great Tales of the Sea.*) Christopher Morley wrote in the *Book-of-the-Month Club News:* "Mr. Cozzens comes to us in this story as a master of the subtlest gifts a writer needs. From the very first sentence we are carried on by the beautiful crispness and decision of his prose, and anyone who has the least acquaintance with the life of ships recognizes at once that he has the feeling for physical things and the meanings under their forms."[26] Morley was writing a sell piece; nevertheless, he was an influential tastemaker. The English reception was just as good. Longmans, Green required two printings in 1931 and a third in 1934. The British reviews were solidly respectful, as in the

Morning Post: "Comparison with Conrad is inevitable in such a case, but it is a comparison from which this young American writer emerges unscathed . . . an unforgettable little epic."[27] Cozzens's photo did not appear on the dust jacket of *S.S. San Pedro,* but it was used in publicity and by the *BOMC News.* It was said that his face helped to sell the book, and he was described as the handsomest novelist in America. At twenty-eight he was just under six feet tall, lean, with dark wavy hair. One young woman at his publisher's office remarked that he resembled an Aubrey Beardsley drawing come to life. Cozzens took no part in promoting his book, having decided that it was his task to write books, not to peddle them. *S.S. San Pedro* became Cozzens's most widely reprinted work; it was published in paperback by Berkeley in 1955 and by the Modern Library in 1956 (with *Castaway*).

Universal Studios acquired the movie rights to *S.S. San Pedro* for $4,000 and invited Cozzens to come to Hollywood to write the screenplay. He asked for $1,000 a week, which was his way of declining. The movie was not made. In 1932 Paramount offered him $400 a week to write a movie about the *Lusitania,* but he wanted $750.

While Cozzens was working on *S.S. San Pedro* in 1929 and 1930, he resumed writing commercial short stories—to master the technique and to earn money.* But the Cozzenses did not have financial worries. In 1930 they spent $10,385.79, a good deal of money for a couple in the first year of the Depression. Through his connection with Brandt & Brandt, his stories began selling to the high-paying magazines. His first appearance in the *Saturday Evening Post* was "Future Assured" (2 November 1929). Cozzens had studied the magazine market carefully—clipping and saving Fitzgerald's stories—and it is a perfect imitation of a certain kind of *Post* story. A young man recently graduated from college is having trouble finding a job in New York, although he was president of his college club and expects to be favored by a wealthy alumnus. In the end he has a promising position and the boss's daughter.

---

*Two prose sketches by Cozzens appeared in *Morrow's Almanac* for 1929 and 1930, "Breaking the Week in Cuba" and "Portrait of a Chief Officer on His Birthday." In the headnote on Cozzens for the latter, editor Thayer Hobson commented that "if he is ever killed in an accident, [Cozzens] will be picked up meticulously attired."[28]

"Defender of the Liberties," a sardonic story about a Latin-American revolutionary, was published by *Alhambra* in January 1930.*

Although Cozzens did not take his short-story work seriously for its own sake, the form interested him as a problem of mechanics. During the summer of 1929 he had explained to his mother that it had a place in his ambitious career plans:

As you know, this business of technique has been obsessing me all summer—it grows steadily clearer to me that nothing can ever take the place of complete mastery of the tricks of the trade—it's what's wrong with half the people writing today—they've gone off half-cocked and only about a quarter prepared. The simple fact is that they don't work hard enough— this absurd and pernicious idea of spontaneous genius which keeps all the boys playing around the Dome has wrecked dozens of them. I think it's probably likely that all the work in the world wouldn't get you there if you didn't have it in you, but I'm surer and surer that simply having it in you is pretty negligible too. To learn to write and write decently is simply a much longer and harder thing than is generally admitted. I shall have to beat the short story to a stand still right now, not simply in the post, but in the so-called respectable magazines—which will probably be easier, because the technique is the same and the material easier for me. I don't want to write short stories, because I know past any dispute that the novel is right for me, but I am going to write them perfectly before I give them up. I suppose, though it gives me the willies to consider it, I shall have to do the same about plays, just as I think I may take up verse again—the content doesn't interest me, but the fact that I never, even when I wrote scores of them, turned out a perfect sonnet, technically speaking, can't, I'm afraid, be allowed to rest—I simply must have it all, because I don't see anyone who writes as well as I'm going to, and the explanation, obvious from the instructive past, is simply that they've never learned how. Certainly there has never been a writing age in English so perfunctorilly and shallowly prepared as the immediately current one. We, as the saying goes, are damn well going to change all that.[29]

Cozzens couldn't bring himself to write more "tripe" stories of "serious accomplishment and proper moral" and shifted to "slightly facetious" fiction.[30] "Lions Are Lower Today," which the *Post* published on 15 February 1930, is an entertaining story in the screwball-humor vein, in which a young man wins a taxidermist's daughter by buying stuffed animals. Bernice provided the idea for

---

*Other 1929–1930 stories are known only by their titles: "Fifty Points for Cinderella" (from an idea suggested by Bernice), "The Turret-Ram *Affondatara*," "The Crabbed Age of Edmond Clancy," and "In at the Death."

"October Occupancy" (*American Magazine,* October 1930): an eccentric young man woos the rental agent for an apartment building by having her decorate the apartment which, unknown to her, will be theirs. Cozzens was uncomfortable with these stories and planned a series of pseudohistorical stories set in Cuba, intending to imitate Marquand's technique. He reported to his mother in February 1930: "this job is precisely nine-tenths work which anyone can do, given the time and patience—the last tenth, which you have to have and cannot learn, I was born completely equipped with, it seems safe to believe."[31]

None of the projected Cuban stories was published, but on 21 June 1930 the *Post* published "Someday You'll Be Sorry," the first of five stories about the Durham School and its headmaster, Dr. Holt.* The Durham stories were recognizably about Kent, and Dr. Holt is a generous portrait of Father Sill. In "Someday You'll Be Sorry," the best of the group, a very successful alumnus, who was the target of Dr. Holt's displeasure at Durham, accepts the invitation to speak at a fund-raising dinner, planning to use the occasion to tell off the headmaster. When the moment comes, the speaker cannot betray the roomful of people who admire him. Instead of denouncing Dr. Holt, he pledges a large sum of money. "It took a long time, but in the end the account seemed somehow to get squared."[32] Old-boy Cozzens squared his own account with Father Sill in the Durham stories—not by providing a characterization of the headmaster at his roaring worst, but through revealing Kent at its best. Father Sill recognized himself as Dr. Holt and was pleased by the Durham stories. In 1933 Cozzens included a generous tribute to Father Sill in "Kent: A New School" for *Town & Country.*

In the fall of 1930 Cozzens broke off writing stories to start a novel, which he described as a "slight satirical exercise."[33] While recognizing that magazine fiction had benefited his plotting, he was galled by the necessity of writing to satisfy the *Post*'s expectations.

---

*"Someday You'll Be Sorry," "We'll Recall it with Affection" (4 October 1930), "The Guns of the Enemy" (1 November 1930), "Son and Heir" (2 April 1938—but written in 1930), "*Candida* by Bernard Shaw" (25 July 1964—written in the thirties). "Total Stranger" (15 February 1936) is about a prep-school boy, but is not set at Durham. Another 1930 Durham story, "Where Your Treasure Is," may have been retitled. An unfinished Durham story, "A Short History of the World," is in the Cozzens Papers.

He was so happy to be free of stories that he claimed the new novel was writing itself and that he wasn't really sure of what he was trying to say with it. On 13 October he wrote his mother: "The work in question goes by the title of a Week in a Store; and if you can outrage your credulity to the point of thinking of a man finding himself (the reasons don't, or won't, when I finish, matter) shut up alone in a shop like Macy's with, on his hands, the problem of working out a living from the stocks, you could doubtless guess the type of commentary on human beings and our civilization which might be evolved—that is, the insanely wide profusion of material things, gathered without regard to the fundemental necessities of life—the idea seems to exhilirate me so much that, on the lines of a perhaps slightly cock-eyed Robinson Crusoe yarn, I daresay I can do a great part of it as fast as I can write." By February 1931 he had 21,000 words, but he was still trying to finish it during the summer. The short novel, which became *Castaway,* went through six drafts before it was published in 1934. Harcourt, Brace did not want it, although they were eager to keep Cozzens on their list. Bernice had to peddle the manuscript around to other publishers, and at one point in the process Cozzens decided to forgo publication. Maxwell Perkins, of Scribner's, admitted that he didn't understand it.

While writing the first draft of *Castaway* he formulated the rationale for his work that would develop into a monastic discipline: "What you get by going away is certainly not that myth called experience; it seems to me that all experiences happen inside your head. The most you can hope for it to jounce your mind around until you bring up a fresh load; and going somewhere else is probably a great help, but you won't get what you haven't got."[34]

A 1931 *Bookman* article, "Thoughts Brought on by 633 Manuscripts," entertainingly draws on Cozzens's experiences as a reader for Brandt & Brandt. It concluded with an appeal to the public "not to falter in its commendable stand against both the principle and practice of book buying . . . so long as one publisher remains solvent, manuscript writing will persist."[35] *Balzac's Masterpieces* was published in 1931 with an introduction by Cozzens. He later ruefully explained:

At the time this—effusion I think is the word—appeared I was doing odd jobs of ms. reading and editing for Brandt & Brandt, the agents. A certain now long deceased rare book dealer had undertaken the Balzac compilation for McKay, providing a foreword. This proved to be so illiterate that the publisher's editor asked B & B for help. I agreed to see what I could do (I was paid, I believe, $250).* I made it my intent to keep as much of the original "thought" as could be made understandable and as much of the wording as could be made to approach sense. The estimate of Balzac (then and now far from mine) I didn't regard as my business. However, the foreword's "writer" seeing his work slightly straightened out looked on it as ruined and though he had been paid to produce a publishable piece more or less furiously refused to sign it. Frustrated, feeling he needed a signature, the publisher asked me if I would sign. Since I'd been paid (and perhaps because I never thought anyone would see or read the stuff anyway) I agreed. Older and more experienced I of course wouldn't have; but that was then; and so that to my own confusion, is now definitely that. My simplicity's condign punishment is the fact that today it must be taken as my very own vapid judgment and abominable prose.[36]

As good as they are, the Durham stories were still high-grade potboilers. During 1931 Cozzens published the first of the short stories that were recognizably his own and not intended to satisfy the commercial market. In "Farewell to Cuba" (*Scribner's,* November 1931) Cozzens expressed his conviction that life is harsh and that people get away with very little. A middle-aged American banker is absconding from Cuba with embezzled money and another man's wife. When he returns to their hotel room after a farewell night of drinking with his Havana friends, he discovers that she has committed suicide because she can't face the life of a fugitive; he then shoots himself. This story received second prize and appeared in the O. *Henry Memorial Award Prize Stories of 1932* volume.

The defining quality in "Farewell to Cuba" and Cozzens's next story, "The Way to Go Home" (*Saturday Evening Post,* 26 December 1931), is a sense of mortality and limitations, a dispassionate acceptance of the conditions of life, remarkable in a twenty-eight-year-old writer. The American manager of a Havana auto agency is anticipating a reunion bender with an old friend, a celebrated rounder. But the friend is now a serious businessman, and the other old drinking pals have disappeared.

You reached a point where peace seemed more important than gayety; there was nothing more to celebrate, only things to fear. Most of those

---

*The fee was fifty dollars.

good fellows had finally to see that they would never be rich, nor greatly successful, nor the free masters of their happy lives. Their aspirations, going out unfounded, came home empty; they must learn to be satisfied with the monotony of mere existence. They must keep their money, guard their health, employ their time to please the people who let them live at all. Apprehensive; with ambitions small enough to be plausible; with pleasures kept small, quiet, unexceptionable; they were said to have settled down. It was spoken of as a virtue, with an approving inflection, but the word, he saw, did not more than give a shoddy gilding to necessity.[37]

He abandons his binge, attends to his business, and goes home to his family.

He was lucky, he guessed, that he had anyone or anything, for this road was one way—not back—and had one end. In spite of everything, he liked now, the present, better than he would like that end; it was a progression, hopeless and natural. He would never meet the bunch at Johnny's again, nor Johnny himself, probably; but he had still a roof over his head, and he would better be careful, for soon enough he'd have only earth there.[38]

Cozzens had written a *Post* story without compromising his material or satisfying a commercial formula, indicating that he might have prospered in the slick market; but he found the form too limiting and thereafter wrote stories when he wanted fast money. Most were declined by the magazines and discarded.

In the fall of 1931 Erd Brandt, who headed the magazine department at Brandt & Brandt, advised him to write a series of Civil War stories, although Cozzens knew nothing about the subject. He began studying the war and eventually decided to write a novel. Planning a visit to the battlefields, he explained to his mother: "It is valuable to the imagination, not because I am much interested in the historical fact, but because it corrects a looseness or vagueness in the imagination itself—in fact, as I have so often preached to you, you see it in terms of you and at once, if you can write at all, you gain a great light, you see how you can really make it clear to someone else, not just mouth a few phrases."[39] Two of his Civil War stories were later published: "Men Running" (*Atlantic,* July 1937) and "One Hundred Ladies" (*Saturday Evening Post,* 11 July 1964).

"Every Day's a Holiday," published by *Scribner's* in December 1933, draws upon the same mood that informs "Farewell to Cuba" and "The Way to Go Home." A twice-divorced young woman is trying to cope with her children, her prospective third husband, and her disapproving father at a summer cottage. During the evening she sneaks off with her father's chauffeur. As the title indicates, her life will be a succession of such holidays—much different from the mood of Rodgers and Hart's "Blue Room," which probably provided the title.

On 79th Street the Cozzenses acquired a Scotch terrier they named Peter. Dogs, he commented, were a satisfactory substitute for children, providing ample cause for worry without promising filial ingratitude. As he withdrew into his writing, he lost interest in the diversions of Manhattan. They bought a used Chevrolet, which was replaced with a sporty new DeSoto convertible, and began exploring the suburbs in search of a farm they could afford. Cozzens missed the country, and Bernice was willing to commute.

In May 1932 Cozzens was called for jury duty in an insurance case. When the lawyer for the plaintiff asked in the panel room if any member of the jury had a prejudice in the case, Cozzens said, "Yes. I think most of these cases are nothing but blackmail. Possibly some aren't, but I don't feel qualified to judge between professional liars."[40] He was dismissed with the warning that he could have been jailed if he had made his remarks before the judge. His fascination with the law was still in the future.

While he was rewriting *Castaway* Cozzens began a novel about a doctor, set in a small Connecticut town: "this setting is imagined to be Kent, Connecticut, with a green like New Milford's along US 7 as it passes through Kent."[41] Published in 1933 as *The Last Adam,* it was a major novel and the first in which he assembled most of the qualities that distinguish his best work: a central figure from one of the professions, complex weaving of cause and effect, close scrutiny of community structure, dispassionate tone, lucid style, precision of statement, objective presentation. The social novel and the novel of manners came together in *The Last Adam.*

The Connecticut novel was first called "Bodies Terrestrial," but Alfred Harcourt and the Book-of-the-Month Club (which paid a $5,000 advance) did not like the title.* The phrase appears in I

---

* The *Book-of-the-Month Club News* felt obliged to explain that the selection was not unanimous: "Three of the judges were immensely impressed with this book of Mr. Cozzens,

Corinthians 15:40 ("There are also celestial bodies and bodies terrestrial: but the glory of the celestial is one, and the glory of the
terrestrial is another"). Bernice spotted "the last Adam" in the forty-
fifth verse and said, "There's your title." He admitted that "it is of
course lousy in point of significance, but it is all right in sound
. . . it will have to be meant to be ironic."[43] Saint Paul's "last
Adam" refers to Christ ("The first man Adam was made a living
soul; the last Adam was made a quickening spirit").[44] But there is
nothing Christlike about Cozzens's doctor. "A Cure of Flesh"—
Cozzens's preferred title—was used when the novel was published
in England. In this phrase "cure" has the meaning of "curacy"; as
a divine has a cure of souls, so a physician has a cure of flesh.*
Although there was nothing salacious in the novel, the Book-of-
the-Month Club and the English publisher insisted that clinical
details be altered.†

Dr. Bull is not the dedicated, heart-of-gold country-doctor figure familiar in fiction. He is barely competent and not overcon-
cerned about his patients. "An old horse doctor like me looks at
them and all he can see is that medical science is perfectly useless
in ninety-five out of every hundred cases" (p. 250). The main action in the novel is a typhoid epidemic in New Winton for which
Dr. Bull is partly to blame because as health officer he had neglected to inspect a work camp, from which the latrine drained
into the town reservoir. Yet he is the one who diagnoses the disease after his aged aunt recalls the smell of typhoid cases. The
novel covers a full month, dictated by the course of the epidemic.
At the end of *The Last Adam,* having faced down a town meeting
called to dismiss him for incompetence, the sixty-seven-year-old
Bull relaxes with his mistress:

There was an immortality about him, she thought; her regard fixed
and critical. Something unkillable. Something here when the first men
walked erect; here now. The last man would twitch with it when the
earth expired. A good greedy vitality, surely the very vitality of the world

---

having the view of it outlined in Dr. Canby's critique above; and one other favored it with
reservations; one of the judges, however, was so definitely opposed to its choice that the
fact, in fairness, should be stated here."[42] The five judges in 1933 were Henry Seidel Canby,
William Allen White, Dorothy Canfield Fisher, Heywood Broun, and Christopher Morley.
*Cozzens's source may have been Thomas Hood's "Ode to Rae Wilson, Esq.": "Quacks—
not physicians—in the cure of souls."
†In 1956 Cozzens restored "balls" in the Harvest paperback edition.

and the flesh, it survived all blunders and injuries, all attacks and misfortunes, never quite fed full. She shook her head a little, the smile half derisive in contemptuous affection. Her lips parted enough to say: "The old bastard!"

The real subject of *The Last Adam* is New Winton. Community—the structure of a tight society and the interrelations of its people—became a principal concern of Cozzens's best work. But he had not yet found his central figure, the man of reason and responsibility operating within his awareness of human limitations. (Lancy Micks, Joel Stellow, and Anthony Bradell are approaches to this figure.) *The Last Adam* is the first of what have been called Cozzens's "professional novels"—studies of men (physicians, lawyers, clergymen, soldiers) who serve their communities. Unlike Dr. Bull, the professionals in subsequent novels adhere to the ethics of duty. Cozzens later insisted that he did not write about professions as such, but about men who had professions.

Near the end of *The Last Adam,* by citing the concluding lines of Milton's *Samson Agonistes,* Cozzens disclosed what he had come to realize was the aim of his writing:

> *His servants he, with new acquist*
> *Of true experience from this great event*
> *With peace and consolation both dismissed,*
> *And calm of mind . . .* [p. 300].

"New acquist of true experience" would become his test of literature: the presentation of convincing characters in convincing action, unimpaired by sentimental theories about human nature, to provide the reader with an undistorted recognition of behavior. *The Last Adam* is populated by accurately observed characters who provide a sense of the community life of New Winton. Cozzens was particularly successful with Henry Harris, the crafty Yankee politician, and Herbert Banning, the ineffectual aristocrat—both of whom represent a worn-out puritanism. Dr. Bull is saved from public censure by Harris, not because he cares about Bull, but because he nurtures a permanent resentment against the Bannings and takes a secret pleasure in manipulation. Mrs. Banning, the local *grande dame,* was a "faithful to fact" portrait of Bertha Wood Cozzens.[45]

For the *Book-of-the-Month Club News* Cozzens submitted to an

The author of The Last
Adam (*Harcourt Brace
Jovanovich*)

interview, which would be his last until 1940. When Ruth Hale—
who described him as resembling a painting by Andrea del Sarto—
complimented him on the intuitive quality of his work, he admitted, "It's that or nothing for me. I try to recreate the thing I have
felt, or retell the thing I have seen. The ordered process is beyond
me."[46] Although Cozzens had not yet mastered the techniques of
construction that would enable him to achieve the effect of simultaneous action within a compact time frame of two or three days—
what he later referred to as "the difficulty of doing things all of a
piece"—the structure of *The Last Adam* is much tighter than that
of his apprentice novels. The meditative telephone operator May
Tupping is effectively used as a linking device; through her Cozzens enunciates his controlling concept of the complexity of causes:
"there had been a point in every course of events (and usually
countless points) at which the littlest, most incidental change in
any one of a hundred interlocking details of time, place, or human
whim, would have turned the whole present into something entirely different" (p. 11 –12).

Published by Harcourt, Brace on 5 January 1933 at $2.50, *The
Last Adam* was Cozzens's first best seller. It appeared on the *Pub-*

lishers Weekly list for three months and reached the number-three position in February. (But *The Last Adam* did not sell nearly as well as Lloyd C. Douglas's medical melodrama *The Magnificent Obsession.*) The American News Company gave *The Last Adam* a triple-a rating and ranked it "second only to the Sinclair Lewis novel [*Ann Vickers*] as an achievement." There were three Harcourt printings (10,000, 6,000, and 4,300 copies) in 1933. The publisher advertised that 25,000 copies were in print during the first week after publication, but this figure included BOMC copies. There was a Grosset & Dunlap inexpensive reissue of 879 copies in 1936, and The Readers Library sold 23,923 paperback copies in 1940. The reviews were excellent across the country, with frequent mention that *The Last Adam* was the sixth novel by an author who had not yet reached his thirtieth birthday. The critics expressed a general recognition that the novel marked the beginning of a major reputation. Joseph Henry Jackson urged his readers in the *San Francisco Chronicle:* "Read this novel, if for no other reason than to meet one of the most important of America's younger novelists."[47] In New York, where most American literary reputations are made, *The Last Adam* received prominent exposure in the Sunday book-review supplements of the *Times* and the *Herald Tribune.* In the *Trib* Isabel Paterson—never a Cozzens partisan—acknowledged the skill of the writing and the excellence of the characterizations, but complained about "deliberate, unnecessary coarseness."[48] Paterson used the opportunity to mount an attack on the hard-boiled school, in which she incorrectly placed Cozzens with Hemingway. The *Saturday Evening Post* book column—cutely called "The Literary Lowbrow Who Reads for Amusement"—also noted "the occasional crudities which, I feel, add to the force of the story."[49] There was a stubborn misapprehension about Cozzens's work during the thirties and forties, when reviewers categorized him as a cold and merciless ultrarealist. They were responding not to his material, but to his dispassionate stance: This is what life is; this is how people behave—take it or leave it. Yet Cozzens is not a reportorial writer; nor is he invisible in his work. The authorial intelligence is pervasive in *The Last Adam,* despite the objective third-person point of view.

Longmans, Green published *A Cure of Flesh* on 23 February 1933. In a joint review of the novel and *S.S. San Pedro* in the *London Sunday Times* Desmond MacCarthy warmly welcomed Cozzens to the select company of imaginative realists and declared: "After reading this book I thought that, on the whole, perhaps I would rather be drawn by Mr. Cozzens than by other living novelists, though one or two others might depict more enthusiastically my better-self. I should, at any rate, be safe with him; I should get quick penetrative justice."[50] But the *Times Literary Supplement* reviewer found the plan of the novel disjointed: "it is not until it is clear that he is giving us a cross section of human society in a limited area that his book is easy to read."[51]*A Cure of Flesh* sold 1,149 copies in 1933, and a 1934 inexpensive issue sold another 256 copies. (In 1945 the Penguin paperback edition sold 84,693 copies.) Perhaps the New England characters were too American for old England. Despite Cozzens's poor sales in England, Longmans continued to publish his novels.

Since Cozzens had worked close to his models in Kent, *The Last Adam* inevitably aroused local curiosity and resentment. Before the novel was published, he advised his mother to assume an attitude of detachment: "The avidity with which people try to see themselves in books is amazing, especially as they work hardest to see themselves in unflattering roles. To a person of any sense at all it is obvious that no writer really uses actual people; who would go to the trouble of attempting a faithful picture when it is so much simpler and more satisfactory just to imagine characters? Naturally there has to be a basis for such imagining, and naturally, too, the basis is doubtless always somebody seen or known somewhere, at some time. I admit that in my mind's eye I saw Arthur Haxton when writing of Mr. Herring and, as it happens, Templeton (ten or twelve years ago) when writing of Henry Harris. But to think that I was attempting a representation of either is fantastic; faces are public property, after all. People do themselves too much honor, really; not one in a thousand is intrinsically interesting enough to hold anyone's attention as he stands. He has to be fixed up until he becomes an entirely different person; just as, if you like, I fixed up Dr. T. [Turrell] until, as Dr. Bull, with everything about him drastically changed, he became somebody worth reading about (or I hope he did). The process is creative; you don't copy, you make."[52] The *Waterbury Republican* devoted three articles—including an interview with Bertha Cozzens[53]—to the resemblances between New Winton and Kent. The novelist responded to the *Republican* with a graceful letter, explaining that his invented characters seemed recognizable because they were based on his observation of New England figures:

I know them well because my people have been New Englanders for two centuries. It is my country; the people are my people and so, of course, they seem to me the only people in the world who are altogether right, the way people ought to be. If I have an eye for their faults, it is because I have them myself and know where to look for faults. If I criticize them or reflect on them, it is because I feel that no one has a better right to. Their virtues I regard with complacency—probably with self-complacency, for that matter; to point them out or to advertise them never seemed to me necessary. My pride in my people is a matter rooted deeper than vanity or any concern about getting them whitewashed for inspection by New Yorkers or Middle Westerners. They will do the way they are; they are as good as any—better than some—indeed. I don't mind saying to me they seem a lot better than most.[54]

A bit of absurdity was provided when the Colgate College *Maroon* revealed that New Winton was really Hamilton, New York, and that Dr. Bull was a portrait of Cozzens's uncle, Dr. Willard Reade, to whom *The Last Adam* was dedicated. (Dr. Reade had moved from Nova Scotia to Hamilton.) Cozzens wrote to the *Maroon*, denying the "diverting but entirely fantastic notion" and explaining that the dedication served only to thank his uncle for longstanding kindness and for his assistance with medical details in the novel.[55]

Fox Studios paid $5,000 for the movie rights to *The Last Adam,* which was produced in 1933 as *Dr. Bull,* a Will Rogers vehicle directed by John Ford from a screenplay by Paul Green. Predictably, the movies made Dr. Bull just what he was not in the novel— a wise, dedicated, and lovable figure.

AFTERNOON

FIVE

The Hermit of Carrs Farm

A T the end of 1932, after *The Last Adam* was off his hands, Cozzens was rewriting *Castaway* and planning the Civil War novel: "The more I get into it, the more the Army of the Potomac seems to me the tragic protagonist—I mean the terrible and bloody way in which its commanders managed to post pone its inevitable victory has perhaps few of the sentimental or dramatic aspects of the Confederate cause, but studying it, I find it more moving—hardly a month passed for four years without an opportunity to win the war but between crushing bad luck and the imbecility of the command they always missed by an hour or a hairsbreadth. You feel a kind of fatal agitation even reading about it as time after time the army gets underway with every prospect perfect yet each time somebody will provide the collosal blunder just in time to bring it all to nothing."[1]

In February and March of 1933 Lynn Riggs's dramatization of *The Son of Perdition* was performed at the Hedgerow Theatre in Moylan-Rose Valley, near Philadelphia. Cozzens discussed the play with Riggs, whom he liked, but did not collaborate on the script and took no interest in rehearsals. He and Bernice attended a performance, and found the country house they wanted to buy while driving around the area. Carrs Farm,* on Goat Hill Road, three miles outside Lambertville, New Jersey, appealed to Cozzens be-

---

*Cozzens's stationery read "Carr's Farm" until 1939, when the apostrophe was dropped.

cause its hilltop situation and view of the Sourland Mountains provided a feeling of "extraordinary repose." The stone house, which dated from 1818, was in disrepair and lacked plumbing and electricity. Mrs. Baumgarten wept when she saw it. They bought the 125-acre farm in April for $6,500, with the assistance of a mortgage to their neighbor Edgar Hunt, a well-to-do lawyer. The house was renovated into nine rooms and three baths—which included servants' quarters. Cozzens calculated that after the work was completed they could live "with the greatest comfort" for $5,000 a year. There was no intention of operating it as a working farm, but he planned an ambitious vegetable garden. Bernice made the 130-mile round trip by train from Trenton to Pennsylvania Station and then by taxi to 101 Park Avenue.

The sixth revision of *Castaway* was finished in May 1933. After it was declined by Equinox Cooperative Press, Bennett Cerf took it for Random House. Cerf knew that there was no chance of luring Cozzens away from Harcourt, Brace; but he liked *Castaway* and owed Bernice a favor for having helped him acquire the rights to Proust. Cozzens was relieved to have *Castaway* off his hands, but he admitted that the novel was "not good enough for me."[2]

Cozzens's only "experimental" novel, *Castaway* has been described as Kafkaesque—a label that annoyed the author because he had not read Franz Kafka and resented the implication that his novel was imitative. The published version of *Castaway* is structurally tighter than the work Cozzens had planned in 1930, but its meanings are deliberately open-ended. The epigraph from *Robinson Crusoe,* in which Providence is thanked for keeping man ignorant of the myriad dangers that surround him, is clearly ironic. Cozzens's modern Crusoe is prey to nameless fears. In 1976 Cozzens explained that *Castaway* "was a semi-symbollic, semi-allegoric fictional demonstration of the proposition that the principle of living adds up to self-killing; with touches of: *If the red slayer think he slays / Or if the slain etc.* * Or, in short I gave way to the writers' always bootless attempt to say more than words can—either by fooling with the language whose end as James Joyce will surely show is on the unread shelf with Lyly's *Euphues His England* or Richard Pettie's *Palace;* or by fooling with 'composition'—unity, emphasis and coherence—what the late Aldous Huxley (how this

---

* From Ralph Waldo Emerson's "Brahma."

ABOVE. *Carrs Farm at time of purchase*   BELOW. *Carrs Farm in the fifties*

puts me back in countenance) ruefully told me once was what he
had to see he'd done in *Eyeless in Gaza*—the fascination point-
counterpoint had for him bringing him to (his phrase) come a
cropper. However *he* never wrote an unreadable line or uttered a
fatuous obscurity. That doesn't go for me, damn it."[3]

Castaway opens with Mr. Lecky*—he has no first name—
emerging into the basement of a vast unpopulated department
store. Almost incapacitated by unknown terrors, he fears pursuit,
but there are no pursuers. His watch has stopped at 5:15. There is
no explanation for Mr. Lecky's situation, and no account of the
outside world is provided.

Mr. Lecky has no survival skills, even surrounded by the material abundance of the store. For the first two days he makes a mess
of whatever he touches while arming himself and fortifying a lav-
atory. During the third day he encounters an apelike figure he
thinks of as "the idiot" and murders him after a terrifying pursuit.
(The contrast with Crusoe's treatment of Friday is obvious.) On
the morning of the sixth day, suffering from an appalling awareness of his isolation and precarious mortality, Mr. Lecky discovers
that his watch is now running—though it still indicates 5:15. He
returns to his victim and studies the face:

. . . Mr. Lecky beheld its familiar strangeness—not like a stranger's face,
and yet it was no friend's face, nor the face of anyone he had ever met.

What this could mean held him, bent closer, questioning in the gloom;
and suddenly his hand let go the watch, for Mr. Lecky knew why he
had never seen a man with this face. He knew who had been pursued
and cruelly killed, who was now dead and would never climb more stairs.
He knew why Mr. Lecky could never have for his own the stock of this
great store [p. 181].

Cozzens did not make it easy for his readers, but his fable is not
baffling. Using the familiar Doppelgänger device, he dramatized
the effects of human isolation resulting from the lack of resources
of mind and spirit. The idiot murdered by Mr. Lecky is himself.
The store is symbolically his body: "Before there was a consciousness to be incarcerated, its prison was built" (pp. 176–177). The

---

*This name may be a reference to the nineteenth-century English moral historian W. E.
H. Lecky, who contended that moral decisions always involve emotion and reason; or it
may have been retained from S. T. S. Lecky's *"Wrinkles" in Practical Navigation* (1881), a
volume Cozzens consulted for *S.S. San Pedro*.

reader's chief difficulty comes in solving the time frame, which may actually be only the moment at 5:15—that is, the entire story may occur in an instant within Mr. Lecky's mind.

Cozzens recognized that he had attempted something "practically impossible" in point of view. With only one character, a first-person narrative would have been the best method; but *Castaway* could not be told by Mr. Lecky because he doesn't comprehend his predicament and is presumably dead at the conclusion. The third-person limited-omniscience narrative was not altogether satisfactory because readers expect more help from it than the material allowed Cozzens to provide.

Castaway was published by Random House on 7 November 1934 at $1.75. The reviews were largely uncomprehending, although the brilliance of the writing was recognized. William Rose Benét described it in the *Saturday Review of Literature* as "a vignette that it is quite possible may become classic."[4] After admitting that he was "not quite sure what it is about," Clifton Fadiman observed in the *New Yorker* that Cozzens had failed to separate the narrative and allegorical levels:

You can't quite swallow it as a straight tale of terror. And if it's all shadowy with meanings, what are they? Is modern man really solitary amid the complexities of civilization? Are things in the saddle, driving him mad? Is he so degenerate that he cannot fend for himself, even in an artificially complete environment? Has he, the effete city man, lost the ability to remain alone? Or, in his neurotic fear, does he turn upon and rend himself to death? If Mr. Cozzens means one or all of these things, he has selected the wrong set of symbols to make his allegory clear. If he doesn't mean any of them, all I can say is that his story is more stimulating than he thinks.[5]

Cozzens felt that his writing was too clear for critics who are impressed by unintelligibility. "One of *Castaway*'s greatest failings is that it's short and perfectly plain reading—I'm not attempting irony at all; it's literally true; it's a serious defect in an out-of-the-way book and the only critics who will treat it kindly are those who have me down as a good writer on their private lists and so know that anything I write must be good."[6]

Most of the reviewers seem to have taken their lead from the dust jacket, which categorized *Castaway* as a "weird tale" for "readers who appreciate the tales of Edgar Allan Poe and Ambrose Bierce." The flap copy also suggested an explanation for Mr.

Lecky's situation: "Is he the only man left alive in all the world?"
A similar clue was provided in the press release included in review
copies. The attempt to establish a realistic background only served
to distract attention from the narrative. Cozzens was not concerned with how Mr. Lecky came to be in the store, and Mr.
Lecky apparently has no memory of what happened to him before
the book opens. *Castaway* is not a disaster story. The outside world
does not exist. The important action is interior, within Mr. Lecky's
consciousness—but not within his stream of consciousness, a technique Cozzens rejected.

The English edition—which preceded the Random House edition by forty-one days—begins with an explanation written by a
Longmans editor:

> Alone in a vast Department Store, the sole sur-
> vivor of a catastrophe that has destroyed
> New York, Mr. Lecky finds himself a com-
> monplace little Robinson Crusoe, cut
> off from his kind amidst the fan-
> tastic plenty of the twentieth cen-
> tury. There is everything to
> sustain life in abundance,
> and nothing to fear —
> except . . . .

Since the English edition was typeset before the American edition,
Cozzens's final revisions for the Random House text reveal that
he deleted clues to the catastrophe explanation. In the concluding
chapter of the Longmans text, after waking with his witch-hazel
hangover, Mr. Lecky wonders about the outside world:

Rain in its desolation would be pouring down all over the city, aug-
menting the catastrophe. That catastrophe it was, Mr. Lecky had never
doubted, though he had wondered so little. It was pressed in with his
misery now, made immediate and overwhelming. He might suppose he
had lived, like those fish he had tried to feed and the birds in their cages
downstairs, a little longer than the world.

Mr. Lecky had not only the sense of catastrophe, but—holding his
head to see better—all the proof he needed of it. How otherwise came
so great a wealth of things, materials, to be untended? Only one concern
could be greater than riches; it must be death. Six days? Who alive could
wait a day to claim and defend so much of value? Granted then, a dead

world. Mr. Lecky lay motionless, for more than the thought of universal
disaster, the misery of his body absorbed him [pp. 174–75].

The Random House text omits this passage. Cozzens decided to
cancel any explanations about the outside world that would engage the reader in extraneous speculation—e.g., where are the store
watchmen?

Castaway marked the termination of Cozzens's lush early or apprentice style. Thus:

Let the man you meet be, instead, a paretic. He has taken a secret departure from your world. He dwells amid choicest, most dispendious super-
latives. In his arm he has the strength to lift ten elephants. He is already
two hundred years old. He is more than nine feet high; his chest is of
iron, his right leg is silver, his incomparable head is one whole ruby.
Husband of a thousand wives, he has begotten on them ten thousand
children. Nothing is mean about him; his urine is white wine; his faeces
are always soft gold. However, despite his splendor and his extraordinary
attainments, he cannot successfully pronounce the words: electricity,
Methodist Episcopal, organisation, third cavalry brigade. Avoid them.
Infuriated by your demonstration of any accomplishment not his, he may
suddenly kill you [pp. 74–75].*

Cozzens later became convinced that style "becomes bad at exactly
the point that a critic says it is brilliant—if you are able to see style
there is something wrong with it."[7]

Castaway sold poorly: 1,410 copies in America and 763 copies in
England. There were Transworld and Bantam paperback editions
in 1952; and the Modern Library paired it with *S.S. San Pedro* in
1956. Cozzens regarded it as a "misstep" and thereafter eschewed
allegory. However, it became something of a cult book after some
critics misread it as a fable about Depression America. Cozzens
did not intend *Castaway* as a political message. In 1934 he in-
structed his mother, an ardent New Dealer: "Don't you worry
about my developing a social conscience at my age—I did it at
sixteen while I was at school and ever since I have got surer and
surer that the poor and wretched are, nine cases in ten, what their
capacities entitle them to be. . . . I think any reasonable person
will agree that it has been again and again proved in this country
that anyone who has the wit to get it can have everything there

* See also the description of the perfume department on pp. 141–43 of *Castaway*.

is—you don't need birth, or money, or education to start with and Lord God how much more equal can you make equality?"[8] He soon modified his position on birth, money, and education. Beginning with his next novel, *Men and Brethren,* he would depict an American aristocracy in which ability and a sense of duty are most frequently found in those who have enjoyed the advantages that attend money and position. Cozzens's political—more precisely, apolitical—views were not shared at home. Bernice was a firm liberal. Edgar Hunt, whom Cozzens called "the Squire," was a staunch opponent of the New Deal's erosion of personal liberty. When the Potato Control Act was enacted in 1935, he drew up a resolution in which thirty-five Hunterdon County farmers declared their intention of openly defying "the unconstitutional measure." Among the signing farmers were Cozzens and Sylvia B. Cozzens, who did not grow potatoes—which brought a headline appearance of his name in the *New York Times.*[9] Cozzens voted for socialist Norman Thomas in 1936 as a protest against being offered the choice between Roosevelt and Landon.

Most of the $20,000 Cozzens earned in 1933 went into improving Carrs Farm, and he wrote stories in 1934 to raise additional money. "My Love to Marcia" (*Collier's,* 3 March 1934) and "Love Leaves Town" (*American,* September 1934) are competent commercial fiction; but two short-short stories for *Collier's*—"Straight Story" (17 November 1934) and "Success Story" (20 April 1935)— are obvious potboilers.*

At Lambertville he established the daily routine he maintained for the rest of his life, except during his 1938 *Fortune* stint and his wartime service in the Air Force. He rose before 6:00 A.M. and prepared tea for himself and coffee for Bernice. Their driver-handyman drove Bernice to the train because Cozzens did not like to have his morning writing delayed. He wrote until lunch, after which he took a short nap and then worked in the garden until it was time for him to meet Bernice's train at 6:00 P.M. He rarely tried to write in the afternoon or evening, having discovered that such work was usually wasted. After dinner Bernice worked on manuscripts, and he either read or vetted manuscripts for Brandt & Brandt. He was usually in bed by ten.

---

*The short-short story was printed on one page of the magazine. Two unpublished short-shorts are in the Cozzens Papers: "Local History," about a small-town newspaper publisher, and an untitled story about a small-town cop.

Bernice at Carrs Farm

There was a succession of live-in servant couples—twenty-four by 1949—who received $60 a month. Cozzens steadily enlarged his vegetable garden because he enjoyed eating food that he had grown; and there were roses. His work on the property kept him in good shape.

They were friendly with the Hunts, but had no social life in the country or in New York. Cozzens rarely went to the city except for dental treatment. The only people they regularly saw were Bernice's sister, Fannie, and her husband, Claude Collins, a newsreel editor, who bought a place nearby, at Pennington, New Jersey. Bernice and Fannie were very close and shared an interest in antique collecting; Cozzens liked Fannie—but not her husband— and called her "Sweetie Pie" when he was in a playful mood.

Their Scotch terriers provided distraction and anxiety. Peter was bred to Peggy, and she produced a litter in 1937. The puppy they kept was killed by a car. Peter was killed by a fox and was replaced by Jock. When an Air Force friend later told him that he was missing a great deal by not having children, Cozzens replied that he knew about the feelings of fatherhood from having raised dogs.

Cozzens kept up with current fiction but returned to Swift, Steele, Gibbon, Hazlitt, and Jane Austen for pleasure. He reread some Shakespeare almost every day. Among contemporary novelists, he admired Aldous Huxley and Somerset Maugham. Apart from gardening, his only hobby was collecting popular records from the twenties. Paul Whiteman, Ted Lewis, and Frank Crumit were his favorites; and it amused him to compare different recordings of the same tune.* Bernice collected eighteenth-century country furniture and Canton china. Cozzens shared her enthusiasm for antiques at first, but he lost interest after he decided that they could not afford the best items. When they attended country auctions he sometimes read in the car. As his interest in the Civil War developed, he collected Currier & Ives battle prints.

During the summer of 1934 Cozzens resumed work on his Civil War novel, which was titled "Captain Cadwallader" and then "Dirge for Two Veterans." In July he postponed the book because of the glut of Civil War novels in progress—particularly because he suspected that William Faulkner's series of Civil War stories in the *Saturday Evening Post* would turn into a novel. (Faulkner's *The Unvanquished,* 1938, consists of loosely connected short stories.) The real problem, Cozzens later admitted, was that he never felt confident with the material: "I wasn't there: I never saw it for myself." [11] Still, he regretted abandoning the subject because, he claimed, he knew more about the Army of the Potomac than anyone else.

Having dropped the Civil War novel, Cozzens began planning a novel based on Dickey Doubs and St. Thomas Chapel, where he had lived in 1927: "the parish of Holy Innocents is imagined to be a combination of St. Bartholomew's and St. Thomas's, with its finances modeled on those of Grace Church in New York City." [12]

---

* In 1957 Cozzens wrote to John McCallum at Harcourt, Brace describing "my really unexampled collection of the records of my youth. (If you want to hear a mint-condition Marian Harris Left All alone Again Blues, or Ted Lewis' original Unreconstructed Margie, or Down the Old Church Aisle; or Paul Whiteman's 1921 Ka-lu-a; or Frank Crumit singing as who else could or would, Sweet Lady, or The Love Nest you have only to stop by)." [10]

He had ample material, for, as he remarked to his mother, "I haven't been bumming around with priests all my life for nothing."[13] The working title was "Humble Access," from the Episcopal prayer; but Charles A. Pearce, his Harcourt, Brace editor, thought it was a poor title, and it became *Men and Brethren.**

The Cozzenses took an apartment at 18 East 64th Street during the winter of 1935 to spare Bernice the trouble of commuting in bad weather, and perhaps also to allow Cozzens to research his novel in New York. He disliked living in the city and was eager to return to the farm.

While writing *Men and Brethren* Cozzens defined genius in writing as "less a matter of emotional intensity—any best-selling tripe novel has plenty of that—than of a talent for saying next not merely the right, the apt, the vivid, or moving thing, but the thing which, having all those qualities, so far transcends your reasonable expectation that you see that it couldn't have been done merely by intelligence, or training, or hard trying, and must simply have been born in a sort of triumphant flash outside the ordinary process of thought."† He identified this quality in Faulkner, Wolfe, and Dos Passos—adding that it is not all there is to literary genius. Even though Fitzgerald had it, he didn't seem to be getting anywhere.[14]

Men and Brethren was ready for Bertha to read in November 1935. Her distress at the identifiable qualities of Doubs and Killian Stimpson (as Doctor Lamb, the rector of Holy Innocents) elicited Cozzens's admission that writers have to work close to their models to achieve convincing figures—a reversal of his 1933 claim that it was easier for him to invent characters than to copy them.

As Somerset Maugham remarked, it's very hard to be a gentleman and a writer. I have long ago given up trying, for if you are going to write honestly at all you cannot show a decent respect for the ordinary obligations of good manners. As I develop more experience I realise that it is not as easy as it looks to change things to make them unrecognizable while still keeping them true—not unnaturally the right and true thing is usually the thing that really happened. It is Maugham again—he is the

---

* Acts 2:36–37: "Therefore let all the house of Israel know assuredly, that God hath made that same Jesus, whom ye have crucified, both Lord and Christ. Now when they heard this, they were pricked in their heart, and said unto Peter and to the rest of the apostles, Men and brethren, what shall we do?"

† Cozzens later observed that a good example of genius was provided when Keats revised "A thing of beauty is a constant joy" to "A thing of beauty is a joy forever."[15]

only person who ever writes anything intelligent about writing—who points out that any real character is always your portrait of someone you have seen and you cannot play tricks with it—any change you make will be a false note, and that the identifying details are by definition the details that matter. Consequently I fear I'll never be through writing about people I know—which ought to be plain, since what do you think the effect would be if I took up writing about people I didn't know? [16]

Men and Brethren covers some twenty-four hours—Friday evening to Saturday evening—in the life of Ernest Cudlipp, vicar of St. Ambrose's Chapel in New York City.* Cudlipp's cure of souls is an Episcopal mission or settlement house funded by the affluent Holy Innocents Church. That Cudlipp has this post at forty-five indicates that he is not likely to rise higher in his profession. His career has been damaged by his prior association with an unorthodox church downtown.† A celibate by conviction, Cudlipp has an unsentimental sense of duty to God's creatures, whom he tries to love but does not particularly like. During the course of the novel he copes with a dozen people and their problems—among them the married woman pregnant by the young poet who is Cudlipp's protégé (a nasty portrait of the young Cozzens); the former Greenwich Village beauty ruined by drugs and drink, whom he supports; the dying parishoner who wants the last rites of the Roman Catholic Church; a bad boy in trouble with the police; a homosexual Episcopalian monk who has left the monastery; Cudlipp's rector, who objects to his having invited a rabbi to speak at St. Ambrose's; a broken missionary; a young curate with Communist enthusiasms; a beautiful married woman who has a crush on Cudlipp. He is never seen in church. Cudlipp copes with everything in a hard-headed way, unencumbered by feelings about the goodness of people. Believing in God's omniscience, he therefore accepts that his duties are preordained. As he explains to the adulterous woman whose abortion he has arranged so that she can return to her husband and children: "A great obligation has been laid on me to do or be whatever good thing I have learned I ought to be, or know I can do. I can't excuse myself from it. I dare not bury it or throw it away" (p. 281). *Men and Brethren* ends with Cudlipp reciting the "terrible" twenty-fifth chapter of Saint Mat-

---

* St. Ambrose was Doubs's favorite saint.
† Doubs had served at St. Mark's-in-the-Bouwerie when Dr. William Guthrie was maintaining an ecclesiastical circus there.

thew: "For the kingdom of heaven is as a man traveling into a far country, who called his own servants and delivered unto them his goods. . . ." This is the parable of the talents, which contrasts the good and faithful servants with the wicked and slothful servant. Cozzens achieved a convincing and admiring portrait of a priest despite his antipathy to religious people, whom he regarded as victims of flawed intelligence or unbalanced nervous systems. As he explained to his mother, "but then, of course, there is something about Our Lord I never liked either, a sort of emotionally intense combination of softness and severity—in point of fact, the same thing that kept me from ever quite liking FHS. . . ."[17]

Men and Brethren is the first novel in which Cozzens fully developed the concept of duty that would become the subject of his major fiction. Cudlipp's deterministic view is that many people "seem to be simply bad stock, bad blood. . . . They have no chance because they are no good" (p. 57). He tries to love them because they are precious to God; his obligation is to employ his talents, which God has provided, since the able and fortunate people who accept the responsibility of privilege make all the difference to society. Many readers have found this position cynical or snobbish or priggish. With the removal of God's omniscience, it was Cozzens's own view of society and his relation to it—which he regarded as "grown-up." He did not love humanity, but he fulfilled the duties of his genius.

Men and Brethren was what critics like to call a break-through novel: the first full-length book in which Cozzens achieved a tight structure to enforce the simultaneity of action and the complexity of causes. Multiple events impinge on one another in *The Last Adam*; but the time scheme is loose, and the focus moves from character to character. *Men and Brethren* is limited to parts of two days (it was originally planned to cover one evening), and the attention is always on Cudlipp. There is no scene from which he is absent. The third-person narrative provides the impression of standing with the author behind Cudlipp and observing everything from Cudlipp's perspective, thereby providing the effect of detachment combined with close participation.

Cozzens felt that *Men and Brethren* was technically successful, but "a little thin, probably because if I got right down to it I find it hard to conceive of a professional Christian who isn't a fool, or a knave—in short, it's largely objective, for I know perfectly how they act and exactly what they say, but I am not really certain at

The author of Men and Brethren
(*Harcourt Brace Jovanovich*)

all what they feel, and not being certain, I realize that when I say what the Vicar is feeling, I am really guessing." [18]

Men and Brethren was published by Harcourt, Brace on 2 January 1936 at $2.50. (After planning to take it as the December 1935 selection, the Book-of-the-Month Club dropped the novel because the material was potentially offensive to its members.) The first printing of 10,000 copies sold out promptly, and a 2,500-copy sec-

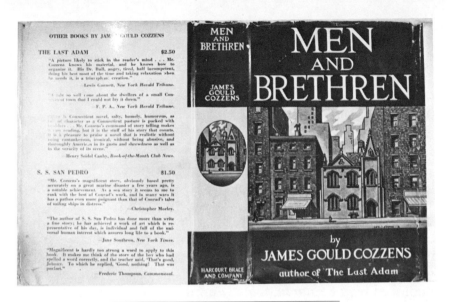

Jacket for first printing of Men and Brethren

ond printing was required in January—after which sales stopped.*
The notices were largely very favorable, with influential reviewers
(Mark Schorer, Louis Kronenberger, R. P. Blackmur, Henry Seidel Canby) recognizing that Cozzens was a steadily improving
writer and "a man to watch." The unsigned *Time* review by T. S.
Matthews, a bishop's son, provided inside information in a scram-
bled sentence: "many an Episcopalian reader would have recognized at least two likenesses—Bishop William T. Manning, one-
time Father Harvey Officer—may think they see in his hero a
similarity to the late Reverend Ralph Pomeroy."† [19] Some reviews
noted that *Men and Brethren* lacked the gusto of *The Last Adam*,
and hinterland reviewers—perhaps expecting a sentimental por-
trayal of Cudlipp—complained that they did not understand the
point of the novel. The church publications did get the point that
Cudlipp combines Christianity with a realistic view of people and
were receptive. *The Churchman*, *Christendom*, and the *Christian
Century* welcomed it as an accurate and moving depiction of a
contemporary man of God. The English reviews were just as good
when the novel was published by Longmans, Green in March

* One of the best sellers of 1936 was *Drums Along the Mohawk* by Cozzens's Harvard class-
mate Walter D. Edmonds.
† Officer, who resigned from the Order of the Holy Cross, was combined with Cuthbert
Wright for the character of Carl Willever, the homosexual monk. Pomeroy, the rector of
Holy Innocents Church in West Orange, N.J., was not the model for Cudlipp.

1936.* The *Times Literary Supplement* praised the novel's remarkable objectivity: "These characters are projected upon the page as human beings embodying no thesis but only life itself. . . ."[20] At the time of publication *Men and Brethren* was identified by several reviewers as the best American novel about a clergyman, a judgment that has been frequently endorsed.

The year 1936 was largely devoted to short stories while Cozzens mulled over possible novel subjects, reconsidering the abandoned Civil War novel. Between 1934 and 1938 Cozzens published twelve short stories, writing them only for money, because the form had ceased to interest him. He found the length too confining, and it became increasingly difficult for him to write about the things the slicks wanted. "Men Running" (written in January 1934 but not published by the *Atlantic Monthly* until July 1937), one of the two published stories he salvaged from his Civil War research, is an account of a volunteer Union battalion at Bull Run. There are no heroics; the battalion tries to reach the battle and is engulfed in the retreat. A 1935 *Redbook* story, "Foot in It," became his most frequently reprinted story under the title "Clerical Error." This uncharacteristic trick-plot story was written from an idea supplied by William Bolitho. An antiquarian bookseller operates a successful racket by sending bills for pornography to the families of recently deceased clergymen, who pay to avoid scandal—until he bills the family of a blind man.

One of Cozzens's most admired stories was "Total Stranger" (*Saturday Evening Post*, 15 February 1936), about a boy being driven to prep school by his severe father. They spend a night at a country hotel and encounter an old flame of the father's; as the man rises to the occasion, the son perceives for the first time that his father is not just a disapproving authority figure. The story ends with a moral plant for the *Post* readership: "Unfortunately, I never did do much better at school. But that year and the year following, I would occasionally try to, for I thought it would please my father."[21] Henry Cozzens is hard to identify in his son's fiction: "In the story Total Stranger I described him as accurately as my boy's-memories would let me."[22]

"Total Stranger" was awarded the O. Henry Prize for the best story of 1936. Cozzens regarded it as "a piece of damned imperti-

*The records of A. M. Heath, Cozzens's English agent, indicate a sale of 736 copies; but the Brandt & Brandt records show that 4,132 copies were sold in England.

nence for anyone to try to give me a prize. I suppose it is a symptom of a vanity so monstrous and excessive as to defy any ordinary classification or expression—just as I don't doubt that fundamentally the reason I prefer to live as nearly like a recluse as possible is that I subconsciously know that people, the world, never would and never will greet my entrances into it with the reverent applause required for my pleasure and if I cannot have that I will not, in effect, play." [23] In statements like this one to his mother he is partly teasing her. Nonetheless, it is true that Cozzens resigned from the literary life in his early thirties. For a self-described recluse he was remarkably well informed about the ego struggles of his fellow scribblers from Bernice's reports, and he found them degrading. With his wife looking after his affairs it was unnecessary for him to involve himself in the tiresome and humiliating business of peddling his wares or his personality and making influential friends. He shared the position of publishers on successful books: if people like an author's previous work they will buy his books. Advertising may make a successful book more successful, but it can't sell a book that people don't want to read. Given these rules, it was much more satisfactory to keep out of the wretched scramble for fame. As the years passed, his reticence hardened into pessimism. ". . . I never—at least not since I was about 14 and had begun to see that the world was not exactly as I had heretofore supposed—seriously expected anything pleasant or good from anything or anyone and when I got things that were either or both I have always more or less felt that it was a pleasant mistake." [24]

In March 1937 Cozzens reported to his mother that he was trying to get started on a novel to be called "Poor Yorick"—a title from Hamlet's graveside speech. "My conception, in so far as I ever have one for a book, was one of mild distaste for a series of scenes and events viewed in retrospect—the parts that were perhaps pleasant at the time becoming by passage of years rather fatuous and sad; the parts that were unpleasant becoming rather fatuous and sad too. . . . I expect I will have a good deal to say about Europe, about money, about the fatuous trade of writing, and about love or the Vale of Lillies and the Bower of Bliss." [25] It drew upon his experiences with the Parishes and Virginia Reiland in

1926–27 and became his closest approach to an autobiographical novel.

Recognizing that it was insufficient to tell just what actually happened, Cozzens continued to ponder the problems of honesty in fiction. The unadorned truth does not make convincing fiction. "You cannot tell what was so, for stating the facts would give the reader a 'false impression'. For a 'true impression' you must say what is calculated to create it, not always, nor indeed very often, what was in fact the case." These ruminations were brought on by his decision to scrap the beginning of "Poor Yorick," in which he had tried to write truthfully about himself. "In effect, the honester I tried to be, the more long-winded and duller I got, and the less sympathetic, until even I could see that the narrator* would have to be definitely not myself, but a fictional character who could be allowed to have attractive and sympathetic qualities which in common honesty it was impossible to allow myself." [26]

The subject of "Poor Yorick" was pride as seen in a young writer sensitive to his relative poverty and obscurity. When published in 1940 as *Ask Me Tomorrow*, the novel carried an epigraph from *Troilus and Cressida*: "Why should a man be proud? How doth pride grow? I know not what pride is."

Ask Me Tomorrow went slowly. A good week's work was four typed pages, and there were some fifteen drafts before publication. Cozzens worked directly on the typewriter. If he got stuck, he would try out wordings in pencil on a slip of paper. The only editorial advice he sought was from Bernice. After the last working draft was completed, he retyped the whole novel himself to give it a final polish. When the typescript was delivered to the publisher, it was finished.

While Cozzens was writing *Ask Me Tomorrow*, he became increasingly sure that his aims were alien to popular and critical tastes. His confidence in his judgments preserved him from doubts about his own standards, and his pride obviated envy. He admitted that it was the writer's job to please readers, but had no intention of trying to become a crowd-pleaser; he insisted that good writers could only write one way. It was impossible for him to provide

---

*The published novel, *Ask Me Tomorrow*, does not have a narrator—that is, a character in the novel who relates the story. It is written in the third person from the central character's perspective. Since none of the working drafts survive, it is impossible to determine whether the first draft employed a narrator. Possibly Cozzens used the term "narrator" to mean the point-of-view character.

sentimental appeal that he did not feel. Thanks to Bernice, he was able to write to please himself.

In April 1937 he observed: "I can support the luck of the deserving as well as the next mean-spirited scribbler, but it has been a hard season when I have to sit by and see John Marquand [*The Late George Apley*] get away with it; and even worse, when the ineffable Steinbeck's exercise [*Of Mice and Men*] with high boo-hoo content in Woollcott-style tripe is hailed as the greatest work of the decade, on one hand; while Virginia Woolf's laborious version of what can only be described as That British Novel [*The Years*] is raised as a great light even by Tom Matthews, on the other; and in the middle Josephine Johnson's appalling prose and nonsensical action [*Jordanstown*] passes as a thing of beauty—it makes effort seem vain and all the world sad & dreary, and one's profession a thing to be changed as soon as possible."[27]

Before it was published, Cozzens regarded *To Have and Have Not* as the most important novel of 1937 because of Hemingway's defiance of the critics. But when he read it, he admitted the critics were right: "the line of thought is hammy and the characters phoney—not that I know what they are really like, but they are human beings, and so it is certain that they are not like that in Key West or anywhere else. . . . I think the plain moral truth is he is reaping what he sowed, and that a writer has to write, not go fishing and bull fighting and defending the oppressed in Spain."[28]

Cozzens declined to make a statement for *Writers Take Sides*, a 1938 symposium on the Spanish Civil War. When the booklet appeared he found that he would have been in a minority of two out of more than 400 American Writers.* He felt that the only chance for an end to the war was for Franco to win; if the Loyalists won, they would begin liquidating each other.[29]

Cozzens had attentively read all of Faulkner until the middle of *Light in August* (1932), which he found boring. "I suppose he believes he can get closer to the truth of feelings and wants by handling words with an eye to their overtones rather than their dictionary meanings, and that by stimulating a pattern of ideas in the mind of the reader he can convey a 'story' without forcing it into the artificial (or if he prefers, false and unreal) forms of the Aristotelean beginning, middle, and end. . . . Faulkner wants writing

---

*Of the writers who responded, 404 declared themselves for the Loyalists and against Franco; seven were listed as "neutral?"; and only Gertrude Atherton was against the Loyalists.

to do something which writing is incapable of doing. . . . Nothing is real on paper, anyway. It is real in the writer's mind, and if he knows his business, it becomes real (though never by any means exactly the same) in the reader's mind."[30]

Surprisingly, the contemporary American work Cozzens most admired was John Dos Passos's *U.S.A.* trilogy (one of Bernice's properties), which he regarded as "the only novel yet published in this century that will be commonly read a hundred years from now." Although "a childish New Masses sort of radicalism" accounts for many absurdities in *U.S.A.*, it is "packed with a sort of distilled experience."[31]

Jerome Weidman has provided a gauge of Cozzens's reputation in 1937. Needing an agent, Weidman was taken to lunch with Bernice Baumgarten by Quincy Howe, the editor-in-chief at Simon & Schuster. "You are the editor of one of America's most important publishing houses," he said to Howe. "Have you ever heard of a writer named James Gould Cozzens?" Howe had not. Then Weidman put the question to Miss Baumgarten.[32]

The first mention of Cozzens in a critical volume came in Harlan Hatcher's *Creating the Modern American Novel* (1935), where he received a one-paragraph discussion as a promising writer who had not yet fulfilled his promise. In 1937 he replied to a questionnaire for Fred B. Millet's *Contemporary American Authors* (1940): "I have no theories about literature and other people's irk me. With great difficulty and uncertainty and much lost motion I write whatever I find that I can. The view I have of writing is that a writer does well to write in a clear and unobtrusive way, trying not to be dull, and being careful to avoid obvious untruths and general nonsense."[33]

Bertha Cozzens's dearest wish was to live near her son, but he took care to forestall any possibility of that. At a distance of some hundred miles he was a dutiful son, supplementing the income from her trust fund—which she was determined to preserve for him—and maintaining a regular schedule of letters about his work. She lived for his letters and was upset whenever one was a day late. His letters closed "Take care of yourself" and "All my love"; and she ended hers with "God bless you darling" and "Devotedly always." Bernice was attentive to Bertha and ran shopping errands for her in New York. A chronic worrier, Bertha literally worried herself to the point of nervous exhaustion. One of her concerns was that her handsome son was losing his good looks. When she worried in 1937 that he was getting stout, he informed her that he was 5'11½" and weighed 152 pounds—observing that the Cozzenses ran to corpulence, which she should have considered before breeding with one. He admitted he was drinking a quart of beer in the evening, but said there was little nutritional value in it. Then, of course, she worried that he was an incipient alcoholic.

In June 1937 Cozzens was invited by Russell Davenport, the Managing Editor of *Fortune*, to become the first writer in a program to bring distinguished writers to the magazine for a year's internship. Bernice warned him he would not be happy writing for the Luce organization. Cozzens declined the offer, but then reconsidered because he thought working for a large magazine would provide him with material. He agreed to try it for three months if *Ask Me Tomorrow* were ready at the end of 1937. It was not finished, but Cozzens joined *Fortune* for a year in January 1938 and was carried on the masthead as an editor starting in the March issue and as an associate editor in May. The salary of $15,000 was a generous figure in 1938, and Cozzens wanted the money to make improvements on Carrs Farm.

He went to work at *Fortune* on the fifty-second floor of the Chrysler Building; the offices were moved to the thirtieth floor of the new Time & Life Building in Rockefeller Center in April. During the winter months the Cozzenses took an apartment at 114 East 40th Street, but the rest of the time he commuted from Lambertville. His first chore was to polish an article on the Navy, for which he spent twelve straight hours dictating revisions. Then he was assigned to write "Oskaloosa vs. the United States," a financial profile of Oskaloosa, Iowa, for the April issue, which required a visit to Oskaloosa. He worked on this article at the office until 5:30 in the morning of the deadline day; then it was rewritten by someone else.

Henry Luce admired *Men and Brethren* and thought Cozzens was the right man for a study of ten great American fortunes, showing what they "really amounted to, what they really controlled, if anything; and what the tie-up between various related interests was in fact as opposed to theory."[34] Cozzens spent several months on this project, but his work never saw print. He was impressed by Luce. "Though in vanity and self-assertion I yield to no man, I well remember while affecting ease and equality in his baronial chambers, at heart I knew all the time that I was not in his class, that I did not think as quickly and forcefully, that painfull as the admission was, he was a more considerable person with a better brain." [35]

The only Cozzens article that appeared in *Fortune* substantially as he had written it was "The Fuller Brush Co." (October 1938). He found the research embarrassing, for he was required to attend salesmen's pep meetings and went out with a door-to-door peddler in Irvington, Maplewood, and Springfield, New Jersey. His article is not stylistically distinguishable from anything else in *Fortune*. After the Fuller assignment he worked on articles about solar energy and the American Arbitration Association, which were written by other hands. Cozzens particularly disliked the monthly deadline crises and all-night conferences.

Cozzens realized that he was not giving *Fortune* what it wanted. He had been brought in to improve the quality of the writing in the magazine; but what was required was someone who could write Fortunese, only better. "The general theory is the more similies, the better or more colorful the writings, while of course the truth is that a similie is a boob trap. What it amounts to is that the writer, unable to think clearly enough or write well enough to say what he means, gets around the impasse by cutely changing the subject. Once in a blue moon a similie will indeed be so perfect, fall so naturally into place—in effect put with one neat stroke the thought on hand, not dragging in extraneous thoughts—that you can use it legitimately. I suppose in a full length book that might happen once or even twice. When it happens twice, or who knows how many times, in every *Fortune* paragraph you begin to see that what, from a writer's standpoint is a vice, has been made into a virtue. If you say that the only result is to interrupt the reader's thought, confuse the point, and weaken the effect of what you're saying, the answer is, sure, fine, never a dull moment." [36]

The *Fortune* editorial staff included John Chamberlain, Ralph Ingersoll, Louis Kronenberger, and Archibald MacLeish; but the only friend Cozzens made there was William B. Harris, who shared his interest in gardening. They lunched together, and Cozzens— always an attentive feeder—regularly ordered the frogs' legs at Longchamps. Harris later joined the brokerage house of Laidlaw & Co., where he managed Cozzens's investments.

There was a power struggle at *Fortune* between Russell Davenport and Eric Hodgins. Cozzens felt that his presence constituted an embarrassment for Davenport. After ten months he offered to resign; somewhat to his chagrin, the offer was accepted. The parting was friendly. Both sides admitted that *Fortune* and Cozzens were not made for each other. He picked up his spare Zeus cigarette holder,* the only personal possession in his office, and returned to his writing regimen at Carrs Farm.

Cozzens had not been able to work on *Ask Me Tomorrow* during his *Fortune* stint. He returned to the novel toward the end of 1938, and by April 1939 had written 201 pages of the penultimate draft. While he was working on it, he explained to his mother—who was concerned that he would offend Mrs. Parish by writing about her too openly—how he had to adapt experience to the purposes of fiction: "alas, when it comes to presenting Mrs. P. or anyone else 'truly', we don't do that in this business—the truth is always too complicated and usually too implausible. It has to be simplified and suggested and the most you can hope for is to present selected material in such a way that an intelligent reader will be conscious of the not-expressed and inexpressible real truth—or at least, and more often, not be too conscious of a falseness." [37]

The novel was at various stages titled "In Praise of Folly," "An Enchanter Fleeing," "To Beg I Am Ashamed" (which was dropped because a London whore named Sheila Cousins had used it for her autobiography), "Pride His Glass," and "It Was the Nightingale" (the working title until Cozzens learned that Ford Madox Ford had pre-empted it).† When *Ask Me Tomorrow* was reprinted in the 1969 Harcourt, Brace & World Uniform Edition, Cozzens added the subtitle *"or The Pleasant Comedy of Young Fortunatus"* as a "touch of formal grave frivolity." Cozzens's preferred title was "Young Fortunatus"; but Alfred Harcourt, who had never heard of Fortunatus, claimed that most readers would be baffled by the title.‡ Thomas Dekker's play *The Pleasant Comedie of Old Fortunatus* (1600) treats pride and wealth; the precipitating event is Fortunatus's choice of riches over wisdom. [38] The final title was selected by Bertha Cozzens when she read the typescript.

Like the author in 1927, Francis Ellery is a young American nov-

---

*The Cozzenses were heavy Philip Morris smokers, and both used Zeus holders.

†*Romeo and Juliet*, 3.5.1–3: "Wilt thou be gone? It is not yet near day. / It was the nightingale, and not the lark, / That pierced the fearful hollow of thine ear." See *Ask Me Tomorrow*, p. 337. See also *Romeo and Juliet*, 3.1.98.

‡ See Cozzens's letter facsimiled on p. 33 of Meriwether's *Checklist*.

elist in Europe with his mother and is compelled by his straitened finances to accept employment as traveling tutor for a crippled boy. Ellery has published two novels and is writing another novel about an 1879 naval battle between Chile and Peru. Like the young Cozzens, Francis Ellery is in love with an American girl touring Europe, and he bitterly resents his inability to be with her. When he finds himself with Lorna Higham at Cap d'Ail, on the Riviera, he neglects his job. Expecting to be dismissed after his pupil almost dies from an asthma attack, Ellery desperately asks Lorna to marry him. "Ask me tomorrow," she replies. He is extricated by his employer, Mrs. Cunningham—an upgraded version of Mrs. Parish. She understands that he is not at fault and asks him if he would like to leave the Riviera with the Cunninghams. He accedes with relief.

Francis Ellery is a study in the defensive pride of a talented young man in reduced circumstances. When an Englishman at a ski resort offers to help the crippled boy, Ellery does not know how to respond: "Relieved or grateful, he simply seemed to find in the forbidding circle of the world one point not definitely hostile, not requiring any new resistance or defiance" (p. 84). Lacking the money to live well while serving his muse, he finds his relative poverty degrading. "The hard fact was that circumstances rarely misled, and appearances were always full of truth. . . . People who are poor, while they may be estimable and virtuous, confess in the fact of poverty an incapacity for mastering their environment . . ." (pp. 157–58). What the reviewers saw as malice in the characterization was Cozzens's chagrined view of himself when young and absurd. Ellery's malaise is reflected in his "blaze of contempt for the whole monkey house of Europe and Europe's mostly undersized, jabbering, mostly not quite clean inhabitants . . . the shoddy posturing bombast of the new Italy . . . La Belle France with its savage avarice and all-pervasive smell of urine; the belching, blockheaded Germans—why should anyone have any patience with any of them? The only demonstrably good reason for their existing was to satisfy the curiosity or serve the convenience of traveling Americans" (p. 104). The novel opens with a disgusted evocation of Florence: * "Even at its occasional best Florence is a forlorn city. It is not sad in any beautiful, comfortable way. It is

---

*This two-page description of Florence, which compared it to "an endless ill-lit cemetery," brought letters of protest from readers, and Cozzens deleted it in 1969.

really sad." The Europe of *Ask Me Tomorrow* is a continent of invalids and decay; and Ellery has a sharp awareness of mortality combined with a fastidious misanthropy:

He thought of the doctor, whose manner with Walter, whose sympathy and intelligence, had been so different from what Francis wildly expected; and yet (how mean and petty to think of it; how impossible not to notice it) the collar, or neckband, or whatever it was, of the shirt worn under his tunic could be seen inside the uniform collar, and it was greasy with dirt. Recoiling in disgust from human beings, you had to recoil, in another disgust, from your own recoiling; and so it went; and after years of distaste, with little done and nothing not somehow spoiled, you could look forward to the appropriate rewarding of patience or effort. You would be old—like Mr. McKellar, with everything going, so that wit began to labor, elegances grew grotesque or sinister, zest for life creaked at the joints—nearly a joke. And then, perhaps, you could hope to grow into an outright joke, like the Admiral at Grindelwald, with everyone secretly laughing; and then (far past a joke, a horror) you might enjoy the longevity of that old man, what was his name, his mother's acquaintance, the friend of George William Curtis, in Florence. Mr. Woodward—[pp. 325–26].

When *Ask Me Tomorrow* was published, Virginia Reiland—the Lorna of the novel—sent Cozzens an unsigned note: "Oh Jimmy how could you—?"[39] It is difficult to gauge the extent to which Francis Ellery is an accurate self-portrait by the artist a dozen years later. The novel can be read as Cozzens's attempt to account for his antisocial behavior in his thirties—that is, to portray himself as having been unsuited to society for a long time. There are ample clues in *Ask Me Tomorrow* to the novelist's awareness that his own character and career had been formed by forces beyond his control—for example, the admission that Ellery, like Cozzens, was published before he had learned how to write. When Ellery finds himself singing a school hymn, he recognizes it as one of "these often-discovered proofs that, too young to have any say in the process, he had been marked for life. . . ." (p. 228).

In *Ask Me Tomorrow* Cozzens enunciated what had been evolving since *The Last Adam* into the central structural and thematic concern of his fiction: the attempt to depict the effect of interlocking simultaneity of events. As Ellery dines with the Cunninghams at an alpine hotel he is struck by "the dramatic inner meaning that lies in the simultaneous occurrence of diverse things" (p. 148). *Ask Me Tomorrow* lacked the scope of action to permit the development

The author of Ask Me Tomorrow (*Harcourt Brace Jovanovich*)

of the epiphany, but Cozzens's subsequent novels would be organized on this structural rationale.

Ask Me Tomorrow was published by Harcourt, Brace at $2.50 on 13 June 1940—the year in which *For Whom the Bell Tolls* and *The Grapes of Wrath* were best sellers. The novel Cozzens had worked longest on, the one he considered as having come closest to fulfilling his intentions, met with a disappointing reception. Thirty-seven years later he advised a professor: "Though not lacking 'literary milage' demands, it's fairly short, a virtue cardinal enough to excuse, perhaps, absence of Relevance ('Modren'), King Cong, sharks & (old aaf term) Nooky. Or do I really mean it happens to be the one book of mine that, finished, left me fairly content—no doubt because, not having tried to do too much, I wasn't forced to see chagrinned how short I came of all I aimed at to start."[40] The 6,500-copy first printing satisfied the demand until 1952. Even the favorable reviews were unenthusiastic. While recognizing the lucidity of the writing, reviewers found Francis Ellery objectionable and some queried the necessity of writing about him at all. Expecting, perhaps, a tragic case history of thwarted genius, they were put off by an ironic diagnosis of pride. Taking their lead from the dust-jacket claim that "Mr. Cozzens could almost be prosecuted for vivisection," reviewers described the novel as "savage" or "clinical." Lewis Gannett delivered a dirge for Cozzens in the *New York Herald Tribune*: "The reader is made aware of his skill as an intellectual juggler, but of his art as a novel-maker [*sic*]. And it never seems to matter. It is a pity; for Mr. Cozzens once seemed to have in him the making of a real novelist."[41] The *New York World-Telegram* reviewer did not think Ellery was worth writing about: "James Gould Cozzens can write; he has a style of his own, but in this case he has wasted a lot of good paper on the analysis of a prig that doesn't even provide a good museum piece."[42] (The term "prig" would become a catchword for Cozzens's critics.)

Some readers assumed that Cozzens had written a delayed version of *The Sun Also Rises*, as indicated by this misleading rhymed review in the *Los Angeles Times*:

> James Gould Cozzens
> Makes epigrams by the dozens
> Describing a young Yankee tutor,
> His mistresses lurid and neuter,
> His rambles in Paris and Venice
> When Fascists were not yet a menace.
> A novel to buy, beg or borrow
> Is J.G.C.'s "Ask Me Tomorrow."
>
> M. B.[43]

Clifton Fadiman explained in the *New Yorker* that Cozzens was a victim of his own bad timing. The world of *Ask Me Tomorrow* was dead, and Europe was in flames: "This isn't Mr. Cozzens' fault; he's a good, honest, able novelist, but he can't compete with a horribly accelerated history. It's simply bad luck that his book about part of Europe's corpse should appear at this particular moment and that reviewers should find it hard to judge his work calmly and objectively."[44]

Despite the disappointing American reception, Longmans, Green published *Ask Me Tomorrow* in October 1940.* The English reviewers were more responsive to Cozzens's irony but echoed the American reviewers in describing the novel as a period piece dealing with familiar American types abroad before the war. L. P. Hartley defended it in the *London Observer*: "But the book is not therefore the less worth reading. Mr. Cozzens is an artist and art is independent of temporal change. Many readers, too, will wel-

---

*The A. M. Heath records indicate that 596 copies were sold; but the Brandt & Brandt records show sales of 2,742.

come the nostalgic pleasure of re-living a day that is dead and find, moreover, in Ellery Francis's [*sic*] state of mind some of the germs of the virulent insanity which has swept over the world."[45]

While awaiting publication of the novel in 1940 Cozzens declined an offer to write a 2,000-word monthly book-review article for *Esquire* at $1,800 a year. He did not admire the magazine, and he knew that his judgments would necessarily involve him in unwanted controversy. Cozzens was not interested in elevating anyone's tastes and had no appetite for literary infighting. He was earning about $1,000 a year reading manuscripts for Brandt & Brandt, and the *Esquire* job would have cut into the time available for that work. His surviving vetting reports make entertaining reading. For a biography of Cora Brown Potter, he advised:

Mrs. Brown Potter was one of the innumerable lays of H.M. King Edward VII when he was Prince of Wales (which he kept on being until he was 59 so maybe his gesture of resignation when he was crowned was half nature's). At any rate the material seems perfectly suited to the style of an author like this one. The degree to which she is dim-witted and scatter-brained exceeds the British average in those no longer young writing about the past and that is saying something. Mrs. B. P. between the Prince's embraces recited verse at gatherings of the Cream of London Society and then took to the stage where the critics panned her savagely but Miss Beamish says the People liked her. She also took up with the Wisdom of the East and finally expired in a villa on the Blue Coast. The general effect, not uninteresting, is a half-wit's account of the goings-on of half-wits in the wonderful days when there was no damn nonsense about merit.[46]

Usually his reports were more succinct, as in this response to a novel: "A returned war veteran here returns (whether actually or in imagination only) to his old college, where he and everyone else are in a trance, indeed, almost a coma. For all I know it is significant as hell; but if you want me to work it out the fee will be $300."[47] On a volume of animal stories he reported "deplorable drivel."[48] The only book he is known to have recommended for publication was a translation of Antonio de Fierro Blanco's *The Journey of the Flame* (1933), a novel set in Spanish California recounting the life of a centenarian.

Dodd, Mead approached Cozzens in May 1940 about writing a

biography of Father Sill. Although the project appealed to him, he recognized that he would have to decline because he would not be able to deliver the requisite exercise in hagiography. "A pretty interesting piece could be made out of it, since the principal point is the demonstration that education is not an intellectual matter, and in fact ought not to be since children have no intellects—but, though greatly to his credit, this approach would hardly be to his taste and a candid and careful study of him as a remarkable human being would probably give nothing but offence."[49]

Cozzens's commitment to using words precisely is documented by his compilation of a typed three-binder loose-leaf dictionary. The dates in these binders indicate that the process was performed twice—in 1940 and again in 1949–56.* Although Cozzens relished rich language, he did not make a display of his vocabulary to impress or intimidate readers; he was seeking greater precision of statement. His aim was to achieve what he found in William Hazlitt: "a kind of marvelous vigor and precision in making complicated thoughts simple."[51]

At the time *Ask Me Tomorrow* was published Cozzens submitted to an interview—his first since 1932 and his last until 1957—with Robert Van Gelder of the *New York Times*. Cozzens had long been convinced that writers made themselves absurd by trying to behave like celebrities and that personal publicity did not sell novels. He told Van Gelder that he was still trying to learn how to write; the bad luck of having *Confusion* published had solidified his natural faults, "and it is taking all of my effort now, in my mid-thirties, to wipe out those faults, to really learn to write." He planned to spend the summer in court assembling material for a novel to be called "The Summer Soldier," a phrase that had been used by Paine to describe part-time patriots. "But as I see it there is a lot to be said for these Summer soldiers. The idealists, the intellectuals, haven't done any too well by the world. My book will be about a lawyer who must make a choice between an ideal and what might be called a selfish, practical consideration. . . ."[52] His original idea was to write about a young lawyer who is compelled to sacrifice some of his ideals for a position with a prosperous law firm.

*The A–L section is dated 12/1/49; M–R, 15/XII/53; S–V 31/VII/56; and W–Z is dated 8/21/40.[50]

Cozzens was slow in coming to his interest in the law. When one of his servants was arrested, in 1933, he observed that "the law is the last place to take anything in which justice is involved."[53] In December 1939 he borrowed from Edgar Hunt volumes of Blackstone and Kent, which he wanted to read for their prose. Cozzens became so engaged by the law that he began studying textbooks with Philip J. Faherty III, Hunt's clerk. During 1940 he spent considerable time at the Doylestown, Pennsylvania, courthouse observing trials. He developed a friendship with Edward Biester, the Assistant District Attorney for Bucks County, who advised him to base his novel on an actual case. The more time Cozzens spent with the law, the more he admired its practical sense. "I can't understand why it did not attract my attention before—it is such an extraordinary compound of baseness and high-mindedness, from one to the other and back again without a change of tone or turn of color. I never realized it before, but in the main, it is, of course, the 18th century speaking and you can hardly help hearing it with pleasure for its perfect sophistication, the way it takes human nature as it is, without evasion or apology, and then sees what can be done by firmness and reason to give it a modicum of dignity and order. There is, I suppose something about it close to what I would have to admit was my own feeling about life—it is absurd to pretend that there is any plan or meaning in it, but never mind, we will make a plan and the meaning will be that we are men and not dogs."[54]

By the twenty-fourth of September Cozzens had started writing about a recent case in Flemington, New Jersey, involving a high-school teacher who had taken indecent photos of female students. But in December he abandoned this main plot—though retaining it as a subplot—to build his novel around *The Commonwealth vs. Martin Farrell and Francis Wiley* (1935), which Biester had called to his attention.* Farrell and Wiley had been tried for participating in the kidnapping and murder of drug dealer Big Nose Weiss. Although not the actual killers, they had been found guilty of first-degree murder under the Pennsylvania felony-murder rule and executed.[55] The work on this version went well "due to my resolution to try for once writing the whole damned thing through as a first draft and doing my fussing afterward. I've never done it be-

---

*Quarter Sessions of Bucks County No. 31 February Sessions 1935.

fore, and I distrust it because it seems so easy just to put it down any old way (which is what it amounts to) and get on without fighting the meaning out in every line. On the other hand I would have to admit that even when I do fight the meaning out I more than half the time change it all when I come to do it over anyway . . ."[56] In December 1940 he reported that he had never written so many pages so rapidly and expected to have a draft ready in two months; but he was unable to stick to his plan and push ahead through a rough first draft. Cozzens admitted in January 1942 that "there is nothing I enjoy more than taking it sentence by sentence and word by word and tinkering with it. . . ."[57]

After his mother urged him to try to make his fiction pleasing to readers by providing more attractive characters, he replied: "Yes, I very well know about the importance of sentimentality, and I also know that it is not people's business to want to read me, but mine to please them. I wish I could say that I avoid pleasing them deliberately, both because it would make me feel good, and because I could then so-easily remedy the defect; but the truth is, I fail because of an inability to write that sort of stuff convincingly. Though you might think you could, you can't put it over without feeling it yourself in just those terms."[58] Neither could Cozzens supply Perry Mason courtroom melodrama. The subject of the novel was "the theory and practice of ethical principles."[59]

The novel was finished in March 1942. It covers three days in 1939 (Tuesday, 13 June–Thursday, 15 June)* during the murder trial of Stanley Howell and Robert Basso at the Childerstown courthouse, in an unspecified northeastern state. The central figure is Assistant District Attorney Abner Coates, six years out of law school. The son and grandson of judges, Abner is in line for the district attorneyship but resists accepting the nomination from the county political boss—even though no quid pro quo is involved. Contingent upon his election is his marriage to Bonnie Drummond, whom he has been tepidly courting for years. As usual, Cozzens had title trouble. After retitling it "The Quick and the Dead," he settled on *The Just and the Unjust*.†

The trial in *The Just and the Unjust* appears to be a routine

---

*Cozzens confused his dates in the novel. On p. 72 he stipulates that the second day of the trial is Wednesday, 15 June.

†Matthew 5:45: "That ye may be the children of your Father which is in heaven: for he maketh his sun to rise on the evil and on the good, and sendeth rain on the just and on the unjust."

matter. Howell and Basso, with Roy Leming and Mike Bailey, kidnapped Fred Zollicoffer, a drug dealer from a nearby city. After the ransom was paid, Bailey murdered Zollicoffer in the presence of the others. Bailey was killed trying to escape from the police. Leming turned state's evidence in return for a reduced sentence of life imprisonment, and the FBI beat a confession out of Howell. The law is clear. Howell and Basso are guilty of first-degree murder, even though they did not shoot Zollicoffer. District Attorney Martin Bunting is confident that the jury will bring in that verdict.

Defense attorney Harry Wurts does not regard the case as open and shut because he believes the jurors may balk at condemning the accused for a murder they did not actually commit. Moreover, he recognizes that the jury is bothered by the circumstances that Leming has saved his skin by ratting on his partners and that Howell was tortured into confessing. Rejecting the law, the jury brings in a verdict of second-degree murder—partly because the District Attorney was a little too confident, but mostly because Wurts worked hard to persuade them that the law is unjust in this case.

When Abner reports the verdict to his father, Judge Coates, who is crippled from a stroke, the Judge counsels:

". . . Justice is an inexact science. As a matter of fact, a judge is so greatly in a jury's debt, he shouldn't begrudge them the little things they help themselves to."

"I don't follow," Abner said.

"The ancient conflict between liberty and authority. The jury protects the Court. It's a question how long any system of courts could last in a free country if judges found the verdicts. It doesn't matter how wise and experienced the judges may be. Resentment would build up every time the findings didn't go with current notions or prejudices. Pretty soon half the community would want to lynch the judge. There's no focal point with a jury; the jury is the public itself. That's why a jury can say when a judge couldn't, 'I don't care what the law is, that isn't right and I won't do it.' It's the greatest prerogative of free men. They have to have a way of saying that and making it stand. They may be wrong, they may refuse to do the things they ought to do; but freedom just to be wise and good isn't any freedom. We pay a price for lay participation in the law; but it's a necessary expense" [pp. 427–28].

This analysis reinforces the irony of the epigraph from Lord Hardwicke: "Certainty is the Mother of Repose; therefore the Law aims at Certainty." There is no certainty where people are involved.

You can never tell about a jury. Judge Coates's concluding instruction to Abner is an echo of Ernest Cudlipp's position in *Men and Brethren*: do your job; employ your talents; fulfill your duties.

"Don't be cynical," Judge Coates said. "A cynic is just a man who found out when he was about ten that there wasn't any Santa Claus, and he's still upset. Yes, there'll be more war; and soon, I don't doubt. There always has been. There'll be deaths and disappointments and failures. When they come, you meet them. Nobody promises you a good time or an easy time. I don't know who it was who said when we think of the past we regret and when we think of the future we fear. And with reason. But no bets are off. There is the present to think of, and as long as you live there always will be. In the present, every day is a miracle. The world gets up in the morning and is fed and goes to work, and in the evening it comes home and is fed again and perhaps has a little amusement and goes to sleep. To make that possible, so much has to be done by so many people that, on the face of it, it is impossible. Well, every day we do it; and every day, come hell, come high water, we're going to have to go on doing it as well as we can."

"So it seems," said Abner.

"Yes, so it seems," said Judge Coates, "and so it is, and so it will be! And that's where you come in. That's all we want of you."

Abner said, "What do you want of me?"

"We just want you to do the impossible," Judge Coates said [p. 434].

If the theme of *The Just and the Unjust* is public and private ethics, the subject of the novel is the community, a subject developed in *The Last Adam* and *Men and Brethren*. As Judge Coates explains, society functions not just because people are interdependent, but because some of the people of necessity do more than their share. By selecting as his central figure a man of public responsibilities on whom many directly or indirectly depend, Cozzens conveyed a sense of the organization of a community. He believed in subordination in the Johnsonian sense of social order; a necessary concomitant is that privilege entails duty.

The plan of *The Just and the Unjust* resembles that of *Men and Brethren*; both novels are structured around a multiplicity of events impinging on the protagonist during a restricted period of time. But the actual time span of the novel is not restricted to the three days of the trial, for Cozzens interweaves expository flashbacks to supplement present-time action. This organizational method would be used to even better purpose in *Guard of Honor* and *By Love Possessed*, and would enable Cozzens to achieve more complexly the effect of simultaneous action that became a chief distinction of his best fiction. His major novels —more than those of any other American writer—simulate the chain of cause and effect (but in Cozzens it is frequently perceived as effect and cause) that determine behavior.

One of the principal aims of Cozzens's mature novels is to convey the thought processes of characters while maintaining the objectivity of the third-person point of view. As in *Men and Brethren*, the reader has the sense of observing the novel from the central character's perspective. In *The Just and the Unjust* this impression is achieved by interruption of the narrative, during which the author summarizes the interior reaction of the character. After Abner Coates considers the improper conduct of a justice of the peace, Cozzens notes that "the long thought filled only part of a second" (p. 67). However, authorial intrusions are infrequent in the novel. Thus when Cozzens inserts his own comment, it seems jarring: "The innocent supposition, entertained by most people, that even if they are not brilliant, they are not dumb, is correct only in a very relative sense" (p. 161). Such violations of point of view were disciplined out of subsequent novels.

The Just and the Unjust became Cozzens's best-received novel up to that time. Harcourt, Brace (which paid an advance of $1,000) published a first printing of 25,000 copies at $2.50 on 23 July 1942;* and the Book-of-the-Month Club distributed 225,000 copies, which earned Cozzens more than $25,000. The novel was abridged in *Omnibook*, but there was no paperback edition. It appeared on the *Publishers' Weekly* best-seller list as number 8 for August 1942. The critical reception of *The Just and the Unjust* was the warmest for a Cozzens novel since *The Last Adam* in 1933. With his tenth novel the thirty-eight-year-old author's label as a promising novelist was altered to that of "one of America's most important serious novelists" (Joseph Henry Jackson, *San Francisco Chronicle*).[60] In the *Harvard Law Review* Zechariah Chafee, Jr., designated it "the best account I know of the daily life of ordinary lawyers" and called it required reading for every law student.[61] Henry Seidel Canby,

---

*Bernice had been planning to move Cozzens to another publisher because she felt that the Harcourt, Brace sales department had deteriorated; but agent and author decided to remain with Harcourt, Brace for the benefit of having his best books under the same imprint. Of the 25,000 copies of *The Just and the Unjust* distributed by Harcourt, Brace, more than half were sold to stores and wholesalers in New York City, Canada, and four states: 9,298 in New York City, 1,560 in Illinois, 955 in Canada, 874 in California, 858 in Massachusetts, 543 in Pennsylvania; 10,923 copies were sold to accounts in the Northeast.

writing for the *Book-of-the-Month Club News*, declared, "If I were asked by an intelligent European to give him a book that would take him into the heart of everyday America, I would give him this one."[62] *The Just and the Unjust* received front-page treatment in the *New York Times* and *New York Herald-Tribune* Sunday book sections, and Cozzens's photograph appeared on the cover of the issue of *Saturday Review of Literature* that had a rambling Joseph Hergesheimer review. Orville Prescott initiated his championship of Cozzens in the daily *Times*; he had found the previous novels "chilly," but *The Just and the Unjust* adds "an undercurrent of tolerant understanding that seems very close to a true and even gentle wisdom."[63] The critical reception was enforced by the trade journals; the *American News of Books* gave it a triple-a rating, and the *Retail Bookseller* announced that it was "sure to be a best seller and probably a best renter." The novel was touted for the Pulitzer Prize, which went to Upton Sinclair's *The Dragon's Teeth*.

Time was disappointed because Cozzens had not produced a new version of *Crime and Punishment*. Describing the novel as "the author's best work" and "the year's most interesting literary disappointment," the reviewer declared that Cozzens poses no profound problems because "the defendants have little moral depth or ambiguity." This unsigned review concluded: "There is not the slightest tremor of human mystery; there is nothing of the fear of God. Lacking these, human life is deprived of its splendor, law of its dignity, society of its tragicomic stature. So is *The Just and the Unjust*."[64] Although some reviewers found the novel hard reading, the most frequent complaint was about the dullness of Abner Coates and his tepid wooing. These reservations were compensated for by the appreciative response to Harry Wurts, the extrovert defense lawyer, who is the kind of mercurial character readers enjoy. It is as though Cozzens was demonstrating that he could provide a crowd-pleasing character when it suited his purpose to do so, but that Wurts could not occupy his full attention. Cozzens was diverted to observe Webster Achey, the Doylestown lawyer on whom he had based Wurts, using verbatim paragraphs from Wurts's speech against the death penalty in a 1948 trial. When Cozzens complimented him on the effectiveness of those passages, Achey replied, "I was afraid they might be a little florid."[65]

The Just and the Unjust was fortunate in its timing, reaping a patriotic response during the first summer of the war. Across the country reviewers praised it as a study of American democracy. Cozzens seems to have shared this reading, as evidenced by his inscription to Edward Biester. The novel was dedicated to Biester with a line from Coke on Littleton: *Cuilibet in arte sua perito est credendum* (Any expert ought to be trusted in his own art). The inscription read:

Dear Ed—it would not have been possible to write this book without your help. I am inscribing it to you in recollection of many agreeable lunches, jobs of legal research, familiar conversations. I never wrote a book I enjoyed getting up so much. More than that, I was greatly and permanently heartened to see in almost two years of your life and work good reasons why America is all right and will be all right
Jim

Lambertville, New Jersey   *1 July 1942* [66]

The *Just and the Unjust* was published in England during April 1943 by Jonathan Cape; Longmans, Green did not have enough paper during the war. It sold 12,296 copies, much better than Cozzens's previous books had done in England; many of these copies were probably bought by American soldiers. It was a Book Society alternate selection, and there was an Australian edition (Angus & Robertson, 1943), which sold 3,450 copies. The *Times Literary Supplement*, moved by a feeling for the Allied cause, described it as "vindication of the American idea." [67]

One reader *The Just and the Unjust* displeased was J. Edgar Hoover, who wrote Cozzens on 31 August 1942:

Apparently in order to inject the FBI into the scenes you manufactured an incident regarding the victim of the murder as being involved in the narcotic business and that the FBI had been on his trail for months. The FBI has no jurisdiction over violations of the Federal Narcotic Law. This, for your information, is under the jurisdiction of the Bureau of Narcotics of the United States Department of the Treasury. There is no excuse for one planning the sale and wide distribution of his writings not to check the facts. Throughout your story with an apparent disregard for the truth you have presented a distorted, false, and extremely prejudicial word picture of the FBI in obtaining a confession from an alleged narcotic dealer, kidnaper, and murderer by using third degree tactics.

. . . .

. . . Further, the statements you make concerning the withholding of evidence by Special Agents of the FBI is malicious and false, and anyone who knows of our work and is acquainted with our methods knows you speak of something of which you know nothing. I am totally at a loss to understand your actions in writing in this manner. Your statements are libelous, malicious, and unfounded. You even go so far in your story as to insinuate that an FBI Agent would "unhesitatingly perjure himself, a risk he was prepared to take in line of duty." Again this is nothing short of libel.[68]

Cozzens, who was by then in the Air Force, was not worried about FBI action against him. He wrote Bernice on 6 September: "Hoover wrote that himself on his own typewriter and I have an idea he may not wish to pursue it. He knows as well as I do that every damn word was the truth—even the line about the narcotics business could have been, in the sense that they were on his trail not for the narcotics but for some illegal action. As I indicated in the book it is almost impossible to prove that the FBI beat anyone up, but they have beaten up plenty of people and I doubt if it is a subject he would like to bring to court."[69] Hoover did not pursue the matter with Cozzens, but made his protests to the publisher and to the Book-of-the-Month Club, which printed an apology in the December BOMC *News*. (Hoover wanted the apology inserted in every unsold copy of the book.)

J. EDGAR HOOVER, chief of the Federal Bureau of Investigation, has protested to James Cozzens, author of *The Just and the Unjust*—and as well to the publishers, Harcourt, Brace & Company, and to the Book-of-the-Month Club—against certain passages in the novel. He calls attention to the fact that the F. B. I. has no investigative jurisdiction over the kind of narcotic case the book deals with, and beyond that, the third degree, which one of the characters claims on the witness stand to have suffered at the hands of an F. B. I. agent, has never been tolerated in his Bureau. Any unfair reflection upon the F. B. I., for which, with the rest of the American public, we have the highest respect and admiration, is—needless to say—regretted.

Cozzens later informed a reader: "In 1942 J. Edgar Hoover wrote me, while I was in the army, to say I was a son of a bitch for suggesting that the FBI ever extorted confessions. Somebody may have identified the case for him and shown him the record, for the rest was silence."[70] When the novel was reprinted in 1950 he revised the text to explain that the FBI became involved in the case because they were after Howell for a mail robbery, but let the beating material stand.*

*In 1950 Cozzens explained to Harcourt, Brace editor Robert Giroux: "I have taken care of it as indicated in four passages, and I thought I might as well throw J. Edgar the sop of changing one word where, as it reads, the author, as opposed to the character, might be thought to say the story of the beating-up was true (he sure as hell so believes but feels no real need to say it)."[71]

A Time of War

Cozzens was considering a political novel to follow *The Just and the Unjust,* but Pearl Harbor put an end to it. He was thirty-eight and was classified 3A (men with dependents). Hoping to avoid being drafted, he tried unsuccessfully for a Navy commission. In May 1942 he learned that the Air Force wanted writers and was accepted for Officers' Training School. While Cozzens was waiting to be called up for service, he accepted an assignment from *Fortune.* Henry Luce had convened a committee to study postwar problems, and Cozzens was paid $750 to prepare *Pacific Relations* for the series *The United States in a New World.* His report was published as a thirty-six-page supplement to the August 1942 issue of *Fortune.*

Answering a questionnaire from *Twentieth Century Authors* (1942), Cozzens played the cranky Tory:

My social preference is to be left alone, and people have always seemed willing, even eager, to gratify my inclination. I am more or less illiberal, and strongly antipathetic to all political and artistic movements. I was brought up an Episcopalian, and where I live the landed gentry are Republican. I do not understand music, I am little interested in art, and the theatre seems tiresome to me. My literary preferences are for writers who take the trouble to write well. This necessarily excludes most of my contemporaries and I think I would do well to skip the presumptuous business of listing the three or four who strike me as good. I like Shakespeare and Swift and Steele and Gibbon and Jane Austen and Hazlitt.[1]

His rare public statements combined self-directed irony with role-playing as a defensive tactic, demonstrating his indifference to popularity by insulating himself from the tastes and fashions of the time. Since this entry in a standard reference book was one of only three personal statements generally available to researchers before 1957, it fostered an image of Cozzens as an eccentric anachronism.*

In January 1943 he accepted election to the National Institute of Arts and Letters, a New York-based group that exists largely to award honors to its members. His willingness to join was uncharacteristic, but he characteristically never attended a meeting and took no part in the Institute's activities.

On 1 August Cozzens (#0912499) reported to Air Force OTS at the Greenbriar Hotel in Miami Beach. After six weeks he was commissioned a first lieutenant and assigned to the Training Literature Section of the Training Aids Directorate (TAD) at Gravelly Point, Washington, D.C., part of the Army Air Forces School of Applied Tactics; his duties were to write manuals and special reports. Bernice closed up the house in Lambertville and moved to a hotel in New York. Her letters repeat the message "Nothing is right when I am not with you."[2] Planning her first visit to him, she wrote: "I ought to warn you that I am nothing to be proud of and if I had any decency I would send down a beautiful blonde as a substitute. But I like to think that you would rather have me, even with all my bones showing."[3] She visited Cozzens every possible weekend for the next three years.

Cozzens began keeping a detailed typed diary on 6 October 1942. Written in narrative form, it chronicled his daily service activities and described the hundreds of people he encountered. He was not yet planning an Air Force novel, but he knew that his experiences were worth banking. By the time he was discharged, Cozzens was sure that his 380 pages of Air Force diaries, especially the Pentagon section, formed a usable historical record.

TAD was not fully operational, and most of the new officers at Gravelly Point had little to do. Cozzens hit on the scheme of finding assignments for himself. He preferred to be occupied, and he discovered that his superiors were relieved to be freed of the problem of making work for him. Also, it was better to find some task

---

* See Fred B. Millett, *Contemporary American Authors* (New York: Harcourt, Brace, 1940) and *Current Biography 1949* (New York: Wilson, 1950).

he did not mind than to be handed an objectionable chore. "You mustn't do too much without orders, but, unless you want to take them, you should never sit around waiting for some" (28 October 1942). One of his jobs was to prepare a lexicon for pilots and control-tower personnel. He was responsible for revising *Radio-telephone Procedure* (TM 1-460) and rewrote *Instrument Flying Technique in Weather* (TO 30-100 D-1) with E. J. Minser of TWA. His most difficult assignment was the revision of the outdated manual *Tactics and Technique of Air Fighting* (FM 1-15), which he struggled with intermittently for almost a year before it was taken away from him. Fighter tactics were constantly changing on the basis of combat experience, and the pilots he worked with were in disagreement with each other as well as with the top brass.

Although he missed the routine of writing and gardening at Carrs Farm, his life was not disagreeable. He was not irked by military protocol; he felt that if you're doing it, you might as well do it right. Moreover, he felt that if he did not serve in the war, he would be "washed out from the standpoint of writing in whatever future there may be."[4] He lived at the George Mason Hotel in Alexandria and had a Ford station wagon, for which he managed to obtain tire and gas coupons. The income from *The Just*

Lt. Cozzens, publicity photo for
The Just and the Unjust
(*Harcourt Brace Jovanovich*)

and the Unjust made him relatively affluent, and he ate and drank in good restaurants. Seafood was his preferred dish, with the lobster at Harvey's in Washington providing a favorite dinner.

TAD was transferred to Orlando, Florida, in November 1942. Bernice flew down on weekends and then joined Cozzens there in a rented house. At Orlando she enjoyed being a housewife for the first time in her marriage. She had resigned from Brandt & Brandt but was occasionally called back to handle problems. The decision to suspend her career was prompted by her recognition that—with his ordered life at the farm removed—her husband needed to be taken care of. As Colonel Ross's sensible wife observes in *Guard of Honor:* "Any woman knows perfectly well that she is either married, and so lives with her husband; or she isn't married at all. It may be very uncomfortable, and very inconvenient; but she ought to be with him, if it is in any way possible. Unless he has been sent overseas, she can always make it possible. She has no right to let him live alone. It isn't good for him; and what isn't good for him will not, in the end, be good for her" (p. 280).

His Orlando assignments included dummying a proposed Air Force magazine and collaborating with Bert Moore of the Civil Aeronautics Administration and Captain L. N. Conklin of the Flight Control Command on *Airways Flying,* a handbook for military pilots. He participated in a series of conferences on the fighter manual, on which he began working in March 1943 with Captain Reade Tilley, Jr., an American who had flown with the British on Malta. (Tilley became the model for Captain Gene Wiley in *Guard of Honor.*) Cozzens found, against the dictates of reason, that he had a desire to learn to fly and began putting in daily stints in a Link Trainer (a device for training in instrument flying). He became fairly proficient at it but never piloted a plane. Although he did considerable flying in the Air Force, he remained nervous in planes and never flew after his discharge.

There was considerable military politics at TAD as career officers jockeyed for power. This was their chance, their reward, for years of patient service between wars. Observing these activities, Cozzens began to sense a novel forming in his mind: "—you could figure some such incident touching off a considerable misunderstanding, and then (if you wanted to figure, and it gave me a vague notion of how sometime, some of this stuff could shape up for a book; that is, a possible pattern to hang the material on could be some such pile-up of cause and effect, extended to any sufficient degree. I even thought it could be called Low in Glory's Lap—I meant; Gash'd with honorable scars etc) * more and more" (1 March 1943).

Cozzens found it impossible to do his own writing during the frequent periods of idleness when it was necessary to look busy. He published nothing during the war years except his Air Force work, but 237,000 copies of *The Last Adam* and *Castaway* were distributed to servicemen in the Armed Services Editions. During one of the office spells of idleness he occupied himself by preparing a 500-word pronunciation test: "Extricating himself by herculean efforts and the operose use of a lever and other apparatus, he was greeted by the canorous denigrating jeers and ribald laughter of the Viscount's suite, a galaxy of moronic catamites, gibbous eunuchs, and dotard fakirs, results of the Viscount's miscegenation with his myriad hetaerae, unsavory maenads who, in a spirit of camaraderie, had shared his whilom orgies, and who spoke only gibberish."[5] He was amused that the document gave a little trouble to Kenneth Gantz, a peacetime college English instructor whose desk was opposite his. They drank beer in the evenings, and Gantz could drink him under the table. Gantz (whose nickname was Dutchman) provided a partial model for Captain Clarence Duchemin in *Guard of Honor*. Cozzens accommodated himself to service life. He was friendly with his officemates and went out with them on evenings when Bernice was not in Orlando.

TAD was relocated to 1 Park Avenue, New York City, in May 1943. Bernice found a penthouse at 121 Madison Avenue and returned to Brandt & Brandt. One of Cozzens's tasks in New York was to write a radio broadcast on Rhode Island for the Office of War Information, which he described as "the most appalling assemblage of obvious crackpots, cranks, chronic literary unemployables, youths with funny shaped beards, Greenwich Village females, liberal professors and the whole range of the intellectual junkpile" (20 May 1943). He remained convinced that "every man is what he looks like if you're old enough to see" (29 December 1976).

Cozzens wrote four articles for Air Force publications during

---

* From James Montgomery's "The Battle of Alexandria" (1801): "Gash'd with honourable scars, / Low in Glory's lap they lie; / Though they fell, they fell like stars, / Streaming splendour through the sky."

the spring and summer of 1943.* In "Writing Clearly" he explained:

Some writers do not make themselves clear because they are not clear in their own minds about what they want to say. Some writers cannot make themselves clear because they never learned enough words to express meanings exactly, or enough grammar to keep the relationship between words straight. In both cases the cure is, if not simple, plain. However, there is one obstacle to writing clearly which is commoner than muddleheadedness or illiteracy among those who regularly turn in reports and memorandums. Doctor Johnson touched on it when he observed that a man could generally improve what he wrote if he would read it over and when he came to any line he particularly liked, strike that line out.

This is a hard saying, and most people who write resist it and its implications. Most writers are by no means content to convey plain information or bare facts. The writer has one eye on his subject, but the other is constantly cocked on himself. Along with his facts he likes to get over the impertinent information that he is a powerful and penetrating thinker, an executive of decision and energy, a master of English prose, and in sum, quite a smart guy. It is a pretty large order. When all or most of this material is added to the actual business on hand it is hardly surprising that readers cannot make head or tail of the thing. The army has the good rule that a communication should deal with only one subject. A writer does well to adhere to it.

By keeping carefully to the real subject of his letter, report, or memorandum, and by resisting the often fierce temptation to give himself a boost on the side, the average writer can greatly simplify his labors. As a rule he knows what he wants to say, and once he is reconciled simply to saying it without wondering how it sounds, or whether the reader is going to form a high opinion of him, he will find that he is no longer at a loss for words or tangled up in relative clauses. Plain facts practically write themselves. After he has put the plain facts down in words he is used to using—sparing himself mental anguish and saving the army's time and paper—he can send them off with sober confidence. The reader, astounded to get something sensible, simple, and short, may even conclude that the writer must be quite a smart guy.

He was promoted to captain in August 1943 and assigned to collaborate with *Fortune* writer William Vogel on "The Air Force

---

*"What They're Reading," *Air Force* (June); "The First Manual," *AFTAD Liaison Bulletin* (29 June); "Writing Clearly," *AFTAD Liaison Bulletin* (9 July); "Airways Flying," *Air Transport* (September), with Bert Moore.

Training Program." Cozzens provided himself with orders that in effect permitted him to write his own orders and began a tour of training facilities that took him to Fort Worth, Orlando, Boca Raton, Miami, Fort Myers, Washington, Baltimore, New Haven, Greensboro, Biloxi, San Angelo, Del Rio, Midland Field (Texas), Lubbock, Sebring, Tallahassee, Maxwell Field (Alabama), Selman Field (Louisiana), and Peterson Field (Colorado). When his plane was landing at Selman Field, another plane dived in front of it, and for a moment he was certain that he was a dead man—an experience that became the triggering event in *Guard of Honor*. The *Fortune* article was published in February 1944 and credited to Vogel with the assistance of Cozzens.

On his return from his travels in October 1943 Cozzens learned that he had been reassigned to the Office of Special Projects, Office of Technical Information (later the Office of Information Services), at Air Forces headquarters in the Pentagon. He was furious at having his comfortable New York life terminated, but there was nothing he could do about it. He reported to the Pentagon and took an apartment at 1524 Mount Eagle Place in the Parkfairfax complex, Alexandria, Virginia. Bernice came down from New York every weekend.

Cozzens later placed the principal figure of *Morning Noon and Night* (1968) in the OIS:

If you supposed, as you reasonably might, that its function was to give out information, you would be much mistaken. What little 'information' it handled was highly classified, prepared for and only available to the offices of the Chief of Air Staff and the Commanding General . . . its principal work was composing speeches for the C.G. and writing articles that he would sign. There was enough of such writing work (by special favor one or another of the Assistant Chiefs of Air Staff was occasionally served) to keep fairly busy five officers in civilian life professional writers, published authors . . . [p. 300].

He described the Air Staff setup to his mother:

There is Mr A [General H. H. Arnold] on top, and then there is Lt Gen Giles . . . who is both Deputy Commanding General and Chief of the Air Staff. As C/AS, he has four brigadier generals as his deputies (Owens, Timberlake, Norstadt, and (until last week) Smith, now replaced by Hood.) Our organization is a so-called exempt organization—that is, not under any of the Assistant Chiefs of the Air Staff (not to be confused with Deputy Chiefs, who are Gen Giles' executives, while the Assistant

At Office of Information Services, Pentagon
Building (Courtesy of Jo H. Chamberlin)

Chiefs head staff sections—Intelligence; Training; Materiel & Services; Operations, Commitments and Requirements; Personnel, and so on).[6]

His fellow writers at OIS were Edward Newhouse, George Bradshaw, Jo H. Chamberlin, and Robert Reeves. The capable Executive Officer was George Haddock, a former newspaper editor, for whom Cozzens developed considerable respect. (Haddock provided the model for Captain Collins in *Guard of Honor*.) Cozzens's closest associates were Newhouse and Bradshaw, who held him in esteem. His friendship with Newhouse developed slowly, partly because Newhouse had recommended him for OIS; Cozzens later remarked that friendship with Ed was an acquired taste, requiring years of exposure. But Cozzens was quickly charmed by Bradshaw, a 1930 Princeton graduate.

Being that rarity, that endangered species of witty man, entertainments he got were very clearly warm-hearted, indulgent; come of a kind-mindedness which, perfectly perceiving what fools these mortals be, watched them in something between pity and paternalism. . . .
. . . We, the Knower of Everybody and I, encountered as Army Air Force majors arbitrarily transferred late in 1943 to Pentagon headquarters staff, fantastically multifarious, and, in record, nowhere through all its strange work and workings explicitly so named, of what by the mil. ser.

George Bradshaw (Courtesy of Jo H.
Chamberlin)

(as orders have it) termed CG/AAF. This diverse, sharply compart-
mented (in fact, aides; but never called that or wearing that insignia)
group did what is most simply and accurately described as just about
Anything—work, paper or flying mission, of true TOP SECRET gravity
now; now turgid mouse-out-of-mountain speech or article farces for favored Chiefs, or Deputy Chiefs, or the Old Man—never anything but
"Mr. A." in our security use; now periods, whole days, of idleness when

we sat feet on desk in our small enclosed (token of our importance) room around the corner from Mr. A's E-ring fastnesses.[7]

Bradshaw did as little as possible—spending whole days "gracefully idling"—but Cozzens preferred to keep busy. Nevertheless, writing for the top brass irked him because they felt obliged to tamper with his speeches and articles.* Arnold was the prime offender, and Cozzens was bemused by the realization that men of proved ability and great responsibility in their fields seemed plainly illiterate when he had to work with them.

There's nothing the matter with Gen Giles except that he is, like Mr. A, illiterate; something which is habitually made too much of by people who do a lot of reading or writing. Either is really a drawback in the strictly practical affair of getting an army together and fighting with it. Everything you do starts chains of irrelevant ideas (derived from reading and extended by attempting to express in words shades of meaning). I have a pet theory that one of the reasons that we are winning the war is that, markedly in the German case, and relatively in the Japanese case, the generals who oppose us have a high proportion of intellectuals. They waste their time weighing complex factors and looking beyond the immediate objective and while they ponder, their simple and single minded opponents take them for all they have. . . . But the fact remains that, by being what he is, Mr. A performed the impossible in building the air force; and Gen Giles who acts as what might be called his general manager, by being what he is, keeps it going.[8]

He decided he could no longer do anything with General Arnold when the Commanding General changed the line "We want you with us when we win" to "We want you with us when we march through Berlin to Tokyo" at a Bolling Field WAC parade.[9] Thereafter he made himself unavailable for General Arnold's speeches by taking over the press briefings.

Two of the Pentagon figures who were exempted from his dismay were Robert A. Lovett, Assistant Secretary of War for Air,† and Brigadier General Frederic H. Smith, Jr., Deputy Chief of Air

---

*Cozzens drafted General Arnold's message to the West Point air cadets in *The Pointer*, XXII (20 October 1944), 1; General Clayton Bissell's statement in *Aerosphere 1943* (New York: Aerosphere, 1944), xcvii; and Robert A. Lovett's "Air Lessons for the Future," *Army and Navy Journal* (Special Number: 7 December 1943–7 December 1944), 22, 162.

†See *Morning Noon and Night*, pp. 303–307 and *Guard of Honor*, pp. 57–58 for impressions of Lovett.

Staff. Cozzens later recalled that Lovett "could handle, really master, in a way no one but George Marshall matched a man, say,
vain & perfidious often like FDR; a table-pounding roaring Hap
Arnold, a braggart & poser like MacArthur. He was so quiet you'd
say he never could until, incredulous (and I'll bet they were too)
you saw he'd, not a hair turned, gone and done it." [10] He enjoyed
handling Smith's press briefings because the young general did so
well with Cozzens's prepared statements. "The object of the conferences, for instance, is to sell the newspaper people in an infor-
mal way those ideas and attitudes about the AAF organization and
operations that we would like them to have. We have been quite
successful, thanks largely to Gen Smith's gifts (and no doubt it
part, to my clear, well-written and well-argued texts)." [11] Cozzens
got them both in trouble in October 1944 by providing General
Smith with a statement about the atomic bomb before there was
any announcement that America was working on it.* It was
deemed necessary to brief Cozzens on the atomic bomb progress
to prevent another inadvertent leak. He later described the flap in
Morning Noon and Night:

Consternation in high quarters when this 'harmless' comment credited
(horrors!) to an Air Staff spokesman of rank came out in a newspaper
was understandable—though maybe high quarters might have reflected
that the perfection of their security measures was demonstrated about to
the hilt when an Air Staff general officer surely on the Top Secret list
could give this innocent proof that he hadn't ever been allowed to know
the atomic-bomb project existed. But now plainly demonstrated, too, was
an overlooked danger in such effective absolute security. It was judged
to be essential for a selected few persons—one having connection with
OIS—to be told that not only were we 'working on it,' but also we had
got so far that our having it was certain. Under absolutely no circumstances was a remotest reference to be made to the work [p. 306].

His promotion to major came in August 1944. In order to avoid
random speech writing, he developed the assignment to prepare
memos for Colonel Rex Smith, the OIS chief, on what was hap-

---

*The *Washington Post* quoted a "high Army Air Forces officer" on 26 October 1944: "Nearly
anything is in the realm of possibility, of course, and I'm not long-haired enough to know
exactly where we stand in working on atomic explosives, but I believe there are many
technical difficulties to be overcome. There is no doubt the Germans are working on atomic
explosives. They'd be foolish if they didn't." [12] This comment was provided by Cozzens in
response to a question submitted before the news conference.

pening in all of the Pentagon Air Forces departments as well as in the combat zones. This job gave him access to virtually anything he wanted to see—bombing statistics, policy decisions, misconduct in high and low places, reports from the theaters of war, and matters such as the menstrual difficulties of women pilots. As described in *Morning Noon and Night*:

From the daily activity reports that all Air Staff sections were directed to send him, and from the Top Secret In and Out Log which he had been cleared to read, one officer [Cozzens] compiled a regular memorandum. Known familiarly as the Scandal Sheet, it called attention to any developments anywhere in the Air Force that could, coming to light, make for unfavorable publicity, harm the AAF. Alerted this way, the high command would not be taken unprepared, could have plans ready to minimize the damage as far as possible if newspapers picked the business up [p. 300].

Cozzens may well have been the best-informed officer in the Air Force—certainly the best-informed officer below the high command—and became privy to some of the best-kept military secrets.* Before Cozzens was discharged he lifted his memos from the Pentagon files, acting on the advice of the Air Inspector.

Even with this dream assignment, there were still idle days when it was necessary to kill time, as noted in this 29 June 1944 diary entry: "Nothing to do all day but we seemed to pass it well enough reading (I was reading Harry Brown's piece on a platoon in Italy [*A Walk in the Sun*] with many good parts and much phoney dialogue—the difficulty a writer has in doing things all of a piece is one of our great literary problems—at what point in realism do you add imagination to fact, and why?—I was glad to go up to the Link Trainer where I got on better for an hour." He kept volumes of Shakespeare in the office as well as a drawer of Everyman volumes for these slack periods. The books he read in Washington included Bishop Burnet's *History*, Latimer's *Sermons*, the memoirs of Colonel Hutchinson, *Locke on Civil Government*, Reynolds' *Discourses*, Fox's *Journal*, *The Memoirs of Sir Thomas Buxton*, and Goldsmith's *The Citizen of the World*. While reading Blackstone he and

---

* Guard of Honor (p. 255) mentions that one of the Allies—obviously the Soviets—had discussed a separate peace with Germany in 1943. This secret did not make the history books until B. H. Liddell Hart revealed it in his 1970 *History of the Second World War*, at which time *Guard of Honor* was cited in evidence.[13]

Bradshaw planned a collection of essays by various hands on American trials. Cozzens completed his study of the 1879 trial of Dr. John Webster, a Harvard Medical School professor who was hanged for murdering a colleague, and planned an epilogue on "the Common Law under evident present insidious change,"[14] but the volume foundered for lack of contributors.*

A perquisite of the OIS staff was the ability to wangle overseas trips, but Cozzens avoided all such opportunities. When he was asked whether he didn't feel that as a writer he ought to see the war, he replied that he already knew all about it. He explained to his mother: ". . . the situation of being there with nothing to do but see the sights while other people were fighting fills me with a sense of awkwardness or discomfort. This would easily be overcome if I were curious, but I have a perfectly positive feeling that I know exactly what it is like—perhaps because I see so many people who have returned from this theatre or that, and have flown in too many planes, and camped out in too many air force posts."[15] The combat pilots interested him because they seemed to be able to perform their duties out of a lack of imagination. "Dumb as a pilot" and "airplane driver" became pet phrases. He noticed that all the good ones had remarkable eyes and concluded that extraordinary eyesight accounted for their success.

An amusement during the hours of office idleness was observing Newhouse's expert teasing of Margaret Johnson, a lively young civilian secretary who became the office pet. Newhouse enjoyed drawing her out through solemn quizzing in which she would guess that Joan of Arc had something to do with the Trojan horse. It was not cruel fun because she obviously enjoyed the attention and there was no intention of humiliating her. Cozzens occasionally joined the game and was pleased to observe her development.

Although Cozzens knew that he really had nothing to complain about in his service life, the prolonged interruption of his writing produced bouts of depression: "To set against happy aspects of freedom are those, less happy, of an existence whose order is fundamental disorder, whose state of no responsibility is essentially a state of solitariness, whose resignation makes for inanition of uncaring, for deep despondencies of what-the-hell, nothing matters."[16] Between Bernice's weekend visits he was often tight in the evenings (he rather prided himself on being able to drive when

* Cozzens's essay was separately published in 1976 as *A Rope for Dr. Webster*.

With Edward Newhouse and Margaret Johnson
(Courtesy of Jo H. Chamberlin)

tight), which resulted in what he referred to as "unplanned war-time connections" with women. The notebooks Cozzens later kept at Williamstown, Massachusetts, include a detailed account of an occasion of alcoholic fornication after which he found himself home with no memory of having driven there. Late one night he arrived at Bradshaw's apartment in distress after seducing a young woman who worked in the Pentagon. He had been drinking, but seemed sober: "How could I have done that to myself?" Bradshaw was amazed to find the normally controlled Cozzens in an emotional condition over this violation of his standards of conduct.

There were evenings spent with the office group. At the end of one party they were singing "Tenting Tonight," and Jo Chamberlin's wife, Mary, noticed that Cozzens was crying. Once Cozzens, who was tight, conducted the Chamberlins and George Bradshaw to the home of newspaper publisher Eleanor "Cissy" Patterson, claiming that he had something to tell her. They were denied admittance.

When Bernice was in Washington they kept to themselves. During her visits she prepared food for him to eat during the week. He was proud of Bernice's "beautiful and sleek" appearance. "She is the same woman I married," he remarked to Mary Chamberlin.

Feeling that the interruption of their Lambertville life had made a resumption of his civilian routine difficult, the Cozzenses put Carrs Farm on the market and sold it, but took it back when the deal fell through. They were considering a move to Virginia for the sake of milder weather and better gardening conditions; but they could not find an affordable farm during their weekend explorations of the Virginia countryside. Bernice was prepared to give up her work, but his earnings were not enough to support them.

As Cozzens's friendship with Ed Newhouse developed, Newhouse kidded him about his misanthropy. Cozzens insisted that "I do too not like people." Newhouse once remarked, "Pick a number, any number, and you'll find fault with it." When he heard Newhouse's young son singing

> There was a jolly miller once,
>   Liv'd on the river Dee,
> He work'd, and sung, from morn till night,
>   No lark more blyth than he.
> And this the burthen of his song.
>   For ever us'd to be,
> I care for nobody, not I,
>   If no one cares for me.*

Cozzens said, "If anyone ever writes my biography, it ought to be called 'The Jolly Miller.'" He told Newhouse, "They got me early, that's my misfortune"—admitting that the forces of conscience had isolated him.[17] Cozzens's sardonic wit sometimes irritated his associates. When Jo Chamberlin was promoted, Cozzens remarked—quoting Lord Melbourne's comment on the Order of the Garter—that promotion in the Air Force involved no damn nonsense about merit. Chamberlin replied, "Jim, every time you say something you make an enemy."

His Air Force novel began to take shape while he prepared memos on the near-mutiny at Freeman Field, in Indiana, in April

---

* From Isaac Bickerstaffe's *Love in a Village* (1763).

1945, when Negro officers tried to force their way into the Officers' Club, which had been designated off-limits to them.*

HEADQUARTERS, ARMY AIR FORCES
WASHINGTON

23 April 1945

MEMORANDUM FOR THE CHIEF, OFFICE OF INFORMATION SERVICES
Subject: Information from AC/AS Offices

1. *Freeman Field Situation.* (Air Inspector) For the record, the recommendations on this matter made by Gen. Giles and approved by Gen. Marshal are:

    a. Release of the 101 negro officers under arrest, and dropping of charges under AW 64 for their refusal to sign the read-and-understood blank attached to Seymour Field Base Regulation 80–2.

    b. Trial of the remaining three officers (who pushed the assistant PM) "if the investigation (by Hq. 1st. AF) indicates the charges can be sustained."

    c. Transfer of the 477th Bomb Group and its supporting units to Godman Field, Kentucky.

    d. Inactivation and demobilization of the units on V-E day or R day, whichever is first announced.

(Policy in regard to the officer's club problem in the future will apparently be guided by Gen. Hedrick's opinion that Par. 19, AR 210–10 "is not interpreted as a requirement that all officers on a base be permitted to use all clubs. It is the view of this office that the mentioned regulation was designed to insure every officer the right to membership in officers' club; but does not prohibit a *reasonable division of club facilities where circumstances make such division necessary or desirable from a practical, disciplinary, or morale standpoint.*" (This disregards the plain meaning of the paragraph, but what the hell?)

2. *Munition Situation on V-E Day.* (OC&R) The Army Service Command has asked the Chief of the Air Staff about the availability of AAF units "to help unload ammunition trains if VE Day should be announced unexpectedly. Because of the tremendous expenditures of bombs and ammunition in Europe, there are constantly on the rails in the US, bound for Eastern ports, great quantities of bombs and ammunition. ASF has

---

*The 477th Composite Group, a trainee group at Freeman Field, was largely Negro. Three officers were court-martialed for jostling a provost marshal while they tried to enter the Officers' Club, and 101 of the officers were confined to quarters. Two of the defendants were acquitted, and the third was lightly dealt with. After the 477th was transferred to Godman Field, in Kentucky, the white commanding officer was replaced by Colonel Benjamin O. Davis, Jr., the son of the first Negro general in the Air Force.

determined if the requirement for this flow suddenly ceases on VE Day, *it will be VE plus 210 days* before the rails are cleared. It is obviously dangerous and impractical to leave these explosives in freight cars in freight yards. ASF requested AAF to designate all possible units to aid in unloading these cars at various points in the U.S." (The ASF was notified that the only troops available would be 2 CM Truck companies—about as much good as nothing.)

3. *Embarkation Port Change.* (M&S) A shift in the point of shipment of material for the India-China-Burma theatre from Los Angeles to New York is underway. It is expected that by 1 June all shipments for the area would be routed through New York.

4. *AAF Losses.* (Management Control)

   a. *Officer Casualties.* "Out of a total of 78,294 officer battle casualties, more than half (53.6%) were suffered by Air Corps officers; 41.2% by Ground officers; 5.2% by ASF officers."

   b. *Planes.* "As of 31 March 1945, more than half (34,557 out of 64,632) of the AAF combat and transport planes dispatched to all theatres since Pearl Harbor have been lost." (Of the 30,075 remaining; 2,300 have been returned to the U.S., 1,116 transferred to allied air forces, 1,371 are en route; 25,288 are on hand overseas. Of the losses, 865 took place en route.)

5. *XB-48.* (OC&R) In line with what appears to be OC&R policy to have as many manufacturers as possible have a try at building planes around jet units, Martin is at work on a medium bomber designed XB-48 to be powered by 6 TG-180 units—two nacelles with 3 units in each. The tactical range is estimated at 2,840 miles, the operational ceiling, 35,000 feet, high speed, 534 mph; cruising speed, 440 mph. The maximum bomb load is 22,000 tons and the bomb bay will allow loading one Grand Slam bomb if desirable. "Except for being considerably larger, the airplane is similar in configuration to other B-40 series bombers." However, a new type landing gear is being tried out. This will consist of two main double-wheeled gears fore and aft in the fuselage, with the front gear steerable; and the bomb bay doors will open by retracting into the bomb bay, instead of dropping down. "In accordance with current military characteristics of medium bombers, only two 50 cal. guns, firing from the tail turret, provide armament. The gunner is the co-pilot, sitting behind the pilot and firing the guns by remote control." The planned crew is three, but in view of the range (7 hours), it is felt that another man should be included and possibly more guns. Martin has been asked to "make a study for another man in the nose, to be visual bombardier."

6. *Reconnaissance Conference.* (OC&R) Representatives of OC&R M&S, and ATSC were summoned by the Chief of Naval Operations last

week for a squawk on subject Subject. "The conference was motivated by a cable from commanders in the Pacific Theatre re the lack of information regarding Japanese installations on Iwo Jima and a request that immediate steps be taken to improve the methods of detecting these installations." Various suggestions were made, most of them, apparently, impractical. "The most useful expedient offered was through low level stereotype photography and visual reconnaissance through high powered (10 power or better) binoculars." (Remaining question in re low level photography and use of binoculars: Who wants to live forever anyway?)

7. *XP-86 Designation Change.* (M&S) The "Bell-fabricated" fighter, with supersonic (speed in excess of 760 mph) characteristics, now in the works (such as they are) will no longer be known as the XP-86. It will be designated S-1; though at the same time, to make it harder, the term "transonic" is being substituted for "supersonic". Presumably to complete the screwing-up, the designation XP-86 will be given to the new North American one-TG-180-unit job.

8. *Notes from In and Out Log.*

a. *CINCPOA 17 April* . . . .The enemy launched heavy air attacks against our forces in and around Okinawa . . . our planes shot down 62 A/E over Okinawa . . . 67 more were shot down in the Ryukus area . . . ships anti-aircraft fire off the Okinawa beaches destroyed 38 . . . (How's that about the Jap air force?)

b. *Paris signed Eisenhower 17 April.* Practicability of earlier movement of 7 remaining HB groups is subject. One group from Italy available after 15 May . . .six groups from Eighth AF could be prepared for shipment 30 days notice . . .

c. *From SHAEF to Gen. Marshal signed Eisenhower 18 April.* . . . I propose to issue instructions that no soldier is to be sent to the Pacific who has fought in both the North African and the European campaigns . . . these men will be retained in the theatre for the occupation forces . . .

JAMES G. COZZENS
Major, Air Corps[18]

Writing to his mother about segregation in the armed forces, he explained: "My own impulse would be to enforce the regulations which prohibited segregation. I can see that it is not practical. Failing that, my next impulse would be to clarify the matter by admitting that we were going to practice segregation. This, too, is wrong, because we then define the issue. For every purpose except that of enjoying a personal sense of virtuous candor, the right policy is to evade the issue, because though slowly and laboriously, the problem is working itself out—there are plenty of AAF fields where colored officers are perfectly free to come into the club and there has been no trouble of any kind. If we point the issue, either by enforcing the regulation and so provoking riot and mutiny at one field, or by changing the regulation to conform to the practice we are in fact allowing, everyone is going to have to take sides. If a thousand white officers are arrested and court-martialled because they do not want to drink beer with negroes we are not going to improve the relations between the races. I find such problems wearing, but I had to see that Gen Hedrick, the Air Judge Advocate, with whom I was discussing it Saturday, is right. Hypocrisy is an essential ingredient in human relationships." [19]

A Negro waiter at Harvey's, who was concerned about getting his sons a fair chance in the Air Force, asked Cozzens for help several times. He looked into their problems and did what he could. These experiences went into the pool of material for his novel; the waiter provided the source for Mr. Willis in *Guard of Honor*.

On 10 May 1945 he noted in his diary: "I had been meanwhile starting to get some stuff together on the Freeman Field business, borrowing Col Scott's file for the purpose and boldly stealing any papers of which I found more than three copies, vaguely feeling that I might like to do a book around that situation, which seemed to have some analogies with the perhaps more general problem of the compromises in life between what you might like to do, and what circumstances make it sensible to do." Ten days later he cleared the project with Bernice: "She seemed to think I might go ahead on my notions about the Freeman Field business in spite of the fact that it was plain that anything, even so remotely connected with the war and the army, when I got it finished, would never sell. It did not make much sense; but I saw that, in psychological self-defense, I would have to start writing or go nuts."

Forty-two-year-old Major Cozzens was discharged on 18 October 1945 because the Air Force was releasing officers who were not needed to wrap up the war. He returned to Carrs Farm and resumed his routine of writing and gardening. Although he regarded his service period as a considerable waste of time in terms of contributing to the war effort, he admitted that the experience had been good for him because it had brought him into close association with a great range of people and activities. Out of Cozzens's thirty-nine months in the Air Force came his eleventh novel, "which pleads the army's case."[20] He had developed a loyal-alumnus feeling about the Air Force, and it was strong enough to make him agree to write General Arnold's farewell speech in 1946.*

---

* Arnold's farewell "To the Men and Women of the Army Air Forces" is dated 8 February 1946 and signed by Captain Loy Singleton. It is not known whether Cozzens contributed to this 269-word statement.

SEVEN

Guard of Honor

As a civilian Cozzens cut back on his drinking and experienced spells of depression. His doctor diagnosed a condition of megaloblastic anemia resulting from a folic-acid deficiency often found in heavy drinkers. The condition was remedied by daily doses of folic acid. Apart from aborted short stories Cozzens had written no fiction during the war. When he returned to his work, he discovered that some of his facility had been lost, perhaps because in "The Tempest"—which became *Guard of Honor* in 1947 when Cozzens thought of the new title while driving—he was dealing with a much larger subject than he had attempted before. Instead of a small-town doctor or lawyer, he was covering the "immense complexity" of an air base—and, by extension, the entire Army Air Forces. He admitted that, after twenty-two years as a novelist, "I still have to depend on the things I never knew I was going to write until I find myself suddenly writing them." [1] Moreover, his craft became more exacting as he practiced it—that is, his own standards had become harder to satisfy: "every paragraph, if it is to hold together, must while carrying one thread keep in touch with ten others and every line must have at least two points. . . ." [2] In October 1946 he described his method of writing *Guard of Honor*:

Monday I wrote out most of the substance and it came to about four pages. I saw Monday night that I did not have quite what I wanted; so

Tuesday I wrote it over and got to about six pages. Wednesday I saw that three of those pages had better come out, I could say that to better effect after I had said something else, which I hadn't yet said, so I said that. Thursday I had four pages plus the three that I wanted later, and it was now necessary to rewrite from the beginning because of the something-else which I had to lead up to. Friday I was able to put it together, doing the whole section over again in the revised order, changing some things, put in (though modified) what I had held out, where I thought it ought to be; and then I had ten pages, though I was actually, in my overall progress, no farther along with the story than I was Monday at noon. It is only right to add that this strive-and-succeed story should be qualified by the good chance that next week or next month or early next year I will see that everything I did this week should be cut or drastically changed in light of what I have come to write since, or of what I then find I had written before. This is not right. It would be smarter and better to do it the first time in a straight and simple way, and not depend for some, at least, of your corrections on the occasional and doubtful aid of a couple of drinks, or any other form of second-guessing.[3]

By December 1946 Cozzens had 300 pages of typescript—which he calculated as half the novel—and 500 pages by March 1947. The novel expanded as he wrote it; in January 1948 he had passed 700 pages, with the end in sight.

The last day of 1947 marked the Cozzenses' twentieth wedding anniversary. For two decades he had been supported and well cared for by a brilliant woman. He had published eight novels since their marriage and with her support had become a major, if unheralded, novelist. Bertha approvingly relayed her son's comment to Bernice: "It is twenty years, all right; and speaking for myself, I think it is chief among the many pieces of luck that have fallen to me."[4] Bernice's business associates thought that she gave more than she got; to outsiders the Cozzens marriage appeared to exist for his work and his comfort. All marriages are collaborations. Bernice had what she wanted, and she told her sister, Fannie, that Jim was the only thing in the world that mattered to her. Outsiders inevitably said that she mothered him. Budd Schulberg, Bernice's client, who lived nearby in Bucks County, detected "a secret bond that was emotional and very strong."[5] According to Schulberg, Bernice saw nothing unusual about her husband's reclusiveness; she thought it was the way writers should live and work. Bernice got all the socializing she wanted at work. Mary McCarthy, another of her clients, speculates that they were both hermits, "except that one was an extrovert hermit and the other an introvert."[6] Fannie never heard them argue; but Carol Brandt reports that Cozzens could be nasty to Bernice when he was in his cups. (On the rare occasions when they came to dinner he stipulated that the Brandts invite no one else.) When there were disagreements at home, Bernice retired to her room. An area of occasional disagreement was what Cozzens called her "money button." She regarded some of his purchases for the farm as extravagant, for he bought on the principle that if one was good then two were better. He sometimes had to hide his mail-order purchases. Bernice's compulsive cleanliness amused her husband. On the housekeeper's day off she scrubbed the kitchen and bathrooms.

While Cozzens pushed through with *Guard of Honor,* he became increasingly confirmed in his belief that the art of literature was an abnormal preoccupation proceeding from personality maladjustment. He only part-jokingly informed his mother:

The whole trouble is that I decided when I was about 15 that I was going to write books. I did not know it then; but I know now that such a decision, seriously made, means that you are going to do it by hook or crook; that, if you stick to it, it is because you have no other real interest and no other real object; that, consequently, you will do whatever you rightly or wrongly feel you need to do to get on with it; and that you will be bound by no obligations and will accept no responsibilities not, as far as you can see, connected with it. With luck, this unamiable program may never need to be pressed to extremes; but I am quite sure it *is* the program of anyone who commits himself, or much more accurately, finds himself by the peculiarities of his nature committed, to one of the so-called arts. I think it has to be his program, because no nature but this self-centered, selfish, unscrupulous, and to all normal people rightly detestable one could stand the incidental gaff, survive the exhausting doubts, bear up under the dreadful discouragements. I don't mean because it is so strong and courageous. Perhaps nobody normal could ever be strong enough and courageous enough. I mean because the conceited mind explains the doubts away and a fundamental insensitiveness does not fully feel the discouragements. In the interests of society, as Plato so well understood, the best course would always be to chloroform any child who showed any sign of artistic talent as soon as he showed it. If he is encouraged in it he is bound to feel that he is a special case, that ordinary rules don't hold for him, that other people are either of no consequence, or means for him to use to his end. I don't say it is the little monster's fault; nobody would practise an 'art' if he weren't psychologically disqualified for getting his livelihood in normal ways; but he is bad news for everyone else and when you raise one I am afraid you have a good deal to answer for. [7]

A working draft of the novel was sent to retired General Hume Peabody—the former commander of the Army Air Forces School of Applied Tactics—for vetting. Apart from possible blunders about the Air Force, Cozzens was concerned about inadvertently working too close to his models. He explained to Peabody that sometimes when a character is invented truly from a model, he proves to be truer than the author supposes.

I think perhaps I should add one thing—a matter usually classified Top Secret in this trade; but I feel sure you have had experience in safeguarding classified material. All prudent writers publically maintain that their characters are completely original and in no way resemble anyone on earth—quite often I must admit they seem to have a point there, too. But in fact I am sure most writers when they see their character see someone a good deal like someone they have seen sometime. Quite often I think it is a kind of composite. You will find in the ms. two regular army air force general officers and I will confess to you that General Beal, as he moved in my mind was in appearance difficult to distinguish from Lauris Norstad, while in speech and attitude he certainly reminded me of Freddy Smith. Similarly, General Nichols kept looking a lot like General Kuter while his observations were, some of them, not too far from some I have heard General Vandenberg make. You no doubt know all these men and perhaps you know one or more of them very well. I know them well only in the sense that I spent a lot of time looking at them and listening to them. Since, I don't have to say, no portrait is intended, I thought I would ask you, if you noticed any detail of the private life or military career of my generals which seemed uniquely or peculiarly true to you with respect to any of those four you might happen to know well to tell me and I will change it. It would only be so by chance; but I have been surprised before this to find that the chance is not quite as remote as you would expect. When you know a person's face and talk and start inventing a 'story' to suit them, what you decide fits best is sometimes better than that—it's perfect, it really happened to them. [8]

General Peabody found no serious errors. (When one Air Force veteran queried the radio procedure in the published novel, citing FM 1-460, Cozzens had the satisfaction of replying that he had been responsible for revising this manual.)

Guard of Honor covers seventy-two hours at Ocanara Air Base, Florida, the second, third, and fourth of September 1943. The 631 printed pages are divided into progressively longer sections: Thursday, 88 pages; Friday, 198 pages, and Saturday, 345 pages. But the time span is not limited to the events of three days; flashbacks provide background on the characters—for example, the extraordinary seven-page account of General Beal's military career near the beginning of the novel (pp. 17–24). Cozzens professed to be chagrined at the self-indulgence of writing such a large novel, and explained to Kenneth Potter at Longmans, Green:

. . . I was disconcerted on my own account to find myself running over 600 pages. I had often contended that there was no excuse for a novel of more than 400 pages. Anything over that was just proof of incompetence . . . but when I came to write Guard of Honor I found myself in a different situation. What I wanted to write about here, the essence of the thing to be said, the point of it all, what I felt to be the important meaning of this particular human experience, was its immensity and its immense complexity.

This feeling had grown on me as my so-called military service drew on and I began slowly to realize that through no fault (or indeed merit) of my own I was being shown the Army Air Forces on a scale and in a way that was really incredible. I was coming to know about, I had to know about, more of its innumerable phases than anyone with real command duties would ever have time to know. Not many officers, and I would guess not any, had reason or opportunity to fly into and look over such a number of airfields and installations of a variety quite unbelieveable. With the exception of the CG himself . . . I don't think anyone had occasion to sit down with and listen to so many of the air generals. I know that no other one person read, as I had to read every morning, yesterday's activity reports from all the Air Staff sections along with the CG's in-and-out log, the messages from and to the commanders in all combat theatres. This, I can tell you, while serving no good purpose toward winning the war, was an experience; and though I did not see how I could stand it much longer I felt at least that writer's excitement of coming to understand things I would want to tell other people about.

With my head full of all this, I could see I faced a tough technical problem. I wanted to show that real (as I now saw it) meaning of the whole business, the peculiar effects of the inter-action of innumerable individuals functioning in ways at once determined by and determining the functioning of innumerable others—all in the common and in every case nearly helpless involvement in what had ceased to be just an "organization" (I think it ceased to be that when it grew past the point where one directing head could keep the whole in mind) and became if not an organism with life and purposes of its own, at least an entity, like a crowd. . . .

. . . .
I saw that I would have to show it, with all that that meant in many scenes, many words, many characters. I would just have to write off as readers everyone who could not or would not meet heavy demands of his attention and intelligence, the imagination to grasp a large pattern and the wit to see the relation which I could not stop to spell out between this & that.[9]

Cozzens told his mother that he was particularly concerned about the long Saturday section in which readers were required "to bear in mind material that was meant to make, remembered as new material came up, pointed parallels or contrasts or both by which I hoped I was going to put over whatever it is I am trying to put over. I suppose my idea is that the obvious or 'natural' dramatic effects strike me always as false (and they damn well are, too) and I am trying to do what they do (engross the interest and involve the feelings) without use of the usual mutually agreed on lies. I'm not sure it isn't hopeless. I'm not sure that people are ever or can ever be moved by what actually happened—they need to misunderstand it and misinterpret it until it touches that maudlin chord which naturally everyone has in one form or another. That way you have them working for you; this way the work is all yours. As I say, if I don't get away with this I will have to reconsider (being now 45) and take steps, if I can, to write what people want to read instead of what I want them to read. They could be right, too. I have not missed the fact that writers as good and as diverse as Shakespeare and Somerset Maugham think so—cheap and silly matter is the best and should always be used. You just give it a competent treatment—that is; write it well and never mind whether it makes any sense or not." [10]

The novel opens on Thursday evening, 2 September 1943, aboard an AT-7 en route to Ocanara, with a tableau signifying military subordination. Major General Ira N. Beal, the Ocanara commander, is at the controls; the co-pilot is war hero Lieutenant Colonel Benny Carricker; the first passenger seat is occupied by Colonel Norman Ross, the Air Inspector; behind him is Captain Nathaniel Hicks, a peacetime magazine editor; behind Hicks is WAC Second Lieutenant Amanda Turck; Master Sergeant Dominic Pellerino, the crew chief, is on a fold-down seat; and symbolically perched on the chemical toilet is Technician Fifth Grade Mortimer McIntyre, a Negro. All are attached to Army Air Forces Operations and Requirements Analysis Division (AFORAD).

Coming in to Ocanara, the general's plane almost crashes when another plane improperly lands in front of them. Beal freezes at the controls, and Carricker saves them. After they land, Carricker punches the Negro pilot of the other plane, breaking his nose.

The ostensible subject of *Guard of Honor* is the testing of General Beal. The youngest two-star general in the Air Forces, forty-one-year-old Bus Beal has been returned stateside after a brilliant combat record in the Philippines, North Africa, and Europe and has been assigned to an administrative job. If he can demonstrate the qualities needed for the responsibility, he will be given a key role in the bombing of Japan. Beal is a born pilot and therefore, in the author's view, not given to complex thinking. The crisis that constitutes his testing is triggered by Carricker's punching of the Negro pilot. The group of Negro officers at Ocanara has been denied use of the officers' club, and the punching results in an attempt by his companions to force their way into the club. Ocanara is in the segregated South, but Air Force regulations prohibit segregation; therefore Beal is required to restore order and maintain the policy of segregation without violating regulations.

Beal actually does nothing about the problem; he leaves it to Colonel Ross, who is in fact, but not in title, the chief administrator at the base. A fifty-nine-year-old veteran of World War I and a judge in civilian life, Ross is the moral center of the novel. He recognizes that "the Nature of Things abhors a drawn line and loves a hodgepodge, resists consistency and despises drama; that the operation of man is habit, and the habit of habit is inertia. This weight is against every human endeavor; and always the best bet is, not that a man will, but that he won't" (p. 572). At a low point of fatigue Ross formulates a deontological code of conduct that epitomizes the mature Cozzens hero: "Downheartedness was no man's part. A man must stand up and do the best he can with what there is. If the thing he labored to uncover now seemed in danger of stultifying him, could a rational being find nothing to do? If mind failed you, seeing no pattern; and heart failed you, seeing no point, the stout, stubborn will must be up and doing. A pattern should be found; a point should be imposed. Was that too much?" [p. 534]. Or, as Cozzens told his mother while the novel was in progress, "I suppose what I am getting at is what I am always getting at in whatever I am writing—a proposition that, in this life, things are indeed tough all over, uncertain, and often disastrous; and that human virtue consists in resisting as far as you can the understandable inclination to sit down and bawl."[11] More formally stated, the principal theme of Cozzens's major novels is the limitations of choice, operating with the imperatives of duty.

An almost idealized Cozzens hero, Ross is a man of ripened reason whose years of experience in the law have taught him that there are times when high principles have to be shelved. Knowing that means become ends, he sees that blacks and whites will be injured if the Negro pilots are allowed to exercise their rights and that, moreover, most whites don't care about black equality: "That big majority may feel that a Negro is a human being all right; but when you add that they want to see him treated fairly, you're wrong. . . . The big majority does not want to insult or oppress him; but the big majority has, in general, a poor opinion of him" (p. 440). Cozzens's own position, as expressed to his mother in 1946, was ". . . I see you point about the black people being unable to help it—it is mine, too; but what about the white people who in a command position like the general's have these alternatives and only these: (a) you can recognize that the majority of them are little or no good in the sense that you can't rely on them and they can't do anything right, and act accordingly—and get yourself denounced for your callous inhumanity (b) you can try to pretend that they are just like everyone else and act accordingly, and when their stupidity and imcompetence has wrecked you, you can take all the blame. Certainly, it's unfair to blame them; but nobody is going to find it unfair to blame you when they do what experience shows they are bound to do, and it won't help you any to say: yes, but given a fair chance for a generation or two, they wouldn't do this. You have to deal with now, not sometime."[12] The segregationists in the novel are bigots or dopes; but Lieutenant Edsell, the champion of justice and equality, is an obnoxious sorehead whose pleasure in making trouble renders his allegiance to liberal principles suspect.

Ross convinces the injured pilot—in return for the prospect of advancement—to persuade his comrades to accept the subterfuge that the officers' club is reserved for permanent base personnel and that a separate club has been provided for the Negro group in order to foster esprit de corps. The irony of the crisis is that Beal was in no special danger of sinking under his problems. At the close of the novel, on Saturday night, he resumes command and even provides a lesson for Ross:

"Even Jo-Jo [General Nichols, the Deputy Chief of Staff who has been sent to report on Beal] knows they could do without him before they could do without me. That's not boasting, Judge. There's a war on. Jo-Jo can talk to Mr. Churchill; but the war, that's for us. Without me— without us, he wouldn't have a whole hell of a lot to talk about, would he?"

. . . .

"I'll do the best I can, Judge; and you do the best you can; and who's going to do it better?"[pp. 630–31].

Guard of Honor is related in third-person omniscient narrative by the recognizable voice of James Gould Cozzens—the voice of an assessing mind, not seeking solutions but identifying limitations in conduct. Cozzens participates in his narrative and controls the point of view by means of style. The form and tone of a sentence extend its meaning—for example, when he incorporates tag lines from verse into his prose. On pages 394–95 Kipling's "Recessional," Longfellow's "The Building of the Ship," G. W. Hunt's "War Song" (a music-hall song that provided the source for the term "jingoism"), and the bawdy poem about "The Good Ship Penis" are echoed:

> Grimacing, Mr. Churchill must taste, too, the gall of his situation. Fine phrases and selected words might show it almost a virtue that, far call'd our navies melt away; that, on dune and headland sinks the fire; but those circumstances also kept him from the leading position. . . .
> Across the table, General Nichols's own side, the Union strong and great, was in a pleasanter position; justifiably cockier. They had the ships, they had the men, they had the money, too! . . .
> Thus, variously hampered and discontented, these great personages showed General Nichols, the errand boy, the perhaps not-unartful nipper, how to make history.

These echoes provide ironic commentary on the subject matter. Thus the application of the 1878 song about England's readiness to go to war, when transferred to the American position during 1943, reinforces the point about the relative strengths of the two nations during World War II. Cozzens knew that unquoted familiar quotations stop or baffle the reader to whom they are unfamiliar. He also recognized that he employed this device partly for his own entertainment and admitted that "entertaining himself is not a writer's job."[13] His mind was a storehouse of remembered lines,

and the connections were so obvious to him that Cozzens probably never realized how many well-read readers would miss his
points.

There is a split focus between two centers of intelligence in
Guard of Honor: Colonel Ross provides the perspective from the
upper echelons, and Captain Hicks represents the viewpoint of the
civilian in uniform. Neither is a professional soldier. Hicks is dismayed by his duties, which include revising FM 1-15, *Tactics and
Technique of Pursuit Aviation* (similar to the manual Cozzens had
worked on at Orlando), and by his subordinate position to career
officers who are plainly not bright. He is permitted partial entry
into the concerns of Beal and Ross through his assignment to arrange for magazine coverage of Ocanara; but his values are those
of a civilian who is outside the tight world of West Pointers and
who would much prefer to be home doing his own work.

The actual subject of *Guard of Honor* is not General Beal's crisis,
but the vast complexity of the Army Air Forces and the operation
of a causal chain within this organization. Cozzens's biggest and
most ambitious book, *Guard of Honor* is nonetheless not a documentary or panoramic work. His method was to exhibit "such parts
of the truth as most nearly produce the effect of the truth and
those and only those."[14] The population of the novel includes fifty
characters, some of whom are studied in detail—Captain Andrews,
the earnest math genius; Captain Duchemin, the ebullient volup-
tuary; Colonel Mowbray, the befuddled old soldier. The most remarkable subsidiary figure is the almost preternaturally intelligent
General Jo-Jo Nichols, who manifests "an undeceived apprehension, a stern, wakeful grasp of the nature of things" (p. 396).

Guard of Honor has no dedication. The epigraph is taken from a
speech by Ariel in *The Tempest*:

> I and my fellows
> Are ministers of Fate: the elements,
> Of whom your swords are temper'd, may as well
> Wound the loud winds, or with bemock'd-at stabs
> Kill the closing waters, as diminish
> One dowle that's in my plume: my fellow-ministers
> Are like invulnerable.

The indirect message of this epigraph is that the men and women
of the novel are all too vulnerable. Far from being ministers of
Fate, they are susceptible to the manifold operations of chance—

or, as Cozzens had come increasingly to regard it, good or bad luck. It is difficult to differentiate the senses in which Cozzens applies luck: luck as fortune (accident) and luck as fate (destiny). Generally, he seems to indicate that fortune is fate.

Cozzens wanted to let *Guard of Honor* age for 1949 publication so he could give it a final polish; but publication was scheduled for 1948 to avoid competing with Hemingway's *Across the River and Into the Trees,* which had been announced for 1949. (It did not appear until 1950.) Harcourt, Brace paid an advance of $2,500, bringing Cozzens's total earnings for 1948 to $2,747. He was deeply disappointed when the Book-of-the-Month Club declined *Guard of Honor* (the grapevine reported that Henry Seidel Canby held out for it but was outvoted); the BOMC might have distributed 300,000 copies. *Guard of Honor* was published in a first printing of 12,500 copies at $3.50 on 30 September 1948, the year that brought Norman Mailer's *The Naked and the Dead* and Irwin Shaw's *The Young Lions.* Unlike Mailer and Shaw, who presented the war from the enlisted man's angle and castigated the military system, Cozzens focused on the levels of command. Although some of his officers are clearly deficient in brains, he regards them as men doing their best within their limitations. None of them would knowingly jeopardize the conduct of the war. He does not attack the system, but anatomizes it to reveal its intricate chain of connections.

Cozzens's dispassionate treatment of segregation aroused no controversy, but *Guard of Honor* was not what the marketplace wanted. It sold 15,000 copies in 1948 (earning the author some $6,000) while *The Naked and the Dead* and *The Young Lions* sold in the hundreds of thousands. The reviews were predominantly respectful but unenthusiastic. Brendan Gill's otherwise strong review in the *New Yorker* judged that it failed to achieve stature as an enduringly great novel because of "an absence of deep feeling . . . of a fastidious shying-off on the part of the novelist, of an inconspicuous but nagging failure to commit himself beyond irony."[15] For this reason, Gill explained, Cozzens was ranked with Marquand instead of with Faulkner or Hemingway. This charge of coldness would become the standard complaint of critics Cozzens regarded as sentimentalists. Marquand's review in the *Book-of-the-Month Club News* called the novel "the writing of a born writer."[16] Other receptive reviewers were Joseph Henry Jackson (*Los Angeles Times* and *San Francisco Chronicle*), John Woodburn

Gardening, 1949

Jacket for first printing of Guard of Honor

(*Saturday Review of Literature*), Charles Poore (*New York Times*), and John K. Hutchens (*New York Herald Tribune*).* Cozzens liked Mark Schorer's review in the *New York Herald Tribune Weekly Book Review,* which identified him as a traditional novelist and praised the book for "its gravity and its special modernity." [17]

In February 1949, five months after *Guard of Honor* was published, Bernard De Voto of *Harper's* addressed himself to the neglect of Cozzens, asserting that the reputation-makers were put off and put out because he deprived them of opportunities to demonstrate their brilliance.

> That explains why criticism shies away from Mr. Cozzens: he is a writer. His novels are written. The word has to be italicized: they are *written*. So they leave criticism practically nothing to do. They are not born of a cause but of a fine novelist's feeling for the lives of people and their destiny—so criticism cannot reproach him for not having made peace with Russia or praise him for having ended anti-Semitism in Coos County. They contain no fog of confused thinking on which, as on a screen, criticism can project its diagrams of meanings which the novelist did not know were there. There is in them no mass of unshaped emotion, the novelist's emotion or the characters', from which criticism can dredge up significance that becomes portentous as the critic calls our attention, and the novelist's, to it. Worse still, they are written with such justness that criticism cannot get a toehold to tell him and us how they should have been written. Worst of all, the novelist's ego has been disciplined out of them, so criticism cannot chant its dirge about the dilemmas of the artist in our time.
>
> . . . .
>
> Apparently he has got to be content with the satisfaction of readers—the most sensitive and intelligent readers—and, for what it is worth, the admiration of writers. He will value the first much more than the second, and the preoccupation of official critical opinion with his inferiors cannot bother him at all. He is not a literary man, he is a writer. There are a handful like him in every age. Later on it turns out that they were the ones who wrote that age's literature. [18]

Perhaps even more than De Voto recognized, Cozzens had written *Guard of Honor* for himself. Writing is always an egotistical occupation, but Cozzens had long since purged himself of the ap-

---

* Cozzens could take satisfaction from the circumstance that his reviewers were not operating on the buddy system. Marquand was a Brandt & Brandt client, but he and Cozzens were not pals. The only reviewer of *Guard of Honor* who knew Cozzens was Lewis Nichols, a Kent classmate, who gave it a mixed notice in the *New York Times Book Review*.

petite for fame. He was honestly indifferent to popularity—apart from the money it brought—and utterly contemptuous of the literary life of self-promotion and reciprocal back-scratching. To be sure, he wrote to be read, but on his own terms. If readers didn't like what he wrote, then the hell with them. It is, of course, possible that Cozzens's indifference to sales figures and reviews was a defense mechanism. Yet when fame came belatedly in 1957 with *By Love Possessed,* he was embarrassed by it.

In May 1949 *Guard of Honor* was the surprise recipient of the Pulitzer Prize for fiction.* Cozzens accepted the award but privately regarded it with mixed feelings. Who were these "second rate newspapermen" to presume to give him a prize? Moreover, he believed that literary prizes were awarded not to the recipient but against someone else. The Pulitzer Prize called attention to the novel, and a third printing, of 5,000 copies, was required in 1949.† *Guard of Honor* did not go into paperback until 1952, but the Permabooks edition did not sell well. By 1966 Harcourt, Brace had sold 39,205 copies of the best novel to come out of World War II. Film rights were sold to Julian Blaustein and Daniel Taradash for $20,000 in 1954, but the movie was not produced.

When *Guard of Honour* was published in England by Longmans, Green in November 1949, it received a warm endorsement by C. P. Snow in the *London Sunday Times.*

Mr. Cozzens is much the soundest of his generation of American writers (which includes Mr. Hemingway, Mr. Faulkner, and Mr. Dos Pasos), and he wears much better. It is difficult to attach an intellectual-journalistic label to his writing, and for that reason and for another which I shall mention later he has been ignored in the train of hysterical New York–London gossip. . . .

. . . And the value of this book, as of all Mr. Cozzens's work, rests in his level, informed, investigatory, trustworthy reports on what individual men look like, say, do and think.

I am judging him by high standards; and I ought to say that, by those standards, he has a deficiency which partly explains why he has been

---

*The jury of Joseph Henry Jackson (*San Francisco Chronicle*), Frederic Babcock (*Chicago Tribune*), and David Appel (*Philadelphia Inquirer*) nominated *Guard of Honor, The Naked and the Dead, The Young Lions,* and Thornton Wilder's *The Ides of March.* The Pulitzer Board selected *Guard of Honor.* Other candidates for the prize were Carl Sandburg's *Remembrance Rock,* Ross Lockridge's *Raintree County,* and Faulkner's *Intruder in the Dust.*

†*Guard of Honor* had made the *New York Times* best-seller list as number 14 on 16 January 1949; it reappeared as number 14 on 22 May.

slow to win overwhelming praise. Warm and human as they are, his books lack impact; they lack the flame, the passionate impulse, which all very great novelists have possessed.[19]

Antonia White was even more enthusiastic in the *New Statesman and Nation:* "The performance is so dazzling that it is almost exhausting. . . ."[20] Nonetheless, English sales were not strong.*

Cozzens reviewed Oliver La Farge's *The Eagle in the Egg* for the *New York Times Book Review* (24 July 1949)—his first book review since Harvard. This book was a history of the Air Transport Command in World War II, and the assignment was offered to him on the basis of *Guard of Honor*. Moved by his alumnus feeling for the Air Force, Cozzens wrote warmly about the work of the ATC and praised La Farge's adult intelligence. Drawing on his own Pentagon experiences, he provided a quick sketch of Jacqueline Cochran: "Practical considerations did, and no doubt always will, take a licking when they come up against what was little less than a blonde vision, exquisite in tailored WASP blue, deliciously scented and sometimes close to tears."[21]

On 19 May 1948 Cozzens was arrested in Trenton when he parked at the Clinton Street Station of the Pennsylvania Railroad to meet Bernice's 6:00 P.M. train, as had been his custom for years. Railroad policeman Lawrence Cunningham ordered him to move his car, and Cozzens said that he would be leaving as soon as the train arrived. Cunningham demanded to see his license. He refused, and Cunningham placed him under arrest but did not say what the charge was. When Cozzens tried to tell Bernice what was happening, Cunningham seized him in a hammer lock and forced him into a baggage room. Bernice saw her husband being taken away in a police wagon and asked Cunningham what had happened, but he refused to tell her. Since Cunningham did not appear at the Trenton police station to charge him, Cozzens was allowed to leave after posting bail of fifteen dollars.

In October Cozzens, represented by Edgar Hunt, appeared at the Trenton Police Court to answer a charge of disorderly conduct

---

*The sales figures are not clear. The first Longmans printing was 5,100 copies, and there was a second printing of 2,990 in 1950. But the Brandt & Brandt records show that 8,973 copies were sold in England and 8,697 were exported.

brought by Cunningham and was found not guilty. Cozzens then brought a $25,000 suit against Cunningham and the Pennsylvania Railroad for false arrest and "great chagrin, shame and mental distress."[22] Bernice separately sued for $10,000, claiming "dread and apprehension that said defendant Lawrence D. Cunningham who is still employed by defendant Pennsylvania Railroad Company as a police officer at said Clinton Street Station, is a person of abnormal mentality and deficient judgment, and unfit to perform police duties, and that he is likely on some future occasion unjustifiably to assault and do serious physical injury to this plaintiff's said husband, who must come to said station several days each week in aiding this plaintiff in her necessary trips to and from New York; and these apprehensions cause continued anxiety to this plaintiff and hamper and interfere with her ability to work and attend to her business in her customary manner."[23] The railroad settled with Cozzens for $3,000 in 1950, but Bernice's claim was denied by the Superior Court of New Jersey. The local papers played up the case, but there was little coverage in New York.

EIGHT

By Love Possessed

I n July 1948—before *Guard of Honor* was published—Cozzens planned a satiric novel called "Fast Falls the Eventide." The contents list indicates the tone of this projected work:

I. Long, Long Ago: or the Pratville Short Line.
II. When Other Helpers Fail: or the Cold Feet.
III. L'Amour Toujours L'Amour: or Some Snap Fastners.
IV. Rise Like Lions: or the Hole in the Head.
V. Light is Her Young Heart: or the Ravished Maiden's Vademecum.
VI. Where Grave Thy Victory: or Left All Alone Again.[1]

He intended to depart from his representational technique:

Instead of trying to harrow the reader by straight accounts of sorrow and disappointment I will have a try at letting him harrow himself if he can by simply presenting my—ah—hero or protagonist and the characters involved with him in what is known as a dead-pan performance at once natural and preposterous—not, I think, by any means the union of irreconcilibles it seems on first statement. The propositions of, say, Catholicism or Communism, as stated by their best apologists, gravely treated need no exaggeration or deliberate fun-making to make a mild sad fun of themselves, if instead of protesting the hearer simply says in effect: is that so? Tell me more. I want to hit somewhere carefully short of farce, with people talking nothing but sense to each other about life, virtue, vice, growing old, and death (or at least what a serious and earnest man could honestly say) but the circumstances and the facts involved point up certain defects in their positions. I agree that it will take a lot of doing, since it will not work if it is prosy and preaching, nor yet if it is too obviously a prolonged joke.[2]

By the end of 1948—after he had accumulated 138 pages of notes and draft openings treating a middle-aged man whose Catholic wife has been killed in a plane crash and whose son is a Communist—Cozzens began to suspect that he couldn't bring it off. "In point of fact I can see that I am really acting on the urge to take a crack at a few things like Communism and the Roman Church which I impatiently think are getting to big for their boots; and it is not a novelist's job to take cracks at things, and the mistaken attempt to do so accounts for practically every bad book by a good man."[3]

On 16 January 1949 he reported to his mother that he had decided to drop "Fast Falls the Eventide." "This is partly because what I have done seems to me not good enough and partly because that subconscious of mine, apparently propitiated, suddenly handed me another derived out of a case I had casually watched in court at Doylestown and (such inconstancy is hard to explain) I suddenly found myself wanting to do it more than the other. I had thought of calling it By Love Possessed,* which will serve for the moment. At any rate, it would be perfectly straight and would allow me at least by implication to shoot my face off along some of the lines that I projected in the other. It amounts to a lawyer in middle life conducting as a favor to his secretary, an action for desertion & non-support against the husband of the secretary's sister; and I am, as I say, much indebted to an unfortunate Bucks County couple named Warren who bared their troubles on the stand some weeks ago.† They weren't exactly the troubles I wanted but by a singularly eloquent despair and bewilderment in expressing them they showed me what I did want." Though he had abandoned the didactic "Fast Falls the Eventide," Cozzens retained a preceptive impulse: ". . . I mean to say something about the cardinal human

---

* Cozzens recalled this phrase from Jonathan Swift but couldn't cite the passage. Prof. Irvin Ehrenpreis suggests that the probable source is: "With friendship and esteem possessed, / I never admitted love a quest" ("To Stella, Who Collected and Transcribed His Poems," ll. 13–14).

† Docket of Domestic Relations Office, Court of Common Pleas of Bucks County, 4 January 1949. Commonwealth of Pennsylvania vs. John Warren: desertion and non-support.

need to do what you want to, at any cost to yourself or to other people; and however indirectly or circuitously, however unreasonably or unwisely, which is what I think is meant by love or being possessed by it."[4]

By October 1949 Cozzens had written the opening paragraph describing the Brocton Courthouse twenty-five times. This seems to be an intermediate version:

All Tuesday morning, in a gloom more like evening than morning, the November rain continued. It came down so hard that a low spray was raised over the pavement of Court Street and the fast run-off of cold water nearly filled the gutters. Across Court Street, behind veil on veil of rain, the white marble shape of the Brocton County Court House loomed dull in its stand of big trees. Higher than the tree tops stripped of leaves the court house roof carried a dome of no great size. The dome, on its summit, carried an effigy: Justice. Wet stone sword and the balances grasped in stone hands, this elevated figure looked east with blindfolded eyes. Intermittently the bad day hid it from sight. Smokes of vapor descended. Forlorn drifts of mist trailed low in passing and then the entire dome would disappear for minutes at a time.[5]

The published version begins Chapter Three of *By Love Possessed*:

The massed foliage of those big trees more than half hid the marble-cased courthouse building, classic in conception, but in execution falsely elaborated. Above the treetops, the structure raised, clear against the sky's hot haze, a small dome. The dome was surmounted by a pillared cupola in whose round base four faces of the courthouse clock were set. Crowning the cupola, stiffly poised on the summit, stood a bronze effigy—Justice. The copper carbonates of time had turned this effigy greenish-blue. The epicene figure's verdigrised hands held the verdigrised sword and balance. The verdigrised head stared south with blindfolded eyes. From the cupola's base now issued a mighty bong, whose power of sound could carry everywhere in the not-very-large borough of Brocton. Given grave deliberation by the full second's pause, another bong followed; and another; and another [p.54].

In 1951 the courthouse opening was replaced by a pedantic declaration of the theme conveyed through Arthur Winner's thoughts ("subject to change without notice, and as likely as not omission altogether"):

Love, Arthur Winner thought, might come to this. By means of love the heart defeated the head. Love was the heart's freedom from the bounds of thought. Love set aside the bitter findings of experience. Love could know for a fact what was not a fact; love, untroubled, believed the unbelievable; love wished, and made it so. Realities assailed in vain love's unrealities. They might as well wound the loud winds, kill the still closing waters—

Was this too much to say? No, Arthur Winner thought, it was not too much to say! His first concern when he entered the bare room with bright lights that Joe Harbison used for his office as Justice of the Peace had been to give Helen Detweiler a look of encouragement or reassurance. . . .[6]

Although Cozzens had predicted that *By Love Possessed* would be published in 1952, it did not appear until 1957.

Cozzens began corresponding with Harcourt, Brace editor Robert Giroux in 1948 about problems of Roman doctrine and canon law. Giroux, a Catholic but by no means an expert, sought the help of priests and provided readings lists. Cozzens's study of Catholicism resulted in Julius Penrose's disquisitions on the Church; but much of the research on particular aspects of Catholic practice was not used—for example, the correct service for the display of a holy relic. In 1950 he sent Giroux a prospectus for his novel.

It has to do, I'm afraid at length, with a lawyer no longer young who finds his personal life in crisis (but you know me; I'll have it so hedged and qualified that the salesmen, poor willing brutes, won't hardly know it's a crisis and will just have to say as usual it's Significant) arising out of a conflict between works of human thinking and the works of human feeling. It has long been my opinion that in the affairs of life the Law's rational design to have the facts and to prevent more from being made of them than unassisted reason makes is in flat opposition to the usually triumphant emotional wish (sometimes merely sentimental; sometimes gravely religious) to do down mere 'facts' and to rise over them by a different logic where feeling counts as higher knowing.

I have to acknowledge that I work under a limitation here in that such Knowing is utterly beyond me; yet I think it is true when I say I have no hostile feelings and no wish to deride what I do not understand; on the contrary, seeing it as I see it, I find it affecting—an example of the general wistful human persistence in make-believe. Naturally I will deal only with what I am able to know, which is the cold dismay or unhappy amazement which those whose minds can get no higher than the Law's level of common sense must find themselves experiencing when they come up against the goings-on whose origin is spiritual—specifically, my lawyer's difficulty in imagining what can possess his wife in slowly going

Catholic. I don't see this as matter to handle with theological arguments or expository conversations on doctrine or discipline, which puts me to the slightly awkward technical necessity of having his wife away when the book opens and still away when it ends. I mean to make what points I can in action—not, I hope I needn't say, the acting-out of tracts or theses, but in my man's relation to a young lawyer son, to another who died in the war, and to a considerably younger daughter, which I will try to illuminate as well as I can by selected developments in the legal cases in which he is at the moment professionally engaged.[7]

After more than two years of writing, in April 1951 he was still wrestling with the almost involuntary desire to instruct the reader: ". . . I have here too damn much material and too many characters—in my recent reconsiderations I found I had twenty six set up for fairly full treatment. Ten would sink any book. In short, I can't tell all about all these people; and also I can't tell *all* about the law, and Roman theology, and what the medical profession is now calling geriatrics or people getting older and not liking it, and sex, and sociology, topped off with my own perennial or only philosophy which seems to be that this is a pretty bad state of affairs with no hope and no sense in it; but still it best becomes a person to keep doing what he can as long as he can."[8]

As he worked on *By Love Possessed,* Cozzens found it got harder to write; he described his method as "taking things that appear simple and reducing them to their essential complexity."[9] By the end of 1951 he had made "at least nine fairly full scale beginnings."[10] Thousands of pages survive from the working drafts of *By Love Possessed,* but they are pages that Cozzens neglected to throw away. He did not attempt to preserve his working drafts systematically. More pages were probably discarded than were saved, and there is no extant complete draft before the final setting typescript. It is therefore impossible to determine how many drafts were written—or even if there were complete drafts—although some surviving episodes were rewritten six or seven times.

In what appears to be the earliest preserved version of the plot, Arthur Winner's wife, Clarissa, is undergoing conversion to Catholicism; Julius Penrose and old Noah Tuttle are members of the Brocton Bar, but not Winner's partners. One opening sequence is Winner's dream about Dunky, which was salvaged for pages 503–505 of the published novel.*

---

*Four draft pages are facsimiled in Richard Ludwig's "A Reading of the James Gould Cozzens Manuscripts," *Princeton University Library Chronicle,* XIX (Autumn 1957), 1–14.

A revised carbon copy for draft sections II–V (pp. 12 –145) represents an intermediate stage of plot evolution. Here Arthur Winner, of Orcutt & Winner, is at the office of Magistrate Joe Harbison on Halloween to represent Ralph Detweiler, his secretary's brother, charged with having raped Veronica Amram. Also present are Helen Detweiler, Joanie Meyer (Ralph's fiancée), Assistant District Attorney Milton Hyman, and Julius Penrose. Penrose is not Winner's partner, nor is he crippled; he is there waiting to attend a meeting with Winner. After a legal wrangle with Hyman, Winner arranges bail for Ralph. Then Penrose and Winner talk outside the courthouse. Their conversation introduces many of the plot elements and provides background for the major characters. Winner is married to Clarissa, presumably his first wife. They have a teen-age daughter, Ann, and a son, Lawrence, just out of law school, who is joining Winner's firm; his son Warren was killed in a wartime plane crash. Penrose is married to Marjorie, by whom he has two children, Priscilla and Stuart. A widower at the time, Penrose had married Marjorie after representing her in a divorce action. His son by his first marriage is a Communist. Penrose is dismayed because Marjorie is planning to join the Catholic Church. He dislikes Catholics and Jews and resents the political power of what he regards as foreign elements. Although Penrose misses the hard brilliance of the Julius Penrose in the published novel, he discourses learnedly on Catholic doctrine. Noah Tuttle—who does not appear in this section—is described as a lawyer going senile, with whom Winner and Penrose are engaged in the Simon Mc-Conkey Estate. Other characters introduced or mentioned are Police Chief Bernie Breck, District Attorney Charles Kovacs (who wants to be a judge), State Senator J. Jerome Brophy, Tipstaff Eph McKim (who talks about the Dummer case), and lawyers Polhemus and Weintraub.

The working papers for *By Love Possessed* include notes for possible plot lines, which show Cozzens's attempts to tie up the strands of action. After forming the firm of Tuttle, Winner & Penrose, Cozzens was undecided as to which partner would be the peculator, but he planned to connect the discovery of the misappropriation with Ralph Detweiler's troubles.

I. R's CASE
Winner Tuttle & Winner
a) R is Helen D's brother—NT was George D's trustee—he was the one who gave Helen her job—his handling trusts is thus in early—
b) R is the bankers son
c) R is the son of Mrs. X, NT's secretary
d) R is NT's nephew—son of a young sister he hadn't spoken to for years because of her marriage etc —'estranged' daughter's son
(she insisted on marrying someone he disapproved of—the [man's] not a gentleman etc—this continuing trait of character in Noah—It is AW who feels something must be done for the boy (The daughter is dead?)
e) R. is the Rector's son
f) R. Marjorie's son by her first marriage—perhaps inherited a touch of his father's 'mental condition'?
g) R son of a woman, now dead, who used to be NT's secretary for years—frightened, he goes to NT. Neither AW nor JP can tell why they should mess into it—NT protests he isn't strong enough to take the thing to trial, do they want to kill him?

III   THE EMBEZZLEMENT
A. *BY NOAH TUTTLE*
a) The old man, his judgment and faculties ruined, has simply got himself into a stupid jam—but it will cost AW all he has because of his partnership liability—the old fool doesn't even know what he's done with it.

B. *BY JULIUS PENROSE*
a) Marjorie's first husband had advanced Marjorie's father $25,000— at the divorce, her problem was to pay this back—JP 'in order to marry her' makes this possible by some expert embezzlement ['This Ruinous Woman'
a) he keeps shifting it around from account to account.
b) he took it outright from the Orcutt Trust, part of Christ Church's endowment and has simply paid the interest ever since [now the new rector wants to put the fund into the Diocesan thing

> and he has to find the money
> [My dear Arthur, I simply haven't got
> it. I think you'd better persuade the
> rector to leave matters as they are

C. *BY ARTHUR WINNER*
  A) the expenses of his new marriage?—money to Lawrence?—same settlements he had made for Warren?

IV THE FIRM
  A. *Tuttle, Penrose & Winner*
    a) NT thinks they have to take R's case—he is not up to it personally, at his age; but JP or AW must—
    b) *R's case precipitates the discovery of the embezzlement*
        (1) JP says they ought not to mess into it, and so angers NT who says he will take it himself—he has long ago found out about JP's embezzlement—now he'll use the knowledge—
        ② R's father (the banker) wants to buy R out of it: because they refuse, he is out to get JP and so digs up the facts
        ③ R's parents feel they'll have to leave Brocton—this will mean that JP must produce the funds he no longer has
    c) *NT took the money*—JP to AW: do you wish to make it good? It will be mainly up to you. I have almost nothing (he has been paying off that debt of Marjorie's, unknown to AW—I think you better cover for him as long as you can [11]

At the end of 1952 Cozzens reported to his mother: ". . . I think I've resolved the conflict that made me my long trouble—I could neither resist the temptation to preach, nor put down the more wholesome instinct that kept stopping me with advices that no, that would not do. This—I don't exaggerate—was gone through fully fifty times while I stubbornly persisted in imagining that I only needed to be more artful about it. . . . It is not practicable to tell my story in any efficient way if I have to lecture the reader, as he goes, on what I feel he may not have got straight about love, human virtue, religious impulse, and indeed life in general. I will recount the goings-on, give him an unobtrusive hint or two about what he ought to think (i.e., what I think), and the rest he'll have to figure out for himself." [12]

In 1948 a consortium of scholars had produced the three-volume *Literary History of the United States,* intended as a standard reference work. Nowhere was Cozzens mentioned. However, the Pulitzer Prize had generated interest in the work of this "overlooked novelist." Stanley Edgar Hyman in 1947 designated *Castaway* "My Favorite Forgotten Book."* In his 1949 essay "James Gould Cozzens and the Art of the Possible" Hyman identified him as "the novelist of [the] American White Protestant middle class" and claimed that Cozzens's most important theme is "the discovery of a moral principle by suffering on its behalf."[14] Writing after *The Just and the Unjust* and *Guard of Honor,* Hyman complained that the longer novels sprawl and that, with the exception of *Castaway,* Cozzens had not yet written a first-rate novel. Wrongheaded as this essay was, it called attention to Cozzens because Hyman's credentials were so good. By fall 1950 Cozzens reported to his mother that "there is a certain steady movement that I get accounts of from Sylvia of the word-of-mouth business. It is mostly a matter of fashion-in-opinion; but it is running my way. . . ."[15] When J. B. Priestley was interviewed by the *New York Times* in 1951 he paid tribute to Cozzens as an "unfashionably good" novelist.[16] Respectful critical judgments were published by Frederick Bracher, Granville Hicks, Louis Coxe, and Orville Prescott in the early fifties.† In December 1956 *The Just and the Unjust* was presented on the "Kraft Television Theatre."

Cozzens's six Harcourt, Brace novels had sold 401,576 hardcover copies (including Book-of-the-Month Club copies) in the United States by 1950. Between 1950 and 1956 Harcourt, Brace reprinted *The Just and the Unjust, Ask Me Tomorrow,* and *The Last Adam* in its Harbrace Modern Classics series. The most successful republication was the 1956 Modern Library paperback edition combining *S.S. San Pedro* with *Castaway,* which sold more than 35,000 copies. The way was being prepared for the reception of *By Love Possessed.*

The twenty-fifth reunion of the Class of 1926 brought Cozzens to Harvard's attention. He was awarded an honorary Phi Beta Kappa key in 1951, although he declined to attend the ceremony. At the June 1952 Harvard commencement Cozzens received an

---

*". . . a social allegory: of the corruption of human relations by property relations, of freedom and personality gained in our society only through murder. . . . It is, equally a psychoanalytic fable of the repression of Id by Ego and the consequent punishment by Super-Ego; or a religious fable of sin and expiation; or even an Evolutionary fable of the development of man."[13]

†The first dissertation was James A. Parrish, Jr., "James Gould Cozzens: A Critical Analysis" (Florida State University, 1955).

Harvard University, June 1952: Cozzens, standing, second from right; Robert A. Lovett, sitting, third from left

honorary doctor of letters degree. The citation read: "A novelist who analyzes the professions: lawyer, doctor, soldier stand sympathetically portrayed by his brilliant pen." Although he said that he accepted the degree mainly to please his mother—who did not attend the commencement—Cozzens was gratified by his alma mater's recognition. Harvard had not played as great a part in shaping him as had Kent, but he retained a deep respect for the academic traditions of the university. Cozzens was in good company; his fellow degree recipients included John Foster Dulles and Robert A. Lovett, his former boss at the Pentagon. But he was bitterly chagrined to find that another doctor of letters degree was awarded to novelist Walter D. Edmonds, '26. Cozzens did not know Edmonds, but he felt that his own work was degraded by being equated with *Rome Haul* and *Drums Along the Mohawk*. When Edward Newhouse phoned to congratulate him, an obviously tight Cozzens said that being paired with Edmonds was condign punishment for his vanity. Nonetheless, Harvard's recognition stimulated his interest in the university. Insofar as his temperament permitted, he became a loyal alumnus.

While Cozzens worked on *By Love Possessed*, he resumed his custom of attending trials at the Bucks County Courthouse, feeling that courtroom observation tempered his isolation: ". . . you can indeed learn a lot about life and observe a lot of people in what is probably their most revealing state—trouble." [17] The Doylestown lawyers were impressed by his ability to sit through boring cases in the Domestic Relations Court with unflagging attention, as well as by the apparent pleasure he took in reading Wigmore and other textbooks in the law library. Cozzens's renewed examination of the legal process resulted in "Notes on a Difficulty of Law By One Unlearned in It" for the November 1951 *Bucks County Law Reporter*. Pondering the rules of evidence, he discussed inconsistencies in the law's attitude toward jurors—that they are not regarded as able to determine what is evidence, but are wise in their verdict. [18] On his court days he usually lunched at the Doylestown Inn, where he became friendly with Luise Porter, whose family owned it. Cozzens ate at the bar with his right side against the wall, and Mrs. Porter protected his left flank from unwanted conversation. His invariable lunch was a rare roast beef sandwich with fresh horseradish and a Beefeater (sometimes two) martini.

After the involuntary camaraderie of the Air Force, Cozzens became increasingly confirmed in his reclusiveness. Except on court days, the only person he saw until Bernice returned from New York was the housekeeper. He cultivated his misanthropic stance, though not without self-directed irony. When, for instance, his mother chided him for claiming that satisfactions such as provided by his well-waxed curly-maple table were "the only true and lasting ones in this life," he elaborated: "I mean that it's my accumulating observation that people who depend on people, though they have their emotional excitements and satisfactions, have more usually, and always in the end, griefs and disappointments that far overbalance; and that those who set themselves objectives or have ambitions will come short of them, or just as unhappily, attain them and see how little they were worth; and, in short, you should as far as possible put your faith in and get your pleasures from material things, the simpler the better. I suspect that well-adjusted people have always known this and done it without discussion. . . ." [19] The self-mocking note is clear, but the role became increasingly comfortable.

Cozzens made use of the Princeton University Library for his research and relied upon the reference librarian, Malcolm Young; but he formed no acquaintances among the faculty. When Professor Carlos Baker invited him to meet with a class that was studying a Cozzens novel in 1953, he declined, explaining that he didn't know how to talk about his work: "in writing a book most novelists who can be considered seriously don't really know what they are doing, and they don't really know how they do it—the process isn't one they use; it uses them."[20]

Bertha Wood Cozzens died of cancer in April 1953. Determined to leave her money in an irrevocable trust for her son, she had lived frugally to preserve her capital. Cozzens had to persuade her to break the trust to pay medical bills, because otherwise he would have had to mortgage Carrs Farm. He later observed in his notebooks: "at any rate, my mother died with every comfort money could provide."[21]

In 1956 the Kent School marked the birthday of Father Sill, who had died in 1952, with a dinner at the Waldorf-Astoria in New York. Cozzens, who did not attend, wrote for the program "FHS: A Faith that Did Not Fail," in which he paid tribute to Pater's "intuitive certainty" but obliquely indicated that the school had changed: "Its author and its instrument, could Pater ever have doubted—should anyone have doubted?—that the superintendent spirit still lived, which, living, informing, guiding, only waiting to draw on its own, would take care that what was Kent's would know Kent's face?"[22]

At the time *By Love Possessed* was delivered to Harcourt, Brace, in February 1957, Robert Giroux had left the firm. Cozzens's new editor was Denver Lindley, but there was little for him to do beyond querying word usage and punctuation. (With his acquiescence, the copy editors overruled Cozzens's custom of using semicolons to introduce dialogue.) The real editing had been done by Bernice. Despite his aloofness toward editorial collaboration, Cozzens maintained cordial relations with his editors. He made a point of being a "good-boy" author and did not intrude in the publishing process. His agent ran interference. When Cozzens saw the jacket flap copy for *By Love Possessed,* he recommended that the theme be more clearly stated and tried his hand at it: "He ends face to face with the fact of this life—the underlying, everlasting opposition of thinking and feeling, with life's simple disaster of passion and reason, self-division's cause."[23] His copy was rejected.

By Love Possessed focuses on forty-nine hours—3:00 P.M. Friday to 4:00 P.M. Sunday—in the life of Arthur Winner, Jr., a fifty-four-year-old lawyer in the Delaware Valley town of Brocton. (Cozzens was fifty-four when the novel was published.) At the opening of the novel Arthur Winner—Cozzens always refers to him by his full name—contemplates an antique French clock with its tableau of a shepherd peeping at a naked maid while Cupid aims an arrow at him, captioned *omnia vincit amor,* love conquers all. Over the next three days he is involved in a complexity of problems resulting from the many varieties of love (altruism; marital, parental, and filial devotion; lust; religion; friendship). The son of a "man of reason," he regards the passions as subverting order. No one is impervious to some form of passion, but Arthur Winner holds that the reasoning man controls—usually—emotions. Reason—sometimes—ripens with experience: "youth's a kind of infirmity" (p. 6). But reason is limited. His partner, Julius Penrose, echoes Fulke Greville: "Passion and reason, self-division's cause!" (p. 547).*

This formula has proved efficacious for Arthur Winner. At fifty-four he is prosperous and respected—in every way a pillar of his profession and of the community. His public esteem is capped by a happy second marriage to a sensible and devoted younger woman. In keeping with his sense of sagesse oblige, he accepts his duty to help the unfortunate. His secretary, Helen Detweiler, has neurotically sacrificed her life to her weakling brother, and she turns to Arthur Winner when Ralph is charged with rape. Marjorie Penrose, the unhappy wife of his partner and closest friend, intends to convert to Catholicism; she asks Episcopalian Arthur Winner to intercede with Julius, who is dismayed by the Roman Church.

Arthur Winner is the central figure in the novel, but Julius Penrose is the dominant intelligence. A brilliant man crippled by polio in his middle years, he expresses scathing contempt for the casualties of unreason and is appalled by the spectacle of human distress: "People, I think, are to be pitied!" (p. 238). Yet Penrose is the most steadfast lover in the novel. While handling Marjorie's divorce from her first husband, he had fallen in love with his alcoholic, latently nymphomaniacal client and compelled her to marry him. When he learns that Arthur Winner has cuckolded him, he is able to understand and forgive the betrayal.

---

*From *Mustapha:* "What meaneth nature by these diverse law? / Passion and reason self-division cause." These lines provided the epigraph for Aldous Huxley's *Point Counter Point,* a book much admired by Cozzens.

At the end of the novel, after Helen Detweiler has committed suicide because of her brother's troubles, Arthur Winner discovers that his senior partner, Noah Tuttle, a paragon of rectitude, has for years been juggling trust funds to conceal a $200,000 embezzlement he made to save investors in a bankrupt trolley line. Another emotional act by another man of reason. Tuttle's behavior is partly attributable to his habit of being right: he perhaps could not tolerate the disclosure that he had committed funds under his trusteeship to a doomed investment. As Arthur Winner sits in his office on Sunday afternoon contemplating the ruin that will attend the exposure of Tuttle—"I am a man alone"—Penrose arrives. He has known about Tuttle's peculations for years and urges Arthur Winner to give Tuttle time to repay his borrowings, as he has been gradually doing. Arthur Winner insists that the only thing to do is the lawful thing: make a full disclosure and accept the consequences. Even though Penrose is legally exempt from guilt because the embezzlement occurred before he joined the firm, he promises that he will demand a share of the guilt and asks Arthur Winner not to ruin him. When Arthur Winner rebukes him for concealing Tuttle's misappropriations from him, Penrose obliquely reveals that he had known about the adultery with Marjorie and has been grateful for the concealment. "If you knew of something that you believed I didn't know, and that you thought it better I should not know, I'm persuaded you'd do as much for me—try every way to keep it from me. . . . Let me be more explicit. I'm persuaded, Arthur, that you *have* done as much for me. And, if unknown to you, I've always thanked you for it" (p. 563). Again, the coldly rational Julius Penrose reveals his capacity for love. Or, perhaps, he is demonstrating the force of his intelligence. Heartened by Penrose's determination to see them through, Arthur Winner formulates a stoic confrontation of his troubles—tempered by Cozzens's rhetorical irony.

Victory is not in reaching certainties or solving mysteries; victory is in making do with uncertainties, in supporting mysteries. Yes, Arthur Winner thought, I must be reasonable. . . . *The question is: What's now the reasonable thing to do?* Is that hollow friend, myself, in spite of me to whine: *I would; but I can't, I dare not, I don't know how?* Never; not ever! (Never say never? Well, then; not for now!) This load, this lading, this burden—the need was only strength. Roused, rousing, he thought: I have the strength, the strength to, to—to endure more miseries and greater far, than my weakhearted enemies dare offer! [pp. 569–70].

Cozzens conveys his understanding of life through the contrapuntal structure of his fiction. Meaning is enforced by organization as well as by style. In *By Love Possessed* Judge Dealey ("I'd really like to be nicer to more people—the stupid bastards!" [p. 439]) delineates a key point and at the same time explicates the novel's structural rationale:

"But, how about what's going to happen? By any chance, could *that* be all over now, too?"

". . . I just notice how often, afterward, you think: If only I'd done this, if only I'd known that! . . . Make you think of anything? *Quaere:* Could you ever have changed what's going to happen? You know this much: Whatever happens, happens because a lot of other things have happened already. When it gets to where you come in—well, it's bound to be pretty late in the day. Things have been fixing for whatever this is for a long time; and that includes you—whether you know it or not, what you're going to do or not do has been fixing for a long time, too. Freedom, I read at college, is the knowledge of necessity" [p. 118].

Whatever happens, happens because a lot of other things have happened already. The structure of *By Love Possessed* is a solution to fiction's endeavor to represent the passage of time and to synchronize simultaneous action. As the epigraph from Shakespeare announces, the novel deals with time and therefore with mortality. The clock is always running; the novel is peppered by time signals.

> Thereby to see the minutes how they run—
> How many make the hour full complete,
> How many hours bring about the day,
> How many days will finish up the year,
> How many years a mortal man may live.
>
> —*Henry VI**

In addition to their general meaning, in the context of the play these lines have a particular application to Arthur Winner. On the battlefield Shakespeare's king longs for the simple, ordered life of a shepherd. So is Arthur Winner almost overwhelmed by his problems, but he stoically confronts them.

The time frame of *By Love Possessed* is not restricted to the 2,940 minutes ticked off by the *omnia vincit amor* clock, which strikes at

---

*The part titles are stage directions from Shakespeare. "Drums Afar Off" (*Coriolanus*) and "A Noise of Hunters Heard" (*The Tempest*) were "picked for sound rather than any special implication."[24] "Within the Tent of Brutus" (*Julius Caesar*) recalls the confrontation between Cassius and Brutus before battle.

the opening and close of the novel. Concerned with the pastness of the present, Cozzens suspends time by building long memory flashbacks into Arthur Winner's ratiocination. The systematic use of flashbacks had begun in *Guard of Honor;* they are much more elaborately orchestrated in *By Love Possessed* to span more than fifty years in forty-nine hours of present time.

Cozzens's strategy in *By Love Possessed*—as in *Guard of Honor*—was to conflate causes and effects as perceived by an intelligent participating observer in a controlled period of time. The view of behavior thereby presented is a species of determinism; but in addition to the familiar complex of environmental and hereditary influences, Cozzens insists on the factor of luck, which often subsumes the other forces. In 1976 he observed, "The longer I watch men and life, the surer I get that success whenever more than minor comes of luck alone. By comparison, no principles, ideas, goals and standards of conduct matter much in an achieving of it."[25] Since this statement was prepared for the Bicentennial Edition of *Who's Who in America,* it was partly intended as a deflating message to his eminent fellow biographees; but it constitutes his valediction forbidding complacency in high place. For Cozzens luck begins at birth. Luck is his form of predestination. As Penrose observes: "What happens to people is simply what was always going to happen to them" (p. 545). Most people are simply born out of luck. But a man is to be judged by what he does with his luck.

Because Cozzens insists on the hierarchical nature of society—a stratification based on character, ability, education, intelligence, and opportunity—he has been variously labeled a snob, an aristocrat, or a reactionary. Egalitarian-minded critics have objected to his equation of merit with breeding and education. (Cozzens never concerns himself with great wealth; his aristocracy is an upper-middle-class aristocracy, in which vocation and character count more than money.) His admirable figures are men who have accepted the duties of their abilities and positions. They are what they do and how well they do it. Free will is a delusion; but it is necessary to behave as though people are responsible for their conduct. When his mother asked him about Paul de Kruif's *The Male Hormone* in 1945, Cozzens replied: ". . . a person's 'character' is humiliatingly bound up with bio-chemical factors, but I don't know that it changes anything. . . . Presumably Jesus, or even D given normal sex impulses, would be a very different character, but deKruif dosing himself in his old age with a few ounces of this or that is a long way from the accumulated forces of a hundred generations of inheritance; and, in short, it is all interesting rather than important. A person may not be to blame for what he is; but it is just as much his 'fault' as it ever was if he does not come up to whatever the local or contemporary standard of proper behaviour may be."[26] Thus Arthur Winner's contempt for the effeminate church organist: "Here was Elmer Abbott, an Orcutt, a well-off man (with all that meant in the way of perfect freedom to quit himself like a man) so tame, so pridelessly relieved at the withdrawal of a false charge, at the permission to continue his namby-pamby round, keep his piffling post, his unpaid job's clung-to prerogative of inflicting on a captive audience his mediocre music, that he cried!" (p. 461). By contrast, there is Garret Hughes, the scrupulously honest and poor young assistant district attorney: "No Lower Makepeace Hughes ever needed watching. For five generations the word of any of them had been as good as his bond; and in that time, to none of them attached a known shame or scandal" (p. 477).

Under the category of sentiment or unreason in *By Love Possessed,* Cozzens placed most forms of liberalism as well as religion. The choicest statements of contempt for these views are made by Julius Penrose: "Not only may each bumptious Catholic freely rate and abuse me if I reflect in the least on his faith; but each self-pitying Jew, each sulking Negro, need only holler that he's caught me not loving him as much as he loves himself, and a rabble of professional friends of man, social-worker liberals, and practitioners of universal brotherhood—the whole national horde of nuts and queers—will come at a run to hang me by the neck until I learn to love" (p. 217). Penrose's animadversions are consistent with his character; but Cozzens clearly relished writing for him and shared many of his judgments. Nevertheless, much of Penrose's rhetoric is self-derisive—a point missed by infuriated readers, despite Cozzens's clear signals: "The well-known habit of the finished phrases, in their level precision almost rehearsed-sounding, the familiar deliberately mincing tones that mocked themselves with their own affectation" (p. 563). In addition to Penrose's learned disquisitions on Catholicism—which he feels demeans its practitioners by depriving them of freedom and dignity—Cozzens's treatment of Polly Pratt, the gushing proselytizer, further angered Catholics. Readers also detected anti-Semitism and racial intolerance. Mr. Woolf, the Jewish convert to Episcopalianism, is shown to be pushy: "Did you forget at your peril the ancient grudge that

might be fed if Mr. Woolf could catch you once upon the hip?"
(p. 63). Yet Woolf is right in challenging Noah Tuttle's irregular
accounts and comes perilously close to exposing him. Alfred Revere, the Negro sexton at Christ Church, is commended for his
dignity in taking communion last so that the sacrament would not
be unpalatable for the white members of the congregation. The
ironies of Cozzens's comment on Revere could be missed only by
those determined to miss it.

What self-respect could that man have who tried to intrude where, he
saw at a glance, he did not belong; who was so lacking in delicacy and
decency, in all proper pride, that he would enter where he was not invited, that he would persist in going where no one welcomed him and
no one wanted him? For the sexton of Christ Church to be a communi-
cant was proper, was needful; but at celebrations of Holy Communion,
Paul then, and Alfred now, with the delicacy, the politeness self-respect
required of them came last to the altar rail. The good, the just, man had
consideration for others. By delaying, he took care that members of the
congregation need never hesitate to receive the blood of Our Lord Jesus
Christ because a cup from which a Negro had drunk contained it [pp.
517–18].

Cozzens was unprepared for the vehemence of the charges of
intolerance brought against *By Love Possessed*. It did him no good
to explain that he had treated individuals, not populations. The
world outside Carrs Farm, and its literature, had changed more
than he realized during the twelve years since his discharge from
the Air Force.* By the standards of 1957 he was bigoted, for he
had the presuppositional biases of his background.

Although Cozzens always insisted that he advocated no political
position in his fiction, he was an apolitical conservative. In 1963 he
noted these definitions:

Conservatism is an attitude of mind of those whose temperament, situation, or both, can keep them feeling that, viewed realistically, society as
it has been gives them in this life quite as much as they deserve, all they
have a right to. Liberalism is the attitude of those whose temperament
and situation can make them take the view, usually (at least to my mind)
most unrealistic, that they somehow deserve, have every right to, a whole
lot more than society as it has been will ever get to give them. In the
case of both, I'm afraid I regard the Erecting of any Standards or the

---

* James Baldwin's *Giovanni's Room* and Allen Ginsburg's *Howl* were published in 1956; Jack
Kerouac's *On the Road* in 1957.

Professing of any High Purpose (even though often done with a sincerity that needn't be doubted) as so much eyewash or so much hogwash.[27]

Cozzens believed in hierarchies and subordination; he respected institutions and traditions; and he was at best indifferent to social amelioration. He accepted original sin, metaphorically if not literally, and therefore regarded all notions of human perfectability as the delusions of weak brains or unbalanced nervous systems. The rebels so dear to many twentieth-century novelists are treated as menaces to. order—opportunists or soreheads—who impede the efforts of serious men. His "burden of guilt" was his duty to his genius. The form of "relevance" that concerned him was the observable truth about how people behaved and, when possible, why.

Another aspect of *By Love Possessed* that attracted attention was Cozzens's objective treatment of sex. Some reviewers felt compelled to warn prospective readers not to leave the book around for the young to see. Considerable space is given to sexual matters in the novel, but it would require an unusual child to be stimulated by Cozzens's treatment of it.* The most passionate scene in the novel occurs when Arthur and Clarissa Winner engage in intercourse.

His as much as hers, the supple and undulous back hollowing at the pull of his hands to a compliant curve; his as much as hers, her occupied participative hips, her obediently divided embracing knees, her parts in moist manipulative reception. Then, hers as much as his, the breath got hastily in common; the thumping, one or another, of the hurried two hearts, the mutual heat of pumped bloods, the start of their uniting sweats. Grown, growing, gaining scope, hers then no less than his, the thoroughgoing, deepening, widening work of their connection; and his then no less than hers, the tempo slowed in concert to engineer a tremulous joint containment and continuance. Then, then, caution gone, compulsion in control, his—and hers, as well!—the pace unreined, raised, redoubled, all measurable measure lost. And, the incontinent instant brought to pass, no sooner his the very article, his uttermost, the stand-and-deliver of the undone flesh, the tottered senses' outgiving of astoundment, than—put beside themselves, hit at their secret quick, provoked by that sudden touch beyond any bearing—the deep muscle groups, come to their vertex, were in a flash convulsed; in spasms unstayably succeeding

*The word *fuck* appears once in the Harcourt, Brace text, at 507.13, and was excised from the Book-of-the-Month Club printings.

spasms, contracting on contraction on contraction—hers! Hers, too; hers, hers, hers![p. 265].*

Cozzens explained: "The reason for that sex scene in the new book is simply this: Hemingway had said that there is nothing new you can say about the sex act. I thought, 'Goddammit, I'll see if I can do it.' I thought: 'You son of a bitch, I can write better than you can, and I'll do it.' Well, I won't do it again. I've covered it as well as I could."[28] The sleeping-bag scenes in *For Whom the Bell Tolls* were meant to be arousing, but Cozzens's scene is not.†

In keeping with the intelligence of his two main characters and with the complexity of their thought processes, Cozzens elevated the style of *By Love Possessed* to a qualifying, meditative, masculine dignity. His writing had evolved from the unadorned style of the thirties; it became a recognizable style in contravention to Cozzens's earlier pronouncements that "it is not the business of style to attract attention."[29] He responded to Charles W. Phillips, a Unitarian minister who had written a lecture and a sermon on him: "I was particularly, I guess, touched—when you constituted yourself what is as far as I know a critical minority of one by apparently seeing without trouble that the 'complications' in certain paragraphs of considering or reflecting were indeed a studied attempt to so reproduce or simulate the process of thought that the reader would go through it instead of just hearing about it."[31] In 1958 Cozzens explained to Frederick Bracher, who was writing a critical book on him:

At any rate, I try hard to fit the wording, the syntax and the structure to the material, so that the manner will vary as the matter varies . . . on pp 404, 405 [Arthur Winner's initial sexual encounter with Marjorie Penrose], my idea was that I'd try to do more than just tell the reader; by breaking up the construction and disarranging the thought I hoped I could bring him, you might say, inside the shaken frightened mind. If only two people got it, that's that. It doesn't work. Similarly, I must ask myself if certain elaborate passages managed what I meant them to manage. The charge, stated or implied, that I look up hard words to impress

---

Time's misleading comment on this passage: "The hour of that art [of love] which the couple share in Cozzens' pages has not been paralleled for clinical candor since Edmund Wilson singed the censors with *Memoirs of Hecate County*."

†Dorothy Parker's wisecrack in *Esquire* about Arthur Winner's lack of passion achieved a certain currency: "He has a child [in fact, three children] by his first wife—I imagine he swam over her . . ."[30]

the boobs I think I can answer by pointing out that normally no boob would so much as try to read beyond a first page of mine. Sometimes the long word will be the one right word and I don't scruple to use it— if the reader doesn't know it, it's time he learned; but such words, if taken as they come in the text, not collected from all over the book and bunched together as some critics bunched them, don't I think really indicate that I'm a lover of long words for their own sake. The elaborations, where I attempted them, were of course directed at the kind of reader I normally do have. With him, I can count on a good meeting of the minds. He is likely to find the sort of mild relish that I myself find in the notes of irony or even sarcasm that fancy or high-falutin phrasings of bold unfancy facts can strike. Still, I confess that tongue-in-cheek stuff comes pretty close to the weakness Fowler describes as Polysyllabic Humor, and I ought to watch it. I will. In this I-can-explain-everything vein I might as well add that studying comments on my alleged complexity of style one other thought came strongly to me. I don't doubt that I nod a normal number of times and really am involved and unclear; but I can't help suspecting that more often what my critic actually means is that he's become used to various loose contemporary styles where you only have to read every other word or even line to follow the as a rule inexact description of what's going on, and my unaccustomed severe demands on his attention irk him.[32]

Among the more noticeable characteristics of *By Love Possessed* are long sentences, frequent use of parenthetical constructions, rhetorical questions, elaborate parallelism, inclusion of unfamiliar words, unacknowledged quotations, ironically intended word choices, the habit of following a formal statement with a clarifying or deflating colloquialism, polyptoton (repetition of a word in different cases and inflections, as in "result's result"), inverted word order ("interest he felt"), double negatives,* the custom of defining a word or providing alternates for it, and periodic sentences in which the meaning becomes clear at the end.[33] The effect of these conjoined elements can be a deliberate density of expression in which Cozzens is mocking not only the content but his own writing as well.

Ah, how wise, how sure, how right, was that genius of the language whose instinct detected in the manifold manifestings of the amative appetite (however different-seeming; however apparently opposed) the one same urgent unreason, the one same eager let's-pretend, and so, wisely

---

* " 'Unlikely' isn't quite the same as 'not likely'; 'likely' is not quite the same as 'not unlikely'." See Appendix, Notebook 5.

consented, so, for convenience covenanted, to name all with one same name! Explaining, sweet unreason excused; excusing, sweet let's-pretend explained. The young heart, indentured (O wearisome conditions of humanity!) to reason, pined, starved on the bare bitter diet of thinking. One fine day, that heart (most hearts) must bolt. That heart would be off (could you blame it?) to Loveland, to feeling's feasts [p. 386].

There are sentences that may require rereading because of Cozzens's reliance on parenthetical structures:

The sweeping voiceless compliment, the silent, single-minded expression of so real a respect (surely real, being silent, being supposed private) could not but gratify; yet, to most people, pause must also be brought— pause, both on one's own behalf (to protest self-consciously: not so! would be a gross gawkishness; while the grave acceptance of no comment must amount to, be the next thing to, the nod complacent, to oneself proclaiming: *I am not as other men are, extortioners, unjust, adulterers . . .*); and on behalf of the single-minded complimenter (not a high look only, but a high aspiration, is apt to go before a fall) [p. 473].*

A tabulation of the novel's stylistic qualities is misleading, for it cites those characteristics that call attention to themselves. Much of the novel is written in Cozzens's straight, unadorned prose. If the critics who have described *By Love Possessed* as "baroque" meant that it was opulent for the sake of opulence, they failed to understand the style. Cozzens's effort with language aims at achieving greater precision of statement. Pondering a world in which nothing is certain, he uses language as a stay against disorder. The qualifying, parenthetical technique achieves the effect of a dignified groping for truth. He insisted that simple truth is not the whole truth in writing; "simple" is not the same as "explicit." But a caveat that Cozzens never really accepted is that irony of style requires readers capable of recognizing it. Never try to kid a dope, he warned himself.†

---

*This sentence is made more difficult by a superfluous semicolon after the second parenthesis.

†The success of *By Love Possessed* resulted in wordplay on its title ("By Syntax Obsessed") and parodies of its style. Cozzens was entertained by the 308-word "By Love Repossessed" in a beer ad: "Victor Summers stared, not unthoughtfully, at the purple-veined, screaming face of the bartender who held him—by the lapels—all desirous of an answer. The bartender said: 'For the last time, *what's yours, chum?*' Quietly, with dignity, Victor Summers' answer came. He said: 'My kind of beer is Schaefer!' " This ad was a sure measure of the novel's visibility.

It was easy for reviewers to compile lists of inkhorn terms in *By Love Possessed*: "presbyopic," "piacular," "autoptic," "temerarious," "longanimous," "volitations," "succussive," "furibund," "vilipending," "vulnerary." Again, these inventories provide a distorted impression. Such words do not appear with frequency. When confronted with lists of his difficult vocabulary Cozzens replied that these words were required for precise meaning. Like his use of unfamiliar words, Cozzens's custom of inserting unattributed phrases from the masters of English literature puzzled or offended readers who felt that he was withholding necessary aid or, worse, was guilty of snobbery. Although Cozzens had always acknowledged that it was the writer's job to please readers, he wrote *By Love Possessed* largely to please himself. As a young man he had expected to be petted and praised; in his fifties he didn't give a goddamn for Goodman Boob.

When the typescript of *By Love Possessed* was read at Harcourt, Brace, the house recognized that it was a major literary property as well as a potential best seller. William Jovanovich, who had become president of the firm in 1955, regarded it as a masterpiece and gave it his strong backing. Concerned that a Book-of-the-Month

Jacket for first printing of By Love Possessed

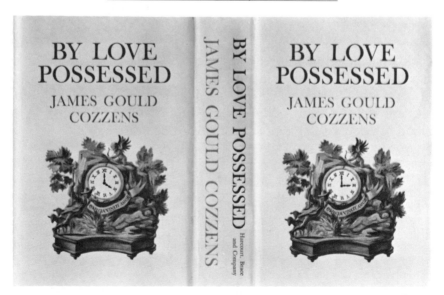

Club refusal would upset Cozzens, Bernice asked Carol Brandt to test the water with BOMC judge John P. Marquand before the novel was formally submitted. (Marquand was Carol's lover.) *By Love Possessed* was the main selection for September 1957, and the BOMC paid an advance of $40,000. Harcourt, Brace ordered a 50,000-copy printing of the 570-page $5.00 novel. (The BOMC printed its own copies.) Julian Muller, who doubled as an editor and advertising director, planned an innovative campaign for a single book, beginning with an unprecedented two-page spread in the *New York Times Book Review* and a full page in the daily *Times*.[34] The first Harcourt, Brace printing sold out before publication day, 26 August 1957, and a second printing of 42,000 copies was manufactured in August. Three more trade printings of 50,000 each were required in September. Muller continued to advertise the novel in the fall and had the unique experience of hearing an author suggest that perhaps it might be well to stop advertising his book. Cozzens told him that it would be a good idea if novels were published anonymously, so that they would not be sold and reviewed as brand-name products.

To the extent that it was possible with an author who eschewed personal publicity, the promotion of *By Love Possessed* was extremely successful. The biggest exposure break was the *Time* cover story. Against Bernice's advice, Cozzens had acceded to Henry Luce's request that he co-operate with *Time*. (Bernice warned him that people found his remarks cutting.) He trusted Luce and perhaps felt that he owed the *Time* organization something. Believing that *By Love Possessed* was his richest work, Cozzens wanted to give it every chance. If he were ever going to achieve a large readership, it would be with this novel. In accordance with *Time* practice, the article was researched by one reporter but written by another. Cozzens had felt reasonably comfortable with the researcher, Serrell Hillman, who spent a week in Lambertville interviewing him. Luce had offered to let him check the piece for accuracy, but Cozzens did not exercise the opportunity and blamed only himself for remarks attributed to him that outraged *Time* readers. Twenty years later Cozzens annotated a copy of *Time* for the Princeton archives: "Let me allow that I gave SH, *TIME* writer on the 'story', a tough time. I don't—doubtless some psychopathic block—ever if I can help it talk about myself, my writing, my 'literary' opinions to anyone. *TIME* got a 'story' only because I liked, much respected for his intelligence and integrity the late Henry Luce, having briefly

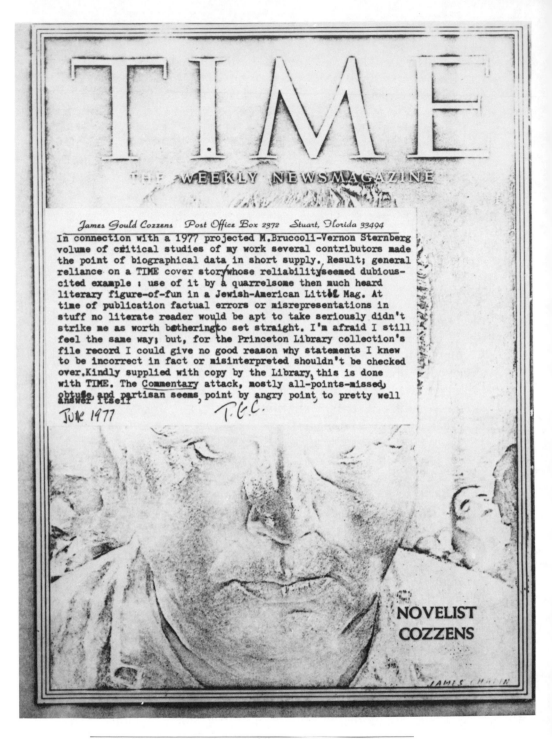

TIME

THE WEEKLY NEWSMAGAZINE

James Gould Cozzens   Post Office Box 2372   Stuart, Florida 33494

In connection with a 1977 projected M.Bruccoli-Vernon Sternberg
volume of critical studies of my work several contributors made
the point of biographical data in short supply. Result; general
reliance on a TIME cover story whose reliability seemed dubious-
cited example : use of it by a quarrelsome then much heard
literary figure-of-fun in a Jewish-American Little Mag. At
time of publication factual errors or misrepresentations in
stuff no literate reader would be apt to take seriously didn't
strike me as worth bothering to set straight. I'm afraid I still
feel the same way; but, for the Princeton Library collection's
file record I could give no good reason why statements I knew
to be incorrect in fact or misinterpreted shouldn't be checked
over. Kindly supplied with copy by the Library, this is done
with TIME. The Commentary attack, mostly all-points-missed,
obtuse and partisan seems, point by angry point, to pretty well
answer itself

June 1977   T.G.C.

NOVELIST
COZZENS

JAMES CHAPIN

Time *photo at Carrs Farm* (*DuBarry Campau*)

served as an editor of his [FORTUNE]; and agreed when he proposed a cover story. SH was agreeable, good company, engag-
ingly—to a point—exuberant; and I'm sure with all good will,
had I taken the trouble to read the copy, would have changed or
dropped anything pointed out to him as said by *him* to *me*, not
by *me* to *him*. He was just doing his job".*

*In October 1963 Cozzens replied to a *Fact* inquiry about inaccuracies in the *Time* cover
story, acknowledging that he was probably more to blame than *Time*. Nonetheless, he
concluded that no one "ever found in TIME anything to approach the conscienceless partisan distorting and misrepresenting done as a matter of course, and indeed, as their very
reason for being, in periodicals of the liberal or sectarian 'little review' type. I'm driven to
say that, all considered, you go a long way before you find editing with consistent basic
regard for truth and respect for fact TIME can generally be counted on to show. I'm sure
the publisher has 'biases'; but who doesn't? Not I? Not you?" *Fact* rewrote Cozzens's letter
for publication.[35]

When he read the published *Time* article, Cozzens found statements attributed to him in Hillman's "phrasing got by saying 'You
mean so & so.' Ans: I suppose you could put it that way. (Of
course dumbly never dreaming I wasn't off the record—and meaning YOU—by no means I.)" For the printed remark that "I like
anybody if he's a nice guy, but I've never met many Negroes who
were nice guys," Cozzens noted: "concluding phrase S. H."[36] *Time*
wanted a picture of Bernice, but she refused to be photographed.
The article appeared with a snapshot of the Cozzenses taken by
Hillman's wife—which they had been assured was not for publication. The writer, T. E. Kalem, also visited Cozzens. Since Hillman's research notes indicated that Cozzens had ethnic prejudices,
the *Time* editors wanted confirmation—which Kalem provided.
(When Cozzens learned that he was half Turkish, he took to referring to him as "the Turk," which didn't amuse Kalem).[37]

The *Time* cover story in the 2 September issue sold thousands
of copies of the novel but confirmed the wisdom of Bernice's
warning.* While recognizing his long dedication to his craft and
acknowledging the achievement of *By Love Possessed*, the article
portrayed Cozzens as what many readers regarded as a crank. Not
the quaint eccentric that authors are expected to be, but a damn-
your-eyes and damn-your-five-dollars arrogant anachronism. Cozzens became briefly famous for his indifference to fame. Although
Time warned that his treatment of Catholics, Jews, and Negroes
might be controversial, no one was prepared for the degree of
controversy. The Book-of-the-Month Club, which was not in the
business of offending customers, had anticipated no problem. Clifton Fadiman's *Book-of-the-Month Club News* piece dismissed the
problem in a parenthesis: "(Intelligent Catholic readers will not
assume that Julius speaks for Mr. Cozzens, any more than those
of the Jewish faith will sense any bigotry in the portrait, not unduly sympathetic, of the converted lawyer Mr. Woolf.)"[39]

The initial reception of *By Love Possessed* was overwhelmingly
favorable across the country. The judgment "masterpiece" was frequently employed, although there were complaints about the difficult style. The best of the early reviews was by Brendan Gill in
the *New Yorker*:

---

*In October Cozzens refused to co-operate with *Life* for a "major photographic essay"
which would use selections from his writings with photos of "people in the locales suggested by the novels."[38] The project was dropped.

No American novelist of the twentieth century has attempted more than Mr. Cozzens attempts in the course of this long and bold and delicate book, which, despite its length, one reads through at headlong speed and is then angry with oneself for having reached the end of so precipitately. No other American novelist of this century could bring to such a task the resources of intelligence, literary technique, and knowledge of the intricate, more or less sorry ways of the world that Mr. Cozzens commands.[40]

Gill was supported by John Fischer, the editor of *Harper's*, whose review was headed "Nomination for a Nobel Prize." Using *By Love Possessed* as a stick to beat the novel of alienation, he wrote: "If your great-grandchild should ever want to find out how Americans behaved and thought and felt in the mid-years of this century, Cozzens' major novels probably would be his most revealing source."[41] The *Saturday Review* ran Cozzens's photo on the cover; Whitney Balliett's review praised Cozzens as "the most mature, honest, painstaking, and technically accomplished American writer alive" but called attention to the dense style and tractarian interruptions.[42] The front-page reviews in the Sunday *Times* (Malcolm Cowley) and *Herald-Tribune* (Jessamyn West) were warmly receptive; and Orville Prescott wrote a strong review in the daily *Times*. West's was the only important review to identify Julius Penrose as the novel's "thematic and spiritual apex."[43]

The critical response was not unanimous. Cozzens assembled a "Kick & Nut File" for *By Love Possessed*, from which he later compiled a sampling of choice abuse.

Item: ARTLESS DODGER. ". . . it is not entirely surprising to discover that these formal and stylistic dodges fail to camouflage a vacuum."

Item: LOOKING BACK IN FAILURE. "He tries prodigiously hard and his reflective processes are Cumbersome (sic) and word-weighted."

Item: BUTYRIC WHIFFS. ". . . a book couched in a style at once soggy with butyric whiffery (sic) and dripping with uncomma'd (sic) commonplaces made to look profound by a certain coy confusion in the phrasing."

Item: OLD EGOCENTRIC'S MISTAKE. "He is woolly minded, packaging his small puzzles of lost past fact in the most execrable style ever devised."

Item: PONDEROSITY. ". . . His sentences are often crudities condited (sic) in the recondite."

Item: A STRONG SMELL OF MEAT. "Nobody would know from reading his accounts that erotic love and fulfillment were an occasion for kindness and joy."

Item: FINGERNAIL ON BLACKBOARD. "The prose is clogged with such words as 'inappetency,' 'inutile,' 'innominate,' 'furibund' and with clod-hopping sentences."

Item: THE ABSENTHEARTEDNESS OF MR. C. "His tragedy is that he simply can't feel anything until he makes his statement about it. He doesn't love people enough to mourn them. He doesn't love life enough even to regret it." (huh?)

Item: THE CASE OF THE CALCIFIED NOVELIST. "Humor might have saved it, because the blackest view of man becomes bearable when lightened or irony. Drama or compassion might have alleviated the dullness. But there is none of these in his novels, books that are bad beyond be-lieveing."

Item: AMIEZ-VOUS BRAHMINS? "All the dismally banal Cozzens prejudices ticked off: sex, FDR, Jewish Intellectuals, Irish Catholic politicians, fatuous liberal intellectual literati. . . ."[44]

Most of these items came from the 1958 counterattacks on *By Love Possessed*.

A frequent charge was that his dialogue was unreal; but Cozzens believed that critics had been trained to judge dialogue by the Hemingway standard. ". . . I couldn't understand how anyone who ever listened to people actually talking could accept the generally accepted critical canon that this was good true reporting, the way people *did* talk: and all writers of fiction must make their characters talk that way—or else! The matter was of course 'brought to my attention' by occasional criticism of dialogue passages of mine which reproduced with I think accuracy talk I knew I had heard as 'unreal'. I was puzzled until I realized suddenly that what was meant was that it didn't sound a bit like Hemingway's dialogue. It had to be 'unreal'."[45]

On 8 September 1957 *By Love Possessed* appeared as number 14 on the *New York Times* best-seller list; the following week it was number 2, behind *Peyton Place*. On 22 September it took the number-1 position, which it retained until 2 March 1958, when *Anatomy of a Murder* replaced it. *By Love Possessed* was on the list for thirty-four weeks. By 1959 Harcourt, Brace had sold 226,969 copies, and the

Book-of-the-Month Club had distributed 270,000 copies.* The sales figures started speculation about whether the novel was actually being read. Newspaper articles based on interviews with bookstore clerks and librarians reported that their patrons were complaining that it was hard to get through.

Harcourt, Brace licensed rights to Reader's Digest Condensed Books (which cut it to 240 pages—double the usual condensation length) for a $100,000 guarantee against five cents a copy royalty; the volume sold 3,094,935 copies.† Paperback rights were auctioned for $101,505—then a record price—and the Fawcett Crest edition was in its fifth printing in 1978. Cozzens was prepared to reject all movie offers. Bernice suggested that he talk to Julian Muller, who broke his resistance by saying, "When you wrote your book you committed an act of art. When you sell film rights you commit merely an act of commerce." The people who read the novel would not be bothered by the movie, but some of the people who saw the movie might be brought to read the book. Before publication the rights were sold to Mirisch–Seven Arts for $100,000 plus bonuses—which brought Cozzens $250,000 total—with Bernice's associate Ray Stark handling the Hollywood end of the deal. The movie was a major release in 1961, with Lana Turner ("The story of a woman who was By Love Possessed!") as Marjorie Penrose, Efrem Zimbalist, Jr., as Arthur Winner, Jason Robards, Jr., as Julius Penrose, and George Hamilton, Susan Kohner, Thomas Mitchell, and Barbara Bel Geddes. *By Love Possessed* was an undistinguished movie; but Cozzens—who went to see it twice—thought that screenwriter John Dennis had done a good job of organizing and condensing the material, despite the impediment that "I write against rather than for movies."[46] A stage version by Ketti Frings was announced in 1958 but canceled.

Though happy to have the "lovely money" *By Love Possessed* brought him, Cozzens retained his conviction that literary success is a matter of luck. Eleven years later, in *Morning Noon and Night*, he expatiated on the lessons of success and failure:

*The success of *By Love Possessed* prompted the Book-of-the-Month Club to offer *The Just and the Unjust* and *Guard of Honor* as a dual alternate selection in December 1957 for $4.95.
†The 1957 American edition combined *By Love Possessed* with condensations of MacKinlay Kantor's *Lobo*, Jürgen Thorwald's *The Century of the Surgeon*, Jan de Hartog's *The Spiral Road*, and Donald R. Morris's *Warm Bodies*. The 1960 edition published in London, Sydney, and Cape Town included condensations of Paul Gallico's *Flowers for Mrs. Harris*, Margery Allingham's *Hide My Eyes*, and Ian Henderson and Philip Goodhart's *The Hunt for Kimathi*.

. . . neither merit as a piece of writing nor excellence, by literary standards of the moment, as a creative work is the determining factor in making a book a best seller. Indeed, as far as merit goes, so many books of no merit (that is, subsequently conceded to be without any) have had very large sales that, considering these alone, the hypothesis that badness does the trick—you find it proposed by almost every failed-writer-turned-critic in the literary-circle jungle—may seem tenable. It is not tenable because, whatever wishful thinking may wish, there are other figures to show that books of much and evident merit (that is, by subsequent critical consensus held so to be) often sell equally well [p. 63].

Cozzens departed from his customary silence to write placating letters to reviewers and readers who charged him with anti-Catholicism. The January 1958 summary article by Jean Holzhauer in the *Catholic Messenger* was a rebuttal to the unfavorable Catholic reviews. She asserted that the novel was accurate and rebuked her coreligionists for wanting only praise: "Here is a state of affairs that could make excellent grist for Mr. Cozzens' next fictional mill, if he were as programatically 'anti-Catholic' as his critics charge. Not without humor, the situation stands for the world to see. We object to a piece of fiction, on artistic grounds, because it contains a Catholic character not consistent, not saintly, not wholly intelligent; because *this* we insist, misrepresents *us*."[47]

Thomas A. Wassmer, S.J., Ph.D., the reviewer for *Best Sellers*, was respectful, though warning that "the several pages of acid contempt for everything Catholic and Julius' reconstruction of the preparation of Marjorie's soul for the 'irrationality' of faith require prudent and mature reading."[48] When the reviewer for *America*, Harold C. Gardiner, charged that Julius's characterization is weakened by his "tactical blunder of estimating his foe, the Church, as being stupid,"[49] Cozzens replied to the editor: "Far from—er—'estimating' the Church as being stupid, his fear for our freedoms was based entirely on his express and explicit opinion that the Church was unresistingly clever, unexampled in its astuteness about human beings and in its intelligent manipulating of human emotions. Surely even Father Gardiner, if he'd happened to read those passages, couldn't ask anyone to say, as touching the Church's brains or lack of them, handsomer than that."[50] Louis McKernan, C. S. P., writing in *Catholic World*, called Cozzens "an intensely opinionated man," but was uncertain whether there was malice in his writing.[51] Cozzens responded: "I would like to answer that, at least as far as my conscious awareness goes, there isn't. I think the human row is a tough one to hoe. I see Rome helping thousands of my fellow men to hoe it cheerfully and hopefully and when that's the case the point of whether or not they may be deluded seems to me quite irrelevant. If Penrose speaks hard words it's because I think his misfortune, his temperament, his background make that the way he would talk. . . . Rome is feared always for the same reasons by those who fear Rome. I'm not one of them".[52]

William Buckley, the Catholic editor of the conservative *National Review* declared that "we do not live in the world of Arthur Winner, Jr., and the least we can do by way of thanksgiving is to refuse to stand idly by while James Gould Cozzens or anybody else so represents our world, and God's."[53] Cozzens replied that "the book wasn't intended at all as an attack on religion, or as any ambitious effort to redesign your world and God's. I simply meant to write of some situations in which human feeling may be observed often to get the best of human reason. If you could manage to view what I wrote this way, the way, I think, that most people who liked it viewed it, I believe you'd see the book's not a bad job as novels go—or at any rate, really nothing you need to get sore about".[54] A friendly correspondence ensued, with Buckley becoming an admirer of Cozzens's subsequent books; but Buckley's attempts to coax him into writing for the *National Review* were unavailing.

On the basis of Mr. Woolf, a minor character, charges of anti-Semitism were brought against Cozzens. (He suspected that these charges were partly triggered by the exclusion of Jews from the gentile society of *By Love Possessed*.) Cozzens categorized these complaints as "crap": "I know that any—well, pontificating, on the subject of yourself is always shaky. You don't see yourself. Yet, in a sense, you *feel* yourself, and I know I wouldn't be anti-anybody by category or class for the bad (not good) reason that this would involve by definition some subscribing to or standing on principle; and I really have no principles. I don't give a hoot in hell about the race, color, religion of individuals. All I go by is whether I find this one agreeable—or, in short; if he be not bad to me, what care I how bad he be?"[55]

The Catholic response was tepid compared to the vehemence of the delayed liberal attack on *By Love Possessed*. *Cozzens delendus est.* The January 1958 issue of *Commentary* ("a journal of significant thought and opinion in Jewish affairs and contemporary issues") published Dwight Macdonald's "By Cozzens Possessed," a rebuttal to the early reviews from the perspective of four months.[56]

Macdonald, a self-described "conservative anarchist,"[57] charged that the novel "falls below any reasonable literary criterion" and that Cozzens "is guilty of the unforgivable novelistic sin: he is unaware of the nature of his characters." Most of the space in this twelve-page article was devoted to four categories of defects in Cozzens's style, which Macdonald derisively discussed with examples: 1) *Melodramatics*; 2) *Confucius Say* ("A queer strangled sententiousness"); 3) *Pointless Inversion*; 4) *Toujours le Mot Injuste*. Macdonald blamed the success of so meretricious a work on the reviewers' desire to compensate Cozzens for their previous neglect and on the "middlebrow Counter Revolution" of the fifties. Cozzens believed that what the enemies of *By Love Possessed* really reacted to was its success—envy among the literati. Quoting Dr. Johnson, he classified it as "criticism enlarged by rage and exclamation."

Concerned that Cozzens might not read the *Commentary* article, Macdonald sent him a copy, which Cozzens acknowledged on 5 March 1958.

Dear Mr. Macdonald—

The copy of COMMENTARY you marked for me finally reached me, thanks. To tell you the truth the 100-critic chorus, though not really driving me off my head the way it drove you off yours, had come to lack freshness, so I found your novel pronouncements a nice change. I see that you don't understand prose structure very well; that shades of meaning in words are, like irony, altogether lost on you; and that your imperceptiveness is, for an educated adult, quite remarkable. Which, I suppose, is why the stylistic claptrap, the crypto-sentimentality, and the just plain childishness in so many of the books you indicate you admire actually can seem to you better 'art' than a Somerset Maugham's lucid thinking and perfect writing. I'm afraid your infirmity here makes me unable to take your 'literary criticism' very seriously. You'd always, it seems safe to guess, be wrong. However, in the field of the philippic (sorry to send you to your dictionary again) I think you're gifted. I haven't in years had the pleasure of reading so refreshingly venomous an outburst. For that, at least, let me award you an earned A—and I'll bet all those little-mag. people are just *loving* you to death!

Yours,
James Gould Cozzens

P. S. I dropped Bill Shakespeare a line to tell him you say "virgin knot untied" won't do.* No word from him yet; perhaps he's out of town.[58]

---

*The awful examples cited by Macdonald included "untied Hope still her virgin knot will keep," an echo of "Untied I still my virgin knot will keep" from Shakespeare's *Pericles*.

Cozzens made no public rebuttal, but he took Macdonald's attack personally. He found out who Macdonald was—Cozzens had never heard of him—and told Buckley that his trouble "is a definite developing paranoid psychosis, the delusion of grandeur being the quite common one of believing himself all-wise, all-learned, all-witty, all-knowing."[59] In 1977 Cozzens sent Princeton the copy of the article Macdonald had provided, explaining in a note:

As noted on the TIME card, comment on this odd outpouring is manifestly needless. You see him able to swallow SH's text which I negligently left uncorrected. In the way of 'literary criticism' any reader soon recognizes the remarkable job of leaving virtually no point unmissed and odd imperceptiveness about people and life worse confounded when all ironies, like all shades of meaning in words (5¢ Or $5), are lost on him. Single possible note-of-use. Q. *Why so hot, Little Man?* Ans: (according to a NYorker staff member): Don't you know what Brendan Gill (writer of the BLP NYorker review) said at the water cooler to Mac about fascination of watching working of second-rate minds? That's what all these pages are really about.*

Macdonald was not a Jew; but the circumstance that his article appeared in *Commentary* and that other unfavorable articles on *By Love Possessed* were written by Jews made Cozzens antagonistic toward what he identified as the Jewish literary establishment. "By Cozzens Possessed" was reinforced by Irving Howe's "James Gould Cozzens: Novelist of the Republic" in the 20 January 1958 issue of the *New Republic*. Howe dismissed the novel as "mediocre and pretentious," but he was more concerned with its deleterious "Philosophy of Limit" than with its literary qualities: "It speaks to a society weary of ideals and dubious of hopes; it helps console people in their prosperous frustrations; it offers conservative wisdom in a moment of liberal twilight." He concluded by identifying Cozzens as the spokesman for "a civilization that finds its symbolic embodiment in Dwight David Eisenhower and its practical guide in John Foster Dulles."[60] There were no prominent replies to the Macdonald and Howe articles. Cozzens's partisans seem to have had no stomach for controversy with such redoubtable foes—or perhaps they had short conviction spans.

When Macdonald collected his article in *Against the American Grain* (1962) he added a footnote acknowledging that Cozzens had provided him with the source for the phrase; but Macdonald argued that the Shakespeare reading was corrupt.

*Gill has no recollection of this exchange.

By the time *By Love Possessed* was published in London by Longmans, Green in April 1958, the English reviewers had been exposed to the initial American reception and to the reappraisal. Evidently they felt that their authority had been pre-empted by the selection of blurbs from the American press used on the Longmans dust jacket, for the English reviews expressed general indignation at being presented with an alleged American masterpiece. Peter Green in the *Daily Telegraph* called the American praise "a species of mass hysteria."[61] Maurice Richardson lumped *By Love Possessed* with two other novels in his *New Statesman* review and spoke for most of his colleagues in dismissing Arthur Winner as a prig and condemning the style as "constipated."[62] His remarks elicited a response from J. B. Priestley, who admitted that the novel had been overpraised in America and stipulated that he disagreed with its "cold conservatism"; nonetheless, Priestley insisted that "it is an unusually massive and intelligent piece of fiction, representing years of work by a novelist of very considerable distinction, and it deserves something better than this flippant dismissal."*[63] The unsigned *Times Literary Supplement* review described the style as "a form of logorrhea" and concluded on a summit of opacity by citing an English solicitor: " 'The dilemma is unreal. The only possible thing was for Winner to explain the situation to the beneficiaries and ask them if they agreed to keep the whole thing dark.' "[64] (So much for Blackstone, Coke, and Hardwicke.) The most favorable and thoughtful English reviewer was D. W. Harding, who defended the style in the *Spectator* and praised the examination of moral complexities, expressing reservation only about whether Cozzens had "ignored the possibility of a subtler intimacy between man and woman achieved by way of sexuality."[65] Despite the bad press, *By Love Possessed* sold 48,899 clothbound copies in England and required four Longmans printings; the 1960 Penguin paperback sold 33,181 copies. The attention to Cozzens generated by this novel resulted in the republication of *Guard of Honour*, *The Just and the Unjust*, *Ask Me Tomorrow*, *Men and Brethren*, and *A Cure of Flesh* by Longmans, Green in 1958. None sold well.

---

*The December 1958 *Encounter* advertisement for *By Love Possessed* quoted Priestley: "I am ready to consider it one of the major pieces of fiction of our post-war age, and prefer it myself to anything by any of America's assorted Nobel Prize winners."

The Winter 1958 number of *Critique*, a journal published at the University of Minnesota, was devoted to Cozzens. It provided a mixed bag of admiration (Frederick Bracher, George Garrett, Louis O. Coxe) and dismay (Maxwell Geismar and Walter B. Rideout), as well as the first checklist of Cozzens's work, by James B. Meriwether. John Lydenberg's "Cozzens and the Conservatives" tried to make him respectable by identifying his values with the "good" conservatism of F.D.R. and Stevenson, rather than with the sickening pieties of Eisenhower Republicanism.[66]

Frederick Bracher, a professor at Pomona College, was writing what would become the first critical book on Cozzens, and John McCallum of Harcourt, Brace arranged for him to meet Cozzens at lunch in New York during February 1958. The meeting was not rewarding for the scholar because Cozzens declined to talk much about his work. When Bracher noted parallels between the garden scene in *By Love Possessed* and *Paradise Lost*, Cozzens denied that there was any connection. He insisted that what matters in a novel is what the reader sees; and he dismissed most literary criticism as attempts to find what isn't there.[67] Cozzens was sufficiently impressed by Bracher's good sense to correspond with him about his approach to writing:

I've never in writing intended any malice and (I could of course be wrong about this) I think readers who credit me with drawing 'malicious pictures' simply give good proof that they didn't read me carefully or would not hear me out. Villains seem to me just figments of an angry, childish mind. I don't mean I feel that everyone is lovely and loveable if you only knew. I am violently against the spirit of the late Will Rogers' dreadful observation that he'd never met a man he didn't like. But I think I can say that since I've been old enough—that's about 20 years now—to recognize most of the manifestations of human nature (when you've learned to recognize a certain number, the rest are so readily predictable you can't be surprised by them) I've never met a man I couldn't, at least to my own satisfaction, understand. Understanding I find perfectly compatible with dislike and people I dislike I always try to have no more to do with; but I find that once you see or think you see why someone is the way he is, active animosity, the urge of malice to make fun of, hurt, or belittle him seems simply silly, a waste of time.[68]

When Bracher's *The Novels of James Gould Cozzens* was published by Harcourt, Brace in 1959, it received generous review space for a critical study; Cozzens attributed that to the controversy generated by Macdonald. On the front page of the *New York Times Book Review*, under the headline "Guardian of Middle-Class Honor," Elizabeth Janeway made the point that Cozzens "arouses such emotions in his critics that he is treated not as a writer but as a moral symbol."[69] Reviewing the Cozzens canon rather than Bracher's study, she cited Cozzens's failure to explore the meanings of power and made the familiar complaint that his heroes are emotionally deficient.

By Love Possessed was nominated for the Pulitzer Prize by judges John K. Hutchens and Robert Gorham Davis, but the recognition went to James Agee's *A Death in the Family*. When the National Book Award was given to John Cheever's *The Wapshot Chronicle*, Macdonald's article was generally credited with having eliminated *By Love Possessed*.[70] Cozzens did not want the award, but he did not want to give Macdonald the credit for depriving him of it. His own explanation was that the NBA judges passed over *By Love Possessed* because they knew he would not attend the ceremony or make an acceptance speech. *By Love Possessed* won the American Academy of Arts and Letters William Dean Howells Medal in 1960 for the most distinguished work of fiction published in the previous five years. Cozzens regarded this award as a reaction against Macdonald; prominent critics who had spoken well of the novel did not relish being stigmatized as incompetents. He did not attend the ceremony. Malcolm Cowley's carefully phrased presentation statement explained: "The Academy is honoring a literary work, not a body of opinion"; and, "the Howells Medal is being awarded to a man who, quite simply and apart from controversy, is the greatest architect in contemporary American fiction."[71] In his letter of acceptance Cozzens wrote: "I am moved by the Academy's vote to honor me. As a token of the consensus of many distinguished members, I accept the William Dean Howells Medal with gratitude."[72] Cozzens was concerned about the danger of the Nobel Prize. He did not want it because he did not respect it and because it would destroy his privacy. Given the literary products of the recipients and his doubts whether the judges could read English, he felt safe. Cozzens composed an imaginary cable: "Glad to have money if you want to forward it. Can't see my way to going to Stockholm for less than $100,000. Are you interested?"[73] He knew that Bernice would not let him send it.

NIGHT

NINE

The Hermit of "Shadowbrook"

C A R R S   F A R M was sold for $50,000 before *By Love Possessed* was published. The local power company had secured the right to erect cable towers across the property, and Cozzens said he was damned if he would spend the rest of his life with his view spoiled. When he left New Jersey after twenty-four years Cozzens donated his papers and some 800 volumes from his library to Princeton in token of his appreciation for the help he had received from the university's library over the years. Once again there is the paradox of an author who scorned fame providing for research on his work and on his life.

The Cozzenses took a Manhattan apartment at 310 West End Avenue while they looked for another country house. On publication day for *By Love Possessed* they were at Block Island, Rhode Island, which they considered as a new location. Cozzens was interested in the Helen Hayes – Charles MacArthur property in Nyack, New York, near Edward Newhouse, because, he claimed, it was enclosed by high walls; but Bernice talked him out of it. Now a relatively wealthy writer, he wanted Bernice to retire, so proximity to New York was not a factor in the choice of a new location. Fannie Collins, with whom Cozzens had always been on excellent terms, had moved from New Jersey to the eastern shore of Virginia. He told Fannie that her sister would never be happy far away from her and asked her to find a place for them in Virginia. In January 1958 the Cozzenses rented "Windingdale," an eighteenth-century house near Belle Haven on Chesapeake Bay.

"Shadowbrook," Williamstown

Bernice continued to handle a few old clients by mail. Always an attentive eater, Cozzens enjoyed the bountiful supply of fresh seafood. He set up a study in the slave quarters, but the structure was uncomfortable in the winter. "Windingdale" was not for sale, and Cozzens wanted his own land where he could garden. After failing to find another suitable property in the area, they were driven north by the bugs and the humidity. In the fall of 1958 while on an antique-scouting trip Bernice found "Shadowbrook" outside Williamstown, Massachusetts, in the Berkshires and per-suaded Cozzens that it would be convenient for him to have access to the Williams College Library. The large hilltop house on Ob-long Road had been built in 1943 and commanded a pleasant view. He paid for it with a check for $55,000.

Although *By Love Possessed* had made Cozzens well off, money had never been a factor in his career. He had always lived com-fortably and, except for the occasional short story, had not written for money. At fifty-four he was at the peak of his power and rep-utation, and he planned to keep on writing. In 1958 he made a start on a novel to be called "A Skyborn Music," about a boy's responses to adult situations.* Sixteen-year-old Richard Maitland and his neuropathologist father are visiting Mt. Zion, a former religious community in New England, now a school for retarded children. The founder, Theophilus Pell, is senile; and Dr. Maitland, whose great-aunt had been one of Pell's polygamous wives, has been asked to observe him. The epigraph from George Santayana† announces that the theme was to be a favorite Cozzens concern: the gap between immaturity and experience.

Cozzens abandoned the novel in December 1960 but kept the title "A Skyborn Music" in reserve. (In 1977 he donated twenty-four pages of the revised typescript to the Friends of the Detroit Public Library benefit auction.) As he explained in the notebooks he began keeping in 1960, "I had at last to decide (or agree to admit) that my several years' effort on the MS. I had been calling: A Sky-born Music couldn't by any means be salvaged. That the 16-year old first-person narrator was going to make things hard was I suppose part of the original attraction. The truth now seems to me; if you're truthful; that is, if you write without sentiment and falsification that marks all books about boys that I've ever read, you must show the boy as dull, tiresome and not worth the adult reader's time." [1]

Williamstown brought no change in Cozzens's habits. He resumed gardening; as always, he enjoyed eating his own vegetables, but his efforts to grow roses were disappointing.‡ Although the college community was prepared to lionize him, his privacy was respected when he made it clear that he wanted to be left alone. He appreciated the welcoming overtures, but he found his own company more agreeable. The Cozzenses exchanged duty visits with President James P. Baxter III, and he accepted membership in the Faculty Club. Williams twice offered him an honorary degree, which he declined, admitting that he didn't know why he found it impossible to accept friendly gestures.

The only official appearances Cozzens made on campus were to attend one of William Jay Smith's English classes and to meet with

---

*The contract, dated 23 July 1958, refers to it as "The Author's Next Novel after BY LOVE POSSESSED." Delivery date was on or before 1 May 1963. The title is from Emerson's "Music": "Let me go where'er I will, / I hear sky-born music still."
†Sonnets Second Series, XXV.
‡In 1967 Cozzens provided a foreword for Roses of Yesterday, a volume of water colors of roses by Nanae Ito with text by Dorothy Stemler. He had long been a customer of Tillotson's rose nursery in California, which Mrs. Stemler operated.

In his "Shadowbrook" study

students of creative writing at the request of Robert Allen. He knew that he couldn't tell anyone how to become a good writer, but it occurred to him that it might be useful to show students what to avoid—"Not that I'd want to try it."

A course that confined itself to a study, not of excellence in writing, but of the ways of going wrong, conceivably could save a would-be writer some time. You could point out to him, by simply exhibiting examples,

Bernice at "Shadowbrook," 1960

a few of the things that his inexperience might make him attempt, in that hope of extra or larger or more exact communication which no one who writes seriously can help having; but which aren't going to work. At random, out of order, and with none of the careful consideration a proper list would need, some examples to exhibit might include: (of course I don't suggest any of these should be read all the way through: a few pages of each ought to be enough) Carlyle's *French Revolution* (Keep calm); Pater's *Marius the Epicurean* (but don't be phony about it); Twain's *Huckleberry Finn* (watch your 'comedy': that king and duke stuff, for example, you don't want): Joyce's *Ulysses* (don't fool with the English language; you can't win); Pearl Buck *The Good Earth* (never try to be biblical); Steinbeck: *Cannery Row* (don't be maudlin); Hemingway's *Across the River and Into the Trees* (check yourself for childishness); Shirley Jackson *The Haunting of Hill House* (trying to say things by not saying them is not a good idea); Dreiser's *An American Tragedy* (you can't get away with never learning to write); Norman Mailer *The Naked and the Dead.* (Feeling is no substitute for fact); Virginia Woolf *Orlando* (let symbolism alone) I'm sure better examples could be found in a number of cases: but I think each of these can be said to have a learnable lesson about writing and a young writer who was taught them effectively would really be ahead in the game that interests him.[2]

At the urging of John P. Marquand, Cozzens accepted appointment to the Harvard Overseers' Visiting Committee for the English Department in 1960, serving until 1966.* This committee met once a year at Cambridge to sit in on classes and discuss problems with the faculty. Walter Jackson Bate, Chairman of the English Department, found him a valuable committee member; in addition to his "unrivalled mastery" of the field, Cozzens "knew Harvard very well, and had an uncanny understanding of the academic mind and of institutions and how they work."[3] Bate arranged for Cozzens to sit next to him at the committee dinners so they could talk about the writers they both admired—Swift, Johnson, Keats. Cozzens was pleased by Harvard's recognition; but when he was nominated as candidate for the Harvard Board of Overseers in 1966, he explained that "neither my experience nor my hermit's temperament at all fit me to assume the public duties and important responsibilities of an Overseer."[4] He privately admitted that the meetings would bore him.

The Cozzenses were invited to the 29 April 1962 White House dinner honoring Nobel Prize recipients. He declined, remarking that he wasn't going to Washington just so Bernice could ask Jackie Kennedy where the ladies' room was. Yet in his isolation he developed epistolary relationships. Jack Iggulden, an Australian novelist and sportsman, had written him fan letters; and when Iggulden was competing in the 1963 World Gliding Championships,

---

* During 1964–65 the committee also included Frederick Buechner, Erwin D. Canham, Lillian Hellman, Frederick W. Hilles, Donald F. Hyde, Howard Mumford Jones, Alfred A. Knopf, Louis Kronenberger, Kemp Malone, Ricardo Quintana, Courtney Smith, Edward Streeter, Robert Penn Warren, Charles F. Adams (chairman), and John Mason Brown (vice-chairman).

he came from Argentina to meet Cozzens. They maintained a correspondence for seven years. Cozzens admonished him that writing was a hopeless and thankless occupation but urged him to settle for nothing less than the best work he was capable of—to test "line by line and word by word, to see if you're really saying, and saying unmistakably, what you mean, what you know to be true."[5] In 1966, referring to his difficulties with his work in progress, Cozzens observed: "One permanent discouragement in writing (and uniquely writing's, I think) is that the more you do of it, the better at least relatively, you get at it, the tougher you may expect to find it."[6] Iggulden sent him boomerangs, which Cozzens dutifully experimented with. Another correspondent was English composer Christopher Whelen, who prepared an unproduced radio script, "Cozzens. Novelist For All Seasons." Cozzens maintained his friendship with Newhouse, who visited him in Williamstown.

The only close friendship he formed after his Air Force service was with William Jovanovich. Seventeen years younger than Cozzens, Jovanovich became President of Harcourt, Brace when he was thirty-five. Himself a writer, Jovanovich had done graduate work at Harvard and Columbia. He was proud to be Cozzens's publisher, and Cozzens responded to him with the respect he reserved for men of great ability and large concerns. They maintained an increasingly warm correspondence, and William and Martha Jovanovich were among the rare overnight guests at "Shadowbrook." In time Cozzens could unembarrassingly write "I love you" to his publisher. Recognizing Jovanovich's pride in his background, Cozzens wrote, "As for Montenegrin embraces, take one of mine. You think you demi-Slavs have a corner on them?"[7] He was deeply concerned about Jovanovich's coronaries and phoned regularly to check on his condition. Yet when his publisher asked for an advance look at his novel, Cozzens explained that he was unable to allow his work-in-progress to be seen by anyone except Bernice: "It's most personally mine and no one else is going to get to finger it."[8]

Even with Jovanovich, Cozzens was more comfortable and expansive on paper. When the Jovanoviches visited for a weekend, Cozzens was effusively welcoming on their arrival but grew increasingly dour. Attempting to rise to the occasion, he drank whiskey after dinner, instead of his customary beer ration. Jovanovich concluded that he saw life as a negotiated truce. Martha Jovanovich's diagnosis of Cozzens during the Williamstown years was that he grew bored with himself.

Fannie Collins lived at "Shadowbrook" after the deaths of her husband and her mother and then bought a house near Williamstown, in Pownall, Vermont, where she was joined by her cousin Annie Reubold. Cozzens was baffled by Fannie's ability with people; everyone she met became her friend. Although Bernice still handled a few clients—she represented Mary McCarthy in the movie sale for *The Group*—Cozzens recognized that she was bored. He encouraged her to start an antique shop with Fannie in Pownall, and she conducted it with her customary energy and taste. They specialized in good pieces of country furniture and primitive paintings. Since the business required considerable scouting for stock, Cozzens occasionally "baby-sat" at the shop while the sisters were attending shows and auctions. He was amused when a customer asked for a clock like the one on the dust jacket of *By Love Possessed* but, of course, did not identify himself.

A puzzling departure from Cozzens's anonymity during his Williamstown years was an almost involuntary writing of public letters. He warned himself that he was getting foolish and speculated on what he regarded as symptoms of senility: "I expect that what you need most to bear in mind, as you get to be an old fool, is: Mail nothing until two or three days have passed." [9] Between 1960 and 1967 he dispatched letters to Princeton's *University* (a comment on the magazine), the *Christian Century* (on his boyhood reading), the *Harvard Alumni Bulletin* (on campus architecture and on President Lowell), *Fact* (on *Time*), *TV Guide* (on his television watching—none), the *Living Church* (on bomb scares and on distributing the Book of Common Prayer), *Forbes* (on American razor blades), the *Bulletin of the Harvard Club of New York* (comment on a recipe), and the *Berkshire Eagle* (on General Charles Lee). Some of these communications were wryly kidding, as in asking the *Living Church* whether, in view of Cranmer's martyrdom, it is "altogether tactful or in good taste to mention him when you offer the non-copyright text of the Book of Common Prayer to our Roman brethren." [10] Judge Henry J. Friendly's *Harvard Alumni Bulletin* letter charging President A. Lawrence Lowell with bigotry for attempting to impose a Jewish quota elicited Cozzens's defense of Lowell's "unbiased intellectual magnanimity." [11] zens was convinced that the "rancor and venom" of anti-anti-Semitism frequently exceeded that of anti-Semitism.

It is difficult to account for these public statements. Perhaps, as the years since *By Love Possessed* extended, he yielded to the writer's compulsion to see himself in print. By 1962 he was working on a new novel with the working titles of "A Skyborn Music" (salvaged from the wreckage of his boy's-eye novel) or "A Thing of the Past," which became *Morning Noon and Night*—but it developed slowly, through false starts.* As Cozzens found it harder to write to his requirements and was increasingly dismayed by the thinking and writing of the sixties, he felt an almost perverse desire to record his disaffections. His public letters can be assigned to the impulse that prompted him to keep notebooks during the same period. Between 1960 and 1965 he filled ten notebooks, in addition to diaries, which were mainly weather and gardening logs. These notebooks included comments on his wide reading, autobiographical vignettes, literary observations, and philosophical and religious speculations. (The Knights of Columbus ads provided a steady source of diversion.) They were really a substitute for writing fiction; only a few entries went into *Morning Noon and Night*. Cozzens subsequently informed Jovanovich that the "quite unpublishable carefully detailed settings-down of personal experience" in his notebooks resulted from the "dismay come suddenly in those years at realizing beyond question that my memory, the only part of me that was Achilles but unappreciated, taken for granted in its close to photographic capacity, was faltering, must soon, like any old man's begin serious forgettings or worse mis-rememberings. Thus past episodes for some reason brought to mind, had best if I hoped to use them someway, be put in writing while I could still be sure the fact remembered really was fact. I can tell you this was damn dismaying, ego wounding, I suppose." [12] Along with a blurring of memory, he felt other depressing symptoms of mortality at sixty. Describing Henry Dodd Worthington in *Morning Noon and Night*, he catalogued his own aging process:

Observed, my image is seen to be large; and, shorter, might appear fat. But I am tall, so my decades of easy living and excellent eating merely make me look a little grosser and meatier than I used to look. Cropped

---

*The 8 October 1962 issue of *Publishers Weekly* carried this news item: "James Gould Cozzens' new novel will shortly be in the publisher's hands, Harcourt, Brace & World announced last week. The author's first novel since "By Love Possessed" (1957), the new one will be titled "Morning, Noon and Night." No further information, such as publication date, is available right now" (p. 35). The novel did not appear until 1968.

short, thinning hair of my image's head is nearly white. My lined face
has to be called old; the cheeks sag lumpily. Under medical examination
my natural body's commencing decrepitude is easy to see. Of earth earthy,
my sixty-odd-year-old image has piffling yet harassing chronic minor
trouble with hemorrhoids and ingrowing toenails. Normal aging's occasional distresses of sudden visceral ill ease, desultory muscle twinge, and
hard-to-diagnose ache of bone and stiffening of joint visit me. Old skin,
now too slowly renewed, suffers routine itches and allergy rashes. The
breath of the image shortens, and, because it now sweats so easily, drafts
need to be guarded against. Long ago glasses began to be required for
reading. In eating employed now are partial dental prosthetic devices.
Hearing may soon have to be aided electrically. Yes, many and sharp, if
not yet very sharp, those numerous ills (the old mind is nervous and
worrisome) inwoven with our frame [p. 6].

The notebooks reiterate that no sane man would choose to be
born and commend suicide as the alternative to lingering illness.

While Cozzens felt that he was at the point in life where he
was waiting to die, he recognized that he really had nothing to
complain about—so far. But he reminded himself that his good
luck was bound to run out; when the reversal came it would
be a lulu. In his sixties he was in the fortunate position of being
able to live very comfortably without worrying about money, for
there was about a quarter of a million dollars in his royalty
account. This 1965 notebook entry describes his Williamstown
situation:

The Human Condition. It is January and half past nine at night with snow
(though less than we often have) covering the ground, and several de-
grees below zero outside. But, indeed, ha, ha, we are warm in my mel-
lowly lighted study with its agreeable walling of books, and 21 original
small folio framed Currier & Ives Civil War Prints, and a lot of pretty
good hybrid African violets flowering in ranks on window shelves; and I
sit at my desk perusing (right word) Dangerfield's *Chancellor Livingston,*
reading about as agreeable as possible, with a mug of Miller's High Life
beer at my hand (it is true that I would prefer National Premium from
Baltimore, if only I could get it) and my Cervantes cigar supplied me by
my Mr. Silverman of Peterson's Ltd and though made in Tampa, still all
Havana (it is true, I would prefer one of the no longer obtainable Romeo y Julietta Numero 57's) and am I content? By God, perfectly! Is this
the best of all possible worlds? Well, at this minute, it is for sure. It
seems right to put this acknowledgement on a record in which I seem to
do a good deal of carping.[13]

"Shadowbrook" in winter

It became apparent that the Williamstown winters were too harsh and that "Shadowbrook" was too much house for Bernice to manage without servants — "a wife-killer," Fannie called it. They considered restoring his great-great-grandfather's Newport house in

1966, but Cozzens couldn't bring himself to live in a city. He was wryly amused by Bernice's concern about finding a safe winter place for him with a study where he could "contentedly occupy myself." A second house, in Florida, was her preferred solution, but they didn't have that kind of money. When he booked them on a winter cruise to the West Indies, Bernice decided against it: "She probably 'has a feeling' that in an uprooted state, I might get out of hand from her standpoint, leaving her in the lurch while I drank with men and fooled with women; and indeed I don't know that this isn't smart of her rather than silly of her." Cozzens was pleased by her concern, "even though recognizing what the object of the Affections of all of us must actually be."[14] He was accustomed to being taken care of by Bernice and yielding to her "whim of iron." If her devotion to him included an admixture of self-love, that was as it should be. When Bernice was leaving "Shadowbrook" to drive her friend Natalie Rogers to the Pownall shop, Cozzens came to the car and cautioned her to be careful on the wet roads. Mrs. Rogers commented on his solicitude, and Bernice said, "He doesn't want me out of his sight."

Bernice proposed a volume of Cozzens short stories to Harcourt, Brace in December 1963, saying that her client did not care either way. Since he did not expect to deliver a novel soon, the story collection might serve to keep his name before the public. She was probably unaware of the literary gossip his six years of silence since *By Love Possessed* was generating—that the Macdonald attack had crushed him and he had quit writing, or that he had become an alcoholic. Cozzens had reverted to his position as America's best unread novelist. In 1963 Harcourt sold a total of 3,852 copies of his books in all editions—including 1,578 of *The Just and the Unjust*, 322 of *By Love Possessed*, and two of *Men and Brethren*.*

Children and Others was published by Harcourt, Brace & World on 29 July 1964 at $5.95; and it was the Book-of-the-Month Club selection for August, which brought a $30,000 advance. Fannie Collins provided the dust-jacket sketch. The collection had seventeen stories—two of which, "King Midas Has Ass's Ears" and "Eyes

---

*Cozzens was not entirely ignored during the sixties, for he was the subject of three critical monographs: Harry J. Mooney, Jr., *James Gould Cozzens: Novelist of Intellect* (University of Pittsburgh Press, 1963), D. E. S. Maxwell, *Cozzens* (Edinburgh & London: Oliver & Boyd, 1964), and Granville Hicks, *James Gould Cozzens* (University of Minnesota Press, 1966). In 1974 a Belgian scholar, Pierre Michel, published *James Gould Cozzens* (New York: Twayne).

The author of Children and Others
in Williamstown (*Harcourt Brace Jovanovich*)

to See," were previously unpublished.* With the exception of "Eyes to See"—which Bernice salvaged from "A Skyborn Music"—none of the stories was written for the volume. Two unsold stories from the thirties—"One Hundred Ladies" and *"Candida* by Bernard Shaw"—appeared just before the book was published. The *Saturday Evening Post* paid $4,000 each for these stories, which it had declined some thirty years earlier.

Children and Others is divided into five sections: I. "Child's Play" ("King Midas Has Ass's Ears," "Child's Play," "Whose Broad Stripes and Bright Stars," "The Animals' Fair," "Total Stranger," and "Something about a Dollar"); II. "Away at School" (four Durham stories—"Some Day You'll Be Sorry," "We'll Recall It with Affection," "The Guns of the Enemy," and *"Candida* by Bernard Shaw"); III. "War Between the States" ("Men Running" and "One Hundred Ladies"); IV. "Love and Kisses" ("My Love to Marcia," "The Way to Go Home," "Every Day's a Holiday," and "Farewell to Cuba"); and V. "Eyes to See." Cozzens explained to Jovanovich: "At the time most of them were done, I'd found I couldn't write with what seemed to me honesty about adults if I wanted real money for my work; but you could tell the truth about children. . . . They're generally, if the truth were told, about myself when young with no more than minor changes in detail." [15]

Jovanovich commented on "Eyes to See": "When I put it down I heard still the countervailing voices, saying and not saying at the same time, of the adults, and somehow I felt all too sad without the slightest trace of sentimentality." [16] At forty-three pages "Eyes to See" is the longest story in the collection. Its subject is not so much the familiar initiation of a child into the adult world, but the development of perception by the young narrator during the events associated with his mother's funeral. The story is about observing and testing observation; it ends with an echo of Cozzens's favorite lines from *Samson Agonistes:* "All passion spent, the past days' task, the new acquist of true incredible experience, could be seen completed." † As the adult Richard Maitland admits in retrospect, "It must follow that much of what I believed true could be untrue; that many opinions of mine could be mistaken; and if I

---

*The collection was planned to include the Durham School story "Son and Heir" and "Introduction to Mammon" (unpublished) and "Lady Love" (possibly "Love Leaves Town"). Cozzens omitted thirteen of his stories from *Children and Others.*

† Cozzens inserted *incredible* in the Miltonic phrase.

wanted to know what I actually knew: why, I knew nothing at all" (p. 307). "Eyes to See" had not been planned to stand alone; it reads like the opening of a novel.

Cozzens sent a copy of *Children and Others* to John O'Hara, whom he regarded as the master of the American short story, inviting his comment on "Eyes to See." * O'Hara replied that he was sorry to say that the balance was wrong for a short story.[17] Cozzens accepted this judgment, replying: "The 'imbalance' might (one could hope) get corrected if I'd gone on as I had intended—of course the boy was to be taken to 'Mount Zion' next summer by his father who wanted to see the idiot child school. The point of the incident on which it now ends was to have been that 'cousin Lois' got knocked-up that night and was slated, under circumstances I meant to try to make those of Pity & Terror to die in childbirth in this fantastic Great House of the defunct religious sect while they boy and his father were there. Those described children of hers, 'Joseph,' and a lot of other stuff you'll recognize, as planted for use later. Unfortunately (or do I mean fortunately) after a silly, stubborn struggle that wasted several years I had to see what I should have seen to start with. A boy that age, if you present him honestly, just isn't of enough interest to the reader of adult intelligence for a long narrative to be based on him."[18]

Children and Others did reasonably well for a collection of stories. The trade printing was 40,000 copies (of which 26,762, in addition to the Book-of-the-Month Club copies, were sold), and Fawcett published it as a Crest paperback in 1965. Longmans, Green published it in England in April 1965 but sold only 2,964 copies. The volume was widely reviewed as "Cozzens's first book since *By Love Possessed.*" The notices were mostly very favorable; but some reviewers complained about the tone of the stories—"dispassionate," "detached," "analytical." Inevitably the reviewers used the occasion to reaffirm their stands on *By Love Possessed* and on Cozzens. The most prominent attack was the front-page article in the *New York Times Book Review* by Frederick C. Crews of the University of California, Berkeley, who identified Cozzens as a "cultural symbol" and described *By Love Possessed* as "a rallying point for literary

---

*Their correspondence was apparently initiated when Cozzens wrote to congratulate O'Hara on the introduction to *The Cape Cod Lighter* in 1962. Although they had lived near each other in New Jersey, they never met.

and social conservatives" because it defended status.* Concentrating on the Durham stories, Crews connected their "old-school-tie attitude" with "the prejudices that mar his later work." [19] Julian Moynihan supported Crews in the *New York Review of Books,* citing Cozzens's defense of institutional authoritarianism, his "stock" ideas, and his "uncertain grasp of either English or American prose idiom or syntax." [20] In the eyes of the left Cozzens was the spokesman for the enemy. Indeed, he was the enemy.

Since Cozzens had earlier written Crews a fan letter on *The Pooh Perplex* (1963), a volume parodying schools of literary criticism, Crews felt obliged to warn him about the forthcoming blast.† Before he saw the review Cozzens replied: ". . . never moving in literary circles and belonging to no group, I have ingenuous trouble in realizing that, as in ward politics, in coterie criticism 'Ingratitude' is the Sin against the Holy Ghost; and when you've scratched someone's back a failure of his to scratch yours is dastardly." He restated his long-standing claim that he had no sociopolitical message. "My only aim and interest is to try to present as exactly as I can people and events as they appear to me. When young, I admit that I imagined such painstaking dispassion, and concern for simple truth, could displease nobody. Of course I know now that, to all who have things to sell or emotional need to write for or against things, such an attitude's simply infuriating." [22]

O'Hara—who was experiencing the displeasure of the left for his interest in upper-class characters—wrote to Cozzens expressing anger at the intolerance of the critical establishment: "You go along with them, or by Christ they will try to destroy you, and not on literary grounds any more. They say quite boldly that if you fail or refuse to conform to their politics, you should not be in business. . . ." [23] Cozzens thanked him for his concern: ". . . I'm if not completely good-and-tough, serviceably tough—at least as long as kind providence or something seems to see to it I'm abused mostly by people I'd far rather have not like my work than like it and whose attacks so consistently go first and foremost to show

---

* Jeffrey Hart's *National Review* article replied to Crews and to Jean Stafford's unfavorable *New York Herald-Tribune* notice: ". . . one of Cozzens' worst crimes in the eyes of reviewers is his awareness of social class. . . . Social class is our unmentionable subject, really; *not,* as Leslie Fiedler's fashionable theory would have it, the wish to have homosexual relations with Negroes and Indians. . . ." [21]

† Cozzens is mentioned on p. 64 of *The Pooh Perplex* (New York: Dutton, 1963).

they're missing my every point. I'd be a liar if I told you decoctions of spleen (courtesy William Hazlitt. I've been rereading him; and how damn well he writes) like Fred Crews' don't make me turn a hair; but I do find it true that when someone's obliging enough to confine himself to half bonehead, half sorehead misrepresentation, and to simple, clear, often comic demonstrable stupidities, he can't very well 'hurt' you. You may get a little sore because it's plain he isn't being fair. But, after all, where's the law that says everybody has to be fair to you?"[24]

The review by the Reverend William Turner Levy in the *Living Church,* praising the "never-faltering details and the never-failing narrative honesty"[25] prompted Cozzens to speculate on the reasons why *Children and Others* had aroused such divergent responses.

I can't but see that this goes directly to some matter of overtones in phrasing, word connotations, impossible to-nail-down conveyings of indefinable attitude in what I write that must account for that on the face of it inexplicable fury the 'liberal intellectual' Jewish critics visit on me. Something sets their teeth on edge. Even when nothing is said that could remotely involve them they can take themselves to be deprived. I must guess it is because my scenes seldom fail to be those into which they cannot see themselves fitting and my people almost entirely those they have reason to feel they couldn't get to know, indeed those by whom, at one time or another, they have been most hurtfully—and also, as likely as not, most unfairly—brushed off. My L. C. reviewer, to the contrary, recognizes himself as fitting in perfectly, as having known these people all his life. Of course what I say about them has that 'look of durability' to him. Of course what I say about them has, to the stung attackers, the look of lousy writing. Worth remembering, I think.[26]

In the fall of 1964 Cozzens shifted *Morning Noon and Night* to the first person, which "seemed to release me at once."*[27] A year later he admitted that he was not satisfied with his work on the novel: "After too many hesitations I've been steadily going ahead with *Morning Noon & Night* for the past weeks. It is not what I wanted and what exactly I wanted I can't say—only: something more than this: no doubt what Marlowe in *Tamburlaine* meant in that passage: 'Yet should there hover in their restless heads / One thought,

* An early surviving version is written in the third person, and the major character is named Henry Maitland. Two pages of this typescript are shown in facsimile in Meriwether's *Checklist,* pp. 49, 53.

one grace, one wonder at the least / Which into words no virtue can digest* but plainly I must accept my limitations and settle, in place of what I would want to do, for whatever I prove able to do."[28] Pondering Aldous Huxley's dictum that "there is no equivalent in literature of sustained counterpoint or the spatial unity of diverse elements brought together so they can be perceived at one glance as a significant whole," Cozzens observed: "But one seems to want to keep trying. He made the point himself in regard to his *Eyeless in Gaza* in the course of a lunch I had with him and Denver Lindley I guess about nine years ago. It impressed me. I made a mental note that someone far abler than I conceded it couldn't be done even by him. But still I seem to have to go ahead with 'Morning Noon, and Night,' I can't stop trying to do what I see very well I'm not going to succeed in doing, and what I know I'm foolish to attempt."[29] The novel was intended as a teleological investigation—a search for design or process. "In *MNN* what I want to do is present stuff in a form of true experience, the happenings of life as I have found them to happen. That is: living, you keep being confronted with facts, things as you discover them to be. Sometimes right then, most often a good deal later, explanations may (or may not, of course) come, showing you, letting you realize, how it happened, why it happened, or even, what really *did* happen (at the time, you may not have been knowing enough to know)."[30]

By May 1967 Cozzens had written 340 pages of the penultimate draft of his thirteenth novel. The final typescript was sent to the publisher in November, and Jovanovich responded warmly: "I read your intention to be that of criticizing life and, at the very same time, of criticizing the *means* by which we chronicle, remember, celebrate the events and circumstances of living. . . . You create characters, situations, and you reflect emotion and temperament; and all the while you are suggesting to the reader how and why this might be done. You *are* speaking to the reader in the direct way that the nineteenth century great novelists did, but I think you are also saying to him, 'let us reflect on how elusively life is lived *and told.*'"[31] *Morning Noon and Night* was published by Harcourt, Brace & World on 26 August 1968 at $5.95. As his first novel in eleven years, it generated considerable prepublication interest and was selected by the Book-of-the-Month Club. The publisher

---

* See p. 401 of *Morning Noon and Night.*

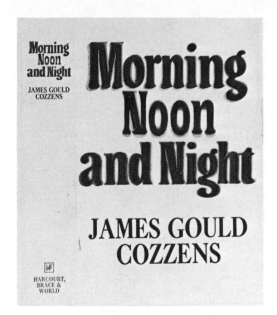

Jacket for first printing of
Morning Noon and Night

sold paperback rights to New American Library for a $76,000 guarantee. The first trade printing was 100,000 copies, in addition to the BOMC copies. Cozzens warned Jovanovich against expecting sales comparable to those for *By Love Possessed:* "I'm trying to see if I can, through a fictional pattern meant to make them readable, lay out observations of mine on human behaviour and the human condition using material taken directly or indirectly from my personal experience. I write in the hope that what I recount may for some people (and I much fear 'some' can't possibly mean 100,000) relate itself rewardingly to their own experience and observation. . . . About fiction-writing my only thought is that writers write whatever they are able to write in whatever way they are able to write it. Asked to pronounce on what the novel ought to be, have or do all I can say is that I think it ought to aim at interesting the grown-up reader."[32]

Morning Noon and Night is cast in the form of a meditative memoir by Henry Dodd Worthington, the sixty-five-year-old founder of a leading management consulting firm. (James Gould Cozzens was sixty-five when the novel was published, and Worthington is the only Cozzens protagonist to use his middle name.) Worthington announces his subject on the third page of the text: *"What is this life? Who am I; what is this 'I' in me?"* That it is the only Cozzens novel written in the first person indicates it is his most personal—though not autobiographical—book, the summation of his broodings on success, reputation, fortune, power, love, marriage, sex, and aging. The title recalls the riddle of the Sphinx solved by Oedipus. What creature goes on four legs in the morning, two legs at noon, and three at night? Answer: man.

The epigraph from Shakespeare's Sonnet 94 defines the renaissance concept of magnanimity:

> They that haue powre to hurt, and will doe none,
> That doe not do the thing, they moſt do ſhowe,
> Who mouing others, are themſelues as ſtone,
> Vnmooued, could, and to temptation flow:
> They rightly do inherrit heauens graces,
> And husband natures ritches from expence,
> They are the Lords and owners of their faces,
> Others, but ſtewards of their excellence:

The intention is ironic. Henry Dodd Worthington, though a powerful and respected figure, claims little virtue for himself. His two marriages were failures (his second wife committed suicide); his daughter is an "incorrigible divorcee"; his business success has been largely the result of good luck. Looking back, Worthington detects no design in life and confronts the future with "apathies of inexpectation." He allegorizes his life as a boat drifting toward a waterfall.

I look around at the twilight, and I look back on my life. I see how it consists of a succession of acts or happenings related in that they were done by or happened to me and were little governed by logic or demonstrable cause and effect—not that there can be effects without causes; still, in the order, may be something of the Queen of Heart's sentence first, verdict afterward. If I have feelings perhaps not consciously known to me of resentment, I have no complaint that I can formulate. Yet I don't doubt, deep down, I harbor a kind of contumacious stubborn persuasion that, given a free hand and almighty means, even with intelligence as limited as mine I could hardly fail to order the order of things better [p. 407].

Morning Noon and Night presents a qualification—if not a negation—of the Cozzens protagonist from Ernest Cudlipp through Arthur Winner. Colonel Ross in *Guard of Honor* insisted that "a pattern should be found; a point should be imposed" on the hodgepodge of life. Worthington—the fount of management wisdom, the solver of other people's problems—sees only all-pervasive good or bad luck. Nevertheless, he does not complain that the struggle naught availeth; there are satisfactions in doing things well for their own sake. The theme of vocation—the interconnections between character and occupation—receives its closest scrutiny in *Morning Noon and Night*.

The novel ends with a rare Cozzens extended metaphor, likening life to Worthington's remembrance of a classic ruin seen in childhood:

—temple columns in twos or threes still loftily upright, damaged capitals held high, while marble drums of others fallen apart lie around them sunk in earth, half concealed by bush and grass. He looks down curving wide ranges of shattered stone steps while he is informed that here had once been a theater. At a distance he can see the tall line of a dozen or more aqueduct arches, commencing suddenly, suddenly ending; coming now from nowhere, now going nowhere. Thin final sunlight of a sort sometimes seen in Canaletto paintings gilds gently enigmatic ancient stone, sere swards of coarse modern grass, and occasional broken hunched old trees. A calling or twittering of skylarks or other birds has ceased; the immense twilight silence settles, and the child must soon be taken away to bed. Yes; good night, good night. Good night, any surviving dear old Carian guests. Good night, ladies. Good night, all.

Appropriately to its subject, *Morning Noon and Night* is an investigation of the memory process. Scene evokes scene in Worthington's meditations, and the first bit of dialogue does not appear until page seventy-one. But it is not cast in stream of consciousness or interior monologue; like the Shakespearean soliloquy, it is exterior monologue. Worthington's memories are developed or staged in complete episodes, although the chronology is associative. The connections exist in the significance of each scene or vignette for Worthington. He explains the structure near the close of his recollections:

That question of causal materiality (or immateriality) presses on me as I come to conclude, much dissatisfied with it, my attempt to put together a meaningful account of my life—how I have drawn breath and walked the earth. Reviewing my passages of writing I am obliged to see I offer little more than a disordered compilation of rough notes, exhibiting frustration rather than accomplished purpose. Perhaps my mistake was in choosing to avoid consecutive narration. I made the choice because I for long have felt that setting out courses of events in the natural, seemingly straightforward way can, oddly enough, distort truth and obscure meaning, at least in the sense of limiting or lessening for a reader his possible new acquist of true experience, since he will not have been told beforehand what he has to know if he is to grasp the real significance in many reported happenings. By imposing an arbitrary order on experience's actual disorder and inconsecutiveness, the consecutive narrative too often sounds that note of falsity, of unpersuasiveness, found in statements or confessions recorded by police stenographers. Even if clearly true transcripts, read or heard they are apt to disturb you with a doubt that it could have been as simple as all that, with a question whether a calculated arrangement, a design of intention (and for what conceivable end but to make a worse appear a better reason?), isn't being imposed on the until now unarranged or designless. Some *post-hoc-propter-hoc* positing, or at least an appearance of it, is hard to exclude—that is, the progressive disclosure of happenings by its mechanical regularity inclines you to presuppose what is not necessarily so, to prevent your seeing where one thing, though it may have followed another, in truth by no means followed as a result [pp. 400–01].

The structure of the novel therefore reinforces Worthington's conclusion that there is no discernable plan in life.

Morning Noon and Night is Cozzens's most sententious work—really, his only deliberately sententious work—with set-piece discourses. The first-person narrative permitted or encouraged him to approach a didactic eighteenth-century flavor in these passages:

[*On Vocation*] When young I managed to believe a man's means of livelihood need be only that. . . . I thought of work as something you did for money to support you while you were living, well apart from the job you happened to have, a 'real' life made up of personal interests and private concerns, intelligent enlargements of physical and mental experience, and selective cultivation of fruitful relations with other people. Apparently I was unable to see that money being what you cannot live without, the means by which you get what you cannot live without is never of no moment. Just as you cannot live without the job you hold, you cannot live apart from it—and, indeed, to say a man holds a job is to misstate the fact. The job holds the man. The job. By 'holding' it he gives his time to it, and what a man spends his time doing is what he is, and through what he is he sees things as he sees them [pp. 37–38].

[*On Puritanism*] In the Puritan tradition, what you took yourself to be superior to was not common man as common man. What you looked down on were personal qualities or practices bad by your standards, not on any human being. You looked down on sloth and ignorance, on fecklessness and vulgarity, on avarice and intemperance. You looked down on lying, stealing, and fornicating. Individuals who exhibited those qualities or indulged in such practices were necessarily held low; yet your own not exhibiting them or not indulging in them never exalted you. You did little more than meet ordinary obligations (or, as at best the case must be, you met many of them much of the time) and from *that* you took no title to glory, laud, and honor. Indeed, in your justifiable looking-down-on, say, the feckless or the fornicators, you were obligated under the code to pause and earnestly pronounce: *There but for the Grace of God, go I* [pp. 41-42].

[*On Writers*] He notices the very noticeable fact (he would prefer not to descend to personalities; but, here, how hard to help it!) that a number of those present fall almost generically into types—the lank and the flat-chested women's-college liberal, looking rather unwashed and rather debauched; the pompous, obstinately humorless revolutionary young man sprouting his bit of beard, yet in his nervous giggle less than virile; the craggy-faced, homespun, virile-indeed buck-fairy on his prowl for boy-does (also sure to be around). Even a few such look-and-act-alikes viewed grouped together can suggest an imitating, a copying of each other—which can in turn suggest (maybe not always fairly) that these are pretenders pretending; fakes, not real writing writers.

My calling attention to generic conference types may, I see, create an impression of the quality of that years-ago summer gathering and of the honesty of those attending that would be both unjust and untrue. To be kept in mind is the newness of the whole concept, the necessarily experimental nature of the agenda, the often extemporized untried and untested methods. Moreover, while quite noticeably present, the generic types were really not there in force, were nothing like a majority. Full-scale musterings of them waited on later-date convocations such as that farcical 'Congress' of the '30's. There the generic types, the more puzzle-headed 'social activists,' and all those human oddities once named by Max Beerbohm *adults of the infantile persuasion* swarmed so numerous that, dominant, they were soon seized of control, magisterially running the close-to-burlesque show, and doing all the fatuous talking for what would be the affair's official record. Indeed, that at our Hank's conference this *wasn't* the case is part of the point I would wish to make. To disturb him seriously, to give him anxious pause, the pretended-writer or doctrinaire-critic suspects needn't be numerous.

I must wonder if the fact doesn't show that, while in his own outward appearance, in what he does and says, he may little resemble the pretenders present, our Hank is not secure in his difference. The show of even a few of their stamp may be judged to speak disturbingly to subliminal doubts of his about his own talent, about whether he, either, has it in him to be a real writer. Is he finding, through watching these people, himself exposed to himself? How can he be sure he isn't what so many of them seem to him to be? Has he a single good reason to believe, if he keeps on writing, he can make himself anything more than they are? The questions shake him; and, shaken, he may begin to realize that by asking themselves they are answering themselves. The inner doubt gives proof positive that, as well as in all likelihood lacking the talent, he most hope-lessly lacks the temperament a writer who is serious about writing has to have.

The temperament is one you must be born with; you can't cultivate or develop it; and if our Hank wonders what signs of being born with it are, he need only look at his friend Knox. At the conference Knox is not failing to see the same things, and he, too, was certainly expecting some-thing else, but his seeing doesn't have the same effect on him. Shaken by no self-distrust, he accepts untroubled, at once perceives as only natural, the straggle of nuts and queers that creative arts must always attract. He is not disturbed by what the pretenders, the half-writers, may do or be like. Sure; the instruction of fools, of the pundits of the little cash-poor magazines, of the radical mouthy doyens of the small-fee sophomore cir-cuit, will be folly—but what the hell else could it be? And what does it have to do with serious writing, with himself as a writer? Egoistically sanguine and confident, he watches them with contempt, sees them as simply good for unkind laughs; and once he is sure that staying in their company offers nothing from which he can profit, nothing to his writing purpose, he drops out. By temperament he is concerned with himself only, and how to express himself. Even if stridulent instruction of the fools turns directly on him and his work (which, should he begin to be successful and celebrated, must be expected; after all, these are self-de-fense's, self-preservation's envious gashes), his born-writer's temperament is a sevenfold shield. He can be hardly pricked to more than flashes of 'ire'—like my grandfather when his critics heaped their rancorous moti-vated abuse on him. The truth in one's heart, we are told, does not fear the lie on another's tongue [pp. 247–49].

As the closing good-night motif suggests, *Morning Noon and Night* can be read as Cozzens's valedictory. Although he expected to continue writing for publication, the novel is virtually an inven-tory of things Cozzens valued (the Puritan ethic, ability, intelligence, reason, the lessons of experience) and deprecated (self-indulgent emotion, youth, the liberal establishment, the literary life). In Worthington's caustic account of a writers' conference and its con-cern over Sacco and Vanzetti, Cozzens indulged the temptation to thumb his nose at the left literary network.* A key word in the novel is *inappetency:* Cozzens delineates Worthington's—and his own—loss of appetite for living. Another personal element in *Morning Noon and Night* is that it provides a reply to the charges of bigotry leveled against *By Love Possessed*. The long account of

---

*Worthington asserts that on the basis of the ballistics evidence Sacco was certainly guilty.

the academic career of Worthington's grandfather, "Cubby," an early traducer of Freud, and his difficulties with anti-anti-Semitism has obvious connections with Cozzens's situation. In commenting on the attacks against Cubby's scholarship—which is in truth bad— Cozzens obviously had his own critics in mind:

Their methodology is by and large one of misrepresentation, and for this purpose a good deal of recourse is had to quotings out of context—often most ingenious; for while rancor may weaken general judgment, it frequently sharpens craft, gives deviousness inspiration. Wonderful to observe are the twists of sense and even total reversals of meaning to be effected in many written lines simply through deleting some that precede and some that follow; or through artful ellipses indicated by a set of points to suggest, all innocence, that phrases or sentences omitted hadn't been relevant [pp. 128–29].

The Cozzens touch is that Cubby is a self-satisfied fool who achieves unmerited renown by surviving to a great age. Since Worthington is the son of a New England college president, Cozzens was able to make use of his Williams observations for the academic background.

Though less dense than *By Love Possessed,* the style of *Morning Noon and Night* is nonetheless authentic late Cozzens—with inverted sentences, occasional unfamiliar words, parenthetical constructions, and borrowings from the classics.* Distilling experience, he required distilled expression. Bernice warned him that no one under forty would understand *Morning Noon and Night,* but he was probably unprepared for the vehemence of the reception. Most of the prominent eastern reviews were denunciatory. In the *New Yorker* John Updike savaged the style as "unique in its mannered ugliness, a monstrous mix of Sir Thomas Browne, legalese, and Best-Remembered Quotations."[33] (Cozzens regarded this review as the "real jewel" of his kick and nut file.)† *Newsweek* described the novel as the "abstracted meanderings of a narrator who recognized early on that he lacked a 'writer's temperament' ";[34] Eliot Fremont-Smith (*New York Times*) called it a "sleeping pill"

---

*Clifton Fadiman tabulated 197 literary allusions and quotations in his *Book-of-the-Month Club News* article.
†Updike listed examples for the following categories of stylistic atrocity: "The Unresisted Cliché"; "The Lame Echo"; "The False Precision, the Legal 'Or' "; "The Vapid Expansion"; "The Inversion Frightful, Capped by Cute Periphrasis"; "The Gratuitous Scientism"; "The Infatuated Sonority."

and "unspeakably sour and sad";[35] John Brooks (*New York Times Book Review*) said it was a failure;[36] Peter S. Prescott (*Look*) branded it a travesty and "bad beyond believing."[37] In the *National Review* Guy Davenport cited the novel's "fog of sentimentality" and classed Cozzens with Howells as a novelist who takes realism to "a kind of ultimate fulfillment" but whose work doesn't seem to matter.[38] The hinterland reviews were no better—warning that the novel was not worth reading and complaining about the fragmentation of the narrative and the coldness of the author. Even Clifton Fadiman had trouble mustering enthusiasm for his report in the *Book-of-the-Month Club News:* "The people so shrewdly drawn in these slow, reflective pages represent the class that up to very recently has owned most of, and operated all of, America, insofar as America is conceived as a business corporation. Whether or not one likes the world that engages Mr. Cozzens' attention, one is forced to admire his capacity to make it live. He is a kind of Sargent of contemporary American fiction."[39]

John Barkham's syndicated review was warmly favorable; other positive reviews were written by Granville Hicks (*Saturday Review*), Clifford A. Ridley (*National Observer*), and Edmund Fuller (*Wall Street Journal*). But even the good notices—which advised that *Morning Noon and Night* was not easy reading—were not what the trade calls selling reviews. It was not a "good read" or "a page-turner." Walter Jackson Bate's letter to Cozzens praised the qualities that discouraged readers: ". . . Swiftian lucidity as a general norm, against which play the allusiveness, the controlled romantic and nostalgic meditations, and an aphoristic richness in the vein of Bacon and Johnson, so that on every page, as in no other novelist of our generation, we are constantly coming upon expression, saturated with thought, that delights both the ear and the mind."[40] Nineteen-sixty-eight was a bad year for thought-saturated expression.

Claiming to be indifferent to the reviews of *Morning Noon and Night,* Cozzens reported to Jovanovich that it had brought him the best fan mail he'd ever had:

I can't pretend I didn't want (or badly need) some of that, but that's really all I ever want or need; and here comes in—it's a hell of a thing to tell one's publisher when he's warmed one's heart with his editor's praise and laid out I hate to think how much promotional dough—the secret truth that I don't *like* books of mine to be Big Best Sellers.

The stand is less than lofty. Damn it, I just don't want what in my

vanity I conceive to be my choice devices and delicate conceits made free
with by hordes of semi-literates who'll simply get fingermarks on them
as they hand them back and forth vacuously dropping their jaws and
grunting: *huh?* Alas, baser still are that stand's underpinnings. That most
of the BLP business gave me nothing but a severe pain in, let's call it,
my mind's ass is no lie, but I loved every bit of that lovely money. What
else, now rather more than doubled for me by Bill Harris at Laidlaw's,
lets me be hoity-toity about who may read my books, and permits me in
lordly unconcern about sales figures? And do these fine pronouncements
come pretty close to: *Screw you Jack I've got mine?* Yes, they do; but all
the while I love you (if that helps).[41]

Cozzens recognized that his lofty disdain for readers was in considerable part a wound-licking mechanism. Finding that his most
mature work repelled readers, he could only say the hell with them.
He took wry comfort in Maugham's observation that writers often
achieve high reputation through longevity—by simply outliving
the bastards. (But so did that old fool Cubby.) Nevertheless, he
lacked Maugham's sustaining egoism. As Cozzens brooded in his
isolation, his thoughts darkened.

The critical disagreement did not generate any real controversy,
and the trade sales never gained momentum. Harcourt sold about
35,000 copies, leaving 65,000 to be disposed of. While insisting
that *Morning Noon and Night* was *"not* a bad book," Cozzens admitted to Jovanovich that its failure showed people didn't want to
read the kind of novel he wrote. The fact that the Book-of-the-
Month Club dropped it from their ads indicated that it had not
been ordered by members: "That would be no matter of Ethnic
Group liberal intellectual trying to do me down."[42] The English
reception when the novel was published by Longmans in January
1969 was no better. The reviews dismissed it as an eccentric work.
Only 5,329 copies were sold, and the Book Club Associates moved
another 5,899.

Harcourt, Brace & World used the publication of *Morning Noon
and Night* to launch a Cozzens uniform edition. Buyers of the
novel were invited to write to the publisher for a free uniform-
edition dust jacket; *Castaway, S.S. San Pedro, Men and Brethren,*
and *Ask Me Tomorrow* were reprinted in the uniform-edition format, but the project had to be suspended.*

---

*By 1962 *Castaway* had sold 4,175 copies; *S.S. San Pedro,* 3,700; *Ask Me Tomorrow,* 932; and
Men and Brethren, 902.

Despite the disappointment of *Morning Noon and Night,* Cozzens informed Julian Muller in November 1968 that he was "mulling over the opening of a new book, perhaps to be called a Skyborn Music. . . ."[43] It was not a return to the Maitland material he had abandoned in 1960. Nothing more is known about it, but it was probably the work that became "The Wind and the Rain." In the fall of 1969 he reported to Jovanovich on his sense of futility:

I do of course write and write away. It's a nervous habit I contracted about age 15 and, 60 years on, I can no more kick it than I can kick tobacco and booze. Still, driven as I am, I have to know I'm not now really getting anywhere, and can't hope I will until my old codger's organism finds means to adjust, to compensate for what I must recognize as natural endocrine deficiencies that too often, with no excuse of pain or illness, no legitimate worries about health or money or Getting Ahead, no discontents with my cozy as possible living conditions, can wake me up at 4 am to ponder until my 6.30 rising hour on what's the use of anything.

However I find this happening now less regularly than 6 months or a year ago. Could be, I see, I'll again get to have my heart in my work. For now, that work's a couple of hundred pages of random or desultory scraps (often ten times rewritten) to which I give the title: *A Thing of the Past,* with for tentative epigraph lines of Santayana's. . . .[44]

The 7 November 1969 contract called for 1 July 1971 delivery. During 1970 and 1971 he wrote hundreds of pages of character sketches for a novel titled "The Wind and the Rain"—almost certainly a retitling of "A Thing of the Past"—but had no schedule for completion. Again he informed Jovanovich of his pervasive despair: ". . . I have my daily moments of wondering what writing *is* worth as a human act—with resulting discouraged spells of not seeming able to get the stuff to suit me. I'm enjoying one of these at the moment and while able as a creature of habit to write all right it's under a cloud (mornings mostly) of pointlessness."[45] After forty-six years as a published novelist he no longer believed in his craft.

"The Wind and the Rain"* survives in 129 pages of revised typescript described by Cozzens as "a few left-behind insubstantial

---

* From the clown's song in *Twelfth Night:* "When that I was and a little tiny boy, / With hey, ho, the wind and the rain, / A foolish thing was but a toy, / For the rain it raineth every day."

JAMES GOULD COZZENS

THE WIND AND THE RAIN.

I. Home is the Sailor.

II. Casca, Be Sudden.

III. Farewell, a Long Farewell.

MXMLXX

Contents page for The Wind and the Rain

pagent racks." These working drafts introduce Admiral Orton and his four sons—a doctor, an Episcopal bishop, an artist, and a politician. A "quarterdeck martinet," retired from sea duty and now in charge of an old sailors' home in New England, the Admiral is disappointed in all of his sons. The point-of-view character—but not the narrator—is Andrew Orton, the politician's son. A major character in the unwritten or discarded sections was to be Lenore Orton, the bishop's daughter who becomes a Washington columnist; she was based on Cozzens's journalist cousin Prunella Wood. The time span of "The Wind and the Rain" would have covered some thirty years. It was his custom to date the pages of his drafts, and the latest date on these pages is 712/6 (6 February 1971).

Cozzens experienced lingering flu symptoms and leg pains in the winter and spring of 1971. His doctor informed him that he was an alcoholic and advised him to quit drinking. To Cozzens's surprise, he was able to give up alcohol without much trouble after decades of methodical drinking. Since uncontrollability is a factor in defining alcoholism, his ability to stop drinking without relapses raises the question of whether he was truly an alcoholic—and if so, for how long.

His alcohol consumption seems to have increased at Williamstown, but the evidence is inconclusive because it comes from visitors whose presence accelerated his drinking. Fannie Collins, who lived with the Cozzenses in Williamstown, reports that his regular ration was a double Scotch with lunch and two doubles before dinner, but he poured with a heavy hand. In the evening he drank three or four beers. He became irritable when his predinner drinks were delayed, but all was serene after two doubles. His postprandial beer intake provided a feeling of well-being: "Pope's phrase: 'a person much bemused in beer' occurred to me for no particular reason last evening when bemusing myself in it. I sat reading Walter Jackson Bate's *Keats*. I could see the phrasing was perfect. Us beer-drinkers, when we've put down whatever our quota is, just sit there, content. You're not in the least befuddled, or otherwise mentally disabled. You're not stirred as hard liquor in the amount you begin to 'feel' may stir you, to ill-advised action and general getting into trouble. You're less than jubilant perhaps: but you feel fine. Every prospect pleases. All looks well in some indeterminate, yet completely reassuring and confidence-inspiring way. Indeed, it *does* do more than Milton can to justify God's ways to man. With a beer mug beside you, it's now whatever o'clock it is, and all's (for the prolonged moment) well."[46] Cozzens never went on benders or got into trouble with the law because of drinking. As his outdoor activities became less strenuous his body was unable to burn up his ration, and he became stout.

It is impossible to discuss Cozzens's alcoholism with confidence.

He was clearly not the kind of textbook alcoholic writer that Fitzgerald, Faulkner, and O'Hara were. If the diagnosis of alcoholism requires only dependence, then Cozzens was an alcoholic. He depended on alcohol to make his life agreeable and, as it turned out, to write. As with many alcohol-dependent people, the factor in Cozzens's case was not so much quantity of consumption, but timing. Methodical drinking after morning writing stints formed part of his creative process. However much good going on the wagon at sixty-seven did for his liver, the deprivation of alcohol was disastrous for Cozzens as a writer. He never felt good again, and he stopped writing. The term *anhedonia*—defined as "total loss of pleasure in acts that normally give pleasure"—describes the condition of "inappetency" Cozzens endured without alcohol. It was never ameliorated.[47]

In May 1971, some ten days after he quit drinking, Cozzens blacked out at the wheel of his Thunderbird. He reported the event to Jovanovich in July:

Thanks for the books & the sympathy. Yes, 'my' accident proved indeed a horrid experience, made worse by the fact that I had and have no idea of exactly what happened or how it happened. I went down to Williamstown to get the mail about two in the afternoon. I did not feel sleepy, I hadn't been drinking (see infra) and there were no warning odd feelings. The sequence as seen by me: driving along everything had been all right, and then without intermission I was lying in the middle of a monumental smash-up. The crash, I gather, had been truly spectacular. I must have hit the concrete wall of a small bridge at around 45 mph. The car doubled up and bounced back across the road, blocking it. US7 is heavily travelled and sheer luck made it one moment when nothing [was coming] was coming the other way—the normal two or three cars coming south fast and we would have had something. As it was, it was good enough—the car, a fairly tough one, a Thunderbird, ended as about as total a loss as anyone ever saw. Perhaps I also had more luck in that not not far behind me drove the man who mows our grass, and not far behind him a physician, not mine but one I knew, and a telephone was not a hundred feet away. I must have been out awhile, though I wasn't aware of it. A line of cars and quite a crowd had gathered to see so exciting an accident, including two ambulances, by the time I came, quite clear-headed to dumbly ask: what happened? and the physician, bent over me, was telling me that I knew him, just lie still. He continued to go over me rapidly (somehow they had got me out) and signed to the stretcher bearers to pick me up. I was taken to the North Adams hospital emergency room, not in any pain, still clear-headed, though my face was good and bloody (right: I hadn't bothered to fasten my seat belt, seeing myself as too skilled and experienced a driver to need to). Here came much delay, since the hospital, though not a bad one, has no resident physicians; and since I seemed nearly suffocating on blood I decided, continuing clear in my mind and to my surprise not at all seriously distressed that I was without doubt dying. Indeed when at last a surgeon, one of my physician's colleagues, turned up that seemed to be his idea too. He took seven quick stitches in my lip and shot me down to the x-ray rooms to be gone over, There, to everyone's incredulity, the pictures showed nothing broken or even ruptured. This incredulity was so great that they kept after me for days with all kinds of fancy tests, imcluding much attention to the skull, employing devices I had never heard of. One, a cumbersome machine, scans the head 20 minutes on the back, 20 minutes on the right side, 20 minutes on the left and draws an amaxingly clear and detailed picture. In another, they paste wires all over the scalp, direct lights of variable intensity into your eyes, asking you from time to time if you feel dizzy (I didn't) and putting sudden questions: eg. what is 100 minus 9; if yesterday was Tuesday what is today? (I refrained from answering: a damn bore) apparently designed to make you think so they can count electric waves. In the end they were driven to conclude that it was true, I had no overlooked injuries; and though they kept me on I.V. bottles for 72 hours, after the stitches in my lip, there was nothing to do—even there, though I badly lacerated my tongue, I didn't lose any teeth. Finally satisfied that the littel miracle was a fact they lost interest in me.

Still, though I came out of it whole—no one knew how—I was soon to find I was very far from having got away with it. I'd taken a terrific if not testable beating which would plague me for weeks, and indeed I now see probably for months and maybe forever. My troubles I know sound insignificant—one of the tongue lacerations was so deep that it could not heal without scar tissue, so I'll have a tiresome lisp for what remains of my life, and succeeding each other are odd assortments of aches and pains in unexpected places that keep you from sleeping. With them, and hardest to stand up under, is such a sunk feeling as I've never known—I can't seem to get back any energy (ten minutes picking peas which are good this year exhausts me) and I find it impossible to take any real interest in anything. My doctor, on his latest checking, beamed with satisfaction assuring me I was in fine physical shape, but I could only answer that I wished he were inside me, and then let him see what he thought. Of course the simple fact, so hard for me to believe even now, is that I am not 48 or 58 but next month 68.

This is about enough complaining. Still the incident seems pretty much to put a period to life up here. We can't stay here if I'm not able to drive a car, and that blackout business persuades me (for the moment) that I never can again—if Bernice had been with me that afternoon she would unfailingly have been killed because it was on her side that the engine moved right into the front compartment. Three physicians have agreed that such a thing was unlikely to recur (nothing of the kind ever happened to me before; I'd never in my life fainted, or been knocked out, or in any other way lost consciousness); but that's hardly enough when you can't be sure it won't, not even when their concensus gets support of sorts from what I've since learned, which suggests it may indeed have been a special case and very much my own fault.

This goes to my physician's advice, given a couple of weeks before, when he couldn't find anything else wrong with me, to stop drinking. Taking it, I was fool enough to do it the wrong way. I just stopped; which I did not find difficult; but that was, I've heard from another physician to disregard the hell of a shock I gave my 'system', accustomed for years to daily little doses of alcohol, and the blacking-out, I'm assured, is a well known side effect. I should have stretched it over a month. slowly reducing the dose. I can partly excuse myself because my doctor authoratatively said and indeed I had heard that there was no such thing as doing it gradually—wrong, I believe, in my case because as I say I quit with no trouble, which I suppose you can't do if you have the addiction he must have supposed I had. He is a very good physician but I should have remembered he is also a bit of a Christer, neither drinking nor smoking himself, and so of course much bent on having other people do likewise. Usually this might not matter, but, again in my case, I much fear I'm going to find it was a very bum idea; that, if unawares, I depended for any creative impulse I had on a mood that depended on a judicious (I think I may claim it was) taking of a few drinks. So while substitution of water may be good for my liver, which he somberly said was becoming enlarged, I must suspect it will be by no means good either for my mind or my work. We'll just have to see, supposing I ever recover anything like a normal feeling.

This collection of circumstances greatly helped to make it seem a sensible idea to get rid of this place. It had long been too big, too expensive, and the winters too tough for old bones. Conveniently it happens that the man who owns the white house on the road, whose ten acres are surrounded by our land has been anxious to buy the place and is well able to afford it, so selling was no bother and we are getting out the 1st of November. Our first plan had been to go down to Sanibel island, which I know and where Fannie has been spending winters; but, untimely, the so-called 'red tide' has hit into Fort Myers this year, meaning no fish and no shellfish for a long time (even without booze ny stomach is still my god) so that will not do. Instead we are trying to locate some place on the keys, perhaps around Marathon. Here I know little having done no more than pass trought to Key West. I remembered your saying you'd visited your son there. Do you know or know anyone who knows anything about the neighborhood? (Key West is too much of a town for me). Our new idea was to go down to Islamorada and look around, but it would be a great help if someone could say first hand which among the many advertised resorts, each represented as a sort of heaven, were actually fit to live in.

I wish I could be definite about plans beyond the winter but clearly what we do must depend on what, come spring, I find I can do. We'll just let it ride, but you'll gather that any new book must be some way off. As a literary property I fear I scrape bottom and may justly be regarded with impatience when I show myself so lacking in grace under stress. If you can write me anything cheerful about yourself please do. I might take heart.

. . . .

I have also forgotten how to type, you'll note.[48]

Cozzens later felt that ". . . I really died in that car and this is someone posing as me."[49] He insisted that he should have died then: it was the right time.

TEN

Mute in Gaza

WHEN "Shadowbrook" was sold the Cozzenses disposed of some 3,000 volumes to a Vermont bookseller and abandoned his record collection.* Many of these books were complimentary copies sent to agents and authors, but the decision to abandon the library he had transported from Carrs Farm indicates that Cozzens knew he wouldn't be needing books in Florida. In November 1971 the Cozzenses rented a house at 1 Harbor Circle Drive, Coconut Park, in Stuart, Florida. They spent the summer of 1972 at Shaftsbury, Vermont, and returned to Coconut Park in the fall. Unwilling to pay the high purchase price for this house, they decided to buy the cheapest comfortable condominium they could find in 1973. Fannie moved to Florida, and they bought apartments in Beacon 21 at Rio, near Stuart. F-1, the Cozzenses' apartment, had a kitchen, living room, Bernice's bedroom, and Cozzens's small bedroom-study facing a fenced-in back patio. His room held the few hundred volumes he had retained—Huxley (19 volumes), Galsworthy (17), Maugham (16), Evelyn Waugh (4), Shakespeare, dictionaries (including the thirteen-volume *Oxford English Dictionary*), reference works, gardening books, and Bernice's collection of cookbooks and

---

*284 of the books were listed in Ken Leach's Catalogue 71-4. Cozzens's phonograph records are in the Bruccoli Collection.

In Rio, Florida
(*Princeton University Library*)

her volumes on antiques—as well as a model of a 1964 Thunder-bird.*

Cozzens felt humiliated by his Florida senior-citizenship, which he described as "the Eyeless-in-Gaza-at-the-mill-with-slaves syndrome" (5 December 1974). Unlike the saga of Milton's Samson, the history of James Gould Cozzens would not conclude with the comfort of "calm of mind all passion spent." By the end of 1974 he had stopped writing, telling Jovanovich that "these days I find myself stultified by seeing I simply have nothing to say to or for contemporary Making-It Literary Establishment, or to satisfy current Intellectual Elite Criticism. . . . In clear fact work of mine's all out of season. . . ."[1]

Having abandoned fiction, he resumed keeping detailed diaries in January 1974 (the old itch to write), which provide an unre-

---

*The only American novels he had were Harold Frederic's *The Damnation of Theron Ware* and Dos Passos's *U.S.A.* trilogy. His reference library included: *New Catholic Edition of the Holy Bible, Dictionary of the Bible, English Prepositional Idioms, Dictionary of Obsolete English, Modern American Usage, Dictionary of American Slang, March's Thesaurus-Dictionary, A Dictionary of Modern English Usage, Harvard Concordance to Shakespeare, The Catholic Encyclopaedic Dictionary, The Oxford Dictionary of English Etymology, The Reader's Encyclopedia of Shakespeare, The Oxford Classical Dictionary, The Shorter Oxford English Dictionary, Webster's Third New International Dictionary,* a Greek/Latin *New Testament, An Elementary Latin Dictionary, A Dictionary of Latin Literature, The New Testament* (Moffat), *The Dictionary of Philosophy,* a Roman Catholic *New Testament, The Apocryphal New Testament, The Oxford Self-Pronouncing Bible,* and several editions of the *Book of Common Prayer.*

lieved chronicle of inappetency, inexpectation, and disrelish for life.* He felt that he and Bernice were under a suspended death sentence. But he was spared the shameful spectacle of his self-pity. Since he had never expected anything good from old age, he did not feel ill-used or betrayed. He had long warned himself that the bill for his good luck would come due. Given his choice, he would have preferred not to have been born. "All I see is Santayana's 'this great disaster of our birth' " (15 March 1974). And "if I could arrange to go to bed to night and just never wake up tomorrow I'd do so instantly, yet the animal [shrinking] from the upsets, inconveniences and invaded privacy of dying isn't gone" (20 September 1974). Thus, "I rather liked death: but eschewed dying" (9 December 1974). Cozzens regularly considered suicide: "since there's nothing here I enjoy, want, feel interest in, or can look forward to but more silly annoyances and unbecoming behavior on my part what the hell is that 12 gauge pump gun in my closet for if not to blow off the top of my head and make these odds at even. Real trouble: those who have wisely done it I find I rather despise?" (4 March 1975). Apart from his reluctance to cause Bernice distress—although he knew that she would get along better without him than he would without her—he was prevented from putting the gun to his head by some unformulated feeling that he had to see his life through.

Writing fiction was impossible without alcohol. And without his work his existence was purposeless: "because in fact I only lived to write, see no sense in life, have only forced 'interests,' wish every night, not urgently but quite definitely I could just not wake up tomorrow" (17 August 1974). Moreover, he missed the sense of well-being that alcohol, especially beer, had provided. He tried an occasional Scotch in Florida but found "alas, that cursed spite is unchanged: the stuff that once made life look worthwhile does nothing at all to my aged physiology" (25 December 1976).

When they moved to Beacon 21, Cozzens was concerned that he would have unwelcome socializing forced on him. He was relieved to find that the condominium residents left him alone after Bernice passed the word that her husband was a writer and required solitude. Mentions of his books were painful reminders of what

*"Foeda in coitu et brevis voluptas est / Et taedet veneris statim peractae" [The pleasure in coitus is brief and repulsive, and when sex is over it immediately disgusts]—from Cozzens's notepad, Princeton University Library.

he once had been. He occupied himself with mild patio gardening and by playing the stock market. In addition to the some $450,000 that was being managed by William Harris, Cozzens maintained a "cat and dog account," in which he speculated in over-the-counter stocks with a local broker. He made a steady profit by buying 500 shares and then selling 400 if the stock rose. His income in Florida was $35,000 a year, and it cost him $15,000 to live. He had nothing to spend money on.

To his real chagrin, television—which he had never bothered to watch before—came to kill a larger and larger part of his time. "Dismayingly, I just can't seem to give a damn about doing anything except somehow getting thru to bedtime" (5 February 1974). He rose before 6:00 A.M. and enjoyed the early-morning hours when he brooded—if not happily, at least tranquilly. But the evenings were long. At first he limited his television watching to news programs, but then began to watch serious dramatizations, which confirmed his long-held conviction that novels and Shakespeare were always better when read. The only mass-entertainment program he found occasionally diverting was the Mary Tyler Moore show.

His growing dependence on television resulted from the circumstance that he had stopped reading books: "senility or something seems to, I guess stultify thinking of the sort that made reading interesting & profitable—indeed I guess I always read mainly, you could say, to write: no longer writing, why read?" (16 May 1976). However, he subscribed to a wide assortment of magazines (*Barron's, Forbes, National Review, Living Church, Scientific American, British History Illustrated, Time, Newsweek, American Heritage, U. S. News, Consumer's Guide, Early American Life, Plants Alive, Civil War Times, Smithsonian, Gourmet, American History Illustrated, Saturday Review*—and other gardening and Episcopal Church journals). The *Wall Street Journal* was his favorite newspaper; Bernice was a loyal reader of the *New York Times,* which he called "The Daily Liar." The "ineffable" Anthony Lewis in the *Times* provided Cozzens with a dependable source for indignation.

He became occupied by the Watergate and Daniel Ellsberg cases—in which he perceived the Democrats, Judge Sirica, Ellsberg, the *New York Times,* and the *Washington Post* as the principal villains. Politicians of all parties were cheap bastards and liars; but "the furibund Dems" were using the Watergate disclosures to get Richard Nixon, whose "vulgar antics" appalled him. (He was also appalled by Jimmy Carter, "the Skipping King.") * Whatever Nixon was, his enemies were worse. Cozzens believed that the Congress had deliberately prevented the Vietnam War from being won by the War Powers Act of 1973. The only public figure he particularly respected was Henry Kissinger, and Cozzens relished the show of the Jewish left turning on their fellow Jew. Having no one to talk to except Bernice—who did not share his political views—he carefully recorded his disaffections in his diaries.

During 1974 Cozzens was bothered by a persistent sore spot on his palate, which he attributed to the after-effects of his 1971 wreck. He suspected a malignancy and rather hoped it would put an end to his increasingly purposeless life. A March 1974 biopsy revealed no cancerous tissue, but he continued to anticipate development of "the customary cancer." At the same time Bernice was troubled with intestinal disorders diagnosed as colitis or diverticulitis. She had always been slim, but her weight fell below ninety pounds. Cozzens had a foreboding that she was seriously ill, but the doctors assured them that there was no evidence of a condition that required surgery.

The sore spot in Cozzens's mouth was removed in March 1975; the biopsy revealed a neoplasm. He was given the choice between radical surgery and less-certain cobalt treatment. "I pointed out at my age life isn't much to use (never mind: but young men think it is and they were young—that's just what I wasn't, I'd had a damn lucky life in point of comfort, success, money. . . . Or, in short: And farewell, world" (13 March 1975). All of his teeth were extracted before he underwent a cobalt series. His doctors reported that he was a good reactor and encouraged him to hope that the thing had been caught in time; but Cozzens assured them that he didn't expect to "win them all. . . . I also remember Lucretious said (roughly) when you finish dinner, stupid, go to bed. That's for me."[2] False teeth were not provided until September, and for five months he spoke in a mumble. After his dentures were fitted, he went without them as much as possible. These discomforts and humiliations intensified his meditations on "the expense of spirit in a waste of shame" and the shotgun in his closet.

Bernice was clearly starving to death in the fall of 1975, and Cozzens managed to function with steady doses of Valium. She was

* Secretary of State Cyrus Vance, Kent '35, irritated Cozzens: "why the hell couldn't he have gone to Choate" (13 January 1977).

operated on in November for removal of a tumorous intestinal obstruction and made a good recovery. Several times in 1976 bone fragments were removed from Cozzens's jaw. He thought it would be well to kill himself after Bernice was stable.

In 1972 James B. Meriwether of the University of South Carolina compiled a book-length checklist of Cozzens's work for a series published by Gale Research and Bruccoli Clark. Since Meriwether was a Cozzens admirer of long standing and had visited him in Lambertville and Williamstown, Cozzens wrote an introduction for the volume. Editorial correspondence with Matthew J. Bruccoli led to Cozzens's November 1973 offer of an unpublished short story for the Bruccoli Clark Collector's Editions series. "A Flower in Her Hair" had been written when letters and photos from his 1925 –26 Cuban residence were turned over to him after his mother's death. "Result was a past recalled with startling force and clarity, and the result's result (how common with writers) an urge to write about, what missed at the time, now brought new understanding."[3] It had been offered to a women's magazine that requested first chance at a Cozzens story, but was declined as "unpleasant." Concerned that publication of the story in 1953 might hurt people he'd liked, Cozzens withdrew it. When he had selected the stories for *Children and Others* in 1964, Cozzens included "A Flower in Her Hair," but it disappeared at the printer's. In 1973 a forgotten carbon copy turned up in the Brandt & Brandt files. Since the story was one of his favorites, the idea of a collector's edition appealed to him. *A Flower in Her Hair* was published in April 1975 in an edition of 350 numbered and signed copies, with an introduction by Cozzens. This three-and-half-page introduction gave him considerable difficulty over four months: not because he had nothing to say, but because writing no longer seemed to matter. "Concentrating on any Purpose in life is clearly unwise—when you lose it, where are you?" (17 April 1974). Based on two of his pupils in Cuba, the story examines the resentment of a girl whose older sister has become interested in boys. The story was written with "every care for verisimilitude" as an exercise in representational fiction; only the violent ending was invented.* "For Deeper

---

*In a draft for the introduction Cozzens wrote that "—as Somerset Maugham once noted no believable character 'created' by any writer lacked an original. Inventions, if truly so, could not be given lifelikeness."[4]

Insight, there can be no prize of recognition that here, retold to relate to modernity's social, economic, ecological, political or ethnic issues, or for some good propaganda purpose, is, say, the great fable of Leda and the swan. Here, what he gets is what he sees—story only."[5]

Cozzens was sufficiently pleased by the format of *A Flower in Her Hair* to offer another unpublished short work to Bruccoli Clark in September 1976. "A Rope for Doctor Webster," dealing with the 1849 execution of Harvard Professor John White Webster for the murder of Dr. George Parkman, had been written for the aborted volume of essays on classic trials he and George Bradshaw had planned in the Air Force. (The essay had been declined by *True Crime Detective* and *American Weekly*.) The case interested Cozzens because it was "the forerunner of a hundred later cases in which expert testimony turned a trifle into the one damning thing no defense could explain away." In his view, Webster "was duly hanged for a crime that, in the law's defining, he almost certainly never committed."[6]

Since Cozzens had become exercised over the "degradation of the Common Law" in the Watergate trials ("Star Chamber judicial usurpation" of the grand jury's historical protection of the accused), he took the opportunity to provide a "Laborious Explanatory Note" expressing his indignation and at the same time rendering affectionate tribute to Bradshaw ("my fellow of infinite jest"—unnamed), who had died in 1973. Recalling the idle Pentagon days when he talked to Bradshaw about the law with "convert-like overplusage of zeal." Cozzens wrote:

Anyway, time passing, our meetings grew farther between—no falling apart; simply he lived in a crowd of chosen friends; I, naturally solitary, needed none—only people to watch and study, preferably always unaware of me.

Of necessity that meant, since I never got my Serious Call into print, he must miss promised entertainments of my I fear irrepressible *I told you so* when successive years came to take the course they have—when that Grand Jury system did exactly what the wise English ending averted, free men's once-shield against the Crown horridly twisted into the very Star Chamber it was meant to quash forever; when the evils flourished, directly or indirectly derived, of anti-Administration legislature (second horrid historic irony) turned Rump Parliament (There, *take it away* . . .) complete with inquisition committees, forceless subpoena, shameless citations for—yes; *contempt*! And so by natural consequence (shades of Dr.

Webster's innovative trial) the swell of the idiot, false-witness bearing, unabashedly (as needed) treasonable 'media' of our times, some baseless Right-of-the-People-to-Know providing color of that patriotism, long last refuge of scoundrels. And why not; when on the high bench could sit long, too long, the legal coxcomb who never blushed to say: *I come here not to follow precedents but to set them;* when the judicature of whole Federal Districts stood sullied by some Maximum John's smiling menace of plea-dealing, intricately 'lawful' yet with its sickish *Code Napoleon* whiff of end justifying means, to break that time-tried honor by practical necessity among political thieves, by losers' sleight of hate the tacit consents of custom made 'felonies'—as though any kid won't spit on squealers, the sneaks who don't cover up for friends; as though any Dante can't tell you hell's bottom holds the faithless, the trust-breakers. (I can hear that excellent fancy saying: *Watergate; yes, odious crime! I speak of its architecture, of course.*) [pp.11–12]

A Rope for Dr. Webster was published in an edition limited to 350 numbered and signed copies in August 1976.* Since such collector editions are not reviewed, neither *Flower* nor *Rope* attracted attention, which suited the author because he had published them for his own pleasure—and to satisfy a chagrinning itch to see his words in print. ". . . I don't much want to publish anything, yet on the other hand, I miss shooting-my-face-off business" (25 January 1975).

By 1975 seven years had elapsed since *Morning Noon and Night,* and Jovanovich recommended that the Williamstown notebooks be published to keep Cozzens's name before the public. Cozzens reluctantly acceded to the plan and arranged for the ten holograph notebooks to be transcribed at Princeton. The Harcourt Brace Jovanovich contract is dated 10 December 1976. Bernice read the Princeton typescripts and expressed reservations about the project. Cozzens suspected she was concerned that his comments on Jewish critics would expose him to more abuse. Bernice advised that his Pentagon diaries be published instead because they had narrative interest. Though Cozzens was careful not to be encouraging, he co-operated with editor Dan Wickenden to the extent of suggesting the titles "These Our Actors" for the Williamstown notebooks and "A Time of War" for the Pentagon diaries. He subsequently requested that Jovanovich suspend work on both volumes.

In January 1976 Cozzens offered Bruccoli Clark the 600 pages

---

* Less 115 copies spoiled at the bindery.

of Pentagon memos he had written for the OIS in 1944–45 for another limited edition, explaining: "You'd be right in seeing you'd get a unique piece of work—nothing in all the published war stuff is like it; nothing tells any person interested what war-waging at Top Echelon was like, uncoloured by self-serving of most General Officer's Memoirs, or by naked & dead hate-that-officer sheer ignorance of never having been there."[7] He wanted them available to what he estimated would be a small number of readers, but he did not want to offend Jovanovich by publishing a trade book with another publisher. HBJ, Cozzens insisted, was his only trade publisher. Bruccoli was eager to publish the memos; but since the documents were stamped SECRET, he asked Cozzens whether they had been declassified. Ruefully admitting that he had ignored the problem, Cozzens suspended the project: "Alas, alas, & My God that 'clearing with the Air Force' will have to stop the plan dead for the time being, and I can't blame Connections I'll leave nameless for thinking I must be losing my mind, if I'd supposed anything else. . . . Did I know nothing of the congressional Church-Pike rat pack leaving nothing done to wreck 'security'? Didn't I get the point that until the Ellsberg case? (merely nol prosed) gets its quietus, and with it the aiding-and-abetting now scared to death Wash Post–NY Times which would use anything to justify itself— in short, until that's all cleared up we must not only stay out of print but forget those papers even exist."[8] He was privately relieved to have found an out. Feeling inimical to the fashions and doctrines of the reigning intellectual establishment, he had no wish to provide them with a target of opportunity. He did not need money—a circumstance he frequently gave thanks for in his diaries and letters—and felt no obligation to his public. So why publish? At this time his diaries recorded incremental dismay as his lifelong self-judging process became increasingly harsh: "I really don't like that 'me' I know so well—not that I ever did—that pet name 'oh you bastard!' is certainly of 50 years standing—but now the liking I thought couldn't be less, is less" (22 August 1976). This voice of self-reproach could no longer be silenced by alcohol or work.

In 1977 Bruccoli and Vernon Sternberg, Director of the Southern Illinois University Press, planned a Cozzens Festschrift, hoping to initiate a critical reassessment of his novels. Apprised of the project, Cozzens said he saw no point in it because his work was all out of fashion, but did not oppose it. At his recommendation Bruccoli and Sternberg discussed the project with Jovanovich, who advised them to make the volume a James Gould Cozzens reader and offered a subvention for joint publication in cloth by Southern Illinois University Press and in paper by Harcourt Brace Jovanovich.*

Jovanovich was in close touch with Cozzens and knew the state of Bernice's health; he thought it would be therapeutic for Cozzens to have a publishing project to occupy him and urged Bruccoli to involve Cozzens in the editing process. During 1977 and 1978 the *Reader* developed through phone conversations among Cozzens, Jovanovich, and Bruccoli. A working table of contents was submitted to Cozzens, who requested that *S.S. San Pedro* be replaced by *Ask Me Tomorrow,* because it was the novel in which he came closest to fulfilling his intentions; he also recommended inclusion of his essay on Father Sill and other uncollected pieces.† Although Cozzens complained in his diary that he didn't know why he was bothering with the *Reader* and wished everyone would just leave him alone, he was consistently co-operative in his calls and notes and kept himself informed about the production of the volume.‡ (Since he sometimes phoned with his dentures removed, the calls were not always helpful.) But Cozzens firmly declined a meeting.

When Bruccoli used "castoff" (estimating the length of a book by means of a typographical character count) Cozzens, who did not know the term, wanted to know how it was done. A characteristic of his conversation was the repetition of "you might say" as a qualifier. After he had said what was on his mind, he hung up without leave-taking. Cozzens selected the title *Just Representations* from Samuel Johnson's Preface to his Shakespeare edition,§

---

*Critical essays commissioned for the original volume were included in *Just Representations: A James Gould Cozzens Reader* (Southern Illinois University Press and Harcourt Brace Jovanovich, 1978) and in *James Gould Cozzens: New Acquist of True Experience* (Southern Illinois University Press, 1979).

†In addition to *Ask Me Tomorrow,* the 602-page collection included excerpts from six novels, three short stories, and seven essays, forewords, or articles by Cozzens. There were also reviews or articles by George Garrett, Jerome Weidman, Noel Perrin, Frederick Bracher, Brendan Gill, and Richard M. Ludwig.

‡When Bruccoli began a descriptive bibliography of Cozzens's published work, the subject advised the bibliographer to work on a more admired author. Nonetheless, he provided information about his unrecorded Air Force publications, as well as copies of his English editions.

§"Nothing can please many, and please long, but just representations of general nature. Particular manners can be known to few, and therefore few only can judge how nearly they are copied. The irregular combinations of fanciful invention may delight a while, by that

Last photograph: Rio, Florida (Courtesy of Fannie Collins)

and provided the dust-jacket photo of himself, taken by Fannie Collins ("the last old sour puss ever purposes to sit for").[9]

He agreed to provide the introduction for *Just Representations* and worked for a month on "About Being Written About: Or, By Nimiety Possessed." As the title indicates, it was a reply to Dwight Macdonald, and catalogued the qualifications for a fit reader of James Gould Cozzens. He admitted guilt, at his "painful awareness of professional wrongdoing, of my habitual unfeeling treatment of the Common or Constant Reader." Nonetheless, these were his requirements.

novelty of which the common satiety of life sends us all in quest; but the pleasures of sudden wonder are soon exhausted, and the mind can only repose on the stability of truth." When Bruccoli suggested that *the stability of truth* might be a better title, Cozzens observed, ". . . I was compelled to see literary judgment was not his, well, strength" (9 January 1978).

One: The reader has simply got to be grownup. This is a hard saying; for grownups are likely to have concluded that books, particularly the creative artist kind, are simply not worth reading (can anyone deny that in nine cases out of ten, or even ninety-nine out of hundred, they're apt to be quite right?) and so will do no reading at all except for technical information, or news reports bearing on their means of livelihood. Two: Though I know of course Demand One decimates—no, that's to underestimate; better say, cuts the adult population by two-thirds as far as a count of potential fit readers goes, the remnant that may have chosen to remain must be sifted out further. Saying that, I'm forseeably pulled up (that sense of, I agree, guilt, naturally). I must be quick to reiterate that 'chosen to remain'; it's not I who sat in the judgment seat. I asked for, reached for, adult intelligence. Granted that plenty of adults have never grown up and so could never be missed, never could be fit—still, ah, pity 'tis, 'tis true that probably more manifest by not troubling to read such stuff as new novels the very fitness they're told so impudently they must have. What I seek, that I lose. However, Demand Two must be made, and it involves a nicer distinction. A reader remains to be read but what is his reading, what has his reading been? A bookful blockhead, load of learned lumber in his head? No, says Alexander Pope, at least if poetry's in question; that makes for being learnedly unread. The reading I expect him to have done includes no learned lumber. I only ask that, when I bring occasion for it before him, that he show himself familiar (meaning as familiar as I myself may happen to be) with books which colleges term the Company of Educated Men are, or used to be, exposed to, perhaps forceably, but had at least the chance to read, mark, learn and inwardly digest. These are writings in English from, say, Shakespeare, the Book of Common Prayer, the King James Version of the Bible through, let's say, A. E. Housman (1859–1936). What I'm demanding comes down to a freedom for the pleasurable to use references, allusions, to imitate, parody, or paraphrase where doing that may point up my meaning in clarities of identity or contrast, that can strengthen light on scenes I present, or add fullness to the expressing of what oft was thought. Of course such use, perhaps serious, perhaps ironic, perhaps special joking—I have a weakness for that particular joke I see in stilted or high-falutin' word terms given to blunt down-to-dirt facts—has risks. Take the disheartening "huh?" to be had from the unread, or, not to mince it, blurted out quite as often by those who underwent modern college English-course conditioning, administered of course almost everywhere by those who in their own time got the conditioning they now superintend. For what this means and what this does I'll call in (or do I mean, pass the buck to?) George Garrett in his study of the phenomenon.* With lucidity and precision I

*"Whatever Wishful Thinking May Wish: The Example of James Gould Cozzens," *Just Representations.*

don't think I could hope to match, he can help those who are curious as much as I gladly acknowledge I myself was helped with the annoying puzzle of why some new-proclaimed Masterpiece just dropped from the press so often proves, when opened, to be what it so dismayingly is, and why that fresh-come Leading Author writes as, just as dismayingly, he writes. Add next the occasional protests, by usually illiterate letter, that I have been plagiarizing, no quotes around what the letter sender some-how found out someone else wrote. Then add, a prestigeous critic be-lieve it or not, citing to illustrate *my* poor powers of expression a line you might imagine no one could fail to know was Shakespeare's. I can only say that the flash of illumination in recognition that I know I can count on the fit reader to accept with pleasure I hold well worth all such risks—they are risks the tactician calls calculated.

Surely I now have done with my demands, in the face of them a God's plenty, to bear out the psychiatric diagnosis of guilt-sense. Alas, I'm not done; only now I can at least say I wish I were, that I would be if only I had full power to write exactly as I decided I wanted to write. I don't have it, and wishing I had would be fool's wishing for the moon. No writer I have ever read, and one needn't hesitate to guess no writer who ever wrote, enjoyed power beyond or other than writing as he was obliged to write, meaning; as individual capacities or talent of his enabled him to (or limited him to) word the saying of what he wanted to say. So the most inconscionable of my too many demands now comes up and before I present it those regrets and apologies I owe beyond question to all surviving applicants for reading-fitness certificates. I'll add to them the penitent assurance that if he now reasonably explodes: *The hell with it!* I regard him as only doing right, indeed, doing wisely and well. This in-ordinate Demand Three is that he pay attention and this attention must be unremittingly close, absolutely unwavering. If he happens to be of those college literary generations whose thought patterns and fashions of taste are explicitly explained in that analysis of Mr. Garrett's to which I made free both with him and with Mr. G. to offer reference, he can know that the exercise, in their own tell-it-like-it-is tongue, may be; *rougher than a cob, pal.* Prose as I write it, protesting honestly, yes; but also when used to excuse, weakly, yes again, is the prose I have to write, what my cast of mind limits me to writing. It is too tight. If you look at the prose (not verse) of John Dryden, of Jonathan Swift, of Samuel Johnson (if only in *Lives of the Poets*), or for modern instance that of William (not Henry) James or Somerset Maugham (he and his material are out of Liberal Intellectual Fashion, but as that and they pass, look for him to be still there, lasting), you will see what I mean. Prose like mine must, as prose of those I mentioned doesn't, preempt more than fair share of the grownup, fitly read, reader's time. You can't find in it the simple considerateness of chances for the reader to take five—or even, two. A skipped page, a paragraph, a line, sometimes even a word, a freedom most new-speak truly modern novels allow him often and nearly anywhere he wants, isn't allowed here. What, after any hiatus, he picks up will have gone so far out of context as to look like, in fact must amount to, sheer nonsense. What the hell is being talked about becomes impossible for anybody to work out. Of course I might claim it was you, by skipping who bamboozled yourself; but just who do I think I am; and now, by God, quit you do! Since I know all this perfectly well, let me ask you—er, dear reader, a favor, little as I've earned one. Now I've told you all about the heat past standing in the kitchen, why not stay out? *

Bernice read the draft of the introduction and "said quite gently: do I smell Sinclair Lewis? Translated: are you going lit'ry Smart Aleck in your dotage? She's right. I was." [10] He killed it and provided instead "Some Putative Facts of Hard Record or He Commences Authour Suae 19–20: Excerpts from 1923 MS Diary and a Few Notes" covering the writing and publication of *Confusion*.† Reading his 1923 Harvard diary "did not fail to give me what might as well be called a turn of my own. Further deciphering [worked] for 'mixed feeling' to my surprise almost painfully strong—My O-you-SOB reaction constant and lively but alternating, a sort of regret perhaps made poignant simply because I couldn't *say* what it was—a sense (basically false [in] fact it [was] I fear) of loss at sight of I guess you could call it Glory-in-the-Grass syndrome—something there *then* now gone out of everything today" (5 July 1977). Cozzens vetted Bruccoli's introduction, correcting details and revising the assessment of his stature.

Cozzens broke his rule in May 1977 and provided an endorsement for Bate's *Samuel Johnson:* "A treat of relish in reading, learning, and inwardly digesting. What Jackson Bate always shows is a really rare maturity of perception in matters of men and women, this life, our literature."‡ He was annoyed when his statement appeared on the dust jacket in the company of one by Robert

---

* Cozzens presented his working draft for this essay to Colin Cass in March 1977. Because the draft is so heavily revised, it has been necessary to emend the text printed here.
† Cozzens edited the diary entries for publication. Two hundred fifty numbered copies of *Some Putative Facts of Hard Record* were published as a keepsake (New York and London: Harcourt Brace Jovanovich / Carbondale and Edwardsville: Southern Illinois University Press, 1978).
‡ Cozzens gave Julian Muller permission to edit his longer statement.

about his work he has stated that he tries only to render life

and people accurately. ~~Nonxght~~ Nonetheless, there is a consistency

of thinking ~~discernible~~ in his work--particularly in the post-appren-

tice novels. Cozzens respects brains and character. He obviously

distrusts the emotions as a guide to conduct. If it is too strong

to attribute Johnsonian subordination to him, it is clear that

Cozzens believes responsibility should be accepted by these best

qualified for it by natural ability and training. He simply regognizes _AB_

that some people *will prove themselves abler* ~~are better~~ than others~~x~~ and *sees no reason to* ~~does not~~ sentimentalize or

aggrandize fools.

    The lessons of James Gould Cozzens' career are clear eoough.

Caring nothing for popularity or those who accord it, he quietly mastered

his craft. He has scorned literary fashions and literary politics.

He has never accomodated temporary concepts of relevance. He ~~has~~ _2 · MB_

is
maintained ~~an~~ indifference to the game of literary ~~s~~success, writing

only to say as precisely as he can what by standards of his own he judges worth saying.
~~to satisfy his own standards.~~ At present his work is disparaged

weighing standards
or ignored by the guardians of literary reputations. The joke--which

theirs, C. must most assuredly want it no other way.
~~Cozzens no doubt appreciates--is that he is one of the greatest American~~

~~novelists.~~ If there is any truth in the rule that all master-

pieces are eventually recognized, the novels of James Gould

have a safe place among ex *spond* _2 · MB_
Cozzens ~~will achieve their~~ proper stature among the ~~highest~~

achievements in American literature.

Cozzen's editing of the introduction to
Just Representations *(Bruccoli Collection)*

Lowell. "How could I like what that—er—fruitcake liked?" (11 October 77).

Bernice was operated on again in June 1976 and made a satisfactory recovery, but she was visibly wasting away in the fall of 1977. She was hospitalized for a week in December and was dosed with morphine after her return to Beacon 21. Their fiftieth wedding anniversary on 31 December passed without celebration. It was clear that she was losing ground through January. Sylvia Bernice Baumgarten Cozzens died at home on 30 January 1978 at seventy-five and was cremated without a funeral service. The next day Bruccoli phoned with a message from Jovanovich. When Cozzens told him that Bernice had died, Bruccoli tried to end the conversation; but Cozzens insisted on discussing the business matter, saying, "Kent boys don't give in." Replying to Dan Wickenden's condolence letter, Cozzens wrote: "It's a happiness to me that I can tell you with *true* truth, if it had to be done, she did it, as everything else, with *expertise* and consideration for others—gently, quietly, with no pain detectable even by her round-the-clock-nurses here at home." [11]

The man who thought of himself as a constitutional misanthrope discovered the meaning of loneliness after his wife died: "my taste & habit of finding it very agreeable to be alone was always underpinned by the assurance that S was simply . . . not present for a period and the peace of solitude, of no run of 'companions' to interrupt my self-centeredness had never had to face the reality of Lear's Thou'lt come no more—never piled on never: and I'm going to find out about the rack of this tough world & not merely as a philosophical concept—or: watch that wounded mind!" (19 February 1978). Three months later: "I miss her more dead than I ever missed her living—more exactly, of course, I never quite appreciated how important not seeing or hearing her, but just knowing she was there if I wanted to say something—and moreover that one in a real myriad I could count on to have the intelligence to know what I spoke of. E. G. I say 'A funny thing about Pascal, I think.' S is *never* going to have to say: Who's Pascal?" (14 May 1978). He showed Fannie lines from Donne's "The Ecstasy" to convey "what I meant about not liking it without S and she somewhat surprised me by having no trouble 'and we said nothing all the day'—observing you know: she said to me: Jim & I don't seem to talk or see each other a lot: but I couldn't live without him: he's my life. . . ." (4 June 1978).

Cozzens had agreed to a 19 August 1978—his seventy-fifth birth-day—publication date for *Just Representations*. Although he said that he had always avoided publishing a book on his birthday, he felt it might be appropriate this time. After Bernice died, Cozzens asked that the volume be dedicated to her; he and Jovanovich decided on the form of the dedication.

For Bernice Baumgarten
30 January 1978
J. G. C.
W. J.
M. J. B.

On the twentieth of March 1978 Cozzens had discovered a lump on his neck; two neoplastic lymph nodes were removed on 14 April. After surgery he decided to wait a year before killing himself: "only subliminally I suspect the ghost of FHS in the boy still in me will give me crap about *Kent Boys Don't Quit*" (29 May 1978). He began disposing of his possessions, sending the *Time* cover portrait to Bruccoli. On 17 June he experienced chest and back pains; within three days he was unable to walk. His final diary entry was written on 20 June.

He was hospitalized on 22 June and operated on for cancer of the spine. He remained in the hospital for six weeks receiving cobalt treatments. James Gould Cozzens died of pneumonia at Martin Memorial Hospital in Stuart on 9 August 1978, ten days before his seventy-fifth birthday. His remains were immediately cremated.

The first obituaries did not appear until 18 August and did not command much space. Because the *New York Times* was on strike, Cozzens did not receive the full *Times* treatment that is regarded as confirming the reputation of a writer—a circumstance he would have relished. *Time*, which had helped to make him a celebrity as well as an anathema in 1957, gave his death four column inches in "Milestones." The *Kent News* printed a memorial article headlined "Kent marked me for life." But the Kent of 1978 had long since ceased to be his Kent.*

After providing for Fannie Collins and Anne Reubold, Cozzens

---

* Cozzens felt that Kent had lost its identity and was now just another prep school. He did not approve of the admission of girls: "the educating of adolescent males is needlessly handicapped and complicated by—er—gratuitous distractions."[12]

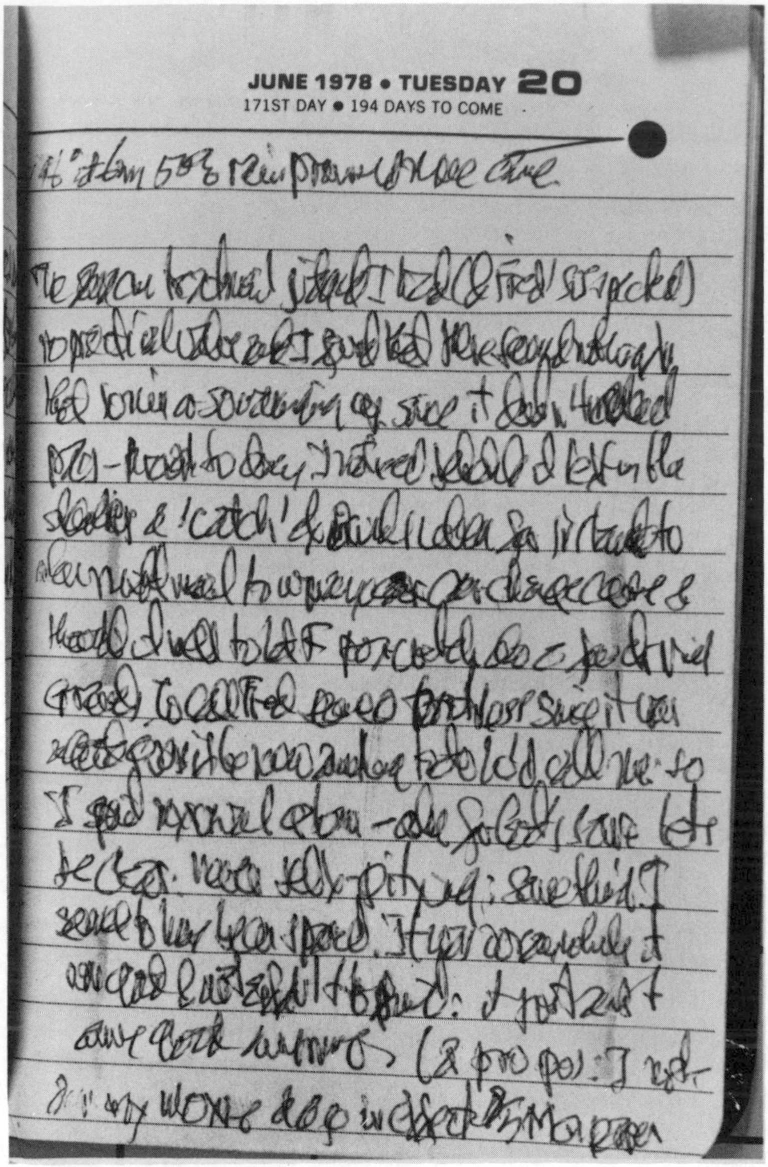

Final diary entry, almost totally indecipherable

bequeathed his estate of almost a million dollars to Harvard—along with Bernice's export china and his Currier & Ives prints. The Matthew Cozzens secretary went to the Newport Historical Society, which appraised it at $75,000. His manuscripts and papers went to Princeton University.

Cozzens died before publication of *Just Representations,* but he had received an advance copy in the hospital. What was planned as a celebratory volume became a memorial. Though not prominently reviewed, it was favorably received by James A. Epperson in the *National Review*, Edward M. White in the *Los Angeles Times Book Review,* Paul Ferris in the *Nashville Tennessean,* John Chamberlain in the *New York Times Book Review,* and by the John Barkham syndicate. Reviewers noted Cozzens's recent death and anticipated that the volume would "fuel debate" and bring about a reevaluation of his work. Nothing of the kind occurred. *Just Representations* sold a total of 2,488 copies in cloth and paper.* Cozzens might well have found mordant satisfaction in this confirmation of his animadversions on the vanity of authorship.

Such was James Gould Cozzens, whose force of mind was formidable, whose veneration for truth was inflexible, whose dedication to the craft of literature was uncontaminated by fashions. His novels have a safe place of proper stature among the sound achievements in American literature.

---

*In 1978 Harcourt Brace Jovanovich sold a total of 2,600 copies of Cozzens's novels—416 in cloth and 2,184 Harvest paperback volumes.

APPENDIXES

NOTES

INDEX

B.B. (*Princeton University Library*)

APPENDIX 1

"The Best Agent in
New York"

Bernice Baumgarten went to work at the Brandt & Brandt literary agency in 1923 as a secretary in the book department under Zelma Brandt, the wife of senior partner Carl Brandt. One of her secretarial chores was to take poems by dictation from Edna St. Vincent Millay, because the poet could not find the texts. When Mrs. Brandt's assistant left, Bernice was asked to take over his work; she promptly placed his backlog of unsold manuscripts.

After the Brandts were divorced in 1926, Bernice became head of the book department. (Brandt suggested that she change her name because Baumgarten sounded too Jewish, but she refused; after her marriage she continued to be known as Miss Baumgarten.) There were periods when Bernice was in charge of the agency while Brandt was being treated for alcoholism. Brandt married agent Carol Hill in 1931; she joined the agency in 1956. Cozzens wanted Bernice to retire, and the income from *By Love Possessed* made it possible. She left the agency soon after Brandt's death in October 1957—when Carol Brandt became the sole proprietor—although she continued to handle a few favorite clients from home.

Over the years her clients included Samuel Hopkins Adams, Conrad Aiken, Margaret Culkin Banning, S. N. Behrman, Stephen Vincent Benét, Bessie Breuer, Walter R. Brooks, Hortense Calisher, Whitaker Chambers, Raymond Chandler, Thomas B. Costain, E. E. Cummings, John Dos Passos, Ford Madox Ford, Shirley Ann Grau, John Gunther, A. B. Guthrie, Jr., Kathryn Hulme, Charles Jackson, Shirley Jackson, Jean Kerr, Josephine Lawrence, Betty Macdonald, Mary McCarthy, Thomas Mann, John P. Marquand, Peter Matthiessen, Edna St. Vincent Millay, Clifford Odets, Aline Saarinen, Budd Schulberg, William L. Shirer,

Frank G. Slaughter, Jerome Weidman—and James Gould Cozzens, for whom she was totally responsible.* Working in the days before the multimillion-dollar deals for "blockbuster" books, she never made big money.† In 1946 her income was $13,000, and by the time of her retirement she was earning $30,000 a year.

Raymond Chandler—who disliked commission men on principle—wrote Bernice in 1949, "You seem to me to achieve what the best film producers achieve even when they don't show it, the ability to be artistically intelligent and maintain a sense of what is practical and possible at the same time."[1] In his essay "Ten Percent of Your Life" (1952) Chandler observed: "Perhaps the three most valuable attributes of an agent are his emotional detachment from a very emotional profession, his ability to organize the bargaining power of his clients, and his management of the business side of a writer's career."[2] Bernice met these qualifications and possessed a fourth attribute: she was a skilled editor with a strong sense of structure. As an editing agent she had the conviction of her judgments and acted on them forthrightly. Her husband described her as "a very honest girl."

It was Bernice's decision to move Chandler from Knopf to Houghton Mifflin with *The Little Sister* (1949), because he would be treated as a serious novelist by a house that did not have a mystery list. But when he sent her *The Long Goodbye* in 1952 Bernice responded: "We [she and Carl Brandt] feel that Marlowe would suspect his own softness all the way through and deride it and himself constantly."[3] This criticism resulted in Chandler's departure from the Brandt & Brandt list.

Cozzens read manuscripts for Brandt & Brandt for twenty-five years, but the extent to which Bernice shared her business decisions with him is not known. However, her comment on *The Long Goodbye* has the ring of her husband's scorn for sentimentality.‡ Carol Brandt has commented that "Brandt & Brandt benefited beyond measure with the editorial gifts of James Gould Cozzens, an unpaid employee to all intents and purposes."[5] During the twenties and thirties he supplied at least two reading reports a week.

Here is the twenty-six-year-old Bernice reporting to John P. Marquand on her meeting with Maxwell Perkins, at which she informed the legendary Scribner's editor that she was moving Marquand to another publisher: "I also reminded him that before publication of "Black Cargo"

---

*An incomplete list of the books dedicated to Bernice Baumgarten includes Schulberg's *The Harder They Fall*, McCarthy's *Cast a Cold Eye*, Shirley Jackson's *The Sundial*, Charles Jackson's *The Sunnier Side*, Calisher's *Tale for the Mirror*, Banning's *The Dowry*, and Brooks's *The Clockwork Twin*—as well as *The Son of Perdition*.

†In 1932 she sold the movie rights to *Mutiny on the Bounty* for $12,500.

‡Chandler thought Cozzens could write a first-rate Hollywood novel because of his "very rare faculty of picking up and rationalizing a complicated background rather quickly."[4]

we had definitely told him that if we were not satisfied with the sales on that book, it would mean a change of publishers. I have talked with Carl about this and our joint opinion is that if they had so much belief in you, it is a little strange that they kept it such a secret from us and from the trade in general."[6] Yet when Marquand submitted a partial draft of *The Late George Apley* in 1935, she regarded it as a misstep because it was a departure from his previous work. Bernice advised him to drop it or use a pseudonym. The novel won the Pulitzer Prize and established Marquand as a serious novelist. Her response cost her the novelist's confidence; he remained with the agency, but his books became Brandt's responsibility.

In 1938 Bernice overcame the reluctance of Harcourt, Brace to publish Dos Passos's *U.S.A.* trilogy as a single volume. Dos Passos subsequently left Brandt & Brandt because he claimed that he could not afford to pay commissions, but he returned to the fold. Her sense of the market extended beyond books. She urged Ray Stark to produce *The World of Suzie Wong* (which became successful as a play and as a movie), and he acknowledges that "if there is anyone I can pin a good part of my success on as a producer, it would be Bernice."[7]

Cozzens—her most editor-resistant client—asserted that Bernice had written more books than anyone else in America and that she had "perhaps the best trained eye of our age for matters of writing."[8] One of her most successful editorial jobs was performed on Betty Macdonald's *The Egg and I* (1946), which became a best seller. Even with established authors, she employed her editorial skills. After reading a draft of S. N. Behrman's profile of Max Beerbohm in 1959, she reported:

There is no danger that the 'I' in this book will be overstressed. The curious effect here is to relate the reader personally to your subject. You never intrude. And of course you must put everything into the book. It is developing into a much bigger thing than the profile your first plan saw. Enchanting as your Max is, I can't wait for more of the two Lady B's.

You have done a remarkable job of compressing the material in your early draft in the opening pages of this section. Later it will want some smoothing, I think. I found the continuity sometimes confusing. The only section I feel is not at its most effective is Sir M. and Kipling, from pages 27 to 29. I'm sure its verbatim, but it gave me a curious twinge, almost dislike. Perhaps it is *too* dramatically presented. If you have the key to this relationship, perhaps you can put it into perspective for us. I'm sure it isn't anything as simple as Sir M's conscious or unconscious enmity because of Kipling's anti-semitism, but if it were I could understand it better.[9]

When Bernice read the typescript of Jerome Weidman's *The Third Angel* in 1953, she phoned him to question a sexual scene: "I think he'd get much further along toward a permanent relationship with the girl if instead of raping her at the first meeting he'd bring her a dozen long-stemmed roses." Weidman explained that it was not a rape and that the man could not afford roses; Bernice firmly replied, "He can certainly afford to bring her a philodendron plant." [10]

Bernice was not a frustrated publisher. She declined opportunities to move into publishing because she enjoyed her work as an agent. Her first priority was to protect her clients' interests, not to teach them how to write. Although she was a shrewd bargainer, Ken McCormick of Doubleday describes her as providing "a bridge between author and publisher." [11] Donald Klopfer, the Chairman of Random House, has said that she was an agent he could always trust. [12] Bernice was a master of contracts and served on the committee that revised the Society of Authors' Representatives standard contract. Al Hart, a publisher who became an agent, recalls that "she took me, step-by-step, through the Macmillan contract. . . . I learned more from her that day than I'd learned in the previous two years. And she was careful to spell out just what a publisher should be entitled to, as well as what the author had a right to expect. She was patient, endlessly knowledgeable, sensible and forthcoming. It may have been Frank Morley who told me she was 'the best agent ever.' . . ." [13]

Bernice was admired for her business ethics and enjoyed a Lincolnesque reputation for probity. When her client James Yaffe's novel *Nothing but the Night* (1957) was in galley proof, Meyer Levin's best-selling *Compulsion* was published. Levin asked her to handle the subsidiary rights—in effect, an invitation to collect the checks for a hot property—but, regarding it as a conflict of interest to represent two novels based on the Leopold-Loeb case, she declined.

Working with emotional people, Bernice insulated herself from involvement with authorial egos by a show of firmness or even toughness. Mary McCarthy recalls her "tremendous, never-failing control" and "straight, reflecting, considering look, as if she always wanted to measure the truth of what she was saying." [14] Shirley Ann Grau admits, "I was a good deal frightened of her. Those ferociously intelligent eyes were the reason, of course." [15] Bernice returned a novelette to Peter Matthiessen with the comment: "James Fenimore Cooper wrote this 150 years ago, only he wrote it better." At the time of her retirement she called him in and said, "I know I've been tough with you, but that is because I think that you're very, very good." [16] When Hortense Calisher was offered a job by a correspondence school for writers, Bernice told her: "When we come to sell your soul, we'll get a damn fine price for it." [17] Calisher, a successful short-story writer, was one of the clients Bernice continued to represent after her retirement from Brandt & Brandt, because she wanted to place her first novel.

Although Bernice had a business lunch nearly every day, she tried to avoid agent-author lunches. (If she was lunching with a male, she expected him to come to her office and escort her to the restaurant.) Her lunchtime tipple was one sherry. Some of her clients became dependent on her, but Bernice did not see them outside working hours. She caught the five o'clock train to Trenton every day. Her husband was the most important thing in Bernice's life. She rigidly separated her two lives and was careful to keep her Lambertville address secure from clients, to prevent weekend drop-ins. Some of Miss Baumgarten's clients did not know that she was married to Cozzens. The only author dinner at Carrs Farm, for Betty Macdonald, was somewhat marred because Cozzens ridiculed *The Egg and I*.

Authors' representatives, even more than editors, operate in anonymity. Except for the celebrity agents who handle celebrities, their reputations do not extend beyond the book trade. Within the trade Bernice was regarded as a champion. There is no way of establishing "the best agent in New York," but authors, publishers, and agents have accorded that distinction to Bernice Baumgarten.

APPENDIX 2

From the
Williamstown
Notebooks

In a 1970 letter draft to William Jovanovich, Cozzens commented on his Notebooks: "I think I am not wrong in saying some of it is quite good. Under a title of, say, Intents and Purposes I can see the possibility of bunching the stuff in several categories: e.g. Doubts & Difficulties; What happened Then; Are we Crazy? This is not a proposal" (Princeton University Library).

No deletions have been made within these entries.

NOTEBOOK I: APRIL–DECEMBER 1960

VIII 6   All I knew is my hair never used to be grey

VIII 8   A principle of today's liberalism seems to be a bowing and scraping to all minority groups—perhaps because liberals themselves are a minority group. If no sadder, I'm at least wiser in knowing now that if you want to offend (which usually means also, infuriate) a 'liberal' a good way to do it is to treat any minority as though people no different from other people compose it.

VIII 30   When Thoreau judged that most men lived lives of quiet desperation I think he failed to consider the fact that, by a merciful provision of Providence, most men have little or no more imagination than an animal. Good reasons for despair may be all around the average man; but he won't see them.

IX 13   The unfortunate fact about 'bias' is that those against whom prejudice is often shown are all too apt, in their pain of wounded feeling, to confirm prejudice's original unfair opinion.

X 3   those depressions which are the natural dead-sea fruit of the introspective and imaginative temperament

X 6   to anticipate the time when the cat, death, will decide to have some fun with the mouse, me.

X 10   my writing aim would be not so much to tell the reader new things as to remind him of what he knows

X 12   the waiting room of this life, where, with that principle of death lurking in you, you must sit until the doctor called your name

X 22   The discomfort, if nothing worse, that a man must generally feel as he looks back on that son of a bitch, himself when young.

X 12   What is called tolerance is in fact a form of indifference. No one is tolerant where his interests are threatened

XII 13 Another point of difference in human temperament might lie in whether the loss of illusions that goes with growing up seems to you a great pity; or, on the contrary, at least a little something gained

NOTEBOOK 2: DECEMBER 1960–JUNE 1961

XII 25 the discovery that with the high brow goes as a rule the bone head

I 18   By sentimentality I suppose I mean feeling that is without discrimination because it is without discernment—feeling, perhaps, for feeling's sake. Why this, or its results, should make me recoil, seem to me so wrong & bad, I find a tough question.

I 24   Writers may do well to try to avoid clichés; but when they do they often also avoid the clearest, shortest and simplest way of stating their meaning.

II 10   I can see that, in reason, allowances ought to be made; that, to myself when young, I should be kinder than my inclination now is. Still, it's hard to be reasonable when I recall, as I suppose most of us must, the innumerable injuries done then to present self-regard or self-respect.

II 15   Prof. Perry's op. cit.* comment on Mark Hopkins suggests that the case was what it must almost always be: any man who has great talents or abilities is bound to be part son of a bitch.

*A. L. Perry, *Williamstown and Williams College* (1904) —MJB.

II 20   This morning when I woke up I remember seeing it was December; how, in the space of a day, it can have come, tonight, to be July I don't know, or perhaps fear to think

II 26   I'm monarch of all I survey—except of course, myself. Myself's monarch of me.

IV 13   By listening to what a man says you may or may not learn what he really thinks; but by watching what he usually does you can tell what he really wants. When you know that, you can tell what he thinks.

IV 16   Returning from Communion, he remarked that Our Lord's veins had apparently been filled with cheap California sherry

 V 18   Why the more solemn and self-important forms of criticism, the critics called by the late Bernard De Voto Deckle Edged, passed him over is plain. Maugham's writing, lucid and explicit, provides no material for their nonsense. In the upside-down world of fashionable letters M's virtues became positive vices
A writer should never come right out and say what he means. This is to be guilty of competence. If you're going to be Great you must leave things uncertain, barely hint at this, vaguely suggest that, offer proper latitude for long speculation on what you really meant
to illuminate the reader's own experience, not to press on him the experiences of the writer
The thing most held against Maugham is obviously the fact that he made critics and criticism unnecessary. He never wrote a line that needed to be explained (or explained away) No 'interpretation' was required. Any adult reader takes his meanings at a glance: he writes to be instantly understood. The literary rubbish of symbolism, of 'levels of meaning' is never allowed to clutter up his prose or obscure his thought

 V 19   *Having it Both Ways at Once*
What shapes you is not the run of ordinary experiences, it's the experience out of the ordinary. Those are the moments you remember. On the other hand, what shapes you is what you do every day. You may remember better what is different: but what you are will always be what you don't remember.

 V 27   Sentimentality is often seen as a fault of kindness, of the soft or warm heart. That is just what it isn't. Sentimentality is basically insensitiveness, undiscerning and imperceptive. When you discover that someone is a sentimentalist, look for him to be stupid, dishonest and cruel too.

VII 5   In judging character, most of us, untaught by experience, persist in what could be called a fallacy of entities. For the honest
man to steal, for the kind man to be cruel, for the brave man
to be cowardly (and, indeed, for the bad man to be good) in
this fallacy is out of character, and so out of the question. The
great truth about character is that no such entities as the honest
man or the bad man exist: there are only men: and in never
learning, or in forgetting, this is the root of all misjudgment.

VII 13 To communicate as clearly as possible what experience has meant
to me

VIII 30 *Henry Miller. Tropic of Cancer* The great trouble here is that the
book must seem tiresome to any adult reader who keeps up
with 'modern' writing because he's read it all so many times
before. Of course, this is not Mr. Miller's fault. If censorship
hadn't prevented American publication when it was written,
the reader would find he'd read it a good many fewer times
than the case is today. However, it occurs to me that it is so
praised by Advanced critics for just that reason. It contains exactly (and all) the stuff that a Work of Genius, by their decree,
must contain. In short, both manner and material are straight
Modern Hysterical; and the one noticeable innovation seems
to be the surely minor one of incessant reference to women as
cunts. This bold stroke serves, at least, as perhaps timely re-
minder that the work, and the rest of the coterie literature like
it, really addresses itself to the young—or, better, the non-adult,
who can still be shocked and still find being shocked an exciting literary experience. Seen this way, the persistence of what
might be called (in Mr. Miller's own language) the Fuck Everything School is easier to understand.

IX 21   I was looking at Henry James' *Daisy Miller* (of course, because
I thought I remembered a point made that I might want to
find a way to make). I could not find it, perhaps because my
memory was some forty years old. Critically, it was respected
then and still, at least in the little mags., seems to be. But what
I was struck by was the obvious truth that nobody, simply
reading as an adult reader, not knowing it was respected and
'ought' to be read, would be likely to read beyond the first few
pages.

IX 24   Putting away some file folders of BLP stuff a number of letters
reminded me of what I'd pretty well forgotten—the real fury
of the attacks on it & me which the book's 'success' had pro-

voked, and how ingenuously unprepared for it I had been. As long as what I wrote was read only by the handful of literate (not literary) grown-ups it was written for I was, you'd gather, unobjectionable. But when, by one of those accidents of publishing, about as impossible to pre-arrange as hitting a slot-machine's jackpot, everyone was brought to read or try to read a book of mine, a slowly growing howl went up. Much like the machine's sudden avalanche of nickles, and evidently triggered by it, a sudden down-pour of partisan abuse began, much of it personal (not real literary criticism), all of it blind, and some of it crazy. Though I'd read about this kind of thing, and how you must expect it, I suppose I couldn't have quite believed those sound advices. It is true that I'd thought very often that other writers' books that were selling a lot were of little merit and didn't hesitate to say so; and since tastes differ, I could well believe the same might be thought and said about me. The active animus that had to go further I wasn't capable (no doubt through indifference) of feeling, so I seem to have doubted that anyone else really felt it.

IX 27   *TIME letters* (in connection with my IX 24 note): one Paul W. Ferris, on the recent 'cover piece' on J. D. Salinger, makes a point: "It will now be fascinating—in a morbid and unrewarding way—to watch the hatchet men of academe attempt to prove that no writer earning a Time cover story can possibly be of literary consequence. Those same precious people who nibbled at James Gould Cozzens will be quoting paragraphs out of context, accusing Salinger of writing like Salinger, reading in their own Freudian fantasies etc" [For some reason I hadn't given much weight to that. Hell, you might say; *Time* has someone on the cover every week: but of course it's true they only have about one writer a year; and, now I think of it, the more crazily abusive critics were always digging out, in my case, hunks of the incredible TIME Crap they seemed to have been able to swallow; and so, in short, the 'success' of the 'cover story' may indeed be what they can't take; not, mere best-selling, or diffused illiberal opinion.

XI 15   The scenes of my childhood (and indeed, youth, and young manhood), when fond recollection restores them to view, I must admit I don't like at all. Most of them make me ejaculate silently: Oh, dear; oh God; or oh Hell. As a rule, you will be closest to the truth if you assume you're no different from everyone else: but here, I wonder. A slightly psychopathic self-conscious, which doesn't need to be general, often seems suggested when I find myself remembering this or that and saying:

'Ah; you son of a bitch!' Why not just forget it? Could it be a subconscious fear that though (or even because) you may have done relatively all right later it may always come out that you really aren't much good, if the truth were known; now, any more than then? [but on the whole, I guess it is just a symptom of what theologians call the Sin of Pride: you think so well of yourself that you feel you should have done better than you know you did.

XI 20 It was a bad day for contemporary letters when the first myth was invented

XI 26 John O'Hara's new book of short pieces seems to be being reviewed with a kind of relief, as though the critics feared a new novel. I can understand. The last three or four very long novels have been, essentially, the same book done over and over about the same unnaturally (at least in print) mean, ugly-mooded and stupid people. Yet it is also a fact that there is not a single contemporary writer I've read over the years who has left me, as a kind of residue of the reading, anything like so many well-remembered lines, tags, and bits of dialogue and description that come often to mind.

XII 3 Ed Newhouse, who is good, shrewd and accurate in relating things about people, gave some examples of things done to hurt and humiliate other people by those who happened to have the power to do it. Pondering the point, I had to see that this seemed to be usually an impulse to torment the weak. It occurred to me that the impulse to torment might not be absent in me—but, fun, if I found it that way, would have to be, for whatever psychopathic reason, in offering to torment the strong. The stern joy, I suppose, that ill-tempered warriors feel in foemen they take to be worth licking

XII 13 He said: To 'celebrate' Christmas a man must be mad. The day should be nothing but one of mourning. That birth—or, since there is no sufficient evidence that it ever actually occurred, let us say, the persuasion that it did—has incontestably been the cause of more human woe, more bestial behaviour, more stupidity and more active suffering than any one other factor in the last 2000 years of history.

XII 22 I began writing long before I'd had enough experience to know truths of life from untruths so my first books weren't and aren't worth any intelligent adult's attention.

XII 31 In practice certain obscurities of style, though they may repel many readers, can and do serve the reputation of several authors very well. They make certain that no one is going to see right away how banal the material is, or how childish or second rate the thinking. And this is not the end. Hardly anyone who has put himself to the long trouble of guessing meanings so hard to get at is going to admit that the findings weren't worth the work—or, bluntly he has let himself be made a fool of. He will in nine cases out of ten save face by being next to the author himself in claiming this work is of Profound Significance.

NOTEBOOK 4: JANUARY–JULY 1962

I 20 The pet name he kept for that long-lost person, himself when young was an unsmiling: *You Son of a Bitch!* A hundred, perhaps a thousand, specific recollections, visiting him in vacant or in pensive mood, flashing on that inward eye could make him pull-up, silently forming the phrase in his mind while in deepest self-dislike he asked (and in vain): how could you ever have said that, how could you ever have done that? To be sure, one (though seemingly not he) might argue that he exaggerated; that he was unduly, improperly hard on that person. Practically all the wounding recollections were of awkwardnesses, stupidities, more or less trivial and momentary meannesses, trifling lies or breaches of faith. What they weighed on, he had to see, was his conceit, not his conscience. They lacked even the dignity of consequence that true crime might have. That is; failing at goodness, he could also be said to have failed at badness; as a villain, never really amounting to anything; never achieving any status higher than that of unsavory, or at most, contemptible, character.

II 6 The observable truth seems to be that almost all failures are demonstrable just deserts; brought about by stupidity or incapacity; earned and meritted. On the other hand, successes, just as observably, don't have to be deserved. Like the rain, they fall on the just and the unjust. You don't have to be intelligent, industrious, or good: you only have to be a certain man at a certain place at a certain time. In short; failure is seldom just bad luck; while success may very well be just good luck.

II 9 There are no new 'truths'; all truths are old and worn: so if it's true it won't be new, and if it's new it won't be true.

II 11 An image of the state of the world. In a sinking boat, the people packed together are engaged in a brawl, actually, a battle-royal. Every man for himself, the fighting maniacs clubbed and stabbed and shot each other, regardless of the inflow of water mounting around their knees.

IV 21 S. hadn't seen the By Love Possessed film and when it turned up (second time around) at the Spring St. theatre today insisted on going. Seeing it a second time, I was again impressed by much really beautiful photography, and a number of excellences of small detail and minor casting—the man, whoever he was, cast as 'Dr. Shaw' in the trifling part allowed him was almost disconcerting, he was so exactly in face and manner what I was seeing as I wrote.* But it was as plain as ever that the job they undertook was impossible: the book defeated them at every turn and was indeed specifically intended to. A play, an acted entertainment by definition can't be 'honest' exhibiting True Experience. Actors act 'parts': plays must provide 'parts'. The whole basis is: Let's Pretend. Anything 'real' or 'true' will destroy or at any rate vitiate this basis. Life is life, not a play: a play is a play, not life. It seems to follow that an effective play must cut loose from considerations of: is this probable? (or even: is this possible?) and proceed on the principle of, say, *Hamlet*. Never mind whether this situation makes sense, never mind if it's obviously impossible. Assume it to be the situation: Now, what next?

V 1 A great many human activities don't interest me at all but why they interest others always does interest me.

V 29 Anyone who enjoys any considerable success in this life must, unless he is a great fool (and of course, that is this point: he *can* be) recognize that merit never determines, nor even as far as you can honestly see, contributes to anything but small successes. There, it seems often essential. To make a thousand dollars you usually have to be fairly smart; to make a million, you must (a much rarer thing) be naturally lucky.

VI 5 Some sad recollection of CA's conversation (supra V 27): † *Item:* speaking of lingering winter in these hills, he mentioned that he had been at Concord, N.H. a few weeks ago and noticed snow remaining in all shaded places. This enabled him to let it be known the S. Paul's School dramatic society had being putting on a play of his. [alas. how hungry for some notice a man must be if he troubles to go to see a secondary school play production and then troubles to let people know he did. *Item*

---

* Everett Sloane —MJB.
† Conrad Aiken and his wife had visited the Cozzenses in May —MJB.

He related how he had gone and spoken to William Faulkner at the Institute 'Ceremonial' and Faulkner had respectfully quoted to him some of his, C.,' verses, only wrong. C. corrected him. F. firmly repeated them as he had first proposed them. Clearly, C said, a man of considerable determination [It was hard to doubt the incident was invented; and that the only point was to have it understood that Nobel Prize Winners got C's poetry by heart

VII 1   *Forbes* in its fairly awful *'Thoughts on the Business of Life'* page quotes William Faulkner: "I believe that man will not merely endure, he will prevail. He is immortal not because he alone among creatures has an inexhaustible voice, but because he has a soul" [no comment seems possible

VII 6   In view of VII 1 supra, William Faulkner's sudden taking-off gave me the least little bit of a turn of the nihil nisi bonum kind; and the newspaper concensus does seem to indicate that I'm about the only person in the world who wasn't edified by his later-day high-falutin sentiments. HT. headline: *'Spoke to Heart of All—Kennedy on Faulkner'* The President: "It can be said with assurance of few men in any area of human activity [this could be F. himself writing] that their work will long endure. William Faulkner was one of these men. Since Henry James no author has left such a vast and enduring monument to the strength of American literature, etc"
[If I feel strong doubt about the 'enduring' of the monument it is, of course, because I lost patience with *Sanctuary* thirty years ago; and after (I think) *'The Wild Palms'* stopped even trying to read him. What had been to me the wonderful, the highly exciting, vigor and effectiveness of the work he was doing in the first books seemed to end with *As I Lay Dying*. This could of course mean a change in my own tastes or interest; but I don't think so. *Sanctuary* shocked me by the cheapness of thinking and feeling—the last thing I had expected. In the next books I found him developing further and further a style, very tiresome to read, whose office appeared to be concealing under piles of words the shoddiness or childishness of what he had to say. It is perfectly true that many, perhaps most, of the realities of this life's complicated thinking and feeling can't be got at with simple statements. To simplify will be to falsify. And I'm also sure F. was honestly wrestling with Marlowe's 'One thought, one grace, one wonder at the least Which into words no virtue can digest'—the hope most writers surely have to make words say more than words are able to say. The result of this effort is usually (Joyce is the perfect example) and, indeed, you

have to see, inevitably, that you will convey less meaning, not more, when you tamper with the language, whether the words themselves, or the structure of the sentences. So I don't agree with the President (and the rest of the world). What will 'endure' seems likely to be what *has* endured. Should Jane Austen perhaps be an object lesson for the kind of writer able to thirst after 'immortality'? (I can't myself seem to give a damn about posterity's opinion).

NOTEBOOK 5: JULY 1962–JANUARY 1963

VIII 17   *FORM LETTER* I've long felt that any novelist's estimate of a novel is bound to be so limited and conditioned by the kind of work he finds himself able to do that opinions he may form about another novelist's novel are worthless: and he should always keep them to himself.

VIII 26   Another note on *The Sound of Bow Bells* * (p. 343) That romanticism of self-pity may perhaps be seen in these passages that argue (I would think rightly) that a writer seldom knows how he did whatever he does. But the implication that 'success' has to be a matter of 'merit' is absurd. All you have to do to see this is to note what *has* paid off for writers. Clearly, the process is hardly different from feeding coins into a slot machine. Of course, the coins probably have to be real and current coins: but the one that releases the jackpot doesn't do it because it is 'better' than previously inserted coins. The book that pays off may be good: but it doesn't *have* to be; and since bad or indifferent books will always greatly outnumber good books; more often than not the jackpot is hit by a book without much merit.

XI 3   Strunk & White *Elements of Style*. On back of paperback: Strunk: 'This book aims to give in brief space the principal requirements of plain English style.' E. B. White 'I shall [Strunk taught him that] have a word or two to say about attitudes in writing: the how, the why, the bear traps, the power, and the glory' [He taught himself that] Dorothy Parker: 'It is a book to put alongside Fowler's works: and I can think of no higher praise'. [Could she ever have read 'Fowler's works'?]
[on all obvious points the 'aim' certainly seems well directed. Simplicity (don't say: *He is a man who is very ambitious*. Say: *He is very ambitious*) and clarity get proper emphasis: but both author and editor seem often to let their enthusiasm for 'simplic-

---

* By Jerome Weidman (New York: Random House, 1962) —MJB.

ity' lead them to suppose it the same as clarity. The simple can't help being clear: but that doesn't mean it won't be also nonsense, or untruth. The simple manner is always good: but matter, not manner, is the important thing. If 'simplicity' involves any sacrifice of the truth, of the significance, of a statement, simplicity just isn't worth it. When, for instance, you insist that something is either 'likely' or 'unlikely' you make for inexactness. 'Unlikely' isn't quite the same as 'not likely'; 'likely' is not quite the same as 'not unlikely'. Advice to avoid such distinctions of meaning in writing is bad advice.

XI 11   Anthony Powell. *The Kindly Ones*. It's obvious that a writer saves himself a lot of work if he writes successive books about the same characters: but this latest Powell suggests to me that for reasons of a more or less mysterious kind, going perhaps to the springs, sources, or basic mechanics of 'creative writing' a writer's well-advised not to do it. First: the books tend to become parts of a serial. Each stands less and less on its own feet: and I very much doubt that when the series is done and they're taken all together they'll cohere into any kind of whole. Second: I suspect the writer may need the renewed exercise of having each time to create from scratch a new world, or at any rate, new people. To use the same old ones is perhaps to let his imagination get flabby; and this will mar the quality or tone of the writing itself in some no doubt subtle way. In the present book, you seem to see both factors working. The narrative lacks firmness and coherence. The material, though still here and there good, is too often listless sounding; or, bluntly, dull.

V 24   The simple statement must always be good writing. *The cat sat on the mat* can fairly be called perfect. Not a word wasted. No possible misunderstandings or confusion of meanings. But simplicity has also made the statement, in the strictest sense, insignificant. You've got simplicity; but at the expense of the specific and the precise. You've confined yourself to abstractions and so defeated the whole real purpose of writing. You've left out what the cat was like; what the mat was like; where the mat was and why the cat's sitting on it was worth reporting at all. Simplicity is not enough?

VI 27   Noting in the Washington Diaries (supra VI 20)* that Washington was only 51 at the end of the revolution, I find myself, as I imagine many people do when they come to be nearly 60, feeling a sort of surprise to realize that I'm older than most of

Diaries of George Washington, ed. John Fitzpatrick (Houghton Mifflin, 1925) —MJB.

the historical figures whose image, if unconsidered, would be that of the boy's-eye-view still. My father, dead 43 years, died, I have to remind myself, 6 years younger than I am now. I know I am old: the figures certify it: but I begin to see that it's only the young or the very young who can see age as a state apart, the state of their masters & pastors, not seriously or convincingly to be conceived by them as ever young. Of course I know already that the grow-old-along-with-me stuff is eyewash and nonsense—it's the worst, not the best, that's sure as hell still to be; yet you can wonder, for example, if Our Lord Jesus Christ in legend supposed, as I remember, to have died at 33, really had enough experience in living to make his pronouncements as the gospels record them worth taking very seriously.

NOTEBOOK 7: AUGUST 1963 – FEBRUARY 1964

VIII 24   I have a letter from a Mr. Applegate of the Syracuse University library suggesting at length and in complimentary terms that they would be in a position to preserve for posterity literary materials of mine if I would honor them by depositing it with them. It's true that I did just this at Princeton: but I reflect now, as I reflected at that time, that I seem to be some kind of exception among 'Authors,'—and I simply could not care less about a posthumous 'reputation'. By all accounts, this unconcern convicts me of a narrow and confined, rather than a wide, ranging and universal 'spirit' (did Shakespeare feel indifferent? The sonnets certainly say no. The idea of outlasting marble and monuments seems to have been to him the most gratifying of all his ideas). I suppose the truth is that subconsciously I come about as close to absolute solipsism as a man can. When I end; everything ends. I can see that thinking so is illogical; but like everyone else, I feel first and think afterward. Clearly, what I feel first is that the one reality is the 'me' of this moment. It seems to give me the best evidence that I've ever seen adduced that a subconscious mind does exist. You can't get at it, or know about it in any rational sense; but *it* gets at, and knows about the conscious you. Could intimations of this kind account for all 'religious' conviction?

IX 28   More on Splendors & Miseries etc (supra IX 23) In a *Newsweek* review of published correspondence of Robert Frost the passing comment is made that when he became old he quarreled with several former literary friends because he felt they had not done all they could to get him a Nobel prize. My first thought was that here, clearly, is a symptom of senility. I don't mean that my own instinct, which would make me do almost anything, if it could be done inconspicuously, to *avoid* getting a Nobel prize is right or normal or due to anything but some self-conscious and surely psychopathic (I wouldn't be at all surprised if a psychiatrist could show me that my real complaint is that I'm so vain or conceited subconsciously that I became miffed at not getting it on the strength of my first book) aversion to mechanical fan-fare (more of the same, no doubt. I don't really object to fanfare: I just want more of it than a prize could get me, if I only knew?). But I do mean that I don't (as usual) see how one could let oneself importune people to do what they'd shown they weren't inclined to do for you. To be any good, any satisfaction, 'honors' would seem to me to have to come to you, not be gone after or wangled for.

But perhaps you need to consider what must have been Frost's special case. He might, and you can see why he might, badly need a sort of justification by prize. Writers being writers, it's easy to imagine the years and years of hardly being able to stand it F. could have spent while all attention, in poetry, went to people like T.S. Eliot or Ezra Pound: and doubtless even worse, to almost every small-fry imitator of them.

XII 28   John O'Hara's *The Hat on the Bed* which (my God) must be his third published book this year, presents a short story collection. All the stuff has the honest qualities of people seen clearly and reported with definitely gifted care and this is good (who does better?) yet the problem persists. What can his experience have been? My own experience (of about the same length as his) has been that 'people' by and large are, as I think Somerset Maugham once said, generally not too bright but generally they have their hearts in the Right Place. O'Hara's procession, literally unbroken, of mean & cheap bastards, all quite convincing and also all wonderfully varied in situation and character is hard for me (for my experience) to accept and credit. It's my experience, so constant that occasional exceptions almost shock me, that if you're honest with a person, he'll be honest right back: that if you're civil and decent in your dealings with him, he'll be the same: that if you need help, most people will, if they possibly can, try to help you. In short, I don't remember ever in my life meeting personally a character of O'Hara's. And yet, as I say, they are so presented that they're perfectly real. I can't for a moment doubt that they do exist, and do behave exactly as he reports.

XII 29   *Note on above.* It occurs to me that what I describe as 'my experience' isn't any absolute observation of life; it's no more than my temperament's view of things and people as they affect me personally. Coloring or conditioning that 'view' may be that (for whatever psychological reasons) I've never wanted much of anything from anyone—except, perhaps, to be left or let alone. I can see that this is abnormal; and what amounts to a defect in me. But if your temperament's such that you *do* want things from other people you no doubt feel differently toward them. Whether you get the things you want may not be of first importance, either. That is: even supposing you do get them, the fact that you *had* wanted them, that your desires had reduced you to wanting them, made you try to get them, could perhaps leave you as resentful as if you hadn't got them.

XII 31   It seems to be the simple perhaps sad fact that our human nature makes it apparently impossible for anyone to really love anyone else. This is an extension of the ruminations above; but not, I think going contrary to them. It's not you who's loved. What your professed lover loves is all too evidently the enjoyment, the good, the use he or she finds you are, or thinks you could be, to him or her. Of course, there's this about it. The feeling's never faked or phony. That's a love that's forever true. And certainly all any human being can be entitled to; since he or she isn't going to be able to return anything different or 'better.' Here, that temperament that 'wants' may have its real trouble. If you want someone to love you for yourself, not for herself or himself, you're crying for the moon—a real expense of spirit in a waste of shame.

I 30   When you get older—and I recognize that I should stop saying 'older'; old is the word—there can be something a little disturbing about what surely ought to be Fond Recollection's show of proof that your luck has been so consistently good as to be almost beyond belief. I must see in my own case that this was always truest when it was most undeserved, when stupid or wanton behaviour of mine got me into fixes (and not all youthful) where bad trouble would seem in right and reason inescapable. But, every time, I escaped; and by no means, not ever, thanks to any resource of my own. So far, so good; all right; but the observations of, say, five decades of reasonable ability to observe must suggest to you that our human life just isn't, just can't be, all like that; and, not without trepidation, you must suspect that when the evening-up comes, necessarily not too long from now, it will be a lu-lu.

NOTEBOOK 8: FEBRUARY–OCTOBER 1964

II 18   Demonstrably, the most dangerous thing anyone can ever do is to be born. You're making a contract, with no escape clause to die at the pleasure of the nature of things. Why do this?

III 12   Inspection of a new issue of the *New York Review of Books* shows again the doyens of the sophomore circuit at their pretentious, labored, and far-too-long-to-read-through self-appointed tasks. However, I read as much as I could; and there didn't seem to be one review really going to the book itself. In every case the 'reviewer' was setting out (and always at that intolerable length) ideas of his or her own on what the book *should* have been if it was being found no good; or if it was being found some good, how he or she, if he or she had been writing it himself or herself, would have made it vastly better.

III 16   a passing crack in the TLS correspondence column about Somerset Maugham's style being 'cliché-ridden' reminds me of a point a wonder more and more about the longer I read and write. Could it be that the cliché is 'bad' only when the writer has nothing, or merely the stupid or obvious, to say and the clarity and simplicity of clichés instantly exposes this fact? Twistings and novelties in language can certainly delay (and for some people, what seems to be indefinitely) any recognition of such thinking basically vapid and action basically false as the later work of James Joyce sets out. But if what you have to say is worth saying, and what you want to show is the truth about life and men, the well-chosen cliché, short, quick, familiar to everyone, certainly may, as I seem to remember Maugham himself quietly suggesting, be the good, right way to convey clear meaning.

NOTEBOOK 9: OCTOBER 1964 – APRIL 1965

XI 14   In Somerset Maugham's *The Summing Up* [one, I come to realize, of the mere handful of books of our time that remain and seem likely to remain really profitable reading] which I was leafing through to check something else (I couldn't find it) I came on his comments p. 76 et seq. on talent, genius, and the 'greatest writers,' one of which he says he sees he cannot hope to be, 'never having felt some of the fundamental emotions of normal men' etc. This may be true, but considering it, wondering if much more can be told you than he tells you so lucidly and well, I had to wonder suddenly if those 'greatest writers' today tell anybody much of anything, because I must suspect that very few of them are generally read. Outside academic circles where reading them may be a professional chore, are Homer, Dante, Cervantes, popular reading anywhere? Is Shakespeare? In my desk-rack of books I have a battered copy of G. B. Harrison's Complete Works and probably there isn't a day (a matter of habit) when I don't (but idly, of course) read a little here or there. That can't be called really 'reading,' and I must wonder just how many people ever look at a line of Shakespeare, let alone ever settle down and read a whole play through.

NOTEBOOK 10: APRIL–DECEMBER 1965

IX 3   In his *Literary Horizons Sat. Review* column Granville Hicks who manages to mention me quite frequently (no doubt because of a 'monograph' on me he is doing for the University of something or other* which he wrote me about early this year asking if I wanted to say anything: I said no) speaks of 'the present-day crisis of values' of which most 'contemporary novelists to whose work (he) is attracted' are acutely aware. "James Gould Cozzens and Louis Auchincloss are exceptions, and that is why I am uneasy with their writings though I admire their craftsmanship and respect their integrity. Both of them it seems to me are writing their novels as if the world in general and the Western world in particular had not gone through a dozen revolutions in the last half century. Cozzens makes a strong case for common sense as the solution of many human problems, but he refuses to look at those problems before which common sense is bankrupt . . ."
[This kind of thing really beats you and I'm certainly 'uneasy with' Hicks' writing as a critic when he makes it so plain that to a novelist attentive to his duty it can't matter a hoot in hell how many revolutions the world has gone through. He has no business looking at 'problems' or offering solutions to them: his proper study is mankind, how men are seen to act and so seem to think. Noting and reporting on that is a whole time job and if he doesn't confine himself to it, while he may attract the momentary attention of our Granville Hickses, he's unlikely to write anything really worth reading.

**James Gould Cozzens* (Minneapolis: University of Minnesota Press, 1966)—MJB.

APPENDIX 3

The Publications of James Gould Cozzens and Books about Him

SEPARATE PUBLICATIONS

Confusion. Boston: Brimmer, 1924.

Michael Scarlett. New York: Boni, 1925; London: Holden, 1927.

Cock Pit. New York: Morrow, 1928.

The Son of Perdition. New York: Morrow, 1929; London: Longmans, Green, 1929.

S.S. San Pedro. New York: Harcourt, Brace, 1931; London, New York, Toronto: Longmans, Green, 1931.

The Last Adam. New York: Harcourt, Brace, 1933; *A Cure of Flesh*. London, New York, Toronto: Longmans, Green, 1933.

Castaway. London, New York, Toronto: Longmans, Green, 1934; New York: Random House, 1934.

Men and Brethren. New York: Harcourt, Brace, 1936; London, New York, Toronto: Longmans, Green, 1936.

Ask Me Tomorrow. New York: Harcourt, Brace, 1940; London, New York, Toronto: Longmans, Green, 1940.

The Just and the Unjust. New York: Harcourt, Brace, 1942; London: Cape, 1943. Abridged in *Omnibook* IV (October 1942).

Technique in Weather. Patterson Field, Ohio: Air Service Command, 1943. Unsigned; with E. J. Minser.

Airways Flying. Training Aids Division, Army Air Forces, 1943. Unsigned; with Bert Moore and L. N. Conklin.

Guard of Honor. New York: Harcourt, Brace, 1948; London, New York, Toronto: Longmans, Green, 1949.

By Love Possessed. New York: Harcourt, Brace, 1957; London, New York, Toronto: Longmans, Green, 1958. *Reader's Digest Condensed Books*. Pleasantville, N.Y.: Reader's Digest Association, 1957; London, Sydney & Cape Town: Reader's Digest Association, 1960.

Children and Others. New York: Harcourt, Brace & World, 1964; London: Longmans, 1965. Stories: "King Midas Has Ass's Ears," "Child's Play," "Whose Broad Stripes and Bright Stars," "The Animals' Fair," "Total Stranger," "Something about a Dollar," "Someday You'll Be Sorry," "We'll Recall It with Affection," "The Guns of the Enemy," "*Candida* by Bernard Shaw," "Men Running," "One Hundred Ladies," "My Love to Marcia," "The Way to Go Home," "Every Day's a Holiday," "Farewell to Cuba," "Eyes to See."

Morning Noon and Night. New York: Harcourt & World, 1968; London: Longmans, 1969.

A Flower in Her Hair. Bloomfield Hills, Mich. & Columbia, S.C.: Bruccoli Clark, 1974.

A Rope for Dr. Webster. Bloomfield Hills, Mich. & Columbia, S.C.: Bruccoli Clark, 1976.

Some Putative Facts of Hard Record or He Commences Authour Aetatis Suae 19–20: Excerpts from 1923 MS Diary and a Few Notes. Carbondale & Edwardsville: Southern Illinois University Press/New York & London: Harcourt Brace Jovanovich, 1978. Keepsake.

BOOKS EDITED OR REVISED BY COZZENS

Lanterns Junks and Jade. Samuel Morrill. New York: Stokes, 1926.

Zoom! George R. White. New York & Toronto: Longmans, Green, 1931.

The United States in a New World II: Pacific Relations. New York: Time, 1942. Supplement to *Fortune*.

FIRST-APPEARANCE CONTRIBUTIONS TO BOOKS

"The Class History," *Kent School Year Book*. Kent, Conn.: Kent School, 1922.

"Breaking the Week in Cuba," *Morrow's Almanack for the Year of Our Lord 1929,* ed. Burton Rascoe. New York: Morrow, 1928.

"Portrait of a Chief Officer on His Birthday," *Morrow's Almanack and Every-Day Book for 1930*, ed. Thayer Hobson. New York: Morrow, 1929.

Introduction, *Balzac's Masterpieces*. Philadelphia: McKay, 1931. Unsigned.

Excerpt from letter, *Contemporary American Authors*, ed. Fred B. Millet. New York: Harcourt, Brace, 1940.

Autobiographical notes, *Twentieth Century Authors*, ed. Stanley J. Kunitz & Howard Haycraft. New York: Wilson, 1942.

Autobiographical notes. *Current Biography*, ed. Anna Rothe. New York: Wilson, 1950.

"FHS: A Faith that Did Not Fail," *Father Sill's Birthday*. Kent, Conn.: Kent School, 1956. *Just Representations*.

Statement, *The Best Short Stories of World War II*, ed. Charles A. Fenton. New York: Viking, 1957.

Excerpt from letter, *Copey of Harvard*. J. Donald Adams. Boston: Houghton Mifflin, 1960.

Excerpt from letter, *Proceedings of the American Academy of Arts and Letters and the National Institute of Arts and Letters*, Second Series, Number 11. New York, 1961.

Excerpts from letters, "The English Editions of James Gould Cozzens," James B. Meriwether. *Studies in Bibliography* XV (1962).

Excerpt from letter, *Roses of Yesterday and Today*. Watsonville, Cal.: Will Tillotson's Roses, 1963.

Statement, *Contemporary Authors . . . Volumes 11–12*, ed. James M. Ethridge & Barbara Kopala. Detroit: Gale Research, 1965.

Foreword, *Roses of Yesterday*, Dorothy Stemler & Nanae Ito. Kansas City: Hallmark, 1967. *Just Representations*.

Introduction, *James Gould Cozzens: A Checklist*, James B. Meriwether. Detroit: Gale Research/Bruccoli Clark, 1972. Also Preface to *The Criticisms of John Keats on English Poetry*, and letters.

Statement, *Who's Who in America . . . 1976–1977*. Chicago: Marquis, 1976.

Statement on dust jacket, *Samuel Johnson*, W. Jackson Bate. New York & London: Harcourt Brace Jovanovich, 1977.

Statement, *The Films of Frank Capra*, Victor Scherle & William Turner Levy. Secaucus, N.J.: Citadel, 1977.

"Some Putative Facts of Hard Record . . ." *Just Representations: A James Gould Cozzens Reader*, ed. Matthew J. Bruccoli. Carbondale & Edwardsville: Southern Illinois University Press / New York & London: Harcourt Brace Jovanovich, 1978.

STORIES

"Remember the Rose," *Harvard Advocate*, CIX (1 June 1923), 395–397.

"Abishag," *Linonia*, I (June 1925), 45–53.

"A Letter to a Friend," *Pictorial Review*, XXVII (May 1926), 116–117.

"Foreign Strand," *Paris Comet*, 11, 4 (September 1928), 4 pp.

"Future Assured," *The Saturday Evening Post*, CCII (2 November 1929), 22–23, 116, 120–121, 124.

"The Defender of Liberties," *Alhambra*, I (January 1930), 14–17, 54–56.

"Lions Are Lower Today," *The Saturday Evening Post*, CCII (15 February 1930), 36, 38, 40, 154, 158.

"Someday You'll Be Sorry," *The Saturday Evening Post*, CCII (21 June 1930), 44, 47, 60, 63–64, 66. *Children and Others*.

"S.S. 'San Pedro' A Tale of the Sea." *Scribner's*, LXXXVIII (August 1930), 113–128, 214–228.

"October Occupancy," *American Magazine*, CX (October 1930), 56–59, 153–158.

"We'll Recall It with Affection," *The Saturday Evening Post*, CCIII (4 October 1930), 12–13, 149–150, 152–154. *Children and Others*.

"The Guns of the Enemy," *The Saturday Evening Post*, CCIII (1 November 1930), 13, 74, 77–78, 80, 82. *Children and Others*.

"Fortune and Men's Eyes," *Woman's Home Companion*, LVIII (February 1931), 29–30, 134, 138, 140.

"Farewell to Cuba," *Scribner's*, XC (November 1931), 533–544. *Children and Others*.

"The Way to Go Home," *The Saturday Evening Post*, CCIV (26 December 1931), 12–13, 59–60. *Children and Others*.

"Every Day's a Holiday," *Scribner's*, XCIV (December 1933), 339–344. *Children and Others*.

"My Love to Marcia," *Collier's*, XCII (3 March 1934), 16–17, 46–47. *Children and Others*.

"Love Leaves Town," *American Magazine*, CXVIII (September 1934), 24–27, 119–121.

"Straight Story," *Collier's*, XCIV (17 November 1934), 22.

"Success Story," *Collier's*, XCV (20 April 1935), 26.

"Foot in It," *Redbook*, LXV (August 1935), 28–29. Reprinted as "Clerical Error."

"Total Stranger," *The Saturday Evening Post*, CCVIII (15 February 1936), 8–9, 96, 98, 100. *Children and Others*.

"Whose Broad Stripes and Bright Stars," *The Saturday Evening Post*, CCVIII (23 May 1936), 16–17, 69, 71. *Children and Others*.

"Something About a Dollar," *The Saturday Evening Post*, CCIX (15 August 1936), 27–28, 62, 64. *Children and Others*.

"The Animals' Fair," *The Saturday Evening Post*, CCIX (16 January 1937), 18–19, 47, 50, 53–54. *Children and Others*.

"Child's Play," *The Saturday Evening Post*, CCIX (13 February 1937), 16–17, 61, 63, 65. *Children and Others*.

"Men Running," *The Atlantic Monthly*, CLX (July 1937), 81–91. *Children and Others*.

"Son and Heir," *The Saturday Evening Post*, CCX (2 April 1938), 10–11, 86, 88–89, 91.

"One Hundred Ladies," *The Saturday Evening Post*, CCXXXVII (11 July 1964), 40, 42–43, 45–47. *Children and Others*.

"Candida by Bernard Shaw," *The Saturday Evening Post*, CCXXXVII (25 July 1964), 50, 52, 54, 57. *Children and Others.*

ARTICLES AND ESSAYS

For unsigned contributions to the *Kent School News* and the *Kent Quarterly* (1920–22), see Bruccoli, *James Gould Cozzens: A Descriptive Bibliography.*
"A Democratic School," *The Atlantic Monthly*, CXXV (March 1920), 383–384. Reprinted as "In Defense of Boarding Schools," *Kent Quarterly*, XII (March 1920), 50–52.
"The Trail of the Lakes," *Kent Quarterly*, XII (May 1920), 86–91.
"A Friendly Thinker," *Kent Quarterly*, XIII (December 1920), 13–14.
"Good Old Main Street," *Kent Quarterly*, XIII (March 1921), 40–42.
"Religion for Beginners: A Nova Scotian Sketch," *Kent Quarterly*, XIV (December 1921), 25–28.
"A Study in the Art of the Novel," *Kent Quarterly*, XIV (July 1922), 77–79.
"The Point of View," *Kent Quarterly*, XVII (June 1925), 55–59.
"Harvard Author Reviews New Work 'The History of Michael Scarlett,' " *Daily Princetonian*, XLVI (12 June 1925), 1, 4.
"What You Should Know About the Club Library," *Winged Foot* (New York Athletic Club), XXXVIII (September 1927), 29–30.
"Notes from the Club Library," *Winged Foot*, XXXVIII (October 1927), 17.
"The Library Talk for the Month," *Winged Foot*, XXXVIII (November 1927), 28–29.
"Notes from the Club Library," *Winged Foot*, XXXVIII (December 1927), 42.
"Notes from the Club Library," *Winged Foot*, XXXIX (January 1928), 20–21.
"Thoughts Brought on By 633 Manuscripts," *Bookman*, LXXIII (June 1931), 381–384.
"Kent, A New School," *Town & Country*, LXXXVIII (1 August 1933), 38–41, 57.
Foreword to *Kent Quarterly*, I (26 November 1936), 3–4.
"The Fuller Brush Co.," *Fortune*, XVIII (October 1938), 69–72, 100, 102.
Work for *Fortune* on "Big Navy" (March 1938), "Oskaloosa vs. the United States (April 1938), "9,000 Billion Horsepower of Solar Energy" (November 1938), "You Don't Need to Sue" (December 1938).
"What They're Reading," *Air Force*, XXVI (June 1943), 28.
"The First Manual," *AFTAD Liaison Bulletin*, no. 41 (29 June 1943), 3.
"Writing Clearly," *AFTAD Liaison Bulletin*, no. 45 (9 July 1943), 4.
"Airways Flying," *Air Transport*, I (September 1943), 39–42. With Bert Moore.
"The Air Force Training Program," *Fortune*, XXIX (February 1944), 147–152, 174, 176, 178, 180, 183–184, 186, 189–190, 193–194. Unsigned; with William Vogel.
"Notes on a Difficulty of Law by One Unlearned in It," *Bucks County Law Reporter*, I (15 November 1951), 3–7. *Just Representations.*

POEMS

"The Andes," *The Quill* (Staten Island Academy), XXX (January 1915), 5.
"Lord Kitchener," *Digby* [Nova Scotia] *Weekly Courier* (16 June 1916), 1.
"The Trust in Princes," *Harvard Advocate*, CIX (1 November 1922), 44.
"Where Angels Fear to Tread," *Harvard Advocate*, CIX (1 December 1922), 86.
"The Passing," *Harvard Advocate*, CIX (1 January 1923), 121.
"Condolence," *Harvard Advocate*, CIX (1 February 1923), 151.
"Two Arts," *Harvard Advocate*, CIX (1 May 1923), 347.
"The Virginia Rose: A Ballad for Eunice," *Harvard Advocate*, CIX (1 May 1923), 338–339.
"For a Motet by Josquin de Pres," *Harvard Advocate*, CIX (1 June 1923), 404.

"The Long Elusion," *Casements* (Brown University), (July 1923), unpaged.
"ΑΦΡΟΛΙΤΗΚΥΠΡΙΑ," *Kent Quarterly*, XV (July 1923), 91.
"Romanesque," *Kent Quarterly*, XV (July 1923), 85.
"Blue Seas," *Palms*, I (Autumn 1923), 110.
"Hail and Farewell," *Harvard Advocate*, CX (1 October 1923), 13. Untitled sonnet.

REVIEWS

The Bright Shawl by Joseph Hergesheimer. *Harvard Advocate*, CIX (1 December 1922), 85–86.
Don Rodriguez: Chronicles of Shadow Valley, by Lord Dunsany. *Harvard Advocate*, CIX (1 January 1923), 120–121.
Love and Freindship, by Jane Austen. *Harvard Advocate*, CIX (7 April 1923), 291.
The Shepherd's Pipe, by Arthur Schnitzler. *Dial*, LXXV (December 1923), 608–610. Signed by Cuthbert Wright, but Cozzens claimed it as his own work.
The Eagle in the Egg, by Oliver La Farge. *New York Times Book Review* (24 July 1949), 1, 17. *Just Representations*.
Reflections on Hanging, by Arthur Koestler. *Harvard Law Review*, LXXI (May 1958), 1377–1381.

INTERVIEWS, STATEMENTS, LETTERS IN MAGAZINES AND NEWSPAPERS

Excerpt from letter about Kent school, "The Contributors' Column," *The Atlantic Monthly*, CXXV (March 1920), 430.
Letter, *Harvard Crimson* (7 March 1923), 2. Reply to review of *Eight More Harvard Poets*.
Interview, "Cambridge Boy Produces Novel Winning Praise" [headline unclear], unlocated clipping, ca. April 1924.
Interview, "Harvard Student to Publish Novel," unlocated clipping, ca. April 1924.
Letter to Harry Salpeter, *New York World* (30 September 1928), 10M. Comment on James Francis Thierry.
Interview, Ruth Hale, "The Author," *Book-of-the-Month Club News* (December 1932), 3.
Letter, *Waterbury* [Conn.] *Republican* (21 January 1933), 8. About setting for *The Last Adam*.
Letter, *New Milford* [Conn.] *Times* (2 February 1933), 4. About setting for *The Last Adam*.
Letter, *Colgate Maroon* (14 March 1933), 2. About model for Dr. Bull in *The Last Adam*.
Interview, Robert Van Gelder, "James Gould Cozzens at Work," *New York Times Book Review* (23 June 1940), 14.
Quoted, "Writer Visits Court Here for Atmosphere," *Doylestown* [Pa.] *Intelligencer* (2 July 1940), 1.
Interview, "Cozzens Was Gardening When Word Came of Pulitzer Prize," *Trenton Evening Times* (6 May 1949), 2.
Interview, Ann Biester, "J. G. Cozzens, Pulitzer Author, Grants Interview to Reporter," *Doylestown High School News* (17 March 1950), 2.
Letter, *New Hope* [Pa.] *Gazette* (15 September 1955), 4. Opposes election of John W. Eckelberry to the Bucks County bench.
Replies to questions, William Dubois, "In and Out of Books," *New York Times Book Review* (25 August 1957), 8.
Based on interviews, "The Hermit of Lambertville," *Time*, CXX (2 September 1957), 72–74, 76–77.
Letters, Richard M. Ludwig, "A Reading of the James Gould Cozzens Manuscripts," *The Princeton University Library Chronicle*, XIX (Autumn 1957), 1–14. Facsimiles, draft pages for *By Love Possessed*. *Just Representations*.

Quoted, "Carl Brandt Dies: A Literary Agent," *New York Times* (14 October 1957), 27.

Quoted, "J. G. Cozzens '22 Pulitzer Prize Winner, Prefers The Quiet Life To Plaudits," *The Kent News* (7 May 1959), 2.

Brief statement, Lewis Nichols, "In and Out of Books," *New York Times Book Review* (9 August 1959), 8.

Letter, *University: A Princeton Magazine*, I (Fall 1960), 2. Comments on the magazine.

Letter, *The Christian Century*, LXXIX (22 August 1962), 1009. Reply to the question "What books did most to shape your vocational attitude and your philosophy of life?"

Letter, *Harvard Alumni Bulletin*, LXV (4 May 1963), 593. On Harvard architecture.

Letter, *TV Guide*, XI (24 August 1963), 6–7. Reply to questions about television preference.

Letter, *The Living Church*, CXLVII (27 October 1963), 17. On evacuating churches during bomb threats.

Letter, *Forbes*, LXXXXII (15 November 1963), 6. About unsatisfactory American razor blades.

Letter, *Fact*, I (January–February 1964), 5. About inaccuracies in *Time* cover story. Text of this letter was rewritten by *Fact*; see Meriwether, *Checklist*.

Letter, *The Living Church*, CXLVIII (22 March 1964), 5. About distribution of the *Book of Common Prayer*.

Letter, *Bulletin* (Harvard Club of New York) (April 1965). Comment on recipe.

Letter, *Harvard Alumni Bulletin*, LXVIII (13 May 1967), 2–3. Reply to letter about President Lowell.

Letter, *Berkshire* [Pittsfield, Mass.] *Eagle* (13 July 1967), 13. Defense of General Charles Lee.

Facsimile of inscription to Edward G. Biester in dedication copy of *The Just and the Unjust*, Wolff, Morris H., "The Legal Background of Cozzens' *The Just and the Unjust*," *Journal of Modern Literature*, VII (September 1979), 508.

Letter, Cass, Colin S., "Cozzens's Debt to Thomas Dekker in *Ask Me Tomorrow*," *Markham Review*, XI (Fall 1981), 11.

BOOKS ABOUT COZZENS

Bracher, Frederick. *The Novels of James Gould Cozzens*. New York: Harcourt, Brace, 1959.

Bruccoli, Matthew J. *James Gould Cozzens: A Descriptive Bibliography*. Pittsburgh: University of Pittsburgh Press, 1981.

————, ed. *James Gould Cozzens: New Acquist of True Experience*. Carbondale and Edwardsville: Southern Illinois University Press, 1979.

————, ed. *Just Representations: A James Gould Cozzens Reader*. Carbondale and Edwardsville: Southern Illinois University Press / New York and London: Harcourt Brace Jovanovich, 1978.

Hicks, Granville. *James Gould Cozzens*. University of Minnesota. Pamphlets on American Writers, no. 58. Minneapolis: University of Minnesota Press, 1966.

Maxwell, D. E. S. *Cozzens*. Edinburgh & London: Oliver & Boyd, 1964.

Meriwether, James B. *James Gould Cozzens: A Checklist*. Detroit: Gale Research/Bruccoli Clark, 1972.

Michel, Pierre. *James Gould Cozzens*. New York: Twayne, 1974.

————. *James Gould Cozzens: An Annotated Checklist*. Kent, Ohio: Kent State University Press, 1971.

Mooney, Harry J., Jr. *James Gould Cozzens: Novelist of Intellect*. Pittsburgh: University of Pittsburgh Press, 1963.

Van Antwerp, Margaret, ed. *Dictionary of Literary Biography: Documentary Series Vol. 2*. Detroit: Gale Research/Bruccoli Clark, 1982.

NOTES

All quotations from James Gould Cozzens's novels in this biography are taken from the first printings. Cozzens usually revised the later editions of his novels. (For collations, see Bruccoli, *James Gould Cozzens: A Descriptive Bibliography*.)

INTRODUCTION

1. *The Idler*, # 102
2. Williamstown Notebooks, 30 January 1962. Princeton University Library.
3. *Time*, LXX (2 September 1957), 78.
4. Johnson, "Preface to Shakespeare."
5. Milton, *Samson Agonistes*, ll. 1755–56.

1957

1. To Emmett Peter, Jr., 19 March 1960. University of Florida Libraries.

CHAPTER I. BOYHOOD AND KENT

1. JGC revision of MJB's Introduction to *Just Representations: A James Gould Cozzens Reader* (Carbondale and Edwardsville: Southern Illinois University Press / New York and London: Harcourt Brace Jovanovich, 1978), xi.
2. *Time*, 74.
3. *Baby's Record*. Collection of Fannie Collins.
4. To D. E. S. Maxwell, 24 July 1963. Carbon copy. Princeton University Library.
5. Dorothy Stemler & Nanae Ito (Kansas City: Hallmark, 1967), 10–12.
6. 4 May 1952. Cozzens's correspondence with his mother is at the Princeton University Library.
7. *Time* research notes. Time Inc., New York.
8. Note pad. Princeton University Library.
9. Collection of Fannie Collins.
10. *Children and Others*, 36.
11. *Time* research notes.
12. B. J. Brimmer files. University of Virginia Library.

13. *The Christian Century,* LXXIX (22 August 1962), 1009.
14. XXX (January 1915), 5.
15. 16 June 1916, 1.
16. 16 July 1916. Princeton University Library.
17. N.d. Kent School.
18. "FHS: A Faith that Did Not Fail," *Father Sill's Birthday* (Kent, Conn.: Kent School, 1956). *Just Representations,* 538–42.
19. "Someday You'll Be Sorry," *Children and Others,* 108.
20. *Children and Others,* 108–109.
21. Princeton University Library.
22. N.d. Kent School.
23. John P. Cuyler, letter to *Kent News* (9 December 1978). 2, 5.
24. CXXV (March 1920), 383–84.
25. Ibid., 430.
26. *Kent School News* (21 April 1922), 2.
27. *Time* research notes.
28. *Morning Noon and Night,* 393.
29. N.d. Princeton University Library.
30. Dudley Fitts Papers, Yale University Library.
31. "A Study in the Art of the Novel," *Kent Quarterly,* XIV (July 1922), 77–79.
32. pp. 9, 11, 13, 15.
33. P. 66. Princeton University Library.
34. 20 June 1922. Kent School.

CHAPTER 2. FAIR HARVARD

1. To Bertha Cozzens, 29 September [1922]. Princeton University Library.
2. 11 October [1922]. Princeton University Library.
3. *Time* research notes.
4. CIX (1 November 1922), 44.
5. CIX (1 May 1923), 338–39.
6. *Ask Me Tomorrow* (Uniform Edition, 1969), 129.
7. To MJB, 6 October 1976.
8. Revised for "Some Putative Facts of Hard Record . . ." *Just Representations,* xxxi.
9. *Ask Me Tomorrow,* 18.
10. "Cambridge Boy Produces Novel Winning Praise" and "Harvard Student to Publish Novel"—unlocated interviews in scrapbook. Princeton University Library.
11. N.d. Princeton University Library.
12. LXXVI (July 1924), 104.
13. CXIX (23 July 1924), 100.
14. 27 April 1924, 14.
15. "The Younger Generation as They See Themselves" (8 April 1924), 11.
16. Williamstown Notebooks, 1 April 1965. Princeton University Library.
17. Ibid.
18. Reproduced in James B. Meriwether, *James Gould Cozzens: A Checklist* (Detroit: Gale Research / Bruccoli Clark, 1972), plates 2–3.
19. N.d. Princeton University Library.
20. N.d. Princeton University Library.
21. N.d. Houghton Library, Harvard University.
22. 1, 4.
23. Bernice Baumgarten to JGC, 19 June 1925. Princeton University Library.

24. 15 November 1925, 8.
25. James B. Meriwether, "The English Editions of James Gould Cozzens," *Studies in Bibliography*, XV (1962), 209.
26. 4 August 1927, 534.

CHAPTER 3. FOREIGN STRANDS

1. Princeton University Library.
2. 25 November 1925. Princeton University Library.
3. To Tom Howard, 11 March 1927. Princeton University Library.
4. Princeton University Library.
5. *Ask Me Tomorrow*, 136.
6. Princeton University Library.
7. *Paris Tribune* (14 October 1926), 2.
8. Collection of Virginia Reiland Watson. MJB telephone interview with Mrs. Watson, 12 March 1981.
9. *Ask Me Tomorrow*, 168.

CHAPTER 4. SYLVIA

1. P. 85. Princeton University Library.
2. N.d. Princeton University Library.
3. N.d. Collection of Fannie Collins.
4. "What You Should Know About the Club Library," *Winged Foot* (New York Athletic Club), XXXVIII (September 1927), 29.
5. To MJB, 13 December 1978.
6. N.d. Princeton University Library.
7. N.d. Princeton University Library.
8. *Morning Noon and Night*, 271.
9. Collection of Fannie Collins.
10. To Bertha Cozzens, 10 February 1930. Princeton University Library.
11. To Bertha Cozzens, 21 March 1928. Princeton University Library.
12. 23 February 1928. Princeton University Library.
13. 4 March 1928. Princeton University Library.
14. 29 September 1928, 9.
15. 4 March 1928. Princeton University Library.
16. 21 March 1928. Princeton University Library.
17. To Bertha Cozzens, 16 April 1928. Princeton University Library.
18. 6 October 1929, 7.
19. 17 September 1929, 15.
20. Princeton University Library.
21. 14 June 1929. Princeton University Library.
22. 5 August 1929. Princeton University Library.
23. To Bertha Cozzens, 12 August 1929. Princeton University Library.
24. Ibid.
25. VIII (12 September 1931), 117.
26. August 1931.
27. Quoted on dust jacket for *A Cure of Flesh* (1933).
28. New York: William Morrow, 1929, p. 220.
29. 23 August 1929. Princeton University Library.

30. To Bertha Cozzens, 17 February 1929. Princeton University Library.
31. Ibid.
32. *Children and Others*, 129.
33. To Bertha Cozzens, 13 October 1930. Princeton University Library.
34. To Bertha Cozzens, 13 January 1931. Princeton University Library.
35. LXXIII (June 1931), 384.
36. Meriwether, *Checklist*, 1.
37. *Children and Others*, 258–59.
38. *Children and Others*, 263.
39. To Bertha Cozzens, 13 September 1932. Princeton University Library.
40. To Bertha Cozzens, 12 May 1932. Princeton University Library.
41. Inscribed copy of *The Last Adam* dated 2 May 1939. Bruccoli Collection.
42. December 1932.
43. To Bertha Cozzens, 25 November 1932. Princeton University Library.
44. See Colin S. Cass, "The Title of *The Last Adam*" in *James Gould Cozzens: New Acquist of True Experience*, ed. Matthew J. Bruccoli (Carbondale and Edwardsville: Southern Illinois University Press, 1979), 63–80.
45. Annotated copy of *Time*. Princeton University Library.
46. December 1932.
47. 8 January 1933, 4 D.
48. 8 January 1933, 6.
49. CCV (21 January 1933), 62.
50. 12 March 1933, 8.
51. 23 February 1933, 124.
52. 27 December 1932. Princeton University Library.
53. 11 January 1933, 8; 15 January 1933, Feature Section, 2; 22 January 1933, 3.
54. 21 January 1933, 8. Cozzens also wrote to the *New Milford Times* (2 February 1933) insisting that "New Winton is not Kent."
55. 14 March 1933, 2.

CHAPTER 5. THE HERMIT OF CARRS FARM

1. To Bertha Cozzens, 6 January 1933. Princeton University Library.
2. To Bertha Cozzens, 21 May 1934. Princeton University Library.
3. To MJB, 22 February 1976.
4. X (17 November 1934), 285, 289.
5. X (17 November 1934), 86–87.
6. To Bertha Cozzens, 12 November 1934. Princeton University Library.
7. To Bertha Cozzens, 26 March 1937. Princeton University Library.
8. 29 April 1934. Princeton University Library.
9. "CURB ON POTATOES DEFIED IN JERSEY . . . Dean Ackerman and James Cozzens Among Signees of Resolution of Revolt" (27 August 1935), 21.
10. 18 June 1957. Harcourt Brace Jovanovich.
11. JGC's note on MJB's introduction to *Just Representations*.
12. Inscribed copy of *Men and Brethren* dated 2 May 1939. Bruccoli Collection.
13. 14 June 1935. Princeton University Library.
14. To Bertha Cozzens, 12 and 15 March 1935. Princeton University Library.
15. Note pad. Princeton University Library.
16. To Bertha Cozzens, 18 November 1935. Princeton University Library.
17. 3 March 1936. Princeton University Library.
18. To Bertha Cozzens, 23 July 1935. Princeton University Library.
19. XXVII (13 January 1936), 66–67.

20. 14 March 1936, 222.
21. *Children and Others*, 89.
22. To D. E. S. Maxwell, 24 July 1963. Carbon copy. Princeton University Library.
23. To Bertha Cozzens, 4 December 1936. Princeton University Library.
24. To Bertha Cozzens, 2 February 1937. Princeton University Library.
25. 2 March 1937. Princeton University Library.
26. To Bertha Cozzens, 23 March 1937. Princeton University Library.
27. To Bertha Cozzens, 13 April 1937. Princeton University Library.
28. To Bertha Cozzens, 10 November 1937. Princeton University Library.
29. To Bertha Cozzens, 30 December 1938. Princeton University Library.
30. To Bertha Cozzens, 24 January 1939. Princeton University Library.
31. To Bertha Cozzens, 30 January 1940. Princeton University Library.
32. "Raise the Banner for Cozzens," *Life*, LVII (7 August 1964), 9, 12. *Just Representations*, 236.
33. New York: Harcourt, Brace, 1940, p. 304.
34. To Bertha Cozzens, 11 February 1938. Princeton University Library.
35. To Bertha Cozzens, 28 March 1939. Princeton University Library.
36. To Bertha Cozzens, 9 December 1938. Princeton University Library.
37. To Bertha Cozzens, 17 March 1939. Princeton University Library.
38. Colin S. Cass, "Cozzens's Debt to Thomas Dekker in *Ask Me Tommorrow*," *Markham Review*, XI (Fall 1981), 11–16.
39. Postmarked 28 June 1940. Princeton University Library.
40. To Colin S. Cass, 15 July 1977.
41. 15 June 1940, 13.
42. 13 June 1940.
43. 23 June 1940, section 3, p. 7.
44. XVI (15 June 1940), 93–94.
45. 27 October 1940.
46. 18 November 1948. Bruccoli Collection.
47. 7 March 1946. Bruccoli Collection.
48. 29 December 1948. Bruccoli Collection.
49. To Bertha Cozzens, 24 May 1940. Princeton University Library.
50. Princeton University Library.
51. To Bertha Cozzens, 1 August 1939. Princeton University Library.
52. "James Gould Cozzens at Work," *New York Times Book Review* (23 June 1940), 14.
53. To Bertha Cozzens, 14 November 1933. Princeton University Library.
54. To Bertha Cozzens, 26 January 1940. Princeton University Library.
55. Morris H. Wolff, "The Legal Background of Cozzens' *The Just and the Unjust*," *Journal of Modern Literature*, VII (September 1979), 505–18.
56. To Bertha Cozzens, 17 December 1940. Princeton University Library.
57. To Bertha Cozzens, 16 January 1942. Princeton University Library.
58. To Bertha Cozzens, 7 February 1941. Princeton University Library.
59. To Bertha Cozzens, 22 February 1942. Princeton University Library.
60. 26 July 1942, "This World" section, 18.
61. LVI (March 1943), 833–36.
62. July 1942, 2–3.
63. 22 July 1942, 17.
64. XL (3 August 1942), 76–77.
65. To Bertha Cozzens, 20 June 1948. Princeton University Library.
66. Facsimiled in Wolff, 508. Biester Family Collection.
67. 17 April 1943, 185.
68. Princeton University Library.
69. Princeton University Library.

70. Inscribed copy of *The Just and the Unjust*, dated 17 July 1960. Bruccoli Collection.
71. 15 April 1950. Harcourt Brace Jovanovich.

CHAPTER 6. A TIME OF WAR

1. New York: Wilson, 1942, p. 323.
2. Summer 1942. Princeton University Library.
3. September 1942. Princeton University Library.
4. To Bertha Cozzens, 26 October 1942. Princeton University Library.
5. Princeton University Library.
6. 29 January 1945. Princeton University Library.
7. *A Rope for Dr. Webster*, 5–12.
8. To Bertha Cozzens, 29 January 1945. Princeton University Library.
9. Ibid.
10. To MJB, 28 February 1976.
11. To Bertha Cozzens, 29 January 1945. Princeton University Library.
12. "U. S. Reported Working on Atomic Bomb," 13.
13. Drew Middleton, "British Book Says Germans and Russians Met in 1943 to Plot a Negotiated Peace," *New York Times* (4 January 1971), 13.
14. *A Rope for Dr. Webster*, 5.
15. 11 February 1945. Princeton University Library.
16. *Morning Noon and Night*, 384.
17. MJB interviews with Newhouse, 15 December 1978, 31 July 1979, and 13 August 1979.
18. Princeton University Library.
19. 23 April 1945. Princeton University Library.
20. To Bertha Cozzens, 27 January 1946. Princeton University Library.

CHAPTER 7. *Guard of Honor*

1. To Bertha Cozzens, 7 April 1946. Princeton University Library.
2. To Bertha Cozzens, 1 February 1948. Princeton University Library.
3. To Bertha Cozzens, 13 October 1946. Princeton University Library.
4. 11 January 1948. Princeton University Library.
5. To MJB, 6 November 1981.
6. To MJB, 3 September 1981.
7. 14 March 1948. Princeton University Library.
8. N.d. Carbon copy. Princeton University Library.
9. N.d. Carbon copy. Princeton University Library.
10. To Bertha Cozzens, 4 July 1948. Princeton University Library.
11. 2 February 1947. Princeton University Library.
12. 27 October 1946. Princeton University Library.
13. To Bertha Cozzens, 30 January 1949. Princeton University Library.
14. To Bertha Cozzens, 22 February 1948. Princeton University Library.
15. XXIV (9 October 1948), 126–28.
16. September 1948.
17. 10 October 1948, 4.
18. LXXXIII (February 1949), 72–73.
19. 20 November 1949, 3.
20. 3 December 1949, 668.
21. "Those Phenomenal Initials—ATC" (24 July 1949), 1, 17.

22. *James Gould Cozzens and Sylvia B. Cozzens* vs. *Pennsylvania Railroad Company and Lawrence D. Cunningham.* Hunt & Faherty, Lambertville, N.J.
23. Ibid.

CHAPTER 8 . *By Love Possessed*

1. Princeton University Library.
2. To Bertha Cozzens, 15 August 1948. Princeton University Library.
3. To Bertha Cozzens, 19 December 1948. Princeton University Library.
4. To Bertha Cozzens, 3 April 1949. Princeton University Library.
5. Princeton University Library.
6. To Bertha Cozzens, 13 May 1951. Princeton University Library.
7. 20 January 1950. Carbon Copy. Princeton University Library.
8. To Bertha Cozzens, 22 April 1951. Princeton University Library.
9. To Bertha Cozzens, 11 February 1951. Princeton University Library.
10. To Bertha Cozzens, 9 December 1951. Princeton University Library.
11. Princeton University Library.
12. 7 December 1952. Princeton University Library.
13. *Tomorrow*, VII (May 1947), 58–59.
14. *New Mexico Quarterly*, XIX (Winter 1949), 476–98.
15. 29 October 1950. Princeton University Library.
16. Harvey Breit, "Talk with J. B. Priestley," *New York Times Book Review* (22 April 1951), 24.
17. To Bertha Cozzens, 1 January 1951. Princeton University Library.
18. I (15 November 1951), 3–7.
19. 13 January 1952. Princeton University Library.
20. 19 February 1953. Collection of Carlos Baker.
21. Williamstown Notebooks, 17 January 1961. Princeton University Library.
22. *Father Sill's Birthday. Just Representations*, 538–42.
23. Bernice Baumgarten to Denver Lindley, 3 May 1957.
24. To Gordon S. Haight, 17 October 1957. Haight Collection.
25. *Who's Who in America . . . 1976–1977* (Chicago: Marquis, 1976), 678.
26. To Bertha Cozzens, 26 May 1945. Princeton University Library.
27. To William F. Buckley, Jr., 8 December 1963. Yale University Library.
28. *Time* research notes.
29. To Bertha Cozzens, 10 March 1936. Princeton University Library.
30. XLVI (December 1957), 64.
31. 22 May 1958. Collection of Charles W. Phillips.
32. 5 June 1958. Collection of Frederick Bracher.
33. Colin S. Cass, "Two Stylistic Analyses of the Narrative Prose in Cozzens' *By Love Possessed*," *Style*, IV (Fall 1970), 213–37; Frederick Bracher, "Style and Technique," *Just Representations*, 379–88.
34. Carl Spielvogel, "How They Sold a Best Seller," *New York Times* (20 October 1957), III, 10.
35. Meriwether, *Checklist*, plates 14, 15.
36. Annotated copy. Princeton University Library.
37. MJB interview with Kalem, 21 August 1981.
38. David E. Scherman to Denver Lindley, 1 October 1957; Lindley to Scherman, 4 October 1957. Harcourt Brace Jovanovich.
39. August 1957, 1–3. Edward Newhouse contributed an article on Cozzens to this issue of the *Book-of-the-Month Club News*.
40. "Summa cum Laude," XXX (24 August 1957), 106–109.

41. CCXV (September 1957), 14–15, 18, 20.
42. XL (24 August 1957), 14–15.
43. 25 August 1957, 1.
44. "About Being Written About: or By Nimiety Possessed," unpublished typescript in the collection of Colin S. Cass. This working draft has been emended in the text printed here.
45. Williamstown Notebooks, 6 May 1964. Princeton University Library.
46. Annotated copy of *Time*.
47. 30 January 1958.
48. XVI–XVII (1 October 1957), 203–204.
49. LXXXXVIII (5 October 1957), 20.
50. To Thurston N. Davis, S.J., 8 October 1957. Carbon copy. Princeton University Library.
51. "Profile of an Aristocrat," CLXXXVI (November 1957), 114–19.
52. 30 October 1957. Carbon copy. Princeton University Library.
53. "Gone Tomorrow," IV (26 October 1957), 380–81.
54. 31 October 1957. Yale University Library.
55. Williamstown Notebooks, 28 November 1964. Princeton University Library.
56. XXV, 36–47.
57. Ann Evory, *Contemporary Authors*, Vols. 29–32 (First Revision) (Detroit: Gale Research, 1978), 417.
58. Yale University Library.
59. 30 November 1959. Yale University Library.
30. "James Gould Cozzens: Novelist of the Republic," *The New Republic*, CXXXVIII (20 January 1958), 15–19.
61. 18 April 1958, 15.
62. LV (19 April 1958), 510.
63. LV (26 April 1958), 533.
64. 25 April 1958, 221.
65. # 6773 (18 April 1958), 491.
66. I (Winter 1958), 3–9.
67. Bracher to MJB, 23 July 1980.
68. 5 June 1958. Collection of Frederick Bracher.
69. 9 August 1959, 1, 18.
70. See John K. Hutchens, "The Case of the One that Didn't Win," *New York Herald-Tribune* (13 March 1958), 23.
71. *Proceedings of the American Academy of Arts and Letters and the National Institute of Arts and Letters*, Second Series, Number 11 (New York, 1961), 38–39.
72. Ibid.
73. Williamstown Notebooks, 8 November 1962. Princeton University Library.

CHAPTER 9. THE HERMIT OF "SHADOWBROOK"

1. Williamstown Notebooks, 6 December 1960. Princeton University Library.
2. Williamstown Notebooks, 4 December 1962. Princeton University Library.
3. Bate to MJB, 2 January 1979.
4. To George R. Clark, Chairman of the Committee to Nominate Candidates for Overseers and Directors of the Associated Harvard Alumni, 22 November 1966. Carbon copy. Princeton University Library.
5. 19 December 1964. Collection of Jack Iggulden.
6. 5 April 1966. Collection of Jack Iggulden.
7. 10 March 1968. Harcourt Brace Jovanovich.

8. 28 October 1966. Harcourt Brace Jovanovich.
9. Williamstown Notebooks, 2 October 1963. Princeton University Library.
10. CXLVIII (22 March 1964), 5.
11. LXVIII (13 May 1967), 2–3.
12. 8 August 1976. Harcourt Brace Jovanovich.
13. Williamstown Notebooks, 14 January 1965. Princeton University Library.
14. Williamstown Notebooks, 14 December 1963. Princeton University Library.
15. 18 January 1964. Harcourt Brace Jovanovich.
16. 24 February 1964. Princeton University Library.
17. 4 August 1964. Princeton University Library.
18. 10 August 1964. Carbon copy. Princeton University Library.
19. 2 August 1964, 1, 20.
20. 10 September 1964, 14.
21. "By Ideology Possessed," XVI (22 September 1964), 825–26.
22. To JGC: 16 July 1964. Princeton University Library. To Crews: 20 July 1964. Carbon copy. Princeton University Library.
23. 4 August 1964. Princeton University Library.
24. 10 August 1964. Carbon copy. Princeton University Library.
25. CLI (1 August 1965), 37.
26. Williamstown Notebooks, 12 August 1965. Princeton University Library.
27. Williamstown Notebooks, 20 November 1964. Princeton University Library.
28. Williamstown Notebooks, 1 November 1965. Princeton University Library.
29. Williamstown Notebooks, 25 December 1965. Princeton University Library.
30. Williamstown Notebooks, 12 November 1966. Princeton University Library.
31. 12 November 1967. Princeton University Library.
32. 10 March 1968. Harcourt Brace Jovanovich.
33. XLIV, (2 November 1968), 197–201.
34. LXXII (26 August 1968), 86 B, 88.
35. 20 August 1968, 39.
36. 25 August 1968, 3, 33.
37. XXXII (3 September 1968), 10.
38. XX (19 November 1968), 1172–73.
39. September 1968, 2–4.
40. 2 July 1968. Princeton University Library.
41. 19 November 1968. Harcourt Brace Jovanovich.
42. 29 September 1969. Harcourt Brace Jovanovich.
43. 5 November 1968. Harcourt Brace Jovanovich.
44. 29 September 1969. Harcourt Brace Jovanovich.
45. 19 November 1970. Harcourt Brace Jovanovich.
46. Williamstown Notebooks, 26 May 1964. Princeton University Library.
47. My comments on Cozzens's alcoholism draw upon discussions with Dr. Michael Sribnick, Dr. Donald W. Goodwin, Dr. David J. Myerson, Dr. William Ober, Dr. Anthony Privitera, and Dr. William Abey.
48. 24 July 1971. Harcourt Brace Jovanovich.
49. To William Jovanovich, 9 April 1972. Harcourt Brace Jovanovich.

CHAPTER 10. MUTE IN GAZA

1. 17 December 1974. Harcourt Brace Jovanovich.
2. To MJB, after 14 March 1974.
3. "Foreword," *A Flower in Her Hair*, (Bloomfield Hills, Mich. & Columbia, S.C.: Bruccoli Clark, 1974), 8–9. *Just Representations*, 544.

4. Bruccoli Collection.
5. "Foreword," 8. *Just Representations*, 541.
6. *A Rope for Dr. Webster*, 17.
7. To MJB, 10 January 1976.
8. To MJB, 29 January 1976.
9. To MJB, before 8 August 1977.
10. To MJB, 20 December 1976.
11. 3 February 1978. Harcourt Brace Jovanovich.
12. To Dominic Rich, 15 June 1959. Carbon copy. Princeton University Library.

APPENDIX I. "THE BEST AGENT IN NEW YORK"

1. *Selected Letters of Raymond Chandler*, ed. Frank MacShane (New York: Columbia University Press, 1981), 200.
2. *Raymond Chandler Speaking*, ed. Dorothy Gardiner and Kathrine Sorley Walker (Boston: Houghton Mifflin, 1962), 159.
3. Frank MacShane, *The Life of Raymond Chandler* (New York: Dutton, 1976), 194.
4. Ibid., 150.
5. Carol Brandt to MJB, 5 February 1982.
6. Millicent Bell, *Marquand: An American Life* (Boston: Little, Brown, 1979), 158–59.
7. Ray Stark to MJB, 7 November 1980.
8. To Richard Ludwig, 1 August 1958. Princeton University Library.
9. 9 April 1959. Humanities Research Center, University of Texas at Austin.
10. Jerome Weidman to MJB, 19 April 1982.
11. Interview with MJB, 3 April 1982.
12. Interview with MJB, 2 April 1982.
13. Al Hart to MJB, 25 August 1981.
14. Mary McCarthy to MJB, 3 September 1981.
15. Shirley Ann Grau to MJB, 7 March 1982.
16. Peter Matthiessen to MJB, 19 September 1981.
17. Interview with MJB, 10 January 1981.

INDEX